D1212610

FOREST
MENSURATION

BERTRAM HUSCH
FORMERLY, UNIVERSITY OF NEW HAMPSHIRE

CHARLES I. MILLER
PURDUE UNIVERSITY

THOMAS W. BEERS
PURDUE UNIVERSITY

SECOND EDITION

JOHN WILEY & SONS
New York/Santa Barbara/Chichester/Brisbane/Toronto

ISBN 0 471 06834-9

Library of Congress Catalog Card Number: 72–178844

PRINTED IN THE UNITED STATES OF AMERICA

10 9 8 7 6 5 4

To
Angelica, Ruth, and Carolyn

Preface

The purpose of this book is to present the fundamentals of measurement and their application to forest mensuration. Designed primarily as a text for undergraduate students, the book should also be useful as a reference guide to both graduate students and professional foresters.

In presenting their material, the authors have followed the approach of the widely used first edition, balancing theory and practice, in the belief that the student should know the theories underlying the methods he employs. This knowledge will enable the student to modify techniques explained in the book and to develop new methods as conditions change and problems arise. Throughout the treatment, a knowledge of basic statistics, plane surveying, and college algebra is assumed.

The widening scope of forestry has created new measurement problems and responsibilities for the mensurationist. This book deals with these areas, as well as with such classic concepts as tree measurement and growth estimation. The reader is given an understanding of the basic aspects of measurement, which are then applied to forest mensuration. In addition, there are discussions on the grading of forest products, forest inventory, point and line sampling, the use of aerial photography in forest inventory sampling, and forest growth and yield. These discussions provide the most comprehensive coverage now available to students in the field.

The authors gratefully acknowledge the valuable assistance of their wives in many phases of the book's development. They also thank their associates and the many readers of the first edition for helpful suggestions in the preparation of this edition. In addition, Bertram Husch wishes to express his appreciation to Harvard University and to the staff of the Harvard Forest for the Charles Bullard Fellowship, so generously granted; and to the Food and Agricultural Organization of the United Nations for granting the leave of absence that made possible his contribution to the book.

BERTRAM HUSCH
CHARLES I. MILLER
THOMAS W. BEERS

November, 1971

Contents

FOREST MENSURATION

1

Introduction

1–1. SCOPE OF FOREST MENSURATION

Forest mensuration has been traditionally concerned with the measurement of trees and stands, or primary products cut from them, and the estimation of growth. Many foresters feel the definition given by Graves (1906) is still adequate. He wrote: "Forest mensuration deals with the determination of the volume of logs, trees, and stands and with the study of increment and yield." The formulation and acceptance of this definition is understandable since for many years forestry has been concerned almost exclusively with the production of quantities of wood products measured in volume units. Mensuration has been the body of knowledge and techniques to service wood-volume estimation needs. However, the scope of forestry has widened and, as its horizons grow, new measurement problems present themselves. Forest mensurationists are faced with the problem of what direction to take and this problem has stimulated a growing introspection. Mensurationists can establish a well-defined, static perimeter of responsibility or they can recognize that new measurement problems have arisen. If they establish rigid bounds, then measurement would remain tree, stand, and primary-wood-product measurement. If they take the dynamic view, then forest mensuration would take as its province the new measurement problems of the expanding field of forestry. They would then consider how far mensuration should concern itself with the measurement problems of wildlife management, watershed management, insect and disease incidence, recreation, in fact any of the mensurational aspects of multiple use forestry. At the same time, they must recog-

3

nize that the traditional measurement problems as expressed by Graves remain a major responsibility, although not the unique goal, of forest mensuration.

An objection to this all-encompassing view of mensuration is that each forestry specialization has its own unique set of measurement problems and techniques and that it is overly ambitious and unrealistic to imagine that forest mensuration can take as its domain such a diverse aggregation. The objection has validity if forest mensuration were to treat all the specialized measurement problems which can occur in the many facets of forestry. The objection is allayed if we consider forest mensuration as the subject which provides the foundation of measurement principles applicable to any forest measurement problem. This approach recognizes that there are fundamental similarities to measurement problems regardless of the specific discipline.

Forest mensuration will be treated in this text from two points of view so as to emphasize:

1. Principles which can provide a foundation for measurement problems in all aspects of forestry.
2. The continuing major requirement for forest mensuration to deal with the growth and yield of forest stands.

For treatment of the subject of forest mensuration in other countries the student is referred to: Prodan (1965), Germany; Pardé (1961), France; Patrone (1963), Italy; Mihailov (1953), Yugoslavia; Anutschin (1960a), Soviet Union; Korf (1953), Czechoslovakia; Gieruszynski (1959), Poland; Seip (1964), Norway; and Carron (1968), Australia. Earlier presentations of forest mensuration in the United States are given by Graves (1906); Belyea (1931); Chapman and Demeritt (1936); Chapman and Meyer (1949); Bruce and Schumacher (1950); Spurr (1952); Meyer (1953); and Husch (1963).

There is no escape from the fact that forest mensuration requires a background of mathematics, the more complete the better. If forest mensuration is considered only as the application of previously devised measurement procedures, it is possible for the practitioner to get by with an elementary knowledge of mathematics. But the basis for solving new and unforeseen problems will be absent. It should be a prime goal of education in forest mensuration to provide the practical skills for routine problems, but at the same time to lay a foundation of basic knowledge for the handling of ever-occurring new problems.

Two important changes have occurred in forest mensuration in the last twenty years: the application of statistical theory, and the use of computers and data processing in measurement problems. Both these applications have wrought a revolution in the solution of forest measurement problems. However, it is fundamental to recognize that they are both tools and not ends in themselves. In other words, forest mensuration is not synonymous with statistics or computer applications. Forest mensuration must make full use of statistical techniques but it must be first grounded on biological knowledge. A forest mensurationist is not equivalent to a statistician, although the more statistics he knows the better mensurationist he can be. Similarly, computers should be used as a tool for calculating, extending, and speeding up logical thought processes. A mensurationist is not equivalent to a computer specialist, although the more computer science a mensurationist knows, the better he can apply this powerful tool.

1–2. IMPORTANCE OF FOREST MENSURATION TO FORESTRY

Forest mensuration has always been one of the main stones in the foundation of forestry. Whether one considers forest mensuration to deal only with the determination of the volumes of logs, trees, and stands and the study of growth and yield, or in a wider, more modern context, its main objective is to provide quantified information for intelligent decision making. Forestry in the broadest sense is a management activity involving land, the plants and animals growing on it, man and his desires to use this land, and the products and services he can obtain from it. In these varied management activities the forester is continually faced with the necessity of making decisions. The possible situations are innumerable but a few typical questions will convey a general idea of the uncertainties he faces:

1. Which silvicultural treatment will result in better regeneration or growth of a particular forest?
2. Which species is most suitable for reforesting an area?
3. Is there sufficient timber on an area to make it economical to harvest it or establish a forest industry?
4. Is the price offered for a tract of forest land satisfactory?
5. Is a given area sufficiently worthwhile for the management of wildlife to warrant the investment of money for that purpose?

To make intelligent decisions for these and countless other problems a forester needs information. This information, whenever possible, should be expressed in quantifiable terms. It has been said, with much truth, that to know what you are talking about you must be able to express it in numbers. In this sense, forest mensuration consists of the application of measurement principles to obtain quantifiable information for decision making. The body of applications which has accumulated over the years has provided information and procedures to acquire this information on the growth and yield of trees and stands. The authors of this text have the view that forest mensuration will expand its information-provision responsibilities. The presentation of material in the following chapters has been organized with this view in mind.

1–3. PRINCIPLES OF MEASUREMENT

Measurement is one of the basic requirements in the extension of knowledge. Mankind's knowledge is to a large extent the result of the acquisition and systematic accumulation of observations of concrete objects and natural phenomena.

Observations and their interpretation are the result of the perceptive abilities of the human mind. The results of this perception may be in the form of qualitative descriptions or of comparisons. For example, the taste of some food may be described as "delicious" or as "better" than other kinds. As the requirements of precision and more advanced interpretations become manifest, qualitative descriptions are supplanted by quantitative or numerical representation. Measurements as they are commonly understood are of this quantitative form. In its broadest sense, measurement consists in the assignment of numbers to measurable properties. These properties may be those of physical objects, characteristics, or the occurrence of events. Ellis (1966) has pointed out that this definition of measurement is too loose and he suggests a better definition: "Measurement is the assignment of numerals to things according to any determinative, non-degenerate rule." "Determinative" means that, provided sufficient care is exercised, the same numerals (or ranges of numerals) would always be assigned to the same things under the same conditions according to the rule. "Non-degenerate" signifies that the rule allows for the possibility of assigning different numerals to different things, or to the same thing under different conditions. Measurement according to this definition implies that we have some kind of scale which allows us to use the rule. Since different rules may be devised, there are different kinds of scales; the choice of scale results in different kinds of numbers and different types of measurements. Each scale has inherent in it a different set of rules which must be adhered to in representing a property by a numerical quantity. Stevens (1946) has considered the question of scales and has presented a summary of the problem formulating a classification for different kinds of scales. Ellis (1966) has pointed out certain deficiencies in this classification. In spite of these shortcomings the system is useful in understanding the measurement process and is briefly summarized here. Four kinds of scales are distinguished: nominal, ordinal, interval, and ratio, as summarized in Table 1–1.

1–3.1. Nominal Scale. This scale is used when numbers are assigned to objects for one of two purposes:

Table 1-1
Classification of Scales of Measurements[1]

Scale	Basic Operation	Mathematical Group Structure	Permissible Statistics	Examples
Nominal	Determination of equality (numbering and counting)	Permutation group $X' = f(X)$ where $f(X)$ means any one-to-one substitution	Number of cases Mode Contingency correlation	Numbering of forest types on a stand map Assignment of code numbers to tree species in studying stand composition
Ordinal	Determination of greater or less (ranking)	Isotonic group $X' = f(X)$ where $f(X)$ means any increasing monotonic function	Median Percentiles Order correlation	Lumber grading Tree and log grading Site class estimation
Interval	Determination of the equality of intervals or of differences (numerical magnitude of quantity, arbitrary origin)	Linear group $X' = \alpha X + b$ $\alpha > 0$	Mean Standard deviation Correlation coefficient	Fahrenheit temperature Calendar time Available soil moisture Relative humidity
Ratio	Determination of the equality of ratios (numerical magnitude of quantity, absolute origin)	Similarity group $X' = cX$ $c > 0$	Geometric mean Harmonic mean Coefficient of variation	Length of objects Frequency of items Time intervals Volumes Weights Absolute temperature Absolute humidity

[1] Columns 2, 3, 4 and 5 are cumulative in that all characteristics listed opposite a particular scale are additive to those above it. In the column which records the group structure of each scale are listed the mathematical transformations which leave the scale invariant. Thus any numeral X on a scale can be replaced by another numeral X', where X' is the function of X listed in this column. The criterion for the appropriateness of a statistic is invariance under the transformations in column 3. Thus the case that stands at the median of a distribution maintains its position under all transformations which preserve order (isotonic group), but an item located at the mean remains at the mean only under transformations as restricted as those of the linear group. The ratio expressed by the coefficient of variation remains invariant only under the similarity transformation (multiplication by a constant). The rank–order correlation coefficient is usually considered appropriate to the ordinal scale, although the lack of a requirement for equal intervals between successive ranks really invalidates this statistic.

SOURCE: Adapted from S. S. Stevens, "On Theory of Scales of Measurement," *Science* 103(2684): 677-680.

1. The numbering of objects for identification. For example, numbering forest types on a stand map.
2. The numbering of a class where each member of the class is assigned the same numeral. For example, the assignment of a code number to species in studying stand composition.

1–3.2. Ordinal Scale. This scale represents an attempt to assign numbers in terms of rank order. Based on subjective consideration, a series of ranks is established, to which are attached numbers. Each individual is then given the number in the rank–order scale to which it best fits. In establishing a scale of this type, it is well to recognize that the successive intervals on the scale are not necessarily equal. Lumber, tree, and log grades are examples of the application of the ordinal scale.

1–3.3. Interval Scale. This scale represents a form in which a series of graduations is established at uniform intervals based on a reference unit of fixed magnitude. The measurement of a particular property is referenced to this scale for the assignment of a numerical quantity. There is no absolute reference point or true origin for this scale. The origin for an interval scale can be arbitrarily chosen. The calibration of the Fahrenheit temperature scale illustrates this procedure. Equal intervals of temperature are scaled off by noting equal volumes of expansion referenced to an arbitrary zero. The scales of time, such as days, months, and years, offer a similar example.

The interval scale may be divided into two subdivisions: the linear interval scale and the logarithmic interval scale. The linear interval scale is described in the previous paragraph. In the logarithmic interval scale, instead of equal intervals there are equal but unknown ratios.

1–3.4. Ratio Scale. This scale is similar to the interval scale in that there is equality of intervals between successive points on the scale. However, an absolute zero of origin is always present or implied. Ratio scales are the most commonly employed and the most versatile in that all types of statistical measures are applicable. It is convenient to consider two types of ratio scales, fundamental and derived.

1. Fundamental scales are represented by such examples as the numerosity of aggregates, length, weight, and period of time.
2. Derived scales are found by combination of measures of several independent quantities, e.g., volume per acre, density determinations, growth per unit of time, etc. These are derived scales in that they are functions of the fundamental magnitudes.

The nominal and ordinal scales of measurement do not use standard reference units having a spatial or physical property. They use the abstract concept of number itself. Such measurement, then, consists in assigning a number on a nominal scale, or ranking items according to an arbitrarily chosen order for an ordinal scale. Measurements of the interval or ratio type are those which are generally thought of as quantitative in nature.

1–4. UNITS OF MEASUREMENT

To describe and carry out calculations with physical quantities requires two elements: a definition of the standard measure of each kind of quantity called the unit, and the number of times the unit occurs in a given amount of the quantity. Thus, if an object has a length of three meters, the meter has been taken as the unit of length and the length dimension of the object contains three of these standard units.

Fundamental and derived units are recognized. The fundamental units in mechanics are measures of length, mass, and time. These have come to be regarded as independent and fundamental variables of nature although they really have been chosen arbitrarily by man. The sizes of these fundamental units have also been arbitrarily established. Besides the three fundamental units of mechanics, other fundamental units have been established for thermal, electrical, and illumination quantity measurement.

Derived units are expressed in terms of the fundamental units or of other units derived from fundamental units. The derived standards include those used in the measurement of volume (cubic feet or meters), area (acres or hectares), velocity (miles per hour, meters per second), force (kilogram-force), etc. All derived units are defined by a relationship between the units in the mathematical expression of some physical law. For example, units of area of a rectangle can be defined by the equation Area $= WL$, where W and L are fundamental units of length.

Measurements of physical quantities such as length, mass, and time are fully defined by the two specifications, the chosen unit and the number of them. These quantities are given the name scalar quantities or scalars. There are other physical quantities which require an additional specification of direction for their complete definition. These quantities are called vector quantities or vectors.

1–5. SYSTEM OF UNITS

When any physical quantity is to be measured, it is necessary to select a unit in terms of which the magnitude is to be expressed. There have been numerous measurement units employed over the course of human history at different times and places. There are two methods of establishing measurement units. We may select an arbitrary unit for each kind of quantity we wish to measure, or we may decide upon certain arbitrary fundamental units and formulate from them a consistent system of derived units. The first method was employed extensively in earlier history and in simplified form is still in general use. For example, measurements of the length of cloth, height of a horse, or land distances were all different and unique. Reference units used in earlier days were those natural objects commonly seen by all, such as the width of a barleycorn, or the length of a man's thumb, foot, or other part of the human body. The definitions of these primitive units were vague and lacking in uniformity. This method is still used extensively in English-speaking countries in the foot, yard, pound, and other units, although modifications have been adopted to standardize the units. Various other systems of weights and measures of this type have been used in different parts of the world. They are primarily of local and historical interest. The second method of establishing a system of measurement units is illustrated by the metric system. In this system, an arbitrary set of units has been chosen that is uniformly applicable to the measurement of any object. Moreover, there is a logical, consistent, and uniform relationship between the basic units and their subdivisions.

In any system of measurement units it is necessary to decide upon at least three units that are entirely arbitrary. The three fundamental units which have been generally used are those of length, mass, and time.

1–5.1. Metric System. The metric system is used in all European countries and is the legal system in all of Latin America and several Asian countries. Practically the entire world with the exception of the English-speaking countries uses the metric system. Even in English-speaking countries it is used for nearly all scientific work.

The fundamental unit of mass is the kilogram, defined as the mass of a certain piece of platinum-iridium in possession of the International Bureau of Weights and Measures. The original unit of mass, the gram, was intended to be equal to the mass of one cubic centimeter of water at maximum density. However, later determinations have shown that a gram of water does not occupy exactly one cubic centimeter. At present, the unit of mass is based upon a kilogram (1000 grams) prototype standard established at the same time as the original platinum-iridium length prototype.

Based upon the metric system, the international MKS system was devised in which the fundamental unit of length was the meter; of mass, the kilogram; and of time, the second.[1] Offshoots of this system have developed to satisfy the needs of engineers and scientists. Scientific measurements utilize the C.G.S. system in which the centimeter is the funda-

---

[1] The International System of Units (S.I.) adopted in 1954 uses these units plus the ampere for electric current, the degree Kelvin for thermodynamic temperature, and the candela for luminous density.

mental unit of length, the gram for mass, and the second for time. The Metric Technical System (MTS) is used principally in engineering. This differs from the MKS system in that the kilogram-force (a unit of weight) is used as a fundamental unit.

In all civilized countries at the present time, the fundamental unit of time is the second, defined until recently as the 86,400th part of a mean solar day or the 86,400th part of the average interval between two successive passages of the sun across the meridian of any given place. In 1960, a new and more accurate unit of time was adopted. The second is now defined as 1/31,556,925.9747 of the period of the earth's revolution about the sun for the standard year 1900.

In the metric system, larger and smaller units are derived from the basic units in decimal steps. Their names are formed by adding the following prefixes to the basic names:

Tera	—	$1,000,000,000,000 \ (10^{12})$
Ciga	—	$1,000,000,000 \ (10^{9})$
Mega	—	$1,000,000 \ (10^{6})$
Kilo	—	$1,000 \ (10^{3})$
hecto	—	$100 \ (10^{2})$
deca	—	10
deci	—	$0.1 \ (10^{-1})$
centi	—	$0.01 \ (10^{-2})$
milli	—	$0.001 \ (10^{-3})$
micro	—	$0.000001 \ (10^{-6})$
nano	—	$0.000000001 \ (10^{-9})$
pico	—	$0.000000000001 \ (10^{-12})$

Secondary units consist of various combinations of the basic metric units. In the C.G.S. system the unit force is the dyne, defined as the force which, when allowed to act for one second on a body of one-gram mass, will impart to that body a velocity of one centimeter per second. The unit of work is the erg, defined as the quantity of work done when a force of one dyne is overcome through a distance of one centimeter. The erg is also the unit of energy, because energy is likewise measured by the quantity of work performed.

In the MKS system, the unit of force is the newton and equals 10,000 dynes. The unit of work is the joule which equals 10,000,000 ergs. The power required to do one joule of work in one second is the watt. Other electrical units such as the ohm, volt, and ampere are part of the MKS system.

1–5.2. English System. The commonly used units in the United States are practically the same as those employed in the early American colonies prior to their independence from Great Britain. The names of these units are similar to those used in the British Imperial System but they differ slightly in their definitions.

In the English system, the fundamental length is the yard. The British yard, as presently established, is the distance between two lines on a bronze bar kept in the Standards Office, Westminster, London. Originally the United States yard was based on a prototype bar but in 1893 it was decided to base both the yard and pound on the meter and kilogram. The United States yard was defined as 3600/3937 meter = .9144018 meter. The British yard on the other hand was 3600/3937.0113 meter = .914399 meter. The foot is defined as the third part of a yard, and the inch as a twelfth part of a foot. In 1959, it was agreed by Canada, United States, New Zealand, United Kingdom, South Africa, and Australia that new values would be adopted of 1 yard = 0.9144 meter (1 inch = 2.54 centimeters). In the United Kingdom, these new values are used only in scientific work, the older, slightly different values being used for other measurements.

In the British system the unit of mass is the avoirdupois pound, defined as the mass of a certain cylinder of platinum in the possession of the British government with an equivalent of .45359243 kilogram. In the United States the unit of mass is likewise the pound, but in 1893 it was defined in terms of the mass unit of the metric system as 1/2.20462234 kilogram = .4535924277 kilogram. Thus the United States and British pound were almost but not exactly equal. The 1959 agreement of English-speaking countries established the new value of 1 kilogram = 2.204623 pounds or 1 pound = .45359237 kilogram which, as with the yard, is used in the United Kingdom for scientific measurements.

The attractive force that the earth exerts upon a pound of matter is often called a "pound." This is incorrect, for the pound is a unit of mass and not of force. The "poundal" is the logical unit of force or weight in the English system, defined as the force which, when acting for one second on a body of one-pound mass, will impart to that body a velocity of one foot per second. The poundal is not in general use since in scientific work the metric system is used.

As in the metric system, the second is the fundamental unit of time.

Secondary units in the English system are also of different sizes in the United States and the United Kingdom. For example, the U. S. gallon is defined as 231 cubic inches. The volume of the British gallon is 277.42 cubic inches. Many of the secondary units used in English-speaking countries are as arbitrary as the gallon. Others are derived from the fundamental units in a definite way. For example, the unit of work and energy in English and United States engineering practice is the foot-pound.

Very commonly, conversions from one system of measurement to another are required. Appendix Table A–1 shows conversions between units of length, area, volume, and mass for the English and metric systems.

1–6. NUMBERING SYSTEMS

The numbering system in general use throughout the world is the decimal system which can probably be attributed to the fact that human beings happen to have ten fingers. The relationship is indicated in English by the use of the term digits for the numerals. The decimal system is merely one of many possible numbering systems which could be utilized. In fact, other numbering systems have been used by earlier civilizations such as the vigesimal system, based on twenty, utilized by the Mayas, and the sexagesimal system of the Babylonians, based on sixty. Our own system of measuring time and angles in minutes and seconds comes from the sexagesimal system. Systems to other bases may have been used such as the duodecimal system, based on twelve, which seems to have lingered on in the use of dozens and gross. For a discussion of the history of number theory the student is referred to Ore (1948).

With the development of the electronic computer, interest has been revived in numbering systems to bases other than ten. Of primary interest is the binary system because electronic digital computers using two basic states have been found most practical.

1–7. CONTINUOUS AND DISCRETE VARIABLES

A variate or variable is a measurable characteristic which varies in amount or magnitude. Some variables are continuous in that they are capable of exhibiting every possible value within a certain range. Height, weight, and volume are examples of continuous variables. Other variables are discontinuous or discrete because they can have only values which jump from one number or position to the next. Employees in a company, number of trees in a stand, or number of deer per square mile illustrate discrete variables.

Data concerning a continuous variable are obtained by measuring magnitudes. Data pertaining to discrete variables are arrived at by counting. The problems of measuring continuous variables are dealt with in Chapters 3, 4, 5, 6, and 7 and will not be discussed here. But it would be worthwhile to consider the measurement of discrete variables in greater depth at this time.

The process of measuring according to nominal and ordinal scales, as shown in Table 1–1, consists of counting the frequencies of occurrence of specified events. Discrete variables describe these events. The general term "event" can refer to a discrete physical standard, such as a tree, which exists as a tangible object occupying space, or to an occurrence which cannot be thought of as spatial, such as a timber scale. In either case, the measurement consists of defining the variable and then counting the number of its occurrences. There is no choice for the unit of measurement—the frequency is the only permissible numerical value.

It is important not to confuse a class established for convenience in continuous-type measurement with a discrete variable. Classes for continuous variables are often established to facilitate the handling of data in computations. Frequencies may then be assigned to these classes. These frequencies represent the occurrence or recurrence of certain measurements of a continuous variable which have been placed in a group or class of defined limits for convenience.

A discrete variable can thus be characterized as a class or series of classes of defined characteristics with no possible intermediate classes or values. A few examples of discrete variables used in forestry are species, lumber grades, and forest-fire danger classes.

At times it may not be clear as to whether a discrete or continuous variable is being measured. For example, in counting the number of trees per acre or per hectare, the interval, one tree, is so small and the number of trees so large that analyses are made of the frequencies as though they described a continuous variable. This has become customary and may be considered permissible if the true nature of the variable is understood.

1–7.1. Forest Measurements on a Nominal Scale. Species names or forest types are excellent examples of the use of nominal scales in forestry with discrete variables. The several tree species or forest types would be the classes of these variables. The order in which the frequencies of the classes can be recorded is not due to the discrete variable itself, which is the species, but is merely a matter of arranging in descending frequency. They could be rearranged without affecting their interpretation. It is frequently more convenient to assign a code number or letter to classes of a discrete variable. Thus, instead of writing out the individual species names, each species could be given a code number. Code numbers are especially useful if data are to be entered on punch cards for machine computation. It is important to be aware that the code numbers have no intrinsic meaning but are merely identifying labels. No meaningful operations can be performed on such code numbers.

1–7.2. Forest Measurements on an Ordinal Scale. Ordinal scales for discrete variables abound in forestry. Examples are lumber grades, log grades, piece products, Christmas tree grades, nursery stock grades, and site quality classes.

The order in which the classes of a discrete variable are arranged on an ordinal scale has an intrinsic meaning. The characteristics of a discrete variable still hold, but the order in which the classes occur conveys an additional meaning not given by a nominal scale. These classes are arranged in order of increasing or decreasing qualitative rank, so the position on the scale affords an idea of comparative rank. The continuum of the variable consists of the range between the limits of the established ranks or grades. As many ranks or grades can be established as are deemed suitable. An attempt may be made to have each grade or rank occupy an equal interval of the continuum. However, this will rarely be achieved, since the ranks are subjectively defined with no assurance of equal increments between ranks.

Chapter 10 discusses in more detail the principles of quality measurement and its most important applications in forestry.

1–8. PRECISION, BIAS, AND ACCURACY

The terms "precision" and "accuracy" are often used interchangeably in nontechnical parlance and often with varying meaning in technical usage (Singer, 1964). In this text they will not be considered synonymous but will have two definite meanings. Precision as used here (and generally accepted in forest mensuration), means the degree of agreement in a series of measurements. The term is also used to describe the resolving power of a measuring instrument or the smallest unit used in observing a measurement. In this sense the more decimal places used in the measurement, the more precise is the measurement.

Bias refers to a systematic error that affects all the measurements in the same way. Bias can occur due to a faulty measurement procedure or instrumental error, flaws in the sampling procedure, or errors in the computational procedure. (See Section 12–3.3 for a discussion of bias in forest inventory sampling.)

In sampling, accuracy refers to the size of the deviation of a sample estimate from the true population mean. Precision expressed as a standard error refers to the deviation of sample values about their own mean, which if biased, does not correspond to the true population value. It is possible to have a very precise estimate in that the deviations from the sample mean are very small yet, at the same time, the estimate may not be accurate if it is far from the true value due to bias.

For example, it would be possible to measure a tree diameter repeatedly with great care to the nearest hundredth of an inch using a caliper which is out of adjustment, every measurement being biased due to the caliper reading .05 inch too high. The results of the series of measurements are precise because of little variation between readings, but they are not accurate, not indicating the true dbh, because of the bias caused by maladjustment of the instrument.

The relative accuracy of a measurement is a function of its actual difference from the true measurement and of the size of the measurement itself. The height of a standing tree can be very carefully measured with a transit and still be a foot or more in error. The diameter of a tree might be ocularly estimated to within an inch or two. It would be deluding ourselves to maintain that the diameter estimate using an inch unit was a more accurate measurement. An evaluation of the relative accuracy can be made by expressing the size of the error as a percentage of the total measurement. Thus, an error of one foot for a tree eighty feet tall would be about 1.2 per cent. An error of one inch for a diameter of twelve inches would be 8.3 per cent. Obviously, the diameter measurement in such a case is less accurate than the height measurement.

1–9. SIGNIFICANT DIGITS

A significant digit is any digit denoting the true size of the unit at its specific location in the overall number. The term significant as used here should not be confused with its use in reference to statistical significance. The significant figures in a number are the digits reading from left to right beginning with the first non-zero digit and ending with the last digit written which may be a zero. The numbers 25, 2.5, 0.25, and 0.025 all have two significant figures, the 2 and the 5. The numbers 25.0, 0.250, and 0.0250 all have three significant figures, the 2, 5, and 0. When one or more zeros occur immediately to the left of the decimal position and there is no digit to the right of the point, the number of significant digits may be in doubt. Thus the number 2500 may have two, three, or four significant digits, depending on whether one or both zeros denote an actual measurement or have been used to round off a number and indicate the position of the decimal point. Thus, zero can be a significant figure if used to show the quantity in the position it occupies and not merely to denote a decimal place. A convention sometimes used to indicate the last significant digits is to place a dot above it. Thus, $5,12\dot{1},000$ indicates four significant digits and $5,121,\dot{0}00$ indicates five significant digits. Another method which can be used is to first divide a number into two factors, one of them being a power of ten. A number such as 150,000,000 could be written as 1.5×10^8, 15×10^7 or 150×10^6. Similarly, .0000015 may be written as 1.5×10^{-6} or in some other form such as 15×10^{-7}. A convention frequently used is to show the significant figures in the first factor and to use one non-zero digit to the left of the decimal point. Thus, the numbers 156,000,000 (with three significant figures), 31.53, and 0.005301 would be written as 1.56×10^8, 3.153×10 and 5.301×10^{-3}.

If a number has a significant zero to the right of the decimal place following a non-zero number, it should not be omitted. For example, 1.05010 indicates six significant digits including the last zero to the right. To drop it would reduce the precision of the number. Zeros when used to locate a decimal place are not significant. In the number 0.00530, only the last three digits 5, 3, and 0 are significant; the first two to the right of the decimal place are not.

When the units used for a measurement are changed it may change the number of decimal places but not the number of significant digits. Thus, a weight of 355.62 grams has five significant figures, as does the same weight expressed as 0.035562 kilograms, although the number of decimal places has increased. This emphasizes the importance of specifying the number of significant digits in a measurement rather than simply the number of decimal places.

1–10. SIGNIFICANT DIGITS IN MEASUREMENT

The numbers used in mensuration can be considered as arising from pure numbers, from direct measurements, and from computations involving pure numbers and values from direct measurements.

Pure numbers can be the result of a count in which a number is exact or they can be the result of some definition. Examples of pure numbers would be the number of sides in a square, the value of π, or the number of meters in a kilometer.

Values of direct measurements are obtained by reading some type of measuring instrument, e.g., measuring a length with a ruler. The numerical values arising in this way are really approximations in contrast to pure numbers. The precision of the approximation is indicated by the number of significant digits used. For example, measurement of a length could be taken to the nearest foot, tenth, or hundredth and recorded as 8, 7.6, or 7.60 feet. Each of these measures implies an increasing standard of precision. A length of 8 feet means a length closer to 8 feet than to 7 or 9 feet. The value of 8 can be considered as lying between 7.5 and 8.5. Similarly, a length of 7.6 means a measurement whose value is closer to 7.6 feet than to 7.5 or 7.7. The value of 7.6 really lies anywhere between 7.5500 . . . 01 and 7.6499 . . . 99, or, conventionally, 7.55 and 7.65. In the measurement 7.60, the last digit is significant and the measurement implies a greater precision. The value 7.60 means the actual value lies anywhere between 7.59500 . . . 01 and 7.60499 . . . 99, or, conventionally, 7.595 and 7.605.

It is incorrect to record more significant digits than were actually observed. Thus, a length measurement of 8 feet taken to the nearest foot cannot be recorded as 8.0 feet since this may mislead the reader into thinking the measurement is more precise than it actually is. On the other hand, one should not omit significant zeros in decimals if significant non-zeros are being written. For example, if one records 135.6 and 78.3, one should also write 112.0 instead of 112, if the zero is significant.

Since the precision of the final results is limited by the precision of original data, it is necessary to consider the numbers of significant figures to take and record in original measurements. It is well to keep in mind that using greater precision than needed is a waste of time and money. A few suggestions follow:

1. A cardinal point to remember is that it is not worthwhile to try to observe measurements to greater precision (more significant digits) than can be reliably indicated by the measuring process or instrument. For example, it would be illogical to try to measure the height of a standing tree to the nearest tenth of a foot using an Abney level.
2. The precision needed in original data may be influenced by how large a difference is important in comparing results. Thus, if the results of a series of silvicultural treatments are to be compared in terms of volume growth response to the nearest cubic foot, then there would be no need to estimate volumes more exactly than the nearest cubic foot.
3. The variation in a population sampled and the size of the sample influence the precision chosen for original measurement. If the population varies greatly or if there are few observations in the sample then high precision is not worthwhile.

1–11. ROUNDING OFF

When dealing with the numerical value of a measurement in the usual decimal notation, it is often necessary to round off to fewer significant figures than originally shown. Rounding off can be done by deleting the unwanted digits to the rigit of the decimal point (the fractional part of a number) and by substituting zeros for those to the left of the decimal place (the integer part). Three cases can arise: (1) If the deleted or replaced digits represent less than one-half unit in the last required place, no further change is required. (2) If the deleted or replaced digits represent more than one-half unit in the last required place, then this significant figure is raised by one. Note that if the significant figure in the last required place is 9, it changes to zero and the digit preceding it is increased by one. (3) If the deleted or replaced digits represent exactly one-half unit in the last required place, a recommended convention is to raise this last digit by unity if it is odd but let it stand if it is even. Thus, 31.45 would be rounded to 31.4 but 31.55 would be 31.6. A few examples are given below:

Number	4 significant figs.	3 significant figs.	2 significant figs.
4.6495	4.650	4.65	4.6
93.65001	93.65	93.7	94
567851	567900	568000	570000
0.99687	0.9969	.997	1.0

1–12. SIGNIFICANT DIGITS IN ARITHMETIC OPERATIONS

In arithmetic operations involving measurements, where figures are only approximations, the question of how many significant digits there are in the result becomes important.

In multiplication and division, the factor with the fewest significant figures limits the number of significant digits in the product or quotient. Thus, in multiplying a numerical measurement with five significant figures by another with three significant figures, only the first three figures of the product will be trustworthy, although there may be up to eight digits in the product. For example, if the measurement 895.67 and 35.9 are multiplied, the product is 32,154.553. Only the first three figures in the product, 3, 2, and 1, are significant. The number 895.67 represents a measurement between 895.665 and 895.675. The number 35.9 also means some value between 35.85 and 35.95. The products of the four possible limiting combinations will differ in all except the first three figures as shown below:

$$(895.665)(35.85) = 32109.59025$$
$$(895.665)(35.95) = 32199.15675$$
$$(895.675)(35.85) = 32109.94875$$
$$(895.675)(35.95) = 32199.51625$$

Thus, these three are the only reliable figures in the product. Similarly, in dividing a numerical measurement with eight significant digits by another measurement with three significant figures, the quotient will have only three significant figures. But, if a measurement is to be multiplied or divided by an exact number or a factor which is known to any desired number of significant digits, a slightly different situation obtains. For example, the total weight could be estimated as the product of the mean weight times 55. However, the 55 is an exact number and could also be validly written as 55.000. The product would thus still have five significant digits. It may be helpful to remember that multiplication is merely repetitive addition and the 55, in this case, means that a measurement is added exactly 55 times. Similarly, if the 55 objects had been weighed, as a group, to five significant digits, dividing by 55 would give a mean weight to five significant figures. In these cases the significant digits are controlled by the number in the measurement. Another case occurs if measurement is to be multiplied or divided by a factor such as π or e (base of Napierian logarithms), which are known to any number of significant figures. The number of significant digits in π or e should be made to agree with the number in the measurement before the operation of multiplication or division so that there is no loss in precision.

A good rule in multiplication or division is to keep one more digit in the product or quotient than occurs in the shorter of the two factors. This is especially helpful in a calculation involving a series of operations, in order to minimize rounding-off errors. At the end of the calculation, the final answer can be rounded off to the proper number of significant figures.

In addition and subtraction, the position of the decimal points will affect the number of significant digits in the result. It is necessary to align numbers according to their decimal places in order to carry out these operations. The statement that measurements can be added or subtracted when significant digits coincide at some place to the left or right of the decimal point can be used as a primary guide. Also, the number of significant digits in an answer can never be greater than those in the largest of the numbers, but may be fewer. As one example, measurements of 134.023 and 1.5 can be added or subtracted as shown below, since significant digits coincide at some place.

$$
\begin{array}{r}
134.023 \\
1.5 \\
\hline
135.523
\end{array}
$$

The sum has only four significant figures and should be expressed as 135.5. The last two significant figures of 134.023 cannot be used, since there is no information in the smaller measurement for coinciding positions. It is desirable to take measurements to uniform standards of significant figures or decimal places to avoid discarding a portion of a measurement, as was done in the case of the last two digits of 134.023. Another example is the addition of a series of measurements, the final total of which may have more figures than any of the individual measurements. The number of significant digits in the total will not exceed the number in the largest measurement. Consider the eleven measurements on page 21.

The total, 10,070.8, contains six digits but only the first four are significant. Each measurement can be thought of as an estimate within a range, as shown in the two right-hand columns. The sum of the lesser values is 10,070.25 and that of the larger is 10,071.35. The total value of the sum of the eleven measurements can fall anywhere within these limits. The significant figures are 1, 0, 0, and 7. Beyond this, the digits are unreliable.

Measurement	*Range*	
845.6	845.55	845.65
805.8	805.75	805.85
999.6	999.55	999.65
963.4	963.35	963.45
897.6	897.55	897.65
903.1	903.05	903.15
986.9	986.85	986.95
876.3	876.25	876.35
863.2	863.15	863.25
931.2	931.15	931.25
998.1	998.05	998.15
10070.8	10070.25	10071.35

2

Computations .

The interpretation of a series of measurements in the form of numerical quantities will invariably involve some computation. Especially with the application of statistical methods, calculations of varying degrees of complexity are required. These may vary from the simple calculation of an arithmetic mean to the solution of a series of simultaneous equations. Regardless of the complexities of the methodology or procedural steps, the numerical operations consist simply of addition, subtraction, multiplication, and division.

When these arithmetical procedures are few in number and simple in their sequence, the basic longhand procedure, using pencil and paper, may be satisfactory. As the number of operations and the complexity of their order increase, faster means of computation become necessary, or the labor and time needed become prohibitive. Machines for calculating have been developed to carry out numerical operations rapidly on large amounts of data and to incorporate some form of "memory" so that the machines can complete a sequence of operations without repeated instructions.

There are available several types of machines which solve these problems to varying degrees: mechanical desk calculators, punched card systems, and electronic data-processing machines including electronic desk-type calculators.

The reduction of numerical data by hand or desk-type calculating machines is practicable for small-scale computing tasks. When there are relatively few computations to be made it is less complicated and cheaper to carry them out using longhand procedures and desk-type calculators than to make arrangements for costlier and more complex machine procedures. However, this entails a higher risk of errors in the computations and requires the establishment of a checking system to detect them.

Hand and desk-type machine calculation may also be usefully combined with more sophisticated data-processing machines. In some cases it may be advantageous to utilize hand procedures for simple calculations, for example, to arrive at total values of some parameter for sampling units, which are then subsequently used in calculations on a more complex computing machine.

2–1. MECHANICAL DESK CALCULATING MACHINES

Mechanical desk calculators provide a tremendous increase in computational capacity over longhand operations. Calculators of this type exercise their function through internal mechanical functions. In recent years, desk-type calculators based on electronic principles have also been developed as mentioned in Section 2–3.

The principal attribute of mechanical desk calculators is their ability to carry out rapidly individual arithmetic operations of addition, subtraction, multiplication, or division. These machines are very limited in "memory" ability and can retain only limited amounts of information. When large amounts of data are to be handled, the operator must introduce the individual numerical quantities into the machine by hand. The operator acts as the memory, recording information from the machine, reintroducing it plus new data, and informing the machine what to do at every step of the procedure. Some machines can carry out a limited series of operations such as three-factor multiplication or two-factor multiplication followed by a division. Machines are also available which can automatically extract square roots.

In using the ordinary mechanical calculator, an operator enters two numbers of an operation into the machine via its keyboard and then starts the operation by pressing one of a series of control keys. At the completion of the operation, the answer will appear on a dial. The operator can then copy it. On some machines, the individual factors and the results are printed on paper tape. Some desk calculators do have sufficient memory or storage capacity to keep this answer while carrying out a subsequent operation and in turn adding or subtracting the series of results.

Machines which will only add or subtract are called *adding machines*. Machines which perform all the arithmetical operations are referred to as *calculating machines*. These machines may be hand operated or electrically driven. The more elaborate machines are all electrically operated. Mechanical calculating machines are made in many countries and vary considerably in design.

2–2. PUNCHED CARD SYSTEMS

Punched card systems have been developed for the processing of large quantities of data. These systems are of two types: (1) hand-operated sorting systems, and (2) mechanical and electrical sorting and computational systems.

2–2.1. Hand-Operated Sorting Systems. The principal objective of this type of data-processing equipment is to enter information of a quantitative or qualitative character on cards in such a way that cards containing specific kinds of desired information can be separated or sorted out of the general file when needed. Information is entered on the cards by utilizing series of punched holes along the margins, as shown in Fig. 2–1. Meanings are assigned to the holes, individually or in combination. The holes which are appropriate for the information to be entered are then clipped open to the edge of the card, forming notches. The basic sorting operation then depends on whether or not an information position has an open notch or a hole. A blunt needle is inserted through the appropriate hole position on a group of cards. When the needle is lifted, the cards which had been notched in this position will drop away. The information on each card obtained in the sorting must then be examined visually. Any computations necessary regarding quantitative data must then be carried out, either by longhand or desk calculator.

There is no standard card design, although there are standard card sizes. A design must be worked out for each application of this system. The design of the card is the most important phase in applying this system. There are several commercial adaptations of this procedure; the two most common are the Keysort and the E–Z–Sort systems.

It is clear that a data-processing system of this type is simply a sorting or classification mechanism and does no computational work. It is best applied when problems necessitate only a sorting operation or selection of chosen categories without the need for subsequent calculations. Casey and Perry (1951) have presented a number of applications of sorting systems in science and industry. Meteer (1953) described an application of the procedure to the handling of continuous inventory data in forest management.

2–2.2. Sorting and Computational Systems. An improvement over the computational abilities of mechanical desk calculators has been achieved by more sophisticated machines utilizing punched cards. Systems of this type have the capacity to handle large masses of data rapidly. They can carry out arithmetical operations many times faster than mechanical desk calculators and have greater memory or storage capacity. Moreover, they can perform operations of which the systems described above are in-

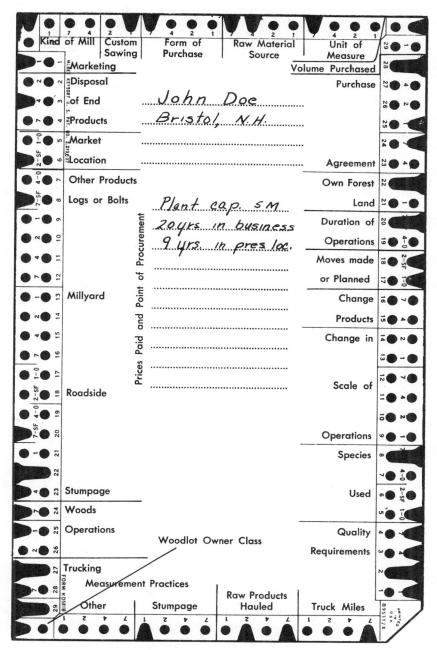

Fig. 2–1. Punch card for hand-sorting system.

capable: sorting, counting, filing, and copying information, and printing totals. These machines antedate electronic computers and are rapidly being replaced by these newer computers. However, equipment of this type is still being operated and warrants a brief description. A description of the International Business Machine system will illustrate the procedure.

The punch cards shown in Fig. 2–2 are standardized in size, $7\frac{3}{8}$ inches long by $3\frac{1}{4}$ inches wide, and .0065 inch thick. They have eighty vertical columns, with twelve punching positions in a column. The twelve punching positions per column make up a unit. Digits are indicated by punching one of the ten positions from 0 to 9, leaving the eleventh and twelfth spaces for other coding.

Original information in numerical form is converted into a pattern of holes in these cards, using a key-punching machine. Another procedure known as mark-sensing has been developed by IBM to allow automatic card punching. In this system, information is entered on the cards as shown in Fig. 2–2(b), using a graphite pencil. The position of the mark with respect to the column and position within a column indicates the numerical value of the recorded information. A maximum of twenty-seven columns is available since the size of the mark-sensing positions occupies three of the ordinary columns. Cards marked in this manner are passed through a machine which electrically senses the graphite marks and punches corresponding holes into the desired position on the same cards. Cards prepared in this way can be used similarly to individually key-punched cards. The International Business Machines Corporation (1959) has available a system which enables data to be punched on prescored cards by hand at the time of an observation. A maximum of forty columns is available on the special prescored cards, shown in Fig. 2–2 (c), rather than the usual eighty on conventional cards. The other columns have been lost because of the space required for prescoring around each punching position. Information is then entered on a card by pushing out the prescored chips from the proper holes with a metal stylus. The cards are held in a punching board called a Port-A-Punch, and a perforated plastic template is placed over the cards so that its holes coincide with the punching positions on the card.

Punched cards, regardless of the manner of punching, are then fed through machines which sense the pattern of holes electrically, by means of wire brushes making contact through the holes. These contacts are converted into a pattern of timed electrical circuits. Electromagnetic relays are employed to route data through the various machines. The machines will read sets of operating instructions as well as measurement data. There are a series of machines in an installation which perform a number of operations. The more important are listed as follows, with their functions.

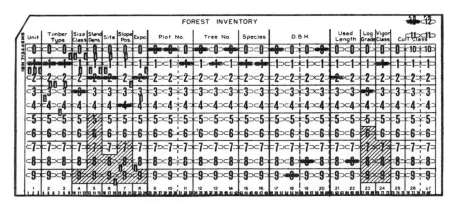

(a) IBM card.

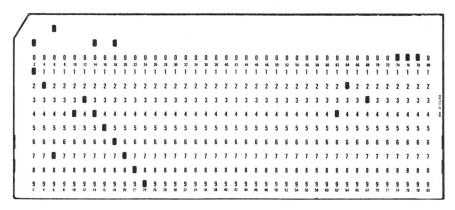

(b) IBM mark sense card.

(c) IBM prescored card.

Fig. 2–2. IBM punch cards.

27

Machine	*Function*
Key punch	Enters data and instructions on cards, in the form of holes
Verifier	Checks original card punching
Sorter	Sorts cards into specified groups
Interpreter	Reads and prints information
Reproducer	Copies card patterns onto other cards
Collator	Sorts, merges, compares, and checks sequences
Calculating punch	Performs arithmetic operations
Tabulator	Totals information and prints

2–3. ELECTRONIC COMPUTERS

The punched card systems previously described provide a great improvement over mechanical desk calculators. However, they are still limited in their storage capacity or memory. This results in complex procedures requiring intermediate steps of reentering information into the machine. In addition, electromagnetic relays are relatively slow, although calculations can be performed many times more rapidly than with a mechanical calculator.

Electronic machines have been developed in the constant search for faster and more versatile methods of processing data. Originally, the electronic circuits in these machines employed vacuum tubes but these have largely been replaced by less expensive, more serviceable transistors. The advantages of electronic computers lie in their storage capacity and in the speed with which they carry out operations. The storage capacity of these machines allows intermediate results to be stored internally until they are needed. In addition, a set of instructions of great complexity can be entered and will be retained internally, to come into play at appropriate times. Electronic computers of this type are called *stored program* machines. Another class of computers is externally programmed in that the instruction device is external to the computer.

There are two general kinds of electronic computers, digital and nondigital. The digital computers depend upon the counting of discrete units and are consequently often referred to as *discrete variable* machines. Calculators based on the measurement of physical quantities are called *continuous variable* or *non-digital* machines. Specific descriptions, together with applications and directions, are provided by the manufacturers of commercially available equipment.

An important advance in computer engineering has been the development of desk-size electronic computers of far greater utility than older mechanical types. These small-scale but true electronic computers are competitive in price with the larger mechanical calculators but embody some of the advantages of faster calculation and greater memory associated with the larger electronic computer installations. They are especially useful for smaller scale problems involving limited size programs and amounts of data.

2–3.1. Digital Computers. This class of computers has the widest application and is the type generally understood when referring to electronic computers. Recent years have seen a proliferation in the number of companies producing computers and in the models available.

Modern, high-speed digital computers generally are of the internally stored program type and consist of five interacting components: input, storage or memory, arithmetic, output, and control. Procedural instructions and data for specific problems are translated into machine language in the input component. The translated input, results of intermediate steps, and final results are held in the storage unit. The arithmetic unit executes the operations of adding, subtracting, multiplying, or dividing, according to the instructions held in the control unit. The output unit takes the results from storage and transforms them into understandable form either by printing out the results or displaying them on a cathode-ray tube.

The functions of electronic computers are not unique. The same operations are carried out by a human operator with a mechanical desk calculator. In this case, the desk calculator serves as an arithmetic unit of very limited storage capability. The human operator serves as the input unit by punching a keyboard. Storage and output are effected by the operator by reading dials on the machine and writing down the intermediate or final results. Control is effected by the operator remembering the steps, either from memory or from a check list.

The storage of information and instructions in these electronic machines is commonly achieved by the use of magnetic storage devices. Information is entered into the machine and recorded as a magnetized or non-magnetized area on some storage device such as magnetic cores or drums or cylinders.

Digital computers are capable of application to many diverse problems. They can carry out long and involved calculations and processes on large amounts of data when given the proper instructions. They will carry out a series of steps involving such tasks as arithmetical operations, sorting, comparing, choosing, ranking, etc., without human intervention once they have been given the proper instructions. However, it is worth mentioning that these machines do not really "think" in a creative sense. They can do operations of astonishing complexity, but only if they have received instructions which have been previously formulated by some human brain.

The development of sets of instructions or job routines for a specific machine or problem has been given the name programming. Each computer has its own set of instructions, which may differ from machine to machine. Nevertheless, all programs have in common that they tell the computer to perform arithmetic or logical operations, or both, in a given sequence. Each step of a program must be very carefully stated in utmost detail, since the machine will do exactly what it is told, no more and no less. Given a problem, a program must be developed to process that problem through a chain of instructions. The program must direct the computer through every step. It must consider the sequence of operations and the arithmetical and logical operations to be carried out at each stage of the sequence. The prepared program must then be put into a language which the machine can understand. The operation of translating a program into machine language is called coding. Certain types of data-processing jobs recur frequently, making it possible to develop a machine program that can be used over and over with different sets of data. Many programs for numerous problems have been developed by the manufacturers of electronic computers and at computing centers. Collections of such programs are called libraries.

Data and instructions can be entered into these machines in several ways. Punched cards of the type described earlier, continuous paper tape, and magnetized tape are commonly used. Paper tape is similar to conventional punched cards in that information is represented by positions of holes in the tape. Magnetized tape consists of a plastic tape coated with a metallic oxide. Data and instructions are represented on this tape in the form of minute magnetized areas. After information enters the machine, it is represented by a sequencing of electrical pulses. Pulse groupings are then interpreted to mean numbers and letters.

The computational speed of electronic computers and their ability to handle masses of data have wrought what can almost be called a revolution in forestry. The powerful techniques of regression and correlation analysis in forest research work have been popularized and made practicable by the preparation of standardized machine programs to handle the immense amount of computations. Forest inventory techniques have also been greatly modified. The long and tedious compilation of volume estimates with their sampling errors can be rapidly accomplished by these computers. The computer revolution was also responsible for the widespread adoption of the continuous inventory system, especially by large industries.

2–3.2. Non-Digital Computers. Machines of this type differ from digital computers in that they carry out their operations by measuring some physical quantity. Electronic non-digital, or continuous variable, computers solve problems by translating measurements of physical quantities into electrical magnitudes. Since these machines operate by means of physical analogy, they are commonly referred to as analog computers. Analog computers are usually designed for the solution of a single problem or class of problems. The machine then gives all desired solutions for varying conditions. Digital machines, on the other hand, can be applied to any problem but will give only the specific solution. The solutions from analog computers are also limited in their accuracy by the precision to which the physical quantity utilized in the computer can be measured.

These analog computers are but one type of non-digital computer, which utilizes electronic principles. Non-digital computers can also be prepared which will carry out calculations based on other physical quantities that may be conveniently measured, such as length or angle. A good example of a non-digital or continuous computer which has been known for many years is the slide rule. This device makes use of the additions of length as the physical quantity to allow numerous arithmetical operations to be performed.

2–4. RELATION OF DATA RECORDING
TO SUBSEQUENT COMPUTATIONS

The design of forms for recording observations or field measurements should always be undertaken with a view to the required subsequent calculations. The following kinds of recording forms should be considered:

1. Recording forms can be designed for entering observations without concern for subsequent calculations. Later calculations are then done entirely separately, extracting the needed information from the array on the form. It is obvious that this may not be an efficient procedure since data may be in sequence or order unrelated to the steps of the calculation procedure. If this kind of recording form is used, it should be designed to harmonize with subsequent calculation procedures. If possible, this type of form should be supplanted by those subsequently discussed.
2. Another type of form can be designed with space for recording observations, carrying out required subsequent calculations, and recording the results on the same form. A form of this type assumes that data reduction will be done by hand or desk-type calculators.
3. If data-processing machines are to be used for calculations, field forms can be designed with the object of allowing the most efficient transfer of data to an input device. For example, observations may be entered in the office on punched cards, punched tape, or magnetic tape from the original recording form. When this transfer sequence is to be followed, it becomes important to design the form so that data can be read from and entered into the machine input device in the simplest and most logical order. If possible, the se-

quence of data positions on the form and the machine input device, such as punch card, should be the same so that transference can be an orderly and efficient operation. In those cases where information must be entered in the computer in code form, it is worthwhile to provide a key with the form so that the appropriate code designations can be immediately recorded at the time of observation.

4. It is also possible to record field observations directly on an input device which can be utilized directly by data-processing equipment. The most successful and generally used devices are mark-sensing cards and prescored cards shown in Fig. 2–2 and described in Section 2–2. The disadvantages of using machine cards for direct recording of observations are threefold: (1) the cards are easily bent or damaged causing difficulty in later machine processing; (2) the amount of information which can be entered on a single card is reduced since the capacity of a mark-sensing or prescored card is, at most, half that of the usual punch card; (3) it is not easy to read and check the original value of a measurement if it is recorded directly on a punch card in the form of a blacked-out space or hole.

2–5. SYSTEMS APPROACH TO CALCULATIONS

The idea of programming—breaking down a complex process into its individual parts and directing how each of these will be carried out—is essential to the use of a computer. One must understand that this process is neither new nor unique to electronic computers, although its necessity is paramount here and has, thus, been given added stimulus with the advent of data-processing machines. Actually, the breaking down of a complex calculation into simpler components has always been used to some extent, albeit in less orderly and systematic fashion. Without attempting to discuss computer programming, which is a specialized skill, it is worth recognizing the fundamental principle of orderly calculation procedures in logical sequence since they should be used for all calculations from longhand operations to the most sophisticated computer. Programming for computers, of course, covers both arithmetical operations and instructions for making logical decisions. These often become very involved and to carry them out in a logical, orderly, and efficient sequence it has been found essential to utilize a systems approach and flow charts. For less complex calculations the necessity of this approach is not so imperative. However, it is still a good idea to think in these terms and to use a programming-type methodology to an extent consistent with the complexity of the calculations. Thus, when a computation is to be executed it should be reduced to a sequence of smaller calculations, preferably not requiring any intermediate steps. A series of arithmetical operations indicated in some manner such as a mathematical formula should be studied to see what is the most efficient way of carrying out the individual indicated operations. For calculation by longhand or with simple desk calculators the best procedure is to set up a calculation form so that the steps can be carried out in an orderly fashion.

3

Linear Measurements

3–1. PRINCIPLES

Length is a fundamental measurement in that it may be observed directly (see Section 1–4). Linear measurement consists of determining the straight-line magnitude of any object from one point to another. The configuration of an object may be curved or irregular, so that the length must be specified as either the straight-line axis connecting the two points, or the equivalent distance as it would be if the curves or irregularities were straightened. An example would be the periphery of a closed figure with curved boundary such as the irregular cross-section of a tree stem or the circumference of a circle. Length measurements can be made directly or indirectly. Direct length measurement is accomplished by placing a prototype standard or copy of a defined unit against the object to be measured. The number of such units and/or fractions of a unit between terminals is the length. This is exemplified by the common use of a foot rule or scale. Indirect linear measurements can be accomplished in several ways. Principles of geometry or trigonometry can be employed to measure a length without physically occupying or touching the object. Linear measurements can also be determined by using knowledge of the speed of sound and light. The recent development of the LASER (Light Amplification by Stimulated Emission of Radiation) offers possibilities of the precise measurement of lengths over great distances (McNish, 1964). The periphery of plane figures, such as shown in Appendix Table A–2, can be determined by formulas. The equivalent length of an irregular, curved boundary may be determined by tracing the line with a wheel of known circumference and reading the number of revolutions, or approximated by dividing the curved line into linear sections and summing their individual measurements.

If a curve is expressible as an equation, its length between any two points can be determined by integration. The length of a curve, $Y = f(X)$ between $X = a$ and $X = b$ is given by:

$$L = \int_a^b \sqrt{1 + \left(\frac{dY}{dX}\right)^2}\, dX \qquad (3\text{--}1)$$

The task of length determination in forestry can be extremely varied. For example, it can consist of such diversified measurements as the height of a tree, the length of a log, the width of a tree crown's image on an aerial photograph, the length of a tracheid under a microscope, the length of the femur of a wildcat, or the length of the boundary of a tract of land.

It should be borne in mind that techniques of measurement are rarely unique to any one measurement activity. Hence, rather than attempt to describe techniques for all measurement tasks, only a limited number are discussed here, with the hope that their wider applications can be appreciated.

A few of the specialized linear measurements most commonly met with in forestry work are covered in this chapter. For techniques or instruments particular to some phase of forestry or an allied subject, the student is referred to specialized texts.

3–2. LAND MEASUREMENT

Forestry as a phase of land management constantly requires distance, area, and volume measurement of portions of the earth's surface. The specific methods and techniques of this activity belong in the realm of surveying, although the constant reference to land measurements makes it imperative that it be briefly mentioned here. For details regarding specialized techniques and instruments, the student is referred to standard texts on surveying such as Davis, Foote, and Kelley (1966). A concise summary of modern procedures used in connection with aerial photogrammetry is given in the Manual of Photogrammetry (1966).

Land measurements require two kinds of linear determination, horizontal and vertical distances. Vertical distances, or differences in elevation of features of the earth's surface from each other or from a datum plane can be determined in the field by spirit leveling, trigonometric leveling, barometric leveling, and such recently developed systems as the Airborne Profile Recorder (APR) and the Airborne Control System (ABC). Elevations can also be determined from stereoscopic pairs of aerial photographs by measurement of parallactic differences. Horizontal distance is the length of a line between points in a plane parallel to the horizon. In land measure this is the distance of primary interest although slope distance, or the length of a line between two points in an inclined plane, is often measured and then reduced to the horizontal. Horizontal or slope distances can be determined by direct measurement with tapes, by various applications of triangulation, or by instruments utilizing the speed of sound and light waves. Shoran and Hiran are radar-type systems used for navigation and the determination of long distances with an accuracy of 1:60,000 and 1:100,000 respectively. The Tellurometer and subsequently developed similar systems are portable electromagnetic distance-measuring instruments with accuracies of 1:100,000 or better (Hilger and Watts, 1965). These instruments determine distance from the time required for a radio wave to travel to and from the point being measured. An earlier developed instrument, the Geodimeter, uses light rays instead of microwaves as the measuring unit (Bergstrand, 1959). The Geodimeter projects a light beam to a distant reflector which reflects the light back to the instrument. A phase comparison is made between the light being projected and being received and is then converted to distance. Since measurements made with any of the electronic instruments are slope distances, they must be converted to the horizontal. Blaschko (1964) described the use of these instruments for forestry purposes in Austria and concluded they were most suitable for surveying work using aerial photogrammetry. It is interesting to note that Bitterlich (1955) described a method of using sound for approximating distances in forest surveying.

In the United States, direct horizontal or slope distances are measured either with the engineer's tape or the surveyor's chain. Most direct measurements are made with the engineer's 100-foot steel tape. The surveyor's chain, a vestige of earlier land measurement, is a steel tape 66 feet long divided into 100 links, each 7.92 inches long. These units are used in the measurements of land areas employing the General Land Office system of land subdivision (U. S. Department of the Interior, 1947). They are also used extensively in forest surveying and inventory work in North America.

3–3. DIAMETER MEASUREMENT

Diameter measurement consists in measuring the length of a straight line passing through the center of a circle or sphere and terminating at each end at the circumference or surface. The most common diameter measurements required in forestry are made on a tree's woody portions: the main stem of a standing tree, its branches, or cut portions. The basic importance of diameter measurement is that it is one of the directly measurable dimensions from which cross-sectional area and volume can be computed.

3–3.1. Effect of Irregularity of Form on Diameter Measurement. The woody parts of a tree commonly approach a circular form in cross-section and for many measurement purposes are assumed to be so. However, the cross-sectional shape frequently departs from the circular and at times this eccentricity may assume importance.

A main objective in the measurement of stem diameter is to determine the cross-sectional area at the point of measurement. When the stem is circular no problem is encountered and any single diameter or circumference measurement will suffice. For those cases when the cross-section is not circular, for practical computational purposes, the formula for the area of a circle is used and the problem is to find some "diameter" which will yield the closest approximation to the true area when employed in the formula.

The departure from circularity will often approach an ellipse although in some cases the cross-section may be completely irregular. Assuming an elliptical shape, calculating the arithmetic mean of the major and minor axis, and subsequently treating this average as the diameter of a circle will always result in an overestimate of the true area of the ellipse. To obtain the true cross-sectional area of an elliptical stem, the appropriate average is the geometric mean, $\sqrt{d_1 d_2}$, and not the arithmetic mean, $\dfrac{d_1 + d_2}{2}$, of the major and minor diameters. If the periphery of an elliptical-shaped stem is measured and then assumed to be the circumference of a circle, the diameter of this circle will always be greater than the diameter of a circle whose area is equal to that of an ellipse. (For a more comprehensive discussion of the effects of eccentricity on cross-sectional area see Section 6–3.1.)

In the case of irregular-shaped cross-sections the appropriate diameter and how to obtain it is not so obvious. Considerable investigation has been carried out to find the best procedure for measuring the diameters of trees which depart from the circular and elliptical shapes to give cross-sectional areas close to the true values (Prodan, 1965; Chacko, 1961; and Matérn, 1958).

There does not seem to be any conclusive evidence for the selection of any one of the many proposed methods as best for the diameter measurement of irregular shapes under all circumstances. Consequently, for practical purposes the best practice is to use the procedure recommended for elliptical-shaped sections. This procedure is recommended since in the majority of cases tree stem cross-sections tend toward a circular or elliptical shape. For a circular shape the geometric mean and the arithmetic mean are equal. It should be obvious that for irregular shapes the correct cross-sectional area will not be obtained. For determinations in some research activities these estimates may not be sufficiently accurate, but for most purposes will be consistent with the other measurements of tree dimensions.

The units used in the United States for tree diameter are inches and decimals thereof. In countries using the metric system, and for scientific work in the United States, tree diameters are recorded in centimeters. The methods and instruments used for measuring these diameters are not unique to trees or logs. They should be considered only as specific adaptations of the general methods of measuring the diameter of any circular object.

3–3.2. Diameter of the Standing Tree. The main stem of a tree is a tapering geometric solid, approaching a form somewhere between a neiloid and a cylinder (see Chapter 8); the diameter of the main stem will normally decrease from its base to its tip. For purposes of standardization, the representative diameter of a standing tree has been accepted as the diameter at a fixed height above ground. In the United States, the diameter is measured at 4.5 feet above ground level and is referred to as diameter, breast high, commonly abbreviated as d.b.h. or dbh. In countries using the metric system, the standard diameter is measured at 1.3 meters (4.3 feet) above the ground level.[1] For trees on slopes, it is recommended that dbh be measured at a point 4.5 feet or 1.3 meters above ground level on the uphill side of the tree. Diameters of the stem at higher points are often required and are referred to as upper stem diameters. Diameter may be qualified as o.b. or i.b., designating outside or inside bark measurement. Bark thickness on a standing tree can be conveniently determined by using a bark gauge. The usual instrument, the Swedish bark gauge, consists of a steel shaft, half-cylindrical in shape, which is pushed through the bark. The cutting edge is dull on one side so that the shaft will penetrate the bark but is stopped at the wood. Doubling the bark thickness and subtracting from the outside bark dimensions gives diameters inside bark.

3–3.3. Measurement of Diameter of the Standing Tree. Diameters of standing trees can be recorded to varying degrees of precision, depending on their intended use. If tree diameters are to be used for estimating the quantity of wood in the tree from volume tables (see Section 9–4), the precision of the measurement should be consistent with the diameter

[1] The abbreviation of diameter, breast height, recommended by IUFRO (1959) is d when measured at 1.3 meters above ground. If the diameter is measured at another point, such as 4.5 feet, it would be indicated by a subscript, e.g., $d_{4.5}$.

classes shown in the table. The presence of buttresses or basal swelling on standing trees, especially as occurs in tropical regions, may invalidate the use of dbh measurements for subsequent tree quantity (e.g., volume) estimation. Buttresses are often of irregular shape with flutings which make a diameter measurement meaningless because buttress or basal swelling dimensions will usually have no consistent relation to the quantity of wood in the tree. Although various practices are followed in dealing with this irregularity, the fundamental idea is to substitute for dbh another diameter measurement at a higher point on the stem which is assumed to indicate what the diameter would be at breast height if the irregularity were not present. There is a risk, of course, in considering diameters taken at variable heights above ground level to be equivalent to dbh determinations for estimating tree quantities from volume tables constructed on the basis of tree dbh as an independent variable. It is doubtful if variable-height stem diameters will maintain the same relationship to height, form, volume, etc., as will diameters taken at breast height. But, for lack of a better procedure, stem diameters are taken above the point where deformation ceases to affect the "normal" stem diameter. In tropical regions this question assumes importance and merits further investigation.

Other conventions have been adopted to deal with other irregularities which may occur in diameter measurements. Trees consisting of two or more stems which fork below the dbh level are considered as separate trees and the diameter is measured for each stem separately. If a fork occurs exactly at the dbh level, the diameter measurement is taken immediately below the enlargement caused by the fork.

Many instruments have been devised for measuring dbh. Descriptions of a few of the most commonly used and practical follow.

Calipers. Calipers are the most commonly used instruments for measuring tree diameters. Their construction varies and modified designs frequently appear. Figure 3–1 shows examples of three of the simplest forms. One form (a) consists of a graduated scale of metal or wood with two arms perpendicular to it. One arm is fixed at the origin of the scale and the other arm slides. For correct readings, the movable arm must form a 90° angle with the scale when the arms are pressed together. The diameter of a circle can be obtained from a single reading. If the cross-sectional form approaches an ellipse, two readings should be taken at right angles to approximate the major and minor axes and the geometric mean used as the diameter. Another type of caliper (b) consists of a set of fixed arms forming a V-shape. The graduations on these arms are so calibrated that, when the instrument is placed on the tree, the points of tangency indicate the diameter of the tree. A similar Finnish instrument (c) consists of a straight and a parabolic scale radiating from a common origin (Wiljamaa,

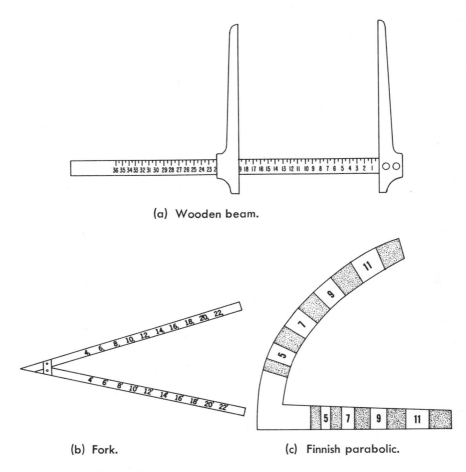

(a) Wooden beam.

(b) Fork.   (c) Finnish parabolic.

Fig. 3–1. Calipers for tree diameter measurement.

1942; Vuokila, 1955). A number of new caliper-type instruments have been developed in recent years. Kondor (1964) described a caliper consisting of two pivoting bow-shaped arms that indicates the maximum diameter of a tree. The lignometer (FAO, 1958) is a caliper with arrangements for automatic tape recording of diameter to the nearest .5 inch. The instrument also has features enabling other data to be tape recorded at the same time. Badan, Henson, and Steward (1961) reported on another caliper which permits the automatic registering of diameter measurements by punching paper tape. Ivanjuta (1964) described a universal mensuration instrument which includes a modified caliper that permits the immediate determination of mean diameter.

Diameter Tape. The diameter tape is a steel tape so graduated that the diameter (at a point corresponding to the circumference) can be read directly by wrapping the tape around the circular object. The graduations are determined by using the relationship: circumference $= \pi \times$ diameter. The diameter inch-divisions are thus described on the tape at intervals of 3.1416 inches. If the cross-section being measured is not a perfect circle, the indicated diameter will always be too large as compared to the diameter of the equivalent area of a true circle.

In the United Kingdom and in some former British colonies, the circumference or girth of a tree is measured rather than dbh. This circumference is then divided by 4 and called Quarter Girth. The Quarter Girth is used in approximating the dimensions of a squared beam which could be obtained from the stem of the tree and in estimating the volume of a tree (see Hoppus foot in Section 7–3).

Biltmore Stick. The Biltmore stick consists of a straight rule which is held horizontally at arm's reach against a tree so that the zero end of the graduations lies on the line of sight tangent to one side of the tree (Jackson, 1911; Bruce, 1916). By shifting the same eye, the intersection of the line of sight to the other side of the tree with the scale of the Biltmore stick will indicate the tree's diameter. This instrument will give approximate values and is useful principally for rough work. Its inaccuracies are due to the necessity of holding the stick at the exact distance (usually 25 inches) from the eye for which it is calibrated and to the difficulty of holding the eye level with the dbh point on the tree.

The graduations for the Biltmore stick can be found from the formula:

$$B = \frac{D}{\sqrt{1 + \dfrac{D}{E}}} \tag{3-2}$$

where:

B = distance from zero point of the stick to the position for a given diameter
D = tree diameter
E = perpendicular distance from eye to stick

Sector Fork. Bitterlich's sector fork (Visiermesswinkel), shown in Fig. 3–2, is a recently developed instrument similar in principle to the Biltmore stick (Bitterlich, 1959). The instrument determines diameters from a sector of a cross-section of a circle. One side of the sector consists of a metal arm and the other side consists of a line of sight. The line of sight intersects a curved scale upon which are printed diameters or cross-sectional areas. It is not necessary to hold the instrument at a fixed distance from the eye because a sighting pin attached to the instrument fixes the line of sight for any distance.

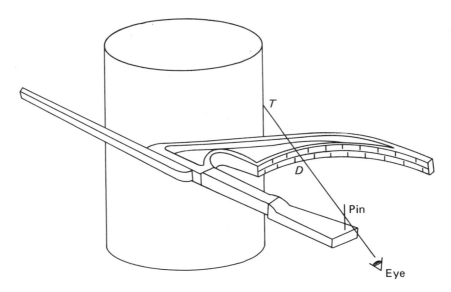

Fig. 3-2. Sector fork (*Visiermesswinkel*). *T* is point of tangency of line of sight; *D* is diameter reading on scale.

When cross-sectional area is the prime consideration, diameter measurements should be taken with the calipers. The measurement of diameter with the diameter tape will result in a systematic overestimate of the cross-sectional area (see Section 6-3.1). The consistency of this error is advantageous when measurements are repeated over annual or longer intervals for estimating diameter growth. Calipers can also be used for this purpose if permanent marks are made on the tree stem so that the points of contact of the caliper arms are at the same spots at successive measurements. Even with a tape it is desirable to mark the position of the measurement so that repeated measurements are truly comparable.

In some instances the average of a number of diameter measurements is required. A good example is the average dbh of a stand of trees. The series of diameter measurements can be considered simply as an array of linear measurements and the arithmetic mean calculated. However, if the primary interest in the measurement of diameter is to permit the subsequent calculation of cross-sectional area and volume (assuming tree circularity), then a better average would be the quadratic mean, Q,

where:

$$Q = \sqrt{\frac{\sum\limits_{i=1}^{n} dbh_i{}^2}{n}} \qquad (3\text{-}3)$$

The quadratic mean indicates the diameter of the cross-section of average area.

3–3.4. Upper Stem Diameters. Tree stem diameters at points above dbh are frequently required, as in the estimation of form or taper. The idea of direct volume computation of sample trees in forest inventory work based on the measurement of diameters at several points along the stem has stimulated interest in devising instrumentation for this purpose. The main difference between dbh and upper stem diameter measurements is that the former can be measured by physically placing the instrument on the stem of the tree, whereas this technique is inconvenient for upper stem measurements. Upper stem diameters can be obtained using the previously described instruments, but this necessitates climbing the tree. For diameter measurements at heights of about 17 feet, as needed for Girard form class determination (see Section 8–7.2), calipers mounted on a pole (Ferree, 1946), or a diameter tape on a pole (Godman, 1949) may be used. Other dendrometers[2] employ optical systems allowing diameters to be measured with the instrument at some distance from the tree. Most of the optical dendrometers that have been devised or proposed over the years have been shown by Grosenbaugh (1963*b*) to be all variations of three main classes: optical forks, optical calipers, and short-base range finders. Much of the following description is based on his presentation.

An optical fork is a dendrometer employing two intersecting lines of sight, tangent at the level of the diameter measurement, with the vertex of the resultant fork angle at the observer's position. The basic geometry is shown in Fig. 3–3. The diameter is determined from the final formula in the figure. The $\mathrm{Cos}\,\dfrac{\alpha}{2}$ is often dropped or can be approximated by using $\mathrm{Cos}\,\dfrac{\theta}{2}$.

Instruments employing this principle vary in design and use depending on whether the fork angle is fixed or variable and if it is coupled to the vertical angle. Using a fixed angle necessitates varying the distance from the tree. With a variable angle a convenient distance can be used and the angle changed. When the fork angle is coupled to the vertical angle, the need to measure it and introduce it in the subsequent calculations is eliminated. Many instruments have been devised on the optical fork principle including the recently developed Spiegel relaskop. It is

---

[2] Considerable ambiguity has occurred in the use of the term dendrometer. The Society of American Foresters (1958) has defined a dendrometer as "an instrument designed to estimate the diameters of standing trees at any given height by sighting from the ground." In common usage, the term has generally meant instruments designed to take diameters at points above dbh. It has also been used to refer to any instrument for measuring tree diameters.

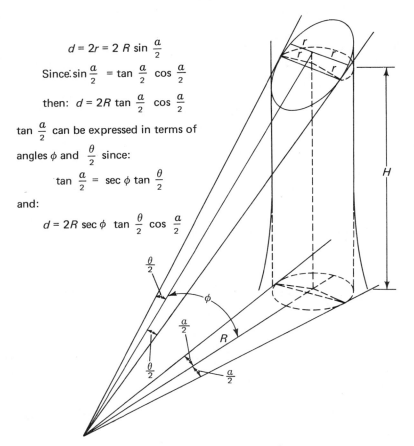

$$d = 2r = 2R \sin \frac{a}{2}$$

Since: $\sin \frac{a}{2} = \tan \frac{a}{2} \cos \frac{a}{2}$

then: $d = 2R \tan \frac{a}{2} \cos \frac{a}{2}$

$\tan \frac{a}{2}$ can be expressed in terms of

angles ϕ and $\frac{\theta}{2}$ since:

$$\tan \frac{a}{2} = \sec \phi \tan \frac{\theta}{2}$$

and:

$$d = 2R \sec \phi \tan \frac{\theta}{2} \cos \frac{a}{2}$$

Fig. 3–3. Principle of optical fork.

worth mentioning that terrestrial photogrammetry utilizes the same basic trigonometry but the angular measurements are made on photographs rather than in the field (Manual of Photogrammetry, 1966; Ashley and Roger, 1969).

A modification of the optical fork principle is exemplified by the use of a transit as reported by Leary and Beers (1963). In this case neither the vertical angle ϕ nor the angle $\frac{\theta}{2}$ need be measured. The horizontal angle is formed on the plates of a transit by sighting two sloping tangent lines to the selected upper stem diameter, these two lines being then projected vertically downward to a horizontal plane. The upper stem diameter is then: $d = 2R \sin \frac{\alpha}{2}$ or for small angles: $d \simeq R \sin \alpha$.

The optical caliper employs two parallel lines of sight, tangent to the tree at the point of diameter determination, whose distance apart can be varied and measured at the observer's position. The principle is illustrated in Fig. 3–4. The two lines of sight can be considered equivalent to the arms of a caliper. The distance between the two lines of sight, d, is equivalent to the tree diameter, regardless of the range from the tree. Several instruments have been devised using this principle, among which is the pentaprism caliper reported by Wheeler (1962). This instrument uses two pentaprisms shown at the bottom of Fig. 3–4 to maintain parallelism in the lines of sight. In this instrument, the left-hand prism is fixed and the right-hand one can be moved along the scale d. The reflection of the right side of the stem is brought into coincidence with the left by moving the right-hand prism. The length of the base limits the usefulness of this instrument to measurements of about 36 inches. The measurement of larger diameters would require a longer base inconvenient for easy portability. The incorporation of a magnification system with the pentaprisms would improve accuracy. Even without the addition of a lens system, preliminary tests indicated that there was less than a 1 in 20 chance that a pentaprism measurement would differ from that of a wooden caliper by 0.5 inch or more (Wheeler, 1962). Two or more observations would reduce this to within 0.2 inch or less.

The application of the rangefinder principle for measuring the upper stem diameters of standing trees is embodied in the Barr and Stroud dendrometer reported on by Hummel (1951), Jeffers (1956), and Grosenbaugh (1963a). In its basic form an optical rangefinder is a triangulation device designed for the measurement of distance from the position of the instrument to some remote point situated at the apex of a triangle, using the measurement of two angles and an included known optical base. The principle is illustrated in Fig. 3–5 (a). The angle A is a right angle, B can be varied to give coincidence. When coincidence of the images is achieved, the distance R to the point E can be found from the known base b and the angle B. The application of the rangefinder principle as a dendrometer is more complicated since not only the distance R from instrument to tree center is desired, but the radius of the remotely located diameter position must be determined. The simplest illustration of the problem can be demonstrated by assuming all sights from the instrument to the diameter position are in a horizontal plane with the tree inside the fixed line of sight as shown in Fig. 3–5 (b). This is referred to as the case of back convergence. Front convergence would occur if the tree was to the left of the fixed line of sight. In this case the formula given for tree diameter in the back convergence case would yield a negative value. In actual practice, angles F and T are in a slant plane at an angle formed by the fixed line of sight and a horizontal line. This results in a much more complicated solu-

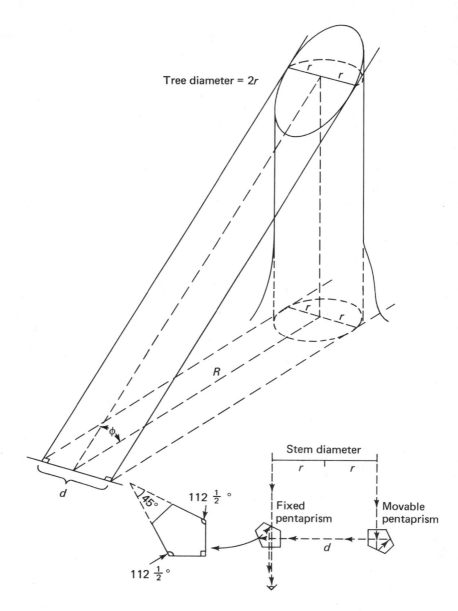

Fig. 3–4. Principle of optical caliper.

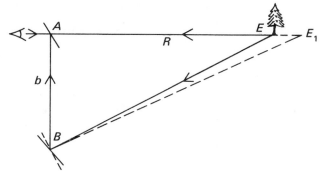

(a)   Principle of rangefinder.

(b)   Principle of rangefinder dendrometer —
assuming all sights in a horizontal plane
and tree inside fixed line of sight
(back convergence).

$$K = \frac{r}{\sin x} = \frac{b-r}{\cos (w+x)} = \frac{b}{2 \sin \frac{1}{2} T \cos \frac{1}{2} F}$$

$$r = \frac{b \sin x}{\sin x + \cos (w+x)} = \frac{b \left(\sin \frac{1}{2} T \cos \frac{1}{2} F - \cos \frac{1}{2} T \sin \frac{1}{2} F \right)}{2 \sin \frac{1}{2} T \cos \frac{1}{2} F}$$

$$d = 2r = b \left(1 - \frac{\tan \frac{1}{2} F}{\tan \frac{1}{2} T}\right)$$

$$R = \frac{b}{2} \left(\cot \frac{1}{2} T - \tan \frac{1}{2} F\right)$$

(when $2r = b$, $F = 0$ and $\tan \frac{1}{2} F = 0$)

(when $2r > b$, $\tan \frac{1}{2} F$ becomes negative)

Fig. 3–5. Rangefinder dendrometer.

47

tion for tree diameter and height, which was explained by Grosenbaugh (1936b).

Mesavage (1965a) pointed out that the ideal dendrometer should be portable, incorporate magnifying optics, and utilize split-image coincidence. At present, the Barr and Stroud dendrometer best fits these specifications although modification of the pentaprism caliper to incorporate these requirements would make it an excellent instrument for all but very large diameters.

3–3.5. Precise Measurement of Diameter Changes. For research purposes, measurement of minute changes in diameter over a short time interval may be required. Measurements may be desired for periods as short as an hour. Diameter changes over brief periods cannot be detected with the usual instruments such as calipers or diameter tapes. Three classes of instruments have been devised to measure minute changes; dendrometer bands, dial-gauge micrometers, and recording dendographs. Dendrometer bands, as described by Liming (1957), and Bower and Blocker (1966), consist of aluminum or zinc bands with vernier scales scratched into the surface. The band is fitted around the stem of a tree and held taut in place with a spring. Changes in diameter as small as .01 inch can be read. Reineke (1932) described a dendrometer utilizing a dial-gauge micrometer and a fixed reference point on a tree. The stationary reference point consists of a screw hook screwed into the xylem. The distance from this point to a metal contact glued to the bark of the tree is then measured with the micrometer. Differences between repeated measurements give the periodic change. Measurements may be taken accurately to .001 inch. Daubenmire (1945) modified this instrument by using three screws inserted into the xylem as the fixed reference. The dial gauge with a three-legged mount is then placed on these reference points for a reading.

Various types of recording dendographs have been developed. Fritts and Fritts (1955) devised a precision dendograph consisting of a pen on an arm, bearing on a fixed point on the tree stem. The pen records diameter changes to .001 inch on a chart mounted on the drum of an 8-day clock. Phipps and Gilbert (1960) designed an electrically operated dendograph similar in principle to the dial-gauge micrometer. A potentiometer is fixed to a tree using two screws anchored in the xylem. A movable shaft is fixed to the outer bark; any displacement in the shaft is measured as a change in electrical resistance and can be recorded on a continuous strip chart.

3–3.6. Diameter of a Cut Section. The measurement of the diameter at the end of a log can be easily determined with an ordinary rule or scale. The measurement can be made in the same way as for a standing tree or by measuring radii, which in this case are visible. Since the center of the section as evidenced by the pith can be found, it is possible to determine the length of a number of radii and obtain their quadratic mean. The radii can be chosen randomly to get an unbiased estimate. The quadratic mean radius would be found from equation 3–3 using radii values instead of diameters.

If diameters, inside or outside bark, are required at points other than the ends of a log, the procedure and instruments described for measuring the diameter of a standing tree can be used.

3–3.7. Crown Diameter. Interest has been stimulated in recent years in the diameter of the crown of a tree as a variable, since it is one of the directly measurable dimensions on an aerial photograph. The value of this variable is that it can be used to estimate stem dbh and, in turn, quantity of wood in a tree. Numerous studies have been carried out indicating that a linear model relating stem diameter to crown diameter (Dawkins, 1963; Vezina, 1962) and a combination of crown diameter and total height (Minor, 1960) is suitable for practical applications over the range of merchantable tree sizes. Crown diameter in relation to stand density has also been investigated by Smith and Bailey (1964).

The measurement of tree-crown diameter by photogrammetric techniques is described by Husch (1947) and Spurr (1960). Crown diameter measurement on aerial photographs or in the field is necessary for obtaining the basic data to establish dbh-crown diameter relationships. Field determination is a difficult problem due to the physical impossibility of making a direct measurement and to the irregularity of the crown outline. The usual procedure is to determine the crown perimeter by projection vertically to the ground and then to make the diameter measurements on this projector. Instruments for determining this vertical projection have been described by Husch (1947), Nash (1948), Raspopov (1955). The quadratic mean radius of the vertical crown projection can also be determined by measuring a number of radii using the tree stem as the center in an analogous manner to that described for the end cross-section of a log.

3–4. HEIGHT MEASUREMENT

The measurement of height is the determination of the linear distance of some object from the surface of the earth or some other datum plane, in a direction normal to that plane. It differs from length only in having a specified orientation.

Vertical distance measurements are based on principles identical to those used in other linear measurements. They differ only in the technique of making the measurement. The difference stems from the fact that one end of the linear distance is usually inaccessible or cannot be physically occupied. For this reason, techniques and instruments have been devised to permit height measurements either from a single terminal of the dis-

tance or from a point remote from either terminal. Other than land elevation, determination of tree height is the principal vertical distance measurement required in forestry. Techniques and instruments devised for
general height measurement can often be applied to the specialized problem of tree-height measurement. Conversely, the procedures used for tree-
height measurement can also be used to measure the heights of objects
other than trees.

3–4.1. Types of Tree Height. The term "tree height" is ambiguous without
defining the terminals of this linear distance. Figure 3–6 shows a suggested
classification for height or length measurements which can be applied to
standing trees of both excurrent and deliquescent form. These linear distances are defined as:

Total Height. The vertical distance between ground level and tip of the
tree. The advantage to this type of height is that the terminals, i.e., the
base and top of tree, can be more objectively determined than for other
points along the stem. On the other hand, difficulties can be experienced
in seeing the top in a closed stand or deciding what is the uppermost limit
of tree crown.

Bole Height. The distance between ground level and the crown point.
The crown point is the position of the first crown-forming living or dead
branch. Bole height expresses the height of the clear, main stem of a tree.

Merchantable Height. The distance between ground level and the terminal position of the last usable portion of a tree. There are several criteria
which can define this upper terminal and the exact location is to a large
extent subjective and further problematical by difficulty, under forest
conditions, of sighting the upper part of a stem in a tree crown. The upper
position may be defined by a chosen minimum top diameter or by branching, irregular form, defect, etc., which limits what is considered the utiliza-
ble wood in a stem. The merchantable height may be up to a minimum top
diameter or below it but never above. The minimum top diameter chosen
will depend on the intended use of the wood in the stem.

Stump Height. The distance between ground level and the basal position of the main stem when a tree is cut.

Merchantable Length. The sum of the lengths of the portion of a tree
which are cut and utilized. This includes material such as trim allowance
which may be wasted in the manufacturing process.

Defective Length. The sum of the lengths of portions of the stem whose
diameter is larger than minimum acceptable, but which cannot be utilized
because of some kind of defect.

Crown Length. The distance between crown point and the tip of the
tree.

If heights or lengths to other positions are needed they may be defined
and added to the list.

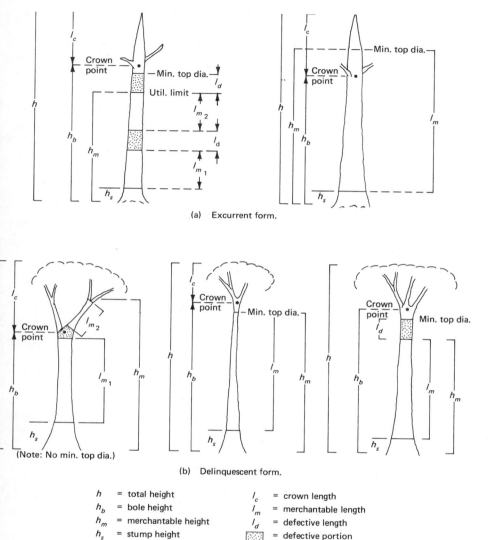

(a) Excurrent form.

(b) Delinquescent form.

h	= total height	l_c	= crown length
h_b	= bole height	l_m	= merchantable length
h_m	= merchantable height	l_d	= defective length
h_s	= stump height	▨	= defective portion

Fig. 3–6. Tree height and stem length classification.

3–4.2. Tree Height and Length Measurements. The measurement of height and length of portions of standing individual trees is a task which has stimulated the ingenuity of foresters for many years. The principle of measuring the height or vertical length of a standing tree does not differ from that of measuring heights of any object. However, other circumstances complicate the situation. The method and instrument must be within economic bounds, field instruments must be light and portable, and the difficulty of sighting in a closed stand must be considered.

In measuring tree heights one should keep a few principles in mind:

1. For the usual instruments used, the top and base of the tree must both be visible.
2. The measurement of the several kinds of height are always taken vertically even if the tree is leaning. Total heights are taken on vertical distance from tip to the ground. This may not be the true length of the stem. The lengths of sections of a stem may be measured or estimated following the axis tree stem or branch. A study of the conditions depicted in Fig. 3–6 will show that the sum of these lengths may not equal height to the same point in the stem.
3. The vertical height of leaning trees should be measured from a point at right angles to the lean. Otherwise, trees leaning away from the observer will be underestimated and trees leaning toward the observer will be overestimated.
4. The total height of trees with cone-shaped tops can be measured more accurately than flat-topped trees.
5. The method and instrument should be consistent with the desired accuracy of the height measurements.

Individual tree heights can be measured from aerial photographs (Spurr, 1960) or in the field. The existence of parallax in stereoscopic pairs of photographs affords an excellent means of height determination. The length of shadows as measured on single aerial photographs can also be used to determine heights. Topographic relief displacement on single photographs is theoretically possible but has not been found practically useful. The techniques and instruments used in height determination from aerial photographs constitute a specialized field which will not be covered here. The following treatment covers only field determination of vertical tree height.

The heights of small trees can be measured directly with a pole or rod. An engineer's self-reading level rod or similar device can be used for small trees. Sectional or sliding poles of wood, fiber glass, or lightweight metal can be used for taller trees. The use of poles is slow for tall trees but often used for continuous forest-inventory plot measurements. Height measurement of tall trees can be taken indirectly with height-measuring instruments called hypsometers. Numerous hypsometers have been devised over the years but they are all based either on the geometric principle of the relation of the sides of similar triangles, or either on the trigonometric principles of the relation existing between the sides and the trigonometric functions of the angles of right triangles, as illustrated in Fig. 3–7. A comprehensive summary describing and evaluating many hypsometers has been compiled by Hummel (1951). Patrone (1963) and

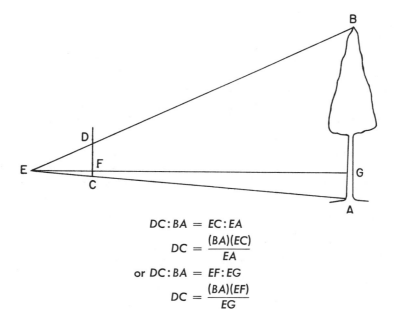

$$DC : BA = EC : EA$$

$$DC = \frac{(BA)(EC)}{EA}$$

$$\text{or } DC : BA = EF : EG$$

$$DC = \frac{(BA)(EF)}{EG}$$

(a) Application of geometric principle of similar triangles to tree height measurement.

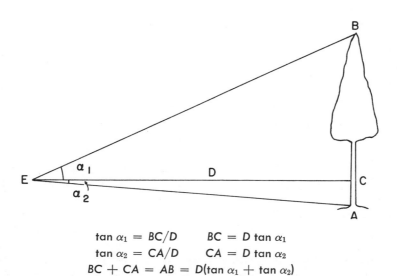

$$\tan \alpha_1 = BC/D \qquad BC = D \tan \alpha_1$$
$$\tan \alpha_2 = CA/D \qquad CA = D \tan \alpha_2$$
$$BC + CA = AB = D(\tan \alpha_1 + \tan \alpha_2)$$

(b) Application of trigonometric relationships of right triangles to tree height measurement.

Fig. 3–7. Tree height measurement.

Pardé (1961) give descriptions of a number of the more popular European hypsometers.

3–4.3. Hypsometers Based on Similar Triangles. Examples of instruments employing the principle of similar triangles are the Christen, Klausner, Merritt, Chapman, and JAL hypsometers. Of these instruments, the only ones in general use in the United States are the Christen and Merritt.

Christen hypsometer. This hypsometer consists of a graduated strip of metal or wood with protruding edges at top and bottom. A pole of known length is held against the tree. The hypsometer is then held vertically at a distance from the tree that will allow the height of the tree to be measured just to fit in between the upper and lower edges of the instrument. The observer need not stand at a fixed distance from the tree. The point of intersection of the line of sight to the top of the pole and the upright hypsometer indicates the height of the tree. The graduations on the hypsometer must be based on the height of the pole used.

Merritt hypsometer. This hypsometer consists of a series of graduations placed on a strip of wood, usually one side of a Biltmore stick. The graduations are commonly in terms of 16-foot logs or half-logs although any linear unit may be used. The stick is held vertically at a fixed horizontal distance from the eye of the observer. The distance chosen is usually the same as used for the diameter graduations of the Biltmore stick, i.e., 25 inches. The observer stands at a fixed distance (1 to 1.5 chains) from the tree and holds the stick vertically so that the lower line of sight to the base of the tree is tangent to the zero graduation of the stick. The intersection of the line of sight to the upper position on the tree with the hypsometer indicates the height. The graduations for the hypsometer and method of use are illustrated in Fig. 3–7 (a).

3–4.4. Hypsometers Based on Trigonometric Principles. Numerous hypsometers employing the principles of trigonometric functions have been developed. There are a wide variety of designs with differing accuracies, ease of use, and portability. All these hypsometers require two readings. The height above eye level is first determined; and a second reading must be either added or subtracted to give the total height of the tree or other object.

Curtis and Bruce (1968) have shown how any clinometer measuring slope in percentage and a pole of fixed length can be used to measure the height in a manner similar to the principle of the Christen hypsometer (i.e., without need for any measurement of horizontal distance from a tree). Using this system, a pole of known length (between a fourth and a fifth of the tree height to be measured) is placed against a tree. The slopes from any convenient point are then read to the top of the tree, α_t, to the top of the pole, α_p, and to the base of the tree, α_b. With p as the known height of the pole the tree height is:

$$h = p \frac{\alpha_t - \alpha_b}{\alpha_p - \alpha_b} \qquad (3\text{--}4)$$

Note that slopes are in per cent and are assigned sign $(+)$ or $(-)$ according to direction of slope.

An engineer's transit may be used but is slow in operation and, for most tree-height measurements, the precision of the instrument is greater than necessary. The most commonly used hypsometers of this type in the United States are the Abney level (Calkins and Yule, 1935), the Haga (Wesley, 1956), and the Blume-Leiss (Pardé, 1955) altimeters. The Spiegel relaskop (Daniel, 1955) and the Barr and Stroud dendrometers also can be used for height measurement by trigonometric means.

Abney level. The instrument shown in Fig. 3–8 (a) consists of a graduated arc mounted on a 6-inch sighting tube. The arc may have a degree,

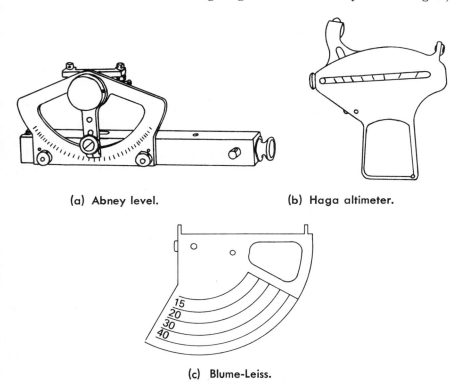

(a) Abney level.   (b) Haga altimeter.

(c) Blume-Leiss.

Fig. 3–8. Examples of hypsometers based on trigonometric principles.

percentage, or topographic scale. The degree scale indicates the angle in degrees for a sight from any horizontal distance. The percentage scale indicates elevation directly when the observer is at a horizontal distance of 100 feet from the object, and the topographic scale does the same for a distance of 66 feet. The instrument is used by centering a bubble in a level tube while sighting to the top or bottom of an object.

Haga altimeter. This instrument, shown in Fig. 3–8 (b) consists of a gravity-controlled, damped, pivoted pointer and a series of scales on an interval, rotatable, hexagonal bar in a metal, pistol-shaped case. The instrument indicates heights directly for several horizontal distances. Sights are taken through a gun-type peep sight and readings are taken by squeezing a trigger which locks an indicator needle at the observed height. A rangefinder can be added to the instrument, eliminating the necessity of using a tape to establish the distance to the tree. With the range finder a bar with markings indicating the several fixed distances must be affixed to the base of the tree.

Blume-Leiss altimeter. This instrument is similar in construction and operation to the Haga altimeter although its shape is somewhat different as shown in Fig. 3–8 (c). The five scales corresponding to five fixed, convenient distances from a tree are all evident at the same time. A rangefinder is incorporated into the instrument and used in the same way as the Haga.

The other available instruments are all similar in principle to those described. Tests of the accuracy obtainable with many of the available instruments (Ker, 1951; Lovengreen, 1952; Soest and Tiemens, 1953; Stoffels, 1955; Wesley, 1956; Abetz and Merkel, 1962; Laar, 1962) indicate that the Abney level, the Haga, and the Blume-Leiss are satisfactory, with the latter two somewhat faster and easier to use. Other hypsometers are more accurate, but the greater accuracy is the result of a more complicated, less portable instrument. In evaluating the usefulness of a hypsometer, as well as other measuring instruments, the time required in its use as well as the accuracy of the measurement must be considered.

3–4.5. Expressions of Stand Height. It is often necessary to use some single value to characterize the height of a forest stand. This value has found principal application in determining the volume of a stand from a stand volume equation or in determining the quality of a site.

A number of ways of expressing the average height of a stand of trees has been used or proposed and opinion varies on what is the most suitable expression. The different averages depend upon which trees in the stand are selected:

    1. The heights of all or a sample of the trees in a stand regardless of size or relative position can be measured but this requires excessive time and effort.

2. A procedure often used in North America is to obtain the mean height only of the dominants or of the dominants and codominants in the stand. The idea in measuring this portion of the stand is that these trees represent the most important component. However, the selection of what is a dominant or codominant is subjective and consequently may not be reproducible by another observer. This height expression is commonly used in determining site index.

3. A procedure used in Great Britain and New Zealand is to obtain the mean height of a fixed number of the largest diameter trees per unit area. The usual number has been 100 per acre. The average height of a fixed number of the tallest trees may be used but this approach has the disadvantage of requiring premeasurement decisions on which are the tallest trees or the postselection of the largest sizes from a large number of measurements.

In European forest practice, stand volume calculation is often carried out by the use of relationship:

$$V = (\bar{h})(G)(f) \tag{3-5}$$

where:

V = volume per unit area
G = total basal per unit area
$\bar{h}$ = average height of the stand
f = form class of the stand

Various expressions for height which will yield the correct volume (assuming appropriate values for G and f) have been investigated. The best known is Lorey's mean height. This expression is the weighted average height using basal area as the weighting factor as shown below:

$$h_L = \frac{n_1 g_1 h_1 + n_2 g_2 h_2 + \ldots + n_z g_z h_z}{G} = \frac{\displaystyle\sum_{i=1}^{z} n_i g_i h_i}{\displaystyle\sum_{i=1}^{z} n_i g_i} \tag{3-6}$$

where:

n_i = number of trees in a diameter class
g_i = average basal area of a diameter class
h_i = average height of the trees in a diameter class

For ease of calculation, a stand can be divided into five classes of equal basal area or five classes of equal number of trees per class (see Prodan, 1965). Lorey's mean height was derived from the stand volume equation 3–5 by considering the stand as made up of a series of diameter classes:

$$G h_L f = n_1 g_1 h_1 f_1 + n_2 g_2 h_2 f_2 + \ldots + n_z g_z h_z f_z \tag{3-7}$$

where f_i is the form factor for each diameter class. By assuming a constant form factor and solving for h_L we obtain equation 3–6. Note that $G = \Sigma n_{igi}$.

It is worth pointing out that the average height of trees selected in horizontal point sampling, as described in Chapter 14, yields Lorey's mean height (Kendall and Sayn-Wittgenstein, 1959).

Several expressions of average stand height have been developed which utilize a height-diameter curve. The height-diameter curve is constructed from sample tree data representing the stand. It is then necessary to decide what diameter is representative of the stand and read the height of a tree of this diameter from the curve. A frequently used procedure is to calculate the average basal area of the stand and use the mean diameter corresponding to this mean basal area. In European forest practice, the diameters of the tree of "central basal area" and Weise's average tree are also used (Prodan, 1965).

4

Time Measurement

4–1. USE OF TIME MEASUREMENTS

Time is of such importance in forestry that there must be a clear understanding of its nature and relationships to other measures. The basic concept of time is utilized in several ways:

1. As a framework within which the occurrence of events can be referenced. It denotes the position in a continuum of time at which some event took place.
2. As a measure of length or duration of a given event. The time is the interval between the inception and cessation of the event under observation.
3. As the basis of determining the speed or rate at which events or physical changes occur within a given period.

4–2. UNITS OF TIME

Fundamentally, time is measured as the duration of an interval between successive recurrences of some accepted event. The accepted event, be it the swing of a pendulum or the passage of the seasons, should recur at uniform stable intervals (Clemence, 1952). The greater the stability and uniformity, the more desirable is the chosen event as a reference standard. All conventional systems of time measurement are based on the observance of some natural phenomenon. The daily rotation of the earth on its axis provides the unit of time which is in everyday use: the mean solar day and its subdivision, the mean solar second, which is 1/86,400 part of the mean solar day. The mean solar day is taken as the mean interval between two successive passages of a fictitious mean sun over a given meridian. Although this unit of time is generally employed and is still the legal standard, it is no longer suitable as the fundamental standard time because the mean solar second is a fractional part of the period of rotation of the earth on its axis, and this period of rotation undergoes various changes causing variation in time units derived from it. The unit that appears to satisfy the requirement for a fundamental standard is the period of the earth's revolution around the sun, called the sidereal year. The sidereal day and the second based upon it are unvarying units which serve as better reference standards.

4–3. TIME MEASUREMENT METHODS

Instruments for the measurement of time have progressed considerably from the sundial, water clock, and sandglass of the past. The common method of time measurement presently in use utilizes either a mechanical or electrical clock. Electronic clocks using an electronic current of a specific frequency are a more recent development resulting in increased precision.

A chronograph is a clock device for recording information according to the time of its occurrence. The chronograph is adapted to the measurement of many transient-type phenomena of interest in foresty.

Instruments incorporating this device are illustrated by weather instruments such as the barograph, thermograph, hygrograph, and recording rain gauges. The dendrograph also utilizes this device in recording changes in the diameter of a tree with the passage of time. The typical chronograph consists of a strip chart wound on a drum. The drum is actually a clock, and rotates with the passage of time. If a recording pen is placed against the chart, its movement will be correlated with the time base. The recording pen is attached to whatever mechanism is being used and will move with changes in the measurements.

The rate of disintegration of radioactive elements provides another means of measuring time. Radioactive elements disintegrate at a constant and determinable time rate. These rates vary with the element, ranging between fractions of a second to many million years. Disintegration consists of the original number of atoms losing particles and being transformed into the next element in the disintegration series. As disintegration continues, after a time only 50 per cent of the original number of atoms will be left. This period in which a given quantity of a radioactive element will be reduced by one-half is called its half-life period. Use of the half-life period has been found valuable in various time-measurement problems. The accumulation of helium and lead from uranium-bearing minerals was one of the earliest applications and found useful in geological dating although other radioactive elements are more commonly used now.

4–4. SIZE AS A FUNCTION OF TIME

Measuring the change in the size of some variable in relation to time is of fundamental interest and importance in all aspects of forestry. For example, in biological terms we may be interested in the physical growth of individual trees or stands over a period of time, or from an economic point of view we may wish to see how the market for forest products has varied over the years. There are certain basic principles in all time relationships of this type regardless of the particular variable expressing size.

4–4.1. Average Rate of Change. If X represents any quantity whose size varies with time, then the average rate of change of X between the limits of a period can be expressed as:

$$v = \frac{\Delta X}{\Delta T} = \frac{X_2 - X_1}{T_2 - T_1} \qquad (4\text{-}1)$$

where:

v = average rate of change of X with time over the period
X_2 and X_1 = the sizes of X at the end and beginning of the period
T_2 and T_1 = the time limits at the end and beginning of the period
ΔX = change in X over the period
ΔT = the length of the period

The rate of change has a sign as well as a magnitude. Thus, a positive sign for v indicates an increase or movement in a positive direction and a negative sign shows a decrease or movement in a negative direction. As an example of the calculation, Fig. 4–1 shows the average rate of change in basal area per acre between ages forty and sixty years for western hemlock, site index 150, in Oregon and Washington.

4–4.2. Instantaneous Rate of Change. If the relation between the size of a quantity, X, and time, T, can be expressed in mathematical terms, the time interval can be shortened until it approaches zero as a limit and we can obtain the instantaneous rate of change. This instantaneous rate of change is the derivative of X with respect to T and is expressed as:

$$\frac{dX}{dT}$$

The relation between the average and instantaneous rate of change is expressed by:

$$\frac{\Delta X}{\Delta T} \to \frac{dX}{dT} \qquad \text{as } \Delta T \to 0 \qquad (4\text{-}2)$$

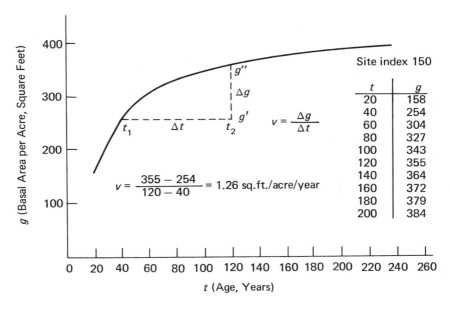

Fig. 4–1. Average rate of change of basal area per acre for western hemlock, site index 150, between 40 and 120 years. Adapted from Barnes (1962).

or:

$$\lim_{T \to 0} \left(\frac{\Delta X}{\Delta T}\right) = \frac{dX}{dT}$$

As a simple example, consider a hypothetical parabolic growth function which states that the size of an organism at age t is represented by $X = .3t^2 + 2t + 3$ as shown in Fig. 4–2 (a). The instantaneous rate of change or growth rate at any time T is given by the first derivative with respect to time:

$$\frac{dX}{dt} = .6t + 2$$

At each age, t, there is a rate of growth given by the formula and we can plot a graph of this rate of change. For the example, this rate of growth is uniform as shown in Fig. 4–2 (b).

4–4.3. Acceleration. The way in which the rate of growth, $\dfrac{dX}{dt}$, is changing is called the acceleration. Consequently it is the second derivative of the original function and is written as $\dfrac{d^2X}{dt^2}$. For the example:

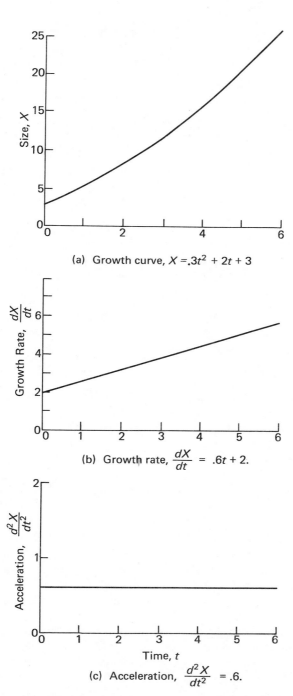

(a) Growth curve, $X = .3t^2 + 2t + 3$

(b) Growth rate, $\dfrac{dX}{dt} = .6t + 2.$

Time, t

(c) Acceleration, $\dfrac{d^2 X}{dt^2} = .6.$

Fig. 4–2. Relationships between growth, rate of growth, and acceleration.

$$\frac{d^2X}{dt^2} = .6$$

It is evident that this is the slope of the line, $\frac{dX}{dt} = .6t + 2$, and shows that the growth rate is constant and increasing .6 units per change in unit of time as shown in Fig. 4–2 (c).

As another example, consider the yield functions devised by Schumacher (1939) to show the cubic volume, V, for a forest stand at any age, t:

$$\log V = a + b \left(\frac{1}{t}\right) \tag{4-3}$$

He employed this function to express the yield of longleaf pine. Using regression analysis, the following equation was prepared for site index 50:

$$\log V = 0.8521 - 20.8837 \left(\frac{1}{t}\right)$$

This equation is shown graphically in Fig. 4–3 (a) with volumes expressed in cubic feet per acre. Its first derivative with respect to age is:

$$\frac{dV}{dt} = \frac{48.0859 \left[10 \left(0.8521 - \frac{20.8837}{t} \right) \right]}{t^2}$$

This derivative is the growth rate and for this example expresses the current annual growth, as shown in Fig. 4–3 (b).

The age of maximum current annual growth can be obtained by taking the second derivative, setting it equal to zero and solving for t. The second derivative can be expressed as:

$$\frac{d^2V}{dt^2} = \frac{48.0859 - 2t \left\{ \frac{48.0859 \left[10 \left(.8521 - \frac{20.8837}{t} \right) \right]}{t^2} \right\}}{t^2}$$

Its maximum value is at $t = 24$ years. This is shown as the high point on the curve in Fig. 4–3 (b). The second derivative is the acceleration and expresses the change in growth of cubic feet per acre per year. The acceleration is shown in Fig. 4–3 (c). If desired, the third derivative could be taken to determine the maximum and minimum values for the curve of acceleration.

The relationship between yield, growth, and acceleration as expressed by the first and second derivatives of a yield function has received little attention in North America forest mensuration, although recent studies by Clutter (1963), Turnbull and Pienaar (1966), and R. O. Curtis (1967) have used this approach.

It is worth pointing out that if we have an expression for a rate of

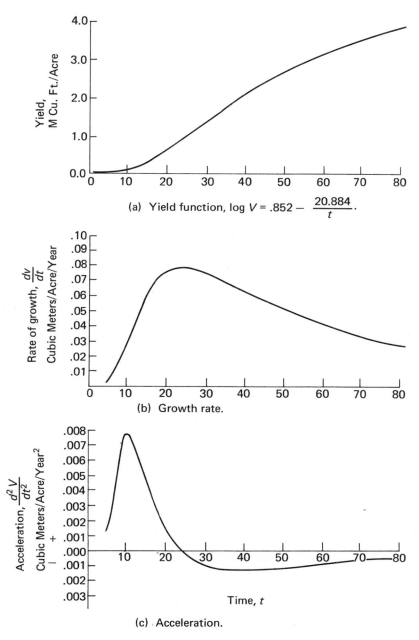

(a) Yield function, $\log V = .852 - \dfrac{20.884}{t}$.

(b) Growth rate.

(c) Acceleration.

Fig. 4–3. Relationships between yield, rate of growth, and acceleration.

change as a function of time we can deduce the function for the size of a variable at any time by the process of integration. Thus, if we had the hypothetical expression of the rate of change, S, of a variable over a certain period of time as $S = kt^{2.1}$, the expression for the size, X, at time t would be:

$$X = \int S \, dt = k \int t^{2.1} \, dt + c$$

$$X = k \frac{t^{3.1}}{3.1} + c$$

where:

k = a constant
c = constant of integration

4–5. TIME RELATIONSHIPS IN THE BIOLOGICAL ASPECTS OF FORESTRY

4–5.1. Growth and Age.

The age of any organism, such as a tree, is considered to be the length of time from its origin to the present or to some stipulated point in time. The age of a tree is reckoned from the germination of the seed. The age of a natural stand is a vaguer concept, since all the trees which comprise a stand usually start growth over a period. In this case, an average age is used as an approximation. Plantations obviously can be characterized by a definite age, since the genesis of the entire stand can be related to a specific date.

The size of a tree is primarily a function of the length of time the plant has been growing, which we designate as its age. Over this period of time, the attained size of the individual will be the result of the interaction of the inherent genetic growth capacity of the tree and the environment in which it is situated. Many of the environmental factors themselves, particularly those relating to climate (such as temperature, moisture, and duration and intensity of light), change and become more or less favorable as time passes. The growing season for any species is the period during which the climatic factors of the environment are sufficiently favorable to allow external measurable growth to occur. The duration of this period is generally taken as the same for all species within a geographical area, although closer observation will reveal differences for the various species. The length of growing season can be described by the dates of initiation and cessation of growth for the growth characteristics under observation. These dates fix the season in terms of a continuing and repeating scale, the calendar. The elapsed period between these dates, in a unit of time such as days, describes the length of the growing season.

Growing seasons are examples of cycles of events, which repeat themselves in a time continuum. A cycle is a term used to describe a uniformly recurring succession of the same kind of event, such as our solar day, lunar day, and lunar month. Our calendar and, in fact, all time measurement rests on this occurrence of cycles. Yearly climatic variation is a type of cycle of paramount importance in the growth of forests. The overall variation is made up of cyclic patterns of the individual climatic factors, such as air temperature, soil moisture, and length of day.

4–5.2. Age Determination. Alternation in the favorableness of environmental conditions causes corresponding periods of growth and dormancy in plants. In many trees, the initiation and cessation of growth are recorded by structural characteristics. The most easily recognized are the annual or seasonal increments of the woody tissue (xylem) of the stem. In some instances, the externally observable increments of internodal lengths are useful.

Most woody plants have a continuous cambium layer which produces the bark and woody tissue. During growing seasons, the cambium is active and produces a distinguishable layer of wood. In temperate climates this layer is quite distinct and is called an annual ring, since one layer is produced per year. Counting annual rings as a measure of age may lead to error in the case of suppressed trees, where an annual increment may not be apparent. In addition, more than one ring may appear per year in exceptionally fast-growing trees, or in years when the growing season may be interrupted by periods of unfavorable growing conditions, such as drought or defoliation by insects. In tropical or subtropical regions having alternating wet and dry seasons, a similar type of wood increment is produced. In tropical regions, not having distinct alternation in growing conditions, this growth characteristic is useless for determining the age of a tree.

The pattern of woody increments can be readily observed on stumps and on the ends of cut sections of tree stems. It is also possible to obtain a sample of the pattern, using an increment borer, shown in Fig. 4–4. The borer consists of a hollow auger which is inserted into the tree by means of a cutting edge and screw-type threads. An extractor is then inserted into the hollow tube and a core removed. If the borer has been properly located and drilled into the pith, a record of growth and age is obtainable for that position on the tree.

If the core and number of annual rings are obtained at some position on the stem, such as the dbh point, then the age refers to the number of years the tree has been growing above the point. The total age of the tree would be the number of years to reach that point, plus the previously determined age. For many purposes, age at a standard point such as dbh is satisfactory without correction for total age (Husch, 1956).

In certain coniferous tree species, e.g., *Pinus strobus* and *P. resinosa,* the annual height increment consists of a single leader or internodal length

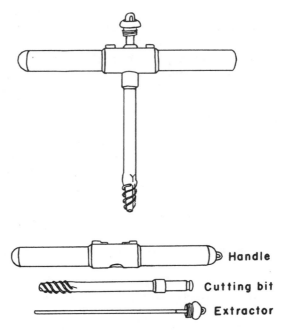

Fig. 4–4. Increment borer.

whose terminals are marked by a whorl of side branches. The age of the tree can be determined by counting the number of these whorls plus an additional two or three years for the period when the seedlings did not develop side branches. As trees grow older, the evidence of whorls disappears as the bark thickens, thereby diminishing the usefulness of this technique. This method is restricted in its applicability since few tree species exhibit this growth characteristic.

The average age of an even-aged stand of trees (see Section 17–1) may be estimated by obtaining the arithmetic average of the ages of a sample of randomly selected trees. For many purposes, such as site index determination of an even-aged stand (see Section 17–3), the average age of the dominants and codominants is used. Another procedure is to compute an average age weighted according to basal area or volume. The age of each sample tree is multiplied by its own basal area or volume, and the sum of all weighted ages is then divided by the sum of the weights. This procedure is preferable if stand age is to be related to stand basal area or volume, since it gives added weight to the ages of trees that contribute the most to basal area or volume.

4–6. TIME RELATIONSHIPS IN FOREST MANAGEMENT

The operation of a forest enterprise requires a number of management decisions concerning length of time. Important parts of management guides are concerned with the length of time a stand is allowed to grow before cuttings of some type are made. Two management specifications expressed as time periods, which control the entire forest operation, are the rotation and cutting cycles.

The rotation is the period of years that elapses between the formation of a stand of timber and the time when it is ready for cutting and regeneration. The concept of rotation is most easily understood and applied in terms of even-aged management. Ideally, the even-aged forest consists of a series of even-aged stands of approximately equal areas. The controlling factor governing operations in each stand is its age.

In uneven-aged management, cutting is not governed by age, but the size and rate of growth of individual trees and another time concept is used. This is the period, called the cutting cycle, between successive cuts in the same stand. These cuts act simultaneously as a stimulus to regeneration, a thinning, and a harvest cut. The cutting cycle concept is really valid only when considering uneven-aged management and should not be applied to intermediate cuttings under an even-aged plan of management. The chosen lengths of rotations and cutting cycles must be based on a thorough consideration of the economical and silvicultural knowledge of the species.

Two widely used expressions of the quality of a forest site for the growth of trees, which strongly influence management decisions, also incorporate the measurement of time. Yield tables for even-aged stands express the characteristics of forest stands, such as volume, number of trees, basal area, etc., at successive ages, on forest land of different qualities (see Section 17–4). Site index indicates the height which trees will attain at a standard age on different forest sites.

4–7. TIME AND MOTION STUDY

Forestry operations, whether in the woods carrying out silvicultural treatments, an inventory, harvesting sawlogs or pulpwood, or producing manufactured products at a sawmill or paper mill, can be thought of as an industrial process that is governed by the same principles as any other industry. As in all industries, the guiding principle is to carry out the given task with the minimum time, cost, and effort possible. The procedures necessary to accomplish these objectives have been known by several names including time and motion study, industrial engineering and methods design, and work measurement. The term time and motion study will be used here. For a comprehensive treatment of the subject the reader is referred to Barnes (1963), while Winer (1961) and Wright (1962) discuss the subject as applied to forest operations.

In application, time and motion study consists of studying the complete production process and dividing it into its fundamental motions or steps. The lengths of time necessary for the individual steps are then obtained. Attempts are made to eliminate superfluous steps or motions and to minimize the work and time of the essential ones by improving the human contribution or possibly by changing machines or the plan of operation.

To determine the time devoted to each step in a production process, either of two procedures may be used: timing or work sampling.

4–7.1. Timing. Using timing, each step of a process is timed with a stop watch with concurrent observation of environmental or working conditions. The influence of the work factors on length of time can then be studied. Stop watches can be operated to stop or start when desired, and readings taken for elapsed time of any particular event or element of the work cycle. Ordinary watches can be used but are not as desirable because the time of the beginning and end of the event must be read. The elapsed time is the difference between the two readings. The observations on length of time for each step in a process can then be analyzed statistically provided the data follow a normal distribution.

Timing procedures can be combined with the measurement of some variable affecting the amount of time required for the operation. In forestry applications, one might wish to measure the diameter of a standing tree, log size, volume per acre, etc., to develop relationships between these variables and the length of time it requires to carry out an operation such as tree felling, hauling, etc. As an example, Fig. 4–5 shows the results of a study by Jensen (1940) relating production time for cutting pulpwood to tree size. Numerous other studies have been conducted for many forest operations, such as length of time for the phases of forest inventory by different methods, length of time to prune different numbers of trees per acre and to different heights, etc.

4–7.2. Work Sampling. Work sampling consists in taking a series of short-interval observations during a production process at random time intervals and noting which step in the process is taking place, with the corresponding environmental conditions. Each observation consists of the discrete variable of occurrence or non-occurrence of a step of the production process at the observation interval. The observation intervals are very short periods, usually a time unit of one minute. The total number of time intervals possible per day would depend on the chosen length of

5

Weight Measurement

The potentialities of weight as a quantitative measurement in forestry, especially in the measurement of wood substance, has only recently been realized. With the increasing value of wood and greater realization of the shortcomings of traditional volume measurements, interest in and use of weight for scaling and other measurement tasks in forestry has grown rapidly since the middle 1950s and its increasing employment seems certain. (See Martin and Simard, 1959; and Taras, 1967.)

5-1. WEIGHT AND MASS

Weight is the force that acts upon material objects, pulling them downward toward the earth. This is the result of the action of gravity upon the mass of the body. Mass should not be confused with weight. The mass of a body remains constant everywhere and under all conditions, as long as no portion of the body is taken away and no matter is added to it. Weight, a force equal to the product of mass times the acceleration of gravity, varies with the locality in which it is measured. As a standard, the gravitational effect of the earth at sea level and 45 degrees latitude is taken as a constant. Since the gravitational effect will vary from place to place on the earth, the corresponding forces or weights of a given mass will also vary.

Since weight is a force, the unit of weight in the metric system should be a kilogram-force. This would be the weight, at any place, of an object whose mass is 1 kilogram. In the United States, the unit of force is taken as the pound. A kilogram-force is taken as equivalent to about 2.2 pounds.

In loose parlance, however, the kilogram-mass has been referred to as a unit of weight rather than the correct kilogram-force. Similarly, the pound unit is basically a measure of mass but through common usage is taken as a unit of force or weight.

The basic procedure in weighing at any locality consists of comparing an object of unknown weight with the weight of an object of known mass. Since the force of gravity at the place affects the standard mass and the unknown object identically, it follows that the weight thus determined is a relative value, independent of this magnitude of the gravitational force. Thus, in actual weighing procedures, an object would weigh the same at any locality, provided the standard used for comparison was of the correct mass.

5–2. INSTRUMENTATION

At present, the measurement of an unknown weight (or more precisely, force) can be carried out using five general methods as described by Doebelin (1966):

1. *By balancing it against the known gravitational force on a standard mass.* This method employs the well-known weighing machines; equal-arm balances, unequal-arm balances, and pendulum scales. Considine (1948) discusses the construction of these machines and their application to the problem of weight measurement in several industries.

2. *By measuring the acceleration of a body of known mass to which the unknown force is applied.* This method which uses an accelerometer for force measurement is of restricted application since the force determined is the resultant of several inseparable forces acting on the mass.

3. *By balancing it against a magnetic force developed by the interaction of a current-carrying coil and magnet.* At present this method is used for the determination of weights of no more than a gram.

4. *By transducing the force to a fluid pressure and then measuring the pressure.* This hydraulic method is exemplified by a container filled with a liquid, such as oil, under a fixed pressure. Application of a load increases the liquid pressure which can then be read on a gauge. Instruments of this type can be constructed with capacities of 100,000 pounds or greater.

5. *By applying the force to some elastic member and measuring the resulting deflection.* This method permits the measurement of both static and dynamic loads while the previously described methods are restricted to static or slowly moving loads. Using deflection transducers the force applied to some elastic element will cause it to move and this motion can then be transformed to an electrical

signal. The various devices differ principally in the form of the elastic element and in the displacement transducer which generates the electrical signal. The movement of the elastic element may be a gross, ocularly perceptible motion, or it may be a very small motion which requires the use of strain gauges to sense the force.

All of the methods of weight measurement will find application in some aspect of forestry. In forest industries and for weighing large, bulky quantities of wood, weighing machines have been and will continue to be widely used. However, the development of instrumentation based on the other methods has made rapid progress and applications to the weighing of wood can be expected.

5–3. THE DECISION TO USE WEIGHT AS A MEASURE

Weight is a quantitative characteristic that may be used because of necessity or because it has certain advantages. Weighing may be a necessity if there is no practical alternative way to measure a quantity; or it may be used if advantages are greater than those of alternative procedures.

For any given substance a decision to use weight as a measurement will depend on several important factors:

1. *Physical Characteristics of the Substance.* Weight is a logical measure to express the quantity of solids which occur as irregular pieces of varying sizes, such as pulpwood, coal, soil, seed, fertilizers, etc. These solids can also be measured in terms of volume by filling a space or container of known volume. However, the ratio of air space to actual material will vary, depending on the shape and arrangement of pieces and their compaction; this can seriously affect the accuracy and reliability of the volume measurement. Weight is a better measure under these circumstances.

2. *Weight as an Expression of Quantity.* Weight should be given prime consideration when it provides the most useful and logical expression of quantity. Thus, weight would be desirable for measuring a substance that cannot be accurately determined by other means. For example, weight measurement of pulpwood is supplanting cord and cubic measurement because with the increasing value of the raw material it can be done more economically and more accurately, and because the derived product, pulp, is expressed in weight. Indeed, when weight is the ultimate expression of quantity in a procedure of several stages, it seems logical to apply it consistently from the beginning.

The movement of materials from one place to another requires work, involving an expenditure of energy. The weight of the material being transported, rather than the volume, is the main factor affecting the amount of work and its cost. This is the reason transportation charges are based primarily on weight.

A material object may be composed of several components which, taken together, have a characteristic appearance. A tree is an excellent example. In its primary form, it consists of roots, stem, and crown. Each part is composed of additional units: the stem of bark and woody tissue, the woody tissue of various cells, etc. The proportion of any component of the whole, for example the proportion of a tree made up of bark, or the part of a tree consisting of usable fiber, can best be expressed by determining the quantities of the parts in terms of weight. This consideration is of increasing importance in forestry. As long as interest is restricted only to the main stem of a tree, volume estimates are practical. But with growing interest in what is considered the usable portion of a tree to include roots, branches, etc., then weight becomes the best means of quantity expression.

3. Feasibility of Weighing. To use weight, the substance in question must be physically separable from other material not relevant to the measurement. In addition, some kind of instrumentation must be available to indicate the weight. For example, it might be desirable to have the weight of the stem portion of a standing tree. Unless one were willing to cut down the tree and separate the portion of the stem in question, it would be impossible to determine directly its weight. However, indirect estimates can be made as discussed in Section 5-7.

4. Relative Cost of Weighing. The decision to employ weight or an alternative expression of quantity will be strongly influenced by the weighing costs and the value of the material. For example, weight might be intrinsically the best expression of quantity rather than volume but, at the same time, the costs of the weighing procedure and instrumentation may be greater than those needed for a volume estimate, such as with low-quality rough wood used for mine props. In another instance, the reverse may be true. But the decision must be further influenced by the value of the material under consideration. When the value is great, then the costlier procedure may be better, provided it gives a more accurate expression of the quantity present.

5-4. FACTORS INFLUENCING WOOD WEIGHT ESTIMATES

It is a comparatively easy and straightforward task to measure physically the gross weight of a quantity of "wood." But an estimate of the dry weight of the cellulose itself is not so simple. The overall weight of a quantity of wood is affected by the following factors:

1. Density
2. Moisture content
3. Bark and foreign material

Since the main objective is to determine the dry weight of the wood substance, excluding bark and any foreign materials when they occur, it is important to understand the meaning and effects of the abovementioned factors.

5–4.1. Density and Specific Gravity. The material substance that constitutes an object can occur in a close-packed structure such as a bolt of wood, or in a very porous form, such as a pile of shredded wood from the same bolt. The difference between the physical conditions illustrated here is described by the term "density." The density of a substance is its mass (or as often expressed, its weight) per unit volume.

In the metric system, density is expressed in grams per cubic centimeter or kilograms per cubic meter. In the English system the expression pounds per cubic foot is used, but since the pound is used as a unit of weight, instead of mass, the quantity can be distinguished from true density by calling it weight density.

The density of water under standard conditions is 62.4 pounds per cubic foot or 1 gram per cubic centimeter. These figures have been taken as standards to which the densities of solids and liquids can be compared. If the density of some other substance is divided by the density of water, the quotient is called the specific gravity or relative density.

$$\text{Specific gravity} = \frac{\text{density of a liquid or solid}}{\text{density of water}}$$

$$= \frac{\text{weight of liquid or solid}}{\text{weight of a like volume of water}} \quad (5\text{--}1)$$

When dealing with wood, specific gravity is the ratio of the oven-dry weight of a given volume of wood to the weight of an equivalent volume of water. Depending on the manner of determining the volume of wood, there can be three types of specific gravities:

1. Current-volume specific gravity
2. Dry-volume specific gravity
3. Wet-volume specific gravity

Current-volume specific gravity (also called basic specific gravity) utilizes the volume of green wood as it comes from the tree. Thus, if the oven-dry weight of the wood of some species was 30 pounds per cubic foot of volume as it comes from the tree, its specific gravity, S, would be:

$$S = \frac{30}{62.4} = .48$$

To determine the current-volume specific gravity, the volume of a sample of green wood is first determined. The sample is then dried at $103 \pm 2°C$ until it reaches a constant weight. This weight and the weight of water equivalent to the original volume are then used in the formula. Unless otherwise defined, the term specific gravity means current-volume specific gravity.

For dry-volume specific gravity, the sample of wood is first brought to oven-dry condition and then its volume determined. For wet-volume specific gravity, the wood is first soaked in water until it is completely swollen and will absorb no additional moisture and its volume then determined. The sample is then oven-dried and weighed. Procedures for specific gravity determinations are given in Forbes and Meyer (1955) and Besley (1967).

Panshin, deZeeuw, and Brown (1964) indicate that the cell-wall substance of woody plants is remarkably uniform. Its specific gravity is about 1.5. A cubic foot of solid wood substance with no air spaces would thus weigh about 95.5 pounds. However, the density of wood as it occurs as plant tissue never attains this figure because wood is a porous structure made up of cells of diverse characteristics. The specific gravities of commercial species in North America range between approximately .29 and .81. Woods from other parts of the world will range between 0.4 and 1.40. However, considerable variation in density between trees of the same species will occur.

For most species there is a tendency for the specific gravity to decrease from base to tip of stem. It appears that this variation is small in comparison to difference between trees. The density of the wood in cross-section of the stem will also show variation with a tendency to increase from the pith to the cambium. Large variations of specific gravity within individual annual rings have also been found but these variations seem to have little effect on the averages for the species.

5–4.2. Moisture Content. The moisture content of wood varies by species, by location in the tree, and by length of time following the cutting of the tree. It is this variability in the moisture content of wood and the difficulty of its practical determination that constitute a major problem with the use of weight as a measure of wood quantity. Moisture occurs in wood as free water in cell cavities and as absorbed water in the cell-wall material. The moisture content when free water has been evaporated leaving only absorbed water is called the fiber saturation point. Its value will vary from 27 to 32 per cent of the dry weight of the wood for most species. The moisture content of wood can be expressed as a percentage of either the dry or wet weight. Usually the percentage is based on dry weight. This is obtained by drying at $103 \pm 2°C$ until no further moisture loss occurs and a stable weight has been reached. This oven-dried weight is also used in the determination of specific gravity, since a standard moisture condition is necessary for calculation. The percentage is calculated from:

$$MC_d = \frac{W_w - W_d}{W_d} (100) \qquad\qquad (5\text{-}2)$$

where:

MC_d = per cent moisture based on dry weight
W_w = weight of wood before drying (in green condition)
W_d = weight of wood at oven-dried condition

In the pulp and paper industry, moisture content is often expressed as a percentage of the wet weight. In other words, the sum of the dry weight plus moisture content. This is expressed as:

$$MC_w = \frac{W_w - W_d}{W_w} (100) \qquad\qquad (5\text{-}3)$$

where:

MC_w = per cent moisture based on wet weight

As an illustration, if the weight before drying of a wood sample is 155 grams and the weight after drying is 85 grams, then the moisture percentages are:

$$MC_d = \frac{155 - 85}{85} (100) = 82.3\%$$

$$MC_w = \frac{155 - 85}{155} (100) = 45.1\%$$

By re-arrangement, equations 5–2 and 5–3 can be used to solve for the dry or wet weight of wood or the weight of water when the other factors are known.

Reports of numerous investigations have shown that the moisture percentages of wood vary with location in standing trees (Besley, 1967; Nylinder, 1967). The moisture percentage in the heartwood of conifers is usually appreciably lower than in the sapwood. In the hardwoods less variation is noted. The wood in the upper portion of coniferous species usually has a higher moisture percentage than the lower sections as a result of the larger proportion of sapwood. Differences in moisture percentages at varying heights of the stem in hardwood species is less pronounced. There are only slight variations in the moisture content by season for most species with several studies indicating a slightly higher moisture percentage in winter and spring than at any other times of the year.

The most marked changes in the moisture content of wood takes place following cutting of the tree. The woody tissue of a tree following cutting will lose moisture gradually and, if permitted to air-dry, its moisture content will reach about 12 per cent. This is always higher than in an oven-dried condition. The rate of loss of moisture and the percentage of moisture content of wood will vary with surrounding air temperature and humidity conditions. This variation can be controlled by the use of dry kilns in manufacturing processes; if left uncontrolled, it will follow atmospheric conditions.

The rates of drying of logs following cutting vary widely by region, species, time of year, and characteristics of the logs such as diameter, length, with or without bark, knottiness, manner of stacking, etc. In the summaries prepared by Besley (1967) and Nylinder (1967) varying weight losses were shown for several species in North America and Scandinavia over different periods with a maximum loss of about 40 per cent of the original green weight over a period of nine months. As an example, the results of a study to determine the loss in weight or logs in relation to time since cutting is given in Fig. 5–1 (Yerkes, 1967). This study for ponderosa pine showed an average loss of 5.3 per cent of the

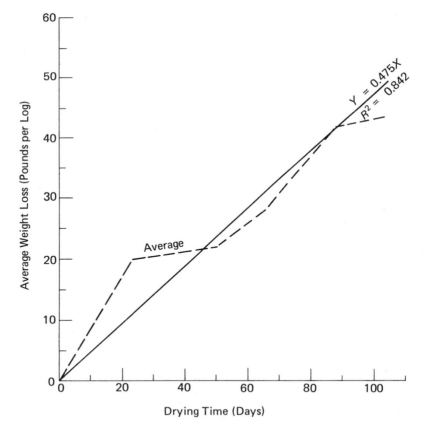

Fig. 5–1. Average and linear model of weight loss per log for 50 woods-stored ponderosa pine logs in the Black Hills (Yerkes, 1967).

initial weight for logs stored up to 108 days through the summer season.

5–4.3. Bark and Foreign Material. When weighing a quantity of wood, bark or foreign material such as ice, snow, mud, or rocks must be removed prior to the measurement or their weight must be deducted from the gross weight to obtain the weight of the wood alone.

Usually, the quantity of bark is of interest only to permit its deduction from a gross estimate to determine the quantity of wood substance. Bark can constitute a sizable percentage of the weight of logs or bolts out from a tree. For example, bark has been found to make up between 9 and 19 per cent of the weight of green, rough pulpwood of hardwood species in Maine, depending on the species (Hardy and Weiland, 1964).

The amount of foreign material on wood such as snow, ice, and mud is variable and depends upon the weather and methods of extraction. Wood cut and piled in the winter will usually have unpredictable amounts of snow and ice adhering. The same is true for mud when logs are ground skidded in wet weather. Thus, if weight scaling is employed, efforts should be made to remove or prevent foreign material from adhering to wood.

5–5. WEIGHT SCALING OF FOREST PRODUCTS

5–5.1. Weight Scaling of Pulpwood. The use of the cord volume unit for scaling bulk forest products, such as pulpwood, has long been accepted as a convenient but admittedly inaccurate means of measuring solid wood content. As long as measurement in the woods may be required, the cord is a satisfactory compromise. However, if determining wood quantity can be done on trucks or at a mill, weighing provides a cheap and accurate method of scaling.

The intent of weighing is to obtain a measure of the solid wood substance which is the source of pulp. It is, therefore, important to know the moisture content of the wood since it is a vital consideration in the pulping process at the mill. Additionally, if purchase and sale transactions of pulpwood are on a weight basis, it becomes important to know the quantity of water involved, since it will affect price. In spite of the problem of moisture content, the use of weight as a measure of pulpwood quantity has a number of advantages which explain its increasing acceptance. The expression of raw material in terms of weight permits the establishment of a more comprehensible and direct relationship to the yield of pulp, which is measured in weight. The use of weight scaling encourages wood suppliers to deliver their product to the mill as rapidly as possible following cutting to reduce weight loss. From the standpoint of the mill, this is desirable since fresh, green pulpwood is preferred. Trucks are usually loaded better for weight scaling since there is no advantage to loose piling with many air spaces. Weight scaling is faster than volume scaling and thus more economical. Weight determination is a more objective procedure than volume scaling since the factor of personal judgment is eliminated.

To employ weight as a satisfactory means of scaling pulpwood some dependable procedure is required to account for the moisture content which will permit an estimate of the dry weight of wood. If unpeeled wood is being handled, then estimates of the contribution of bark to total weight must also be made.

There are two ways to deal with these problems:

1. Develop average moisture and bark percentages for green wood at the time of cutting and according to length of time since cutting

To use the percentages for reducing fresh, greenwood weight to dry-wood weight, it is necessary that weighing be done immediately following cutting. In practice, the actual conversion of green weight with bark to dry weight without bark may not be executed. Rather, procedures may be established requiring that wood be weighed as soon after cutting as possible and prices are then established for wood in this condition. Although the quantity of dry wood is not explicitly determined, it is implicit in its effect on the price per unit weight.

An example of average moisture percentages for several species used for pulpwood in the southern and northeastern parts of the United States is shown in Table 5–1 derived from data from

Table 5–1
Sample Weights and Moisture Contents of Some Species Used for Pulpwood
(All weights are per cord.)

Species	Weights per Cord Green, Pounds			Oven-dry Weight, Pounds, Barked Wood	Percent of Moisture Content, Barked Wood
	Unbarked	Bark	Barked		
Longleaf pine	6374	660	5714	2920	95.7
Shortleaf pine	5669	675	4994	2037	145.1
White ash	5031	795	4236	2992	41.5
Beech	5584	446	5138	3157	62.7
Grey birch	5690	677	5013	2700	85.6
White birch	5731	705	5026	2788	80.3
Yellow birch	6090	786	5304	3013	76.0
Elm	5857	763	5094	2627	93.9
Red maple	5482	720	4762	2877	65.5
Sugar maple	5977	801	5176	3178	62.0

Taras (1956) and Swan (1959). The percentages shown are based on freshly cut green wood without bark.

When weighing is done at varying times following cutting, moisture and bark percentages according to length of time since cutting are required for a reduction to dry-wood weight. Percentages for the moisture component are more variable and less reliable than those for fresh green wood since season of the year, weather, location of wood since cutting, etc., will affect moisture content (Hall and Rudolph, 1957; Martin and Simard, 1959; Tuovinen, 1965; Besley, 1967; Nylinder, 1967).

2. Determine current moisture and bark percentages at the time of weighing

This approach requires that an estimate be made, at the time of weighing, of the moisture and bark contributions to the total weight. For practical purposes, this means that some type of sampling procedures be utilized which will provide these estimates. When moisture percentages have been determined, the dry weight of wood can be calculated using either equation 5–2 or 5–3, depending on the type of moisture percentage. The relationship expressed by equation 5–2 is shown graphically in Fig. 5–2. Nylinder (1958) found that the moisture content of sample disks

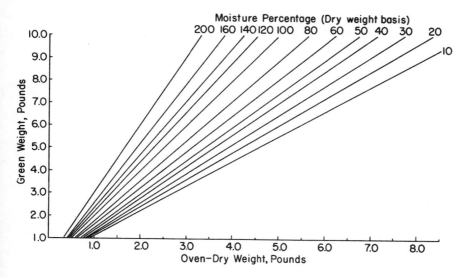

Fig. 5–2. Relationship of green weight, moisture percentage, and oven-dry weight of wood.

cut ten centimeters from the ends of logs gave satisfactory estimates of the moisture content of the log. Braathe and Okstad
(1967) used both a chain chipper which removed a thin triangular
segment of about thirty degrees of the cross-section of a log and
a drill which removed a sample from the radius, from which the
moisture percentage was determined.

Electrical moisture meters to indicate the moisture content of wood are
available but their suitability for moisture determinations of wood in
pulpwood or sawlog form has not been fully demonstrated (see Besley,
1967).

Since about 1950 pulpwood scaling on a weight basis has been practiced
or is being considered by many of the larger companies in North America
and northern Europe (Robinson, 1967; Taras, 1967; Curtis, 1965; Hardy
and Weiland, 1964; Tuovinen, 1965; Dietz, 1966; Jansson, 1964; Braathe
and Okstad, 1964). A convenient way of doing this is to use large platform
scales capable of determining the gross weight of an entire truck and
load. The weight of the empty truck, called the tare weight, subtracted
from the gross weight, gives the net weight of the wood. Dry weight of
wood substance can then be estimated by corrections for moisture percentage and bark.

Weight scaling is not practical or convenient if it is necessary to determine small quantities of pulpwood at scattered locations in the woods
as is the case when cutters are paid on a piece-work or production basis.
In this case the older volume scaling procedure using cord units is more
practical. When pulpwood operations are so organized that quantity determinations can be done at a central location, such as the mill, then the
advantages of weight scaling can be realized. Portable platform scales,
such as described by Lange (1962), are also available which permit weighing of truckloads in the woods.

Since pulpwood quantity expression in volume terms may be required,
converting factors of weight per unit volume have been determined as
shown in Table 5–1. (See also Hardy and Weiland, 1964.) However, there
seems little advantage in weighing as a means of indirectly estimating
volume since converting factors will be variable depending on species,
size and shape of individual bolts, manner of piling, moisture content,
bark, and specific gravity.

5–5.2. Weight Scaling of Sawlogs. Weight scaling can be used for sawlogs with two objectives in mind:

1. To estimate the usable product, such as board feet of lumber, de-
   rivable from the logs.
2. To determine the total quantity of wood substance present in the
   logs.

In both cases, the determination of weight is usually considered only as an intermediate step in the estimation of volume. This is the case since the lumber industry, particularly in North America, has established the custom of measuring sawlog raw material in volume units. For this reason, weight scaling of sawlogs usually consists of weighing them and then, by the use of an appropriate volume-weight relationship, converting the weight to volume.

It should be pointed out that the same problems with regard to moisture content, bark, and foreign material, as were mentioned for pulpwood scaling, also pertain to weight scaling of sawlogs.

As most commonly applied now, weights of entire truckloads are determined and converted to volume equivalents although individual log determinations can also be made. Weight scaling in truckload lots is most suitable when dealing with a single species and logs of uniform diameter, length, and quality. This explains why this procedure has been most widely used in southern pine in the southeastern United States. Weighing eliminates the need for individual measurement of logs in a load, speeds up the scaling time, and reduces personal judgment. Weight scaling is also a stimulus to the delivery of freshly cut logs, especially when weight is based on the green condition with no determination of moisture content and dry weight. However, when logs are variable in size and quality, some adjustment must be made. Otherwise, lower quality logs would command the same price as premium logs. For this reason objections have been raised to weight scaling of hardwood logs since they exhibit greater variation in size, shape, and defectiveness than softwood logs (Trimble, 1965).

In North America most attention has been concentrated on weight scaling of logs as a procedure which may give volume estimates more rapidly and cheaply than by the application of log rules. For this reason, most efforts have been directed toward the development of weight-volume relationships which will show the number of volume units of manufactured products (e.g., board feet) obtainable per unit of weight. In the United States, this has generally meant the development of board foot per pound ratios or regressions to relate the two. These relationships can be developed from studies involving the weighing of sawlogs, followed by tallying the actual number of board feet sawn from these logs. A ratio of this type shows the mill-tally yield rather than an estimate from a log rule. Consequently the ratio is dependent on species, log dimensions, and local milling practices. Guttenberg, Fassnacht, and Siegel (1960) developed a regression showing the relationship of board feet, mill tally, to weight in pounds, for individual logs of shortleaf and loblolly pines in Arkansas and Louisiana. Board-foot yields for different weights are shown in Table 5–2.

For industrial application of weight scaling of sawlogs, it is advan-

Table 5–2
Board-Foot Lumber Yields from Loblolly and Shortleaf Pine

Log Weight, Pounds	Predicted Green Lumber Yield, Board Feet
200	9
600	51
1000	94
1400	134
1800	184
2000	207
2200	231
2600	278
3000	328

SOURCE: Guttenberg et al., 1960.
Based on equation:
Board feet = [(Weight, lbs.)/9.88] + [(Weight, lbs.)^2/254,362] − 10.96

tageous to develop ratios of board feet to weight for truckloads of logs.

For suggested model equation to relate board foot scale to weight for individual logs and for total truckloads, see Row and Guttenberg (1966) and Row and Fasick (1966).

With the growing awareness of the weakness of the board foot as a volume unit (see Section 7–3), attention has been given to developing weight-cubic volume relationships to meet the second objective of estimate of total wood quantity. Thus the total quantity of wood in cubic volume can be determined from its weight. Yerkes (1966) developed an equation expressing the relationship between weight and cubic contents, as obtained from Smalian's formula, for ponderosa pine logs which states:

$$Y = -2.09 + 0.020X_1 \qquad (5-4)$$

where:

Y = cubic foot volume
X_1 = total log weight in pounds

5–6. WEIGHT ESTIMATION OF TREES AND STANDS

As Young pointed out (1964), the increasing value of wood as a raw material makes it imperative that recognition be given to the complete tree. Past and present utilization practices and technology utilize only a portion of the tree; that contained in the main stem above a variable stump to a chosen upper limit of utilization. The remainder of the cellulose material in roots, stump, and branches is usually left in the woods as waste or unusable material. This unused material constitutes a sizable portion of the total quantity of a tree as is evident when one measures the weight of the various fractions of a standing tree. Young, Strand, and Altenberger (1964) have shown the fresh and dry weights of eight components for seven tree species in the northeastern United States. Table 5–3 derived from their data gives an idea of the proportions these compo-

Table 5–3
Example of Proportional Weights of a Tree in 8 Components

Tree Component	Weights[1]			
	Red Spruce 12-Inch dbh, 70 Feet Total Height		Red Maple 12-Inch dbh, 70 Feet Total Height	
	Pounds	Per cent	Pounds	Per cent
Roots less than 1 inch in diameter	55	3	62	3
Roots from 1 to 4 inches diameter	115	6	96	5
Roots larger than 4 inches to base of stump	115	6	115	6
Stump—from 6 inches above ground to large roots	109	5	159	8
Merchantable stem from stump to 4 inches upper diameter	1218	60	1224	63
Branches larger than 1 inch diameter	76	3	109	6
Branches smaller than 1 inch diameter including leaves	320	16	118	6
Stem above merchantable portion	20	1	58	3
Total tree	2028	100	1941	100

[1]Weights are based on moisture conditions when freshly cut and include bark.
Data taken from Young et al., 1964.

nents constitute of the entire tree. Percentages for other species and sizes will vary but the order of magnitude will be similar. The model equation used in their study was:

$$\log X = a + b \log D + c \log H \qquad (5\text{–}5)$$

where:

X = weight in pounds of tree component
D = dbh in inches
H = total height in feet

Additional studies are reported on by Samset (1962), Baskerville (1965), Young and Carpenter (1967), and Attiwill and Ovington (1968).

5–6.1. Tree Weight Relationships. With the increasing use of weight as a measure of wood quantity, a need has developed for the estimation of the weight of wood in standing trees. Just as relationships can be developed to show the volume of wood in a tree correlated with measurable tree dimensions, a similar approach can be used for weight estimation. Several studies have been carried out using regression analyses to relate the weight of the various components in a standing tree to directly measurable tree variables. Several of these studies have concentrated on the weight of the merchantable stem. McGee (1959) has prepared a table of freshly cut merchantable wood weight for slash pine in the Carolinas, shown in Table 5–4, based on the dbh and total height of the tree.

Table 5–4
Merchantable Wood Weight of Freshly Cut Slash Pine
According to Dbh and Total Weight

Dbh	Total Tree Height in Feet					
	20	30	40	50	60	70
Inches			Weight in pounds			
6	81	131	183	235	287	
8		252	344	436	528	620
10			552	696	839	983
12				1012	1220	1429

Line indicates extent of basic data.
Top diameter, 3.0 inches outside bark.

SOURCE: Adapted from McGee, 1959.

Husch (1962) developed tree-weight relationships for permitting estimation of the oven-dry weight of wood in the merchantable stem in standing white pine trees in southwestern New Hampshire. Figure 5–3 can be used for estimating these weights based on dbh and total tree height.

As weight measurement of forest products gains acceptance it is a logical development that estimates of quantities of standing timber use this measure. The freshly cut or oven-dry weight of wood in a stand can be estimated in either of two ways. The volumes of tallied trees can be found from conventional volume tables and then converted to weight using a weight-volume relationship. A second and more direct way would be to utilize tree-weight expressions of the type shown in Table 5–4 and Fig. 5–3. Weight of freshly cut material would be obtained from a relationship exemplified by Table 5–4, while Fig. 5–3 shows oven-dry weight of wood. Inventories could be designed in which the parameter to be estimated is weight rather than volume. The principles and procedures of the inventory would be similar to volume inventories although sampling unit sizes and intensity may be different. Few inventories have been carried out for weight estimates, although Curtis (1965) reports its use by one company in southeastern United States.

In recent years forest ecological studies have utilized dry weight as a

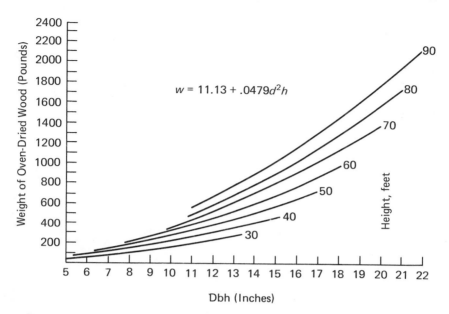

Fig. 5-3. Weight (w) of oven-dried wood in merchantable stem of standing white pine trees according to dbh (d) and total height (h). Weight includes stem without bark from stump to top d.o.b. of 3 inches (Husch, 1962).

measure of tree biomass per unit area of land. Tree biomass is here defined as the total quantity of dry material in the trees on an area of land. The total biomass consists of the sum of the components such as foliage, living branches, dead branches, stems, roots, etc. Baskerville (1965) and Attiwill and Ovington (1968) prepared regression equations for the estimate of the dry weight of these components using the model:

$$X = aD^b \qquad (5\text{--}6)$$
$$\log X = \log a + b \log D \qquad (5\text{--}7)$$

where:

X = oven-dry weight of the tree component
D = diameter (or girth) at breast height

They then estimated total stand weights of the components and biomass by summing weight estimates for each sampled tree.

A number of other tree weight studies has concentrated on the foliage and branch components of trees and stands especially in relation to estimation of the quantity of forest fuel for fire-hazard determination. For example, Wendel (1960) developed a prediction equation for estimating the weight of oven-dry foliage and foliage plus branchwood, W, for individual trees of *Pinus serotina,* based on dbh outside bark. His equations were of the form of:

$$W = a(\text{dbh})^b \qquad (5\text{--}8)$$

Other studies have been carried out to determine the weights of branches and foliage of individual trees and stands from diameter measurements (Kittredge, 1944; Satoo, 1962; Smirnov, 1963; Attiwill, 1966).

5–7. YIELD AND GROWTH STUDIES USING WEIGHT

Increasing interest has developed in expressing the yield of stands in terms of weight rather than the older expression of volume. Zobel, Ralston, and Robards (1965) carried out a study of the effects of site, age, and stand density in wood yields in oven-dry weight per acre for loblolly pine. A portion of their yield table is shown in Table 5–5. Maeglin (1967) used weight as the expression of quantity in a study of the effect of spacing on yields of plantation grown *Pinus resinosa* and *Pinus banksiana.*

Another logical step is the expression of tree and stand growth in weight. Only a limited amount of work has been done in this field, primarily in

Table 5–5
Yield of Dry Wood Per Acre in Tons for Loblolly Pine

Age Class	Site Index	Stand Density—Basal Area Per Acre (Sq. Ft.)				
		60	80	100	120	140
15	70			10.72	18.80	26.89
	80		11.71	19.79	27.88	35.96
	90	12.70	20.78	28.87	36.96	45.04
20	70		8.11	16.20	24.28	32.37
	80	9.10	17.19	25.27	33.36	41.44
	90	18.18	26.26	34.35	42.44	50.52
25	70	5.50	13.59	21.68	29.76	37.85
	80	14.58	22.67	30.75	38.84	46.92
	90	23.66	31.74	39.83	47.92	56.00
30	70	10.98	19.07	27.16	35.24	43.33
	80	20.06	28.15	36.23	44.32	52.40
	90	29.14	37.22	45.31	53.40	61.48
35	70	16.46	24.55	32.63	40.72	48.81
	80	25.54	33.62	41.71	49.50	57.88
	90	34.62	42.70	50.79	58.87	66.96

$W = -219384.0163 + 808.5691(\text{Stand Density}) + 2191.8590(\text{Age}) + 1815.4474(\text{Site Index})$
where:
    W = yield in lbs./acre

$S_{y.123}$ = 26066.8241 lbs./acre, R^2 = 0.7301
Adapted from Zobel et al., 1965.

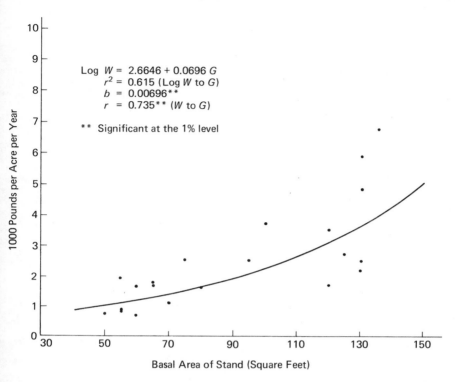

Fig. 5–4. Growth of loblolly pine expressed as pounds (W) of dry wood per acre per year in relation to basal area of stand in square feet (G) (Zobel et al., 1965).

Japan. An example of this approach is a study reported by Hirai and Aizawa (1966) showing average, current annual and total increment in kilograms for several species of *Populus*. Iizuka (1964) studied the theoretical relationship between volume and weight growth for sections and the entire tree stem, applying this result to *Cryptomeria japonica* trees. He determined the ages of the culmination of mean annual increment in both volume and weight. Zobel et al. (1965), in their study mentioned previously, showed the annual growth of loblolly pine per acre in weight as related to stand density, expressed as basal area. Figure 5–4 reproduces their findings.

6

Area Measurement

6–1. PRINCIPLES

Area is the two-dimensional extent of a plane or curved surface. It is a measurement derived from the fundamental measurement of length, using a ratio-type scale. The square of any unit of length yields the corresponding unit of area.

The areas of many plane figures can be most conveniently calculated by using the appropriate formulas shown in Appendix Table A–2. Areas of many other plane figures and curved surfaces bounded by curves and/or straight lines require the use of the calculus.

Area measurements basically require knowledge of the linear magnitude of two dimensions. Derived procedures have been developed which, in operation, eliminate the physical necessity of measuring these two dimensions, although it is still the fundamental basis for area determination. Several procedures are available to meet practical problems of frequent recurrence. Some of the procedures are here discussed.

6–1.1. Area by Counting. If a plane figure is drawn on rectangular coordinate paper consisting of uniform squares whose unit area is known, then the total area of the figure can be estimated by counting the numbers of whole squares which fall within the boundaries of the figures. When the lines marking the boundary of the figure divide one or more squares, it is necessary to estimate their fractions and add them to the number of whole squares. If the drawn figure represents some larger area to scale, the represented area can be obtained by the approriate converting factor which depends on the scale of the drawing.

If a dot were placed in the center of each square of the rectangular coordinate paper, and if the lines were then removed, a dot grid would be formed. This dot grid can then be used in a similar fashion to estimate area. Each dot represents a square of a certain area. The area of a figure can be estimated by counting the number of dots falling within the boundaries and multiplying this number by the area per dot. Dot grids on transparent plastic sheets, of varying densities or number of dots per unit area, are easily prepared or can be purchased. Dot grids can also be used in a sampling procedure to develop area percentages. A dot grid is placed over a figure made up of several component areas, such as a forest-type map. The number of dots falling in each component is then counted. These numbers are then expressed as percentages of the total number of dots falling within the overall figure. If the area of the total figure is previously known, the component areas can be obtained by multiplying by the several percentages. This procedure is frequently used with aerial photographs as described in Section 13–4, although it has numerous other applications. (See Section 9–3 on cord volume determination.)

Another procedure that also develops area percentages makes use of line transects. It is of primary utility, again, in determining areas for component parts of a plane figure. Equally placed lines are drawn through a figure, producing a gridiron effect. The lengths of lines falling in the component parts are then measured. Percentages are developed by making ratios of the total lengths of lines falling within a given component to the total length of all transects.

6–1.2. Area by Weighing. A weighing procedure can be employed to estimate the area of a plane sheet of uniform thickness (uniform weight per unit area) such as the area of a figure drawn on paper. A ratio of area to unit weight is first developed for the paper or other material. Areas of figures of any configuration can then be cut out and weighed. The total weight times the area per unit weight will then give the total area.

6–1.3. Area by Coordinates. If an XY axis system is established, the area of a polygon of any shape can be easily computed. Given the direction and distance between two points, A and B, as indicated on Fig. 6–1, then the X and Y components of the line can be calculated. The north–south component or vector is Y and the east–west component is the X vector. The coordinates of all vertices of the figure can then be obtained by addition or subtraction of successive vectors. The area of a closed figure can then be calculated by the continuous product method. If the X coordinates are designated as $X_1, X_2, X_3, \ldots, X_n$ and the Y coordi-

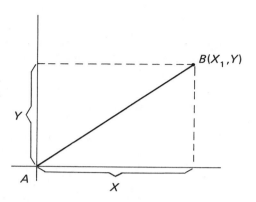

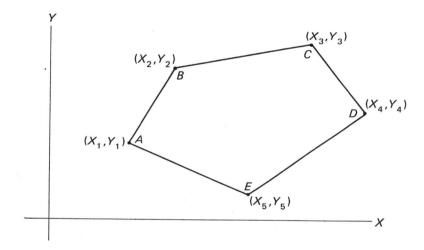

Fig. 6–1. Coordinates for vertices of a polygon.

nates are $Y_1, Y_2, Y_3, \ldots, Y_n$, then the the area of the polygon whose vertices are $(X_1, Y_1), (X_2, Y_2), (X_3, Y_3), \ldots, (X_n, Y_n)$ is:

$$\text{Area} = \frac{1}{2}(X_1Y_2 + X_2Y_3 + \ldots + X_nY_1)$$
$$- (X_2Y_1 + X_3Y_2 + \ldots + X_1Y_n) \quad (6\text{--}1)$$

This method is frequently used in surveying to calculate land areas.

6–1.4. Area by Integration. If the area of a plane surface is bounded by
known functions it can be found by solution of the definite integral:

$$A = \int_a^b f(X)\, dX \quad \text{or} \quad \int_c^d f(Y)\, dY \tag{6--2}$$

The simplest illustration is the area under a curve plotted from a known function and bounded by the X axis and ordinates at $X = a$ and $X = b$. Areas bounded by intersections of curves or straight lines of known functions can be found in this way by setting up the appropriate $f(X)$ or $f(Y)$ to define the area of interest. In forest mensuration, the method is useful when the function can be shown on a graph and the enclosed area is geometrically related to some variable of interest. One application is the calculation of the total volume of a fully regulated forest from an even-aged yield relationship expressible in equation form. The total volume in a fully regulated forest of rotation age n (or n units of area) would be the area under the curve of the yield function bounded by the ordinates at the initial stage, n_o, and rotation, n. Curtis (1967) utilized the approach of evaluating the area under a curve, setting up the expression, $\int_{A_o}^{A}$ (increment function) dA, to obtain cumulative cubic volume growth by age, A, for douglas fir.

The plane area of a figure represented in polar coordinates can also be determined by integration. The plane area bounded by a curve, $\rho = f(\theta)$, between the radius vectors, $\theta = \theta_1$, and $\theta = \theta_2$ is given by:

$$A = \frac{1}{2} \int_{\theta_1}^{\theta_2} \rho^2\, d\theta \tag{6--3}$$

Matérn (1958) used this method in his study of the cross-sectional area of tree stems. He used several functions in polar form to describe the contour of a tree's cross-section.

In the plane area defined by a continuous curve, expressed as $Y = f(X)$, the X axis and the ordinates $X = a$ and $X = b$ can be revolved about the X axis and will generate a solid of revolution (see Section 7–1.1.). The surface area of this solid, excluding the ends, can be determined from:

$$S_X = 2\pi \int_a^b Y \sqrt{1 + \left(\frac{dY}{dX}\right)^2}\, dX \tag{6--4}$$

If the curve is $X = g(Y)$ and it is revolved about the Y axis, the surface area between abscissa values c and d is:

$$S_Y = 2\pi \int_c^d X \sqrt{1 + \left(\frac{dX}{dY}\right)^2}\, dY \tag{6--5}$$

Since tree stems approach the forms of solids of revolution this method is useful in approximating the total surface or cambial area of a tree stem (see Section 6–3.2.).

6–1.5. Approximate Integration. When it is impossible or difficult to integrate by means of elementary functions, the area in a plane figure may be approximated using either the Trapezoidal or Simpson's Rules. In applying these rules, a plane figure is divided by a series of equally spaced chords at a known distance h, as shown in Fig. 6–2. (Using a set

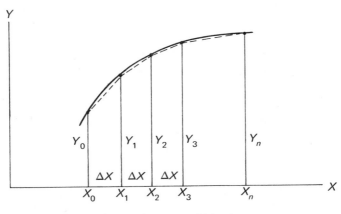

(a) Area by trapezoidal rule.

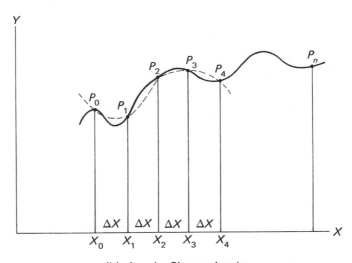

(b) Area by Simpson's rule.

Fig. 6–2. Area by approximate integration.

of XY axes, the length of each chord is an ordinate value, Y_i, and the spacing distance, h, is the value ΔX.)

The basis of the Trapezoidal Rule is that the extremities of the ordinate lines are formed by straight lines forming trapezoids. Since the area of a trapezoid is one-half the product of the sum of the parallel sides multiplied by the altitude, the total area is the sum of the areas of the individual trapezoids as expressed in the formula:

$$\text{Area} = \left(\frac{1}{2} Y_o + Y_1 + Y_2 + \ldots + Y_{n-1} + \frac{1}{2} Y_n\right) h \qquad (6\text{--}6)$$

The greater the number of intervals, the smaller becomes ΔX, and the closer the sum of the areas of the trapezoids will approach the true value. An example of the application of the Trapezoidal Rule is given by Davis (1957) for the calculation of the total volume of growing stock for a fully regulated forest based upon yield-table data. Note that the approximation procedure is used since no yield function in equation form is available.

Simpson's Rule is used when there are an even number of intervals. It assumes that the terminals of each set of three successive ordinates are connected by arcs of parabolas. The areas of the successive "double parabolic strips" are summed yielding the formula:

$$\text{Area} = \frac{h}{3} (Y_o + 4Y_1 + 2Y_2 + 4Y_3 + \ldots + 2Y_{n-2} + 4Y_{n-1} + Y_n) \qquad (6\text{--}7)$$

6–1.6. Area by Planimeter. The planimeter is an instrument which mechanically determines the area of a closed figure by integration. The enclosed area is determined by moving the tracing point of the instrument around the perimeter. The instrument is particularly useful for determining the areas of irregular plane figures plotted to scale on drawing paper. There are several types of planimeters available. The design of the commonly used compensating polar planimeter is shown in Fig. 6–3. In using this planimeter its pivot point, P, is established outside the area to be measured. A starting point, A, is chosen on the perimeter, a reading taken on the recorder, R, and the tracing point, T, is then carefully moved around the perimeter until it returns to A and a second reading taken. The difference between these two values is the effective planimeter reading, n. As the planimeter was moved around the perimeter, the wheel, W, combined sliding, positive, and negative rotations to give the algebraic sum of the rotation, n, which was registered on the recorder. The area is then determined from:

$$\text{Area} = 2\pi r(AB)n \qquad (6\text{--}8)$$

where:

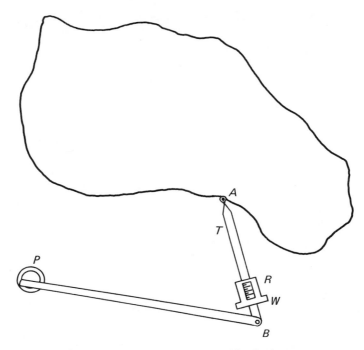

Fig. 6–3. Area measurement with planimeter.

r = radius of the wheel
AB = length of planimeter arm
n = algebraic sum of rotations of wheel

The value $2\pi r(AB)$ is constant for a planimeter and, once known, the area is simply determined by multiplying this constant times the planimeter reading, n.

The hatchet planimeter is a small, extremely simple, and inexpensive instrument which approaches the accuracy of a polar planimeter. It consists merely of a steel rod bent in the shape shown in Fig. 6–4. The two

Fig. 6–4. Hatchet planimeter.

vertical arms can be of any convenient height to permit clearance of the fingers, such as 3 to 3½ inches (approximately 7 to 9 centimeters). The horizontal bar may also be of any length although 10 inches (approximately 25 centimeters) is a convenient length and has the advantage of speeding calculation, since this length is used as a multiplier. In essence, the operation of this instrument requires tracing the perimeter of a figure, using a special procedure described by Dickerson (1942). The total lateral movement of the knife edge multiplied by the length of the horizontal bar gives the area. Tests by Eckel (1953) and Dickerson (1942) showed that surprising accuracy could be obtained in about the same time as required with a polar planimeter. The theory behind the instrument is described by Satterly (1921).

6–2. LAND AREA MEASUREMENT

Area determinations of the earth's surface usually consider the area of the orthogonal projection of the irregular land surface to a datum-level plane. Actual surface area rather than the planar projection may be required in special cases, as in watershed management.

Area determination for portions of the earth's surface can be expressed as the square of any of the linear units. However, in various countries particular units have become standard through common usage. In the United States the acre, consisting of 43,560 square feet or 10 square chains, is the most common area unit. In countries using the metric system, the hectare of 10,000 square meters and the are of 100 square meters are the common land area units. Converting factors for area units are shown in Appendix Table A–1.

In the subdivisions of public lands in the United States, the following units are used:

1 acre	= 43,560 square feet	=	10 square chains
1 section	= 640 acres	=	1 square mile
1 township	= 36 sections	= 23,040 acres	
		= 6 × 6 miles	
		= 36 square miles	

Land area determinations are especially important in forestry. The specialized techniques of field surveying can be found in Davis et al. (1966). These include the analytic procedure of Section 6–1.3. and the approximate integration methods of Section 6–1.5.

For land area determination based on aerial photographs, the reader is referred to Chapter 13 and to Spurr (1960) and the Manual of Photogrammetry (1966).

6–3. TREE AREA MEASUREMENTS

6–3.1. Cross-Sectional Area. The area of a plane passed through the stem of a tree at right angles to its longitudinal axis is called its cross-sectional area. In many instances this cross-section approximates a circle and its area can be computed from the standard formula. If the cross-section is taken at breast height of a standing tree, it is called its basal area. The total basal area of all or specified classes of trees per unit area of land, such as basal area per acre or per hectare, is a useful characteristic of a forest stand. It is directly related to stand volume and is also a measure of stand density (see Chapter 17).

When the cross-sectional form of a tree stem is circular, there is no difficulty in measuring its diameter or circumference and then computing the cross-sectional area. The basic relations are:

$$g = \frac{\pi}{4} d^2 \qquad\qquad (6–9)$$

and, since $d = \dfrac{c}{\pi}$

$$g = \frac{c^2}{4\pi} \qquad\qquad (6–10)$$

where:

g = tree cross-sectional area
d = diameter
c = circumference

The above measurements indicate breast height at 1.3 meters. In American forest practice, basal area is commonly expressed in square feet at 4.5 feet above ground level. Since diameter at this level, dbh, is commonly measured in inches, the basic formula for the area, g, of a circle can be modified to express the result conveniently in square feet:

$$g = \pi \, \text{dbh}^2/4(144) = .005454 \, \text{dbh}^2$$

Using the metric system, with diameter measured in centimeters, basal area in square meters is expressed by: $g = .00007854 \, d^2$.

Cross-sectional areas at the ends of cut sections of a tree, such as logs or bolts if circular, are calculated in identical fashion. The cross-sectional area of sawn products, such as cross ties or timbers, can be simply calculated by using the formula or procedure appropriate to the shape of the cross-section.

Unfortunately, tree stem cross-sections often are not circular. Thus, if it is assumed to be circular, an error of varying magnitude, depending on the irregularily of the shape, will result.

When the cross-section is elliptical, measurements of the major and minor axis d_a and d_b, as shown in Appendix Table A–2, give the necessary information for computation of the correct area.

The area of an ellipse is:

$$g_1 = \frac{\pi}{4} d_a d_b \tag{6–11}$$

A common practice is to take the arithmetic mean of the two diameters and use this average in the formula for the area of a circle:

$$g_2 = \frac{\pi}{4} \left(\frac{d_a + d_b}{2} \right)^2 \tag{6–12}$$

Another procedure uses the arithmetic mean of the squares of the two diameters:

$$g_3 = \frac{\pi}{4} \frac{(d_a{}^2 + d_b{}^2)}{2} \tag{6–13}$$

When the cross-section is elliptical, these latter two practices will always yield overestimates of the true area as expressed by equation 6–12, in the following relation:

$$g_3 > g_2 > g_1$$

since:

$$\sqrt{\frac{d_a{}^2 + d_b{}^2}{2}} > \frac{d_a + d_b}{2} > \sqrt{d_a d_b}$$

i.e.:

quadratic mean > arithmetic mean > geometric mean

For this reason, as mentioned in Section 3–3, the geometric mean of the two diameters should be used for an elliptical shape.

$$g_1 = \frac{\pi}{4} (d_1)^2 \tag{6–14}$$

where:

$$d_1 = \sqrt{d_a d_b}$$

If the cross-sectional shape is either circular or elliptical, this procedure will yield the correct area, whereas any other procedure when used for elliptical shapes will result in an error.

If the circumference of an elliptical shaped section is measured and then assumed to be the circumference of a circle, the diameter of this circle will always be greater than the diameter of a circle whose cross-sectional area is equal to that of the ellipse. In other words, the resulting area will be greater than the true area.

If the shape of tree cross-sections were always either circular or elliptical, the estimation of cross-sectional area would be simple. Unfortunately, the problem is complicated by the fact that actual cross-sectional shapes are often irregular.

Matérn (1958) pointed out that for irregular shaped stems, as shown in Fig. 6–5, a band could be passed around the tree forming the "convex

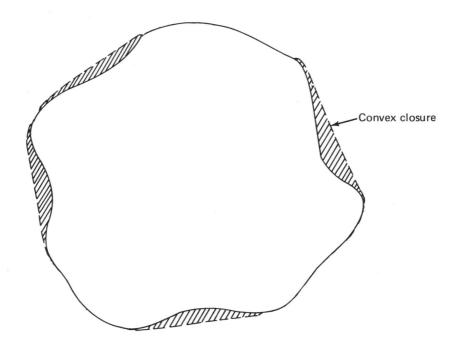

Shaded area indicates convex deficit.

Fig. 6–5. Convex closure of an irregularly shaped stem cross-section.

closure of the region." The difference between the area of the convex closure and the true cross-sectional area he calls the "convex deficit."

If a diameter tape measurement is taken on an irregular cross-section, the perimeter of the convex closure is determined. If the cross-sectional area is calculated using the perimeter as though it represented a circle, this value will always be larger than the true cross-sectional area. The difference between the estimated and calculated areas is called the "isoperimetric deficit." If diameters of irregular cross-sections are taken with a caliper or other diameter measuring instrument and then used in the calculation of area using either the formula for a circle or ellipse, the estimated area can have a positive or negative error depending on

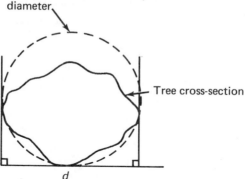

Circular cross-section of equivalent diameter

Tree cross-section

d

(a) Area of assumed circle larger than true area.

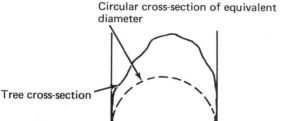

Circular cross-section of equivalent diameter

Tree cross-section

d

(b) Area of assumed circle smaller than true area.

Fig. 6–6. Area of irregular cross-sections determined from a single diameter measurement.

where the diameters are taken. A single measurement can result in very large errors as shown in Fig. 6–6. At least two measurements and determination of the geometric mean will reduce the error.

The reason for the many investigations of the way in which to measure the diameter of a tree is to minimize the effects of these irregularities. The intent is to find some simple means of obtaining a representative diameter which can then be used in the formula for a circle and yield a close approximation to the true cross-sectional area of the irregular shape.

For most practical work, if cross-sectional area is the prime consideration, the geometric mean of two diameters (see Section 3–3.1.), taken
with a caliper, will give the most accurate results. For a detailed consideration of this subject, the student is referred to Matérn (1958), Chacko
(1961), Prodan (1965), and Patrone (1963).

The basal area of a forest stand can be estimated by measuring the
diameters of all or a sample of trees using the forest inventory procedures described in Chapters 11, 12, and 14. The "horizontal point" application of p.p.s. sampling, described in Section 14–4, is an especially
efficient method of estimating this stand parameter.

Cross-sectional areas at the ends of cut sections of a tree such as logs
or bolts, if circular or elliptical, can be calculated using the formulas for
these shapes. If the shape is irregular, a more accurate procedure is to
measure several radii of the section. On a cut section a fixed point, the
pith (which may not be the geometric center or centroid), can be located.
A number of radii taken in random directions may be measured from
which an unbiased estimate of the area can be obtained from the equation:

$$g_4 = \pi r^2$$

where:

$$r = \text{quadratic mean radius} = \sqrt{\frac{r_1^2 + r_2^2 + r_3^2 + \ldots + r_n^2}{n}} \quad (6\text{--}15)$$

6–3.2. Bole Surface Area. The exterior surface area of the stem of a
tree approximates the growing or cambial surface. To be more exact, it
would be area under, rather than outside, bark. This area is of interest
since it represents the surface upon which wood substance accumulates
and can be used in the estimation of tree and stand growth (Anutschin,
1960b). For trees which assume the shape of a geometric solid, the surface
area can be computed by using the calculus or the formula for the surface
area of the solid of appropriate form (Lescaffette, 1951).

As an example, suppose the form of a tree approximated the paraboloid
generated by revolving the stem equation $Y^2 = .066X$ about the X axis
as shown in Fig. 6–7. In this equation, Y is the radius of the stem and X
is the distance from tree tip to some point in the stem. The surface of
the tree between $Y = 2$ feet and the tip of the tree can be determined
using equation 6–4 and evaluating:

$$S_X = 2\pi \int_0^{60} \sqrt{.066X} \sqrt{1 + \left(\frac{\sqrt{.066}}{2\sqrt{X}}\right)^2} \, dX$$

$$= 2\pi \int_0^{60} \sqrt{.066X + .00435} \, dX = 2\pi \left[10.10\sqrt{(3.96 + .00435)^3}\right]_0^{60}$$

$$= 159.4\pi \text{ square feet}$$

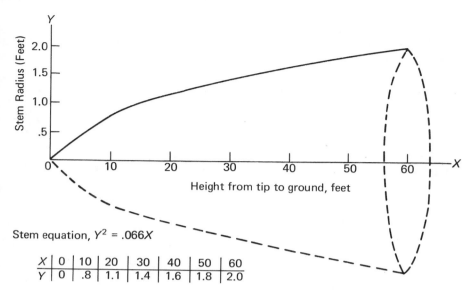

Stem equation, $Y^2 = .066X$

X	0	10	20	30	40	50	60
Y	0	.8	1.1	1.4	1.6	1.8	2.0

Surface area

$$S_x = 2\pi \int_0^{60} \sqrt{.066X} \ \sqrt{1 + \left(\frac{\sqrt{.066}}{2\sqrt{X}}\right)^2} \ dX$$

Fig. 6–7. Surface area of a tree stem of paraboloid form.

In this example, the same value could also have been obtained using the standard formula for the surface area of a paraboloid given in Appendix Table A–3. However, for more complex stem equations, use of the calculus as shown here would be necessary. Lexen (1943) has shown that surface area can also be conveniently approximated, using either Huber's or Smalian's formulas, by substituting observed circumferences for cross-sectional areas and then summing the surface areas for all sections in a tree. It can also be obtained by plotting the observed circumferences at several points along the stem on rectangular coordinate paper and planimetering the area below the curve drawn through these points. The empirical relation of bole area to the height and diameter of a tree can be expressed by substituting bole area for volume in any of the standard tree volume equations (see Section 9–5.1.). Grosenbaugh (1954) presents tables of surface area, allowing this characteristic to be estimated for trees of any size. The horizontal or vertical line application of p.p.s. sampling described in Section 14–4 can also be used for estimating the bole surface area of a stand.

6–3.3. Leaf Area. The surface area of the foliage of forest trees is a useful measure to foresters concerned with studying the interception of precipitation, light transmission through forest canopies, the development of forest litter accumulations, and moisture evaporation from soil surface. Several investigators have devised methods of estimating leaf area. Cable (1958) developed a regression to estimate surface area of individual ponderosa pine fascicles from their oven-dry weight. From this equation the surface area of an entire tree can then be estimated from the weight of sample fascicles and the estimated number of fascicles per tree. Additional work on surface area determination of pine needles has been carried out by Madgwick (1964) and for leaf area of broadleaved species by Cummings (1941).

Less attention has been paid to the surface area of the root portions of trees. Since this parameter represents the moisture or nutrient-absorbing surface of a tree, it will undoubtedly come under closer scrutiny.

6–3.4. Crown Coverage. Crown coverage is the proportion of forest land area covered by tree crowns, a measure of importance in the use of aerial photographs. It is a measure of the relative density or occupancy of a land area by tree crowns and has been used principally in its relation to volume of timber per unit area. Crown area estimates can be more easily made from aerial photographs than directly in the field. Dot grids and crown density scales allow rapid estimation from vertical aerial photographs. In use, these measures indicate the percentage of the area covered by crowns. Area in units is then determined by multiplying the total area by the percentage covered.

A field device called the "moosehorn" crown closure estimation allows estimates to be made in the forest (Garrison, 1949). The instrument is held in a vertical position, and the operator looks through a side aperture and counts the number of dots, on a transparent upper surface, that are covered by tree crowns. This number in relation to the total number of dots is an estimate of the percentage of the total area covered by crowns.

Lemmon (1957) devised the "spherical densiometer" for estimating forest overstory density. The instrument uses a mirror with a spherical curvature which reflects a large area. A grid of squares or dots is scratched either on the mirror or on a transparent overlay. By counting squares, the percentage of the overhead area covered by crowns can be estimated.

7

Volume Measurement

Volume has been the traditional measure of wood quantity and its importance will continue even with the increasing use of weight. This chapter discusses some of the principles of volume measurement and volume units which have been utilized in forest mensuration. Chapters 8 and 9 then take up their applications to the task of estimating tree and log volumes.

7–1. METHODS

Volume is the three-dimensional magnitude of an object. It is expressed in cubic units which are derived from any of the fundamental units of length. If the lengths, in similar units, of the three dimensions of height, width, and thickness of any object are known, their product is its volume. Volume determination methods of importance in forest mensuration can be classified as: standard formulas, integration, liquid displacement, and graphical estimation.

7–1.1. Standard Formulas. Solid objects can assume many forms such as polyhedrons, solids of revolution, and solids of irregular shape. The standard formulas shown in Appendix Table A–3 can be used to compute the volumes of many polyhedrons such as cubes, prisms, pyramids; and the volumes of solids of revolution such as cones, cylinders, spheres, paraboloids, and neiloids and frustums of these solids, when certain dimensions of the solid are known. Special adaptations of these formulas are of particular importance in forest mensuration and are summarized in Table 8–1.

7–1.2. Integration. There are several procedures available through the use of integral calculus for the determination of the volume of a solid. The volume of a solid with known cross-section can be obtained by summation of the volumes of its slices through an evaluation of the definite integral:

$$V = \int_a^b A\ (X)\ dX \qquad (7\text{--}1)$$

in which the area of the cross-section, or its slice is expressed as a function, $A\ (X)$ of X, times the thickness, dX, where this thickness approaches zero, giving the volume between limits $X = a$ and $X = b$. This procedure can be used for solids of any shape, provided the cross-sectional area can be expressed as a function.

Rotating a plane curve $Y = f\ (X)$ around the X axis which becomes the central axis of the solid (or $X = f\ (Y)$ about the Y axis) generates a solid of revolution. The general formula for the total volume contained within the surface between limits formed by planes at $X = a$ and $X = b$ in the integral:

$$V = \pi \int_a^b Y^2\ dX \qquad (7\text{--}2)$$

In the integral, Y, the ordinate or radius of the solid of revolution may vary and must be expressed as a function of X. Some common solids of revolution are the cylinder, cone, sphere, and paraboloid. The cylinder can be visualized as formed by rotating a rectangle around one side; a cone by rotating a right triangle around one side (not the hypotenuse); a sphere by rotating a semicircle around the diameter; and a paraboloid by rotating a second-degree polynomial about its axis. It is worth pointing out that the generalized formulas for the volumes of solids shown in Appendix Table A–3 can be derived from the integral shown above by substituting the appropriate $f\ (X)$ for Y. For solids of revolution formed by curves of other shapes, general formulas, such as these, are not available and integration is required. This concept has been applied to the volume estimation of the main stem of a tree. The difficulty with the practical application of this approach is expressing the longitudinal profile of a tree relating height and diameter in a functional form (see Grosenbaugh, 1966).

To illustrate the procedure, the tree stem depicted in Fig. 6–7 will be used. Assume we wish to compute the volume between a one-foot stump and an upper position on the stem ten feet from the top. The volume would then be expressed as:

$$V = \pi \int_{10}^{59} .066X \, dX$$

Integrating and evaluating yields:

$$V = \left[\frac{\pi \, .066X^2}{2} \right]_{10}^{59} = \left[.104X^2 \right]_{10}^{59}$$
$$V = (.104)(59^2) - (.104)(10^2)$$
$$= 351.6 \text{ cubic feet}$$

Note that since this is the frustum of a paraboloid, equation 8–5 will yield the same volume.

7–1.3. Displacement. A direct determination of the volume of solids can be obtained by liquid displacement. If a solid is completely immersed in some liquid, it will displace a volume of this liquid equal to its own volume. This procedure is of particular value in determining the cubic contents of irregularly shaped objects not easily handled by standard formulas or with surfaces not expressible as mathematical functions.

7–1.4. Graphical Estimation. The solid contents of an object, circular in cross-section, but varying in diameter along an axis at right angles to the cross-section, can be easily determined graphically. The graphical solution is more flexible than the formula method since it is applicable to all solids of revolution, regardless of their surface characteristics. The graphical solution consists in plotting a series of diameter measurements, in terms of cross-sectional area, over height, and then graphically determining the area under the curve. The area under the curve is then converted into cubic volume, using an appropriate converting factor. Ordinary cross-section paper can be used by graduating the ordinate axis in terms of the square of the diameter and the abscissa in terms of length. In Fig. 7–1, diameter squared is plotted over length for the frustum of a solid of revolution. The area under this curve can be accurately obtained by using a planimeter or a fine dot grid. Rougher approximations can be obtained by counting squares on the cross-section paper. The area under the curve can be converted to cubic volume by multiplying by the converting factor C:

$$C = AL$$

where:

A = cross-sectional area per inch of ordinate scale
L = length per inch of abscissa scale

Note that A must be expressed as the square of the unit in which L is expressed. For the example given in Fig. 7–1, the converting factor in terms of cubic feet per inch of area under the curve is:

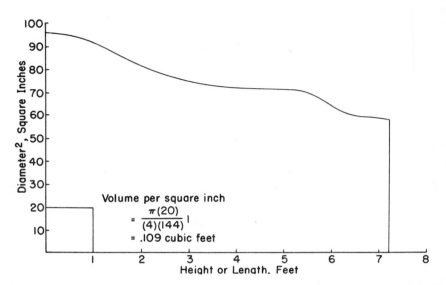

Fig. 7–1. Graphical estimation of the volume of the frustum of a solid of revolution.

$$C = \frac{\pi\,20}{4(144)}\,(1) = \left(\frac{20}{183.345}\right)(1) = \frac{20}{183.345} = .1091$$

The term $\dfrac{\pi}{(4)\,(144)}$ is necessary to convert the square of the diameter in inches to square feet.

7–2. VOLUME UNITS

Units of volume are derived and, hence, not represented by absolute standards but are calibrated against the fundamental units of mass and length.

The metric unit of volume is the liter, defined as the volume occupied by a mass of 1 kilogram of pure distilled water at maximum density (4°C) and at a pressure of 1 atmosphere.

The imperial gallon of the British system is the volume of 10 pounds of distilled water at 62°F and 30 inches of barometric pressure occupying 277.42 cubic inches. The United States gallon occupying 231 cubic inches is defined as 8.345 pounds of distilled water at maximum density.

The units commonly used to express volume of solid objects in the metric system are the cubes of the linear units, e.g., cubic centimeters, cubic meters, while in the English system the units are the cubes of inches, feet, and yards.

For conversions between volume units of the metric and English systems see Appendix Table A–1.

7–3. VOLUME UNITS USED TO MEASURE WOOD

7–3.1. Cubic Units.
In the United States, the cubic foot is often used as the volume unit to express total wood substance in a tree or cut portion. (A cunit is a unit of 100 cubic feet, sometimes employed in measuring bulk quantities of wood.) In countries using the metric system, the cubic meter is commonly employed as the unit of wood volume.

A volume unit used in Great Britain, and to some extent in countries formerly under British rule, is the Hoppus foot. The Hoppus foot gives an estimation of the cubic contents less about 21.5 per cent of the total cubic contents expected to be lost in the manufacture of lumber. The number of Hoppus feet in a log is determined by the formula:

$$\text{Hoppus feet} = \left(\frac{C}{4}\right)^2 \frac{L}{144} \qquad (7\text{--}3)$$

where:

C = overbark circumference in inches at center of log
L = length of log in feet

For conversion, the Hoppus foot equals 1.273 cubic feet of solid wood.

7–3.2. Board Feet.
A board foot is a piece of lumber 1 inch thick, 12 inches wide, and 12 inches long, or its equivalent. In surfaced lumber the board foot is based on the measurement before surfacing. The board foot is, therefore, not an exact unit of volume. Nevertheless, it is widely used in North America where it was devised in the early part of the nineteenth century. The generalized formula for the volume in board feet of a sawn board is:

$$\text{Board feet} = TWL_i/(12)(12)(1) = TWL_i/144 = TWL_f/12 \qquad (7\text{--}4)$$

where:

T = thickness in inches
W = width in inches
L_i = length in inches
L_f = length in feet

For boards cut exactly 1 inch thick, there are as many board feet as there are square or surface feet on one face of such boards. This fact has caused some to think of board feet and surface feet as being the same. Actually, they are the same only for boards exactly 1 inch thick.

Lumber is often intentionally sawn to differing thickness and width than precisely to the inch, e.g., ¾- or ⅝-inch thick boards. In transactions involving lumber of this type the board-foot contents are often calculated as though the thickness and width dimensions were actually to the full inch. For example, a board referred to as 1 inch by 12 inches by 12 feet would probably have dimensions of ¾ by 11¼ by 12 but would be taken as having 12 board feet.

The determination of the number of board feet in a board can be simplified by the use of a board rule. This is a flat stick on which are engraved board-foot volumes corresponding to the dimensions of length, width, and thickness. The stick is placed on the width dimension and the board-foot contents read directly from the figures corresponding to the length and thickness of the board.

Since commercial transactions involving lumber and logs are usually made in large quantities they have given rise to the use of the term thousand board feet and to the abbreviation M.bd.ft. or M.B.F. Lumber and logs are customarily bought and sold per M.bd.ft.

The use of the board-foot measure, when applied to logs, has a serious shortcoming. The unit attempts to state the volume in terms of the ultimate product which can be cut from the log. The board-foot unit is unique in this way. None of the other units of volume does this, with the possible exception of some piece products. The principal objection to the use of the board-foot unit, when applied to standing timber or logs, is that it does not give the entire volume of wood in the tree or log. This is the result of stating volume in terms of the ultimate product. Board-foot volumes disregard all material wasted in the process of manufacture, such as sawdust, slabs, and edgings.

Naturally, the number of board feet contained within a log, or the logs in a tree, will depend primarily on the sizes of the logs, i.e., the length and diameter dimensions. The larger the log is, the more board feet it contains. However, within logs of exactly the same dimension there can be considerable variation, depending on the following factors:

1. The amount of defect, such as rot, and the straightness of the log.
2. Thickness of the saws used in milling.
3. The amount of waste in slabs and edgings.
4. Thickness of lumber sawn.
5. Width of narrowest board sawn.
6. Skill of the sawyer.
7. Efficiency of the milling machinery.
8. Amount of taper in log.

7–3.3. Cord Pen and Stere Units. The necessity for measuring the bulk quantity of relatively small pieces of irregular wood in unmanufactured form gave rise to the cord unit. Wood in this rough form is of low value per piece and a measurement method must be rapid and inexpensive. The measurement of the cubic volume of each piece is physically possible but economically impractical. The cord measure is a substitute in the interests of speed and economic practicality. The fundamental concept of a unit standard cord is a pile of 4-foot-long pieces of wood, 4 feet high and 8 feet long, occupying 128 cubic feet of space. In reality, the cord is not a reliable measure of wood volume, because within the unit of space a range of actual wood volumes can be enclosed, depending on the form of the wood and the method of piling.

Often, pieces less than, or longer than, 4 feet are cut, piled, and measured in cords. When pieces are less than 4 feet long, a stack 4 feet high and 8 feet long is called a short or face cord; when pieces are longer than 4 feet, a similar stack is called a long cord. Commonly, long cords consist of bolts 5 feet and 5 feet 3 inches long, comprising 160 and 168 cubic feet of space, respectively.

An approximate piled volume used in the southern United States is the pen. A pen is a pile of wood 6 feet high, consisting of two sticks to a layer, each layer at right angles to the one beneath. Five pens are assumed equal to a standard cord.

In countries employing the metric system, the stere unit is used analogously to the cord. The stere is a pile of wood 1 meter in length, width, and height. As with the cord, there will be variable solid volumes of wood within this cubic meter of space.

7–3.4. Assumed Standards. Several other volume units have been employed in the measurement of wood volume in the form of logs. In the early days of logging in the United States, the custom arose of accepting a log of some specified dimensions as unity rather than using some unit such as the cubic foot. The volume of any log could then be expressed as multiples or fractions of the standard. Examples of rules of this type are the Adirondack, Saranac, and Quebec standards (Belyea, 1931).

In the New England states, a volume unit for logs called the Blodgett foot is still employed. The Blodgett foot is arbitrarily defined as a cylindrical block 16 inches in diameter and 1 foot long. This is equivalent to 1.4 cubic foot. Blodgett feet are often converted to board feet, using a conversion factor of 10 board feet per Blodgett foot.

7–3.5. Comparison of Units. The continued use of the board foot rather than the cubic foot (or the cubic meter when the metric system is adopted) in North American forestry, in spite of the obvious disadvantages, is an indication of the power of custom and tradition over logic. It would be a boon to forestry and forest industries if the cubic foot were the generally accepted volume unit. The cubic foot is an absolute measure of volume, in contrast to the board foot, which depends upon the standards of utilization, the product to be made, and the efficiency of the manufacturing process. Cubic-foot measurement is simple and exact, eliminating the confusions of different rules and the subjectivity, skill, and experience necessary for board-foot scaling. It would be desirable to use the cubic foot as the general standard for all volume measurement, which could then be converted to whatever units individuals or organizations might desire for a specific reason (Barnes, 1945; Rapraeger, 1950).

The obvious inaccuracies of the cord or board-foot units for expressing wood volume point out the desirability of using better units whenever possible and practical. Weight is a much better measure of bulk wood products than cord volumes, especially if the wood is in small pieces and handled in bulk. If payments are to be made to individual wood workers on the basis of quantity produced, however, it may be necessary to continue to use the cord, since weight measurement in the woods in relatively small and scattered quantities is impractical. If the system of piecework payment could be abandoned, this need would be eliminated. But it is probable that the cord unit will continue to be used for the measurement of minor quantities of low-value material, such as fuel wood, or in any woods operation where limited production will make it uneconomical to use weight scaling.

7–4. VOLUME UNIT CONVERSION

7–4.1. Board Foot–Cubic Foot Conversions. According to the standard definition, 12 board feet are exactly equivalent to 1 cubic foot. But it is impossible to saw 12 board feet from a solid cubic foot of wood because of loss from sawdust and slabs in the converting process. Cubic volume is independent of shape, whereas board-foot volume, in practical terms, exists only where sawn lumber is obtainable. For example, a crooked bolt of wood, averaging 3 inches in diameter, has a definite measureable cubic volume but has no board-foot volume in a practical sense. Thus, the number of board feet per cubic foot will vary, depending on the size and shape of the wood volume. Table 7–1 (a) illustrates the changes in ratios for logs as the diameter of the log increases. It should be observed that ratios also depend on the estimates of board-foot contents indicated by the various log rules (see Chapter 9).

In standing trees, the ratio depends not only on the log rule under comparison but also on the comparative merchantability limits used for the cubic and board-foot volume. Table 7–1 (b) shows board-feet-per-cubic-foot ratios for standing trees according to tree diameter and number of 16-foot logs in the tree. These ratios are based upon coniferous species in the Lake States (Gevorkiantz, 1950). Holsoe and Longacre (1949) reported average ratios for Appalachian hardwoods from 3.62 for 8-inch

Table 7–1
Board-Foot—Cubic-Foot Ratios

(a) For 16-foot logs.

Diameter i.b. Small End (Inches)	Volume[1] (Cubic Feet)	Board feet per Cubic Foot		
		Int. ¼″	Doyle (Ratios)	Scribner
10	11	5.9	3.3	5.4
20	39	7.4	6.6	7.2
30	84	8.0	8.0	7.8
40	147	8.2	8.8	8.2

(b) For standing trees. (Conifers in Lake States)[2]

Dbh o.b.	Board Feet per Cubic Foot by Number of 16-Foot Logs			
	1	2	3	4
Inches		Ratios		
10	4.7	5.0	—	—
20	3.4	5.1	6.2	6.4
30	3.0	4.8	5.8	6.1
40	—	—	5.6	6.0

[1] Volume by Smalian's formula; taper allowance, 2 inches per 16 feet.
[2] Gevorkiantz, 1950. Board foot volumes according to Int. ¼ inch rule.

trees to 6.88 for 24-inch trees. In general, the ratios increase rapidly with increases of diameter for small trees but level off for the larger diameters.

7–4.2. Cubic Foot—Cord Conversions. The number of cubic feet of wood per cord is not constant but varies with the characteristics of the bolts and methods of piling. The total space enclosed by the outside dimensions of a standard cord unit is 128 cubic feet, but the solid wood content never attains this figure. Numerous studies have been conducted to develop ratios, and a variety of converting factors have been developed (Mesavage, 1947; Mountain, 1949; Fenton, 1948; Bickford, 1957; Institute of Forest Products, 1957). Converting factors range from 64 to 91 cubic feet per cord, depending upon the sizes and shapes of individual pieces, presence and thickness of bark, and the method of piling. This means that air space in piles will range from about 50 per cent for crooked and knotty wood to about 29 per cent for straight wood with well-trimmed knots. Piles of split wood contain less solid volume than round wood. The relative amount of space in a cord will also increase as the diameter of the pieces decreases.

7–4.3. Board Foot—Cord Conversions. The conversion of cords to board feet, and vice versa, also incorporates the complexities of trying to relate units which do not have any fundamental similarity. In converting from board feet to cords, the best approximation can be arrived at by first converting to cubic feet, considering 12 board feet as equivalent to 1 cubic foot. The cubic feet can then be converted to cords, using an appropriate factor. In converting from cords to board feet, again, only an approximation can be made since the actual number of board feet producible from a cord of wood depends on the form of the wood. An overall average converting factor of 500 board feet per cord is often used. Gevorkiantz (1956) reported on a study in the Lake States which related number of board feet per cord to the number of bolts per cord and manner of piling. He found a range from 295 board feet per cord for loosely piled small bolts to a maximum of 550 board feet per cord for closely piled large bolts.

8

Cubic Volume and Measures of Form

8–1. THE PARTS OF A TREE

It is convenient to think of the tree as consisting of four parts: the *roots*, the *stump*, the *stem*, and the *crown*.

The *roots* are the underground part of the tree that supply it with nourishment. The *stump* is the lower end of the tree that is left above ground after the main part has been cut off. The *stem* is the main ascending axis of the tree above the stump. Trees that have the axis prolonged to form an undivided main stem, as exemplified by many conifers, are termed *excurrent*. Trees that have a central stem in the lower portion that becomes indistinguishable in the upper portion due to branching, as exemplified by many broadleaved species, are termed *deliquescent*. The *crown* consists of the primary and secondary branches growing out of the main stem, together with twigs and foliage.

The most important portion of a tree, in terms of usable wood, is the stem. Since the roots and the stumps of trees are less often utilized, less attention has been given to the determination of their volume. There is, on the other hand, often a need to determine the volume of crowns. Crown-volume data may be used to describe fuel hazard, estimate volume of material left from line-clearing operations, and determine volume of pulpwood and fuelwood in crowns.

Since the stump, stem, and branches are all covered with bark, they are, when utilized, generally peeled in the woods, or hauled, bark and all, to the mill where the bark is removed before the manufacturing process begins. Thus, it is necessary to determine, at one time or another, unpeeled volume and bark volume.

8–2. DIRECT DETERMINATION OF THE CUBIC VOLUME OF TREE PARTS

Direct volume determinations of parts of trees are usually made on samples which provide the basic data for the development of volume relationships for estimating volumes of other standing trees, as explained in Chapter 9. In the past sample-tree measurements were often taken on trees cut in harvesting operations. Such measurements, however, may lead to bias because they may not be representative of the trees to which the volume relationships will be applied. Thus, there is a growing tendency to take measurements on a representative sample of standing trees.

The direct determination of the volume of any part of a tree involves clearly defining the part of the tree for which volume is to be determined, and carefully taking measurements in accordance with the constraints imposed by the definition. For example, for purposes of measurement we might include the portion of the stem above a fixed-height stump to a minimum upper-diameter outside bark, or on stems that do not have a central tendency, to the point where the last cut can be made. For roots we might include roots larger than some minimum diameter; for tops we might include all branches and the tip of the stem to a minimum upper-diameter outside bark. For tops note that we include the tip of the stem and a portion of the crown. But in defining the portions of interest such combinations are common.

Generally speaking, the tree must be felled and the limbs cut into sections before one can directly determine crown volume. To directly determine root volume, the roots must be lifted from the ground and the soil removed. But, as indicated in Section 8–3, there are methods of directly determining stem and stump volume that may be applied either to the standing or to the felled tree.

The stems and stumps of trees closely resemble certain geometrical solids. Thus, their cubic volume may be determined, either before or after they are felled, by formulas (Section 8–3). It is not feasible, however, to determine the volume of roots by formulas because they do not, either in their entirety or in portions, closely resemble any known geometrical solids. Practically speaking, this is also true of crowns.

Thanks to the reasonably regular form of stems, it has been possible to develop convenient graphical techniques to obtain the cubic volume of the stem and stump of a standing or felled tree (Section 8–4). But again this technique is unsuitable for determining the volume of roots or crowns, because for each set of roots, or for each crown, it requires an inordinate number of diameter measurements and an excessive number of graphs to obtain satisfactory results. The displacement method (Section 8–5), on the other hand, can be used to obtain accurately the cubic volume of any part of the tree. It is applicable only to cut trees, however, and it is a relatively slow and expensive method.

To use formulas or graphical techniques to determine the volume of a stem, it is necessary to have individual-tree taper measurements—that is, diameter measurements at various intervals along the stem. Both inside and outside bark measurements are desirable. The measurements may be made on down or standing trees, as explained in Chapter 3. On standing trees, when it is convenient to obtain only outside bark measurements, inside bark diameters, and thence inside bark volumes, may be calculated by use of bark factors (Section 8–6).

Finally, it is important to note that the volume of roots and crowns, or stumps and stems, for that matter, may be indirectly determined by weighing and then converting from weight to volume as explained in Chapter 5.

8–3. DIRECT DETERMINATION OF CUBIC VOLUME BY FORMULAS

The stems of excurrent trees are often assumed to resemble neiloids, cones, or paraboloids, solids that are obtained, as shown in Fig. 8–1, by rotating a curve of the general form, $Y = K\sqrt{X^r}$, around the X axis. Indeed, whenever the profile of a tree can be expressed by an equation, the formula for the stem volume obtained by rotating the graph of the equation $Y = f(X)$ about the X axis (between $X = a$ and $X = b$) may be written:

$$V = \pi \int_a^b Y^2 \, dX,$$

and the volume of the solid of revolution obtained by integration.

As the form exponent, r, changes in the equation, $Y = K\sqrt{X^r}$, different solids are produced. When r is 1, a paraboloid is obtained by rotating the curve of the equation around the X axis; when r is 2, a cone, when r is 3, a neiloid, and when r is 0, a cylinder. But the stems of excurrent trees are seldom cones, paraboloids, or neiloids; they generally fall between the cone and the paraboloid. The merchantable portion of stems of deliquescent trees, on the other hand, are assumed to resemble frustums of neiloids, cones, or paraboloids, or occasionally, cylinders. But they generally fall between the frustum of a cone and the frustum of a paraboloid.

It is more realistic, however, to consider the stem of any tree to be a

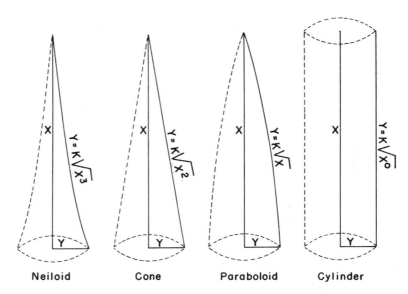

Fig. 8–1. Solids of revolution descriptive of tree form.

composite of geometrical solids, as shown in Fig. 8–2. For example, when the stem is cut into logs or bolts, as cut sections are known in the wood-using industries, the tip approaches a cone or paraboloid, the central sections resemble frustums of paraboloids, or in a few cases, frustums of cones, or even cylinders, and the butt log resembles the frustum of a neiloid. Although the stump approaches the form of the frustum of a neiloid, it is, for practical reasons, considered to be a cylinder.

Formulas to compute the cubic volume of the solids that have been of particular interest to mensurationists are given in Table 8–1. Newton's formula is exact for all the frustums we have considered. Smalian's and Huber's formulas (equations 8–5 and 8–6) are exact only when the solid is the frustum of a paraboloid.[1] For example, if the surface lines of a tree section are more convex than the paraboloid frustum, Huber's formula will overestimate the volume while Smalian's formula will underestimate the volume. But if the surface lines of a tree section are less convex than the paraboloid frustum, as they often will be, Smalian's formula will overestimate the volume and Huber's formula will underestimate the volume. Assuming Newton's formula gives correct volume values, it can be shown by subtracting Newton's formula first from Smalian's formula and then from Huber's formula that the error incurred by Smalian's formula is

---

[1] Newton's, or the prismoidal, formula is attributed to Sir Isaac Newton. Prodan (1965) claims that Huber's formula came into use in 1785 and Smalian's in 1804.

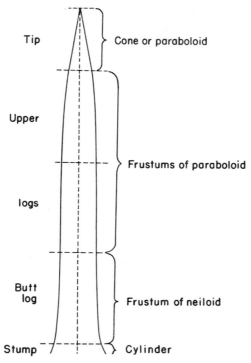

Fig. 8–2. Geometric forms assumed by portions of a tree stem.

twice that obtained by Huber's formula and opposite sign. Indeed, results of two studies tend to confirm this observation. In a study by Young, Robbins, and Wilson (1967) on 8- and 16-foot logs of 4- to 12-inch diameter, in which volumes calculated by Newton's, Smalian's, and Huber's formulas were compared with volumes determined by displacement, average per cent errors of about 0 were obtained for Newton's formula, +9 per cent for Smalian's formula, and −3.5 per cent for Huber's formula. Young found, as one would expect, that there were no significant differences between errors for the three formulas on 4-foot bolts. In comparing computed volumes of 16-foot hardwood logs, diameters from 8 to 22 inches, Miller (1959) found average per cent errors to be about +2 per cent for Newton's formula, +12 per cent for Smalian's formula, and −5 per cent for Huber's formula.

It should now be apparent that in calculating cubic volume of trees and logs, the mensurationist should select his methods carefully. Unless one is willing to accept a rather large error, Smalian's formula should not be

Table 8–1
Equations to Compute Cubic Volume of Important Solids

Geometrical Solid	Equation for Volume, V, in Cubic Units		Equation Number
Cylinder	$V = A_b h$		(8–1)
Paraboloid	$V = \frac{1}{2}(A_b h)$		(8–2)
Cone	$V = \frac{1}{3}(A_b h)$		(8–3)
Neiloid	$V = \frac{1}{4}(A_b h)$		(8–4)
Paraboloid Frustum	$V = \frac{h}{2}(A_b + A_u)$	(Smalian's Formula)	(8–5)
	$V = h(A_m)$	(Huber's Formula)	(8–6)
Cone Frustum	$V = \frac{h}{3}(A_b + \sqrt{A_b A_u} + A_u)$		(8–7)
Neiloid Frustum	$V = \frac{h}{4}(A_b + \sqrt[3]{A_b^2 A_u} + \sqrt[3]{A_u^2 A_b} + A_u)$		(8–8)
Neiloid, Cone, or Paraboloid Frustum	$V = \frac{h}{6}(A_b + 4A_m + A_u)$	(Newton's Formula)	(8–9)

h = height
A_b = cross-sectional area at base
A_m = cross-sectional area at middle
A_u = cross-sectional area at top

used unless it is possible to measure the sections of the tree in 4-foot lengths. For 8- or 16-foot logs, Newton's or Huber's formula will give more accurate results.

Newton's formula will give accurate results for all sections of the tree except for butt logs with excessive butt swell. For such butt logs Huber's formula will give better results. Either the formula for the volume of a paraboloid or the volume of a cone would be appropriate to determine the volume of the tip. Although the stump actually approaches the neiloid frustum in form, its volume would normally be computed by the formula for the volume of a cylinder.

Newton's and Huber's formulas cannot, of course, be applied to stacked logs, because it is not possible to measure middle diameters. However, these two formulas are as well suited as Smalian's formula to determine the volume of unskidded logs or standing trees.

Newton's formula may be used to compute the volume of the merchantable stem, or of the total stem—accuracy is best when short sections are measured. If the sections are of the same length, the procedure can be summarized in a single formula. To illustrate, consider a stem with diameters in inches from top of stump to a point where the last merchantable cut will be made, d_o, d_1, d_2, d_3, d_4, d_5, and d_6, located at intervals of h feet. To give each section three diameters, the volume is computed by sections of $2h$ length. Thus, with Newton's formula the volume in cubic feet, V, is:

$$V = \frac{2h}{6}\,(.005454)(d_o{}^2 + 4d_1{}^2 + d_2{}^2) + \frac{2h}{6}\,(.005454)(d_2{}^2 + 4d_3{}^2 + d_4{}^2)$$

$$+ \frac{2h}{6}\,(.005454)(d_4{}^2 + 4d_5{}^2 + d_6{}^2)$$

$$= h(.001818)(d_o{}^2 + 4d_1{}^2 + 2d_2{}^2 + 4d_3{}^2 + 2d_4{}^2 + 4d_5{}^2 + d_6{}^2)$$

$$= .003636h\left(\frac{d_o{}^2}{2} + 2d_1{}^2 + d_2{}^2 + 2d_3{}^2 + d_4 + 2d_5{}^2 + \frac{d_6{}^2}{2}\right)$$

(The constant, .005454, comes from the expression, cross-sectional area in square feet $= \left(\dfrac{\pi}{4(144)}\right) d_i{}^2 = .005454 d_i{}^2$. If the metric system is used, d_i will be in centimeters and h in meters, and to obtain volume in cubic meters the constant will come from the expression, cross-sectional area in square meters $= \dfrac{\pi}{4(10,000)}\,d_i{}^2 = .00007854 d_i{}^2$.) This formula can be extended for as many sections as desired, provided there is an odd number of diameters, that is, an even number of sections of h length.

If the number of diameters measured is even, the last interval of h cannot be computed by Newton's formula, because it will have only two end diameters. Thus, its volume must be found by Smalian's formula and added to the previous formula. For eight diameters, or seven intervals of h length, the formula is:

$$V = .003636h\left(\frac{d_o{}^2}{6} + 2d_1{}^2 + d_2{}^2 + 2d_3{}^2 + d_4{}^2 + 2d_5{}^2 + \frac{5d_6{}^2}{4} + \frac{3d_7{}^2}{4}\right)$$

Grosenbaugh (1948) described a systematic procedure using this method.

The volume of the merchantable stem can also be calculated with good accuracy using Smalian's formula if the stem is divided into short sections. To illustrate, consider a stem with diameters in inches, from top of stump to a point where the last merchantable cut will be made, d_o, d_1, d_2, . . . , d_n, located at intervals of h feet along the stem. Then, according to Smalian's formula:

$$V = .005454h\left(\frac{d_o{}^2}{2} + d_1{}^2 + d_2{}^2 + \ldots + d_{n-1}{}^2 + \frac{d_n{}^2}{2}\right)$$

To adapt Huber's formula to the computation of merchantable stem volumes, the diameter measurements are taken at the midpoints of the sections. Thus, when diameter measurements, d_{m_1}, d_{m_2}, . . . , d_{m_n}, are taken at the midpoints of sections h length, Huber's formula yields:

$$V = .005454h(d_{m_1}^2 + d_{m_2}^2 + \ldots + d_{m_n}^2)$$

8–3.1. Determination of Volume by Height Accumulation. The height accumulation concept was conceived and developed by Grosenbaugh (1948, 1954), who stated that the system can be applied by selecting tree diameters above breast height in diminishing arithmetic progression, say 1- or 2-inch taper intervals, and estimating, recording, and accumulating tree height to each successive diameter. The system uses diameter as the independent variable instead of height, is well adapted to use with electronic computers, and permits segregation of volume by classes of material, log size, or grade. But since optimum log lengths for top log grades depend on factors other than diameter, the best grades may not be secured.

To apply the system one must know the number of sections, L, in some unit height, between taper steps, the cumulative total, H, of L values, the cumulative total, H', of H values, and if inside bark volume is desired, the mean bark factor, $k = $ dib/dob (see Section 8–6). This requires that one collect the following sample tree data: dbh to nearest 0.1 inch, length of merchantable stem between successive taper steps to nearest unit height, and measurements to compute mean dib/dob ratio. For example, if one used 2-inch taper steps and 4-foot unit heights, a feasible practice, dbh would be rounded to the nearest even inch, and the first unit-height, L, the 4-foot section between stump height and breast height, would be 1. The unit-heights to each taper step might be estimated, but to obtain acceptable accuracy, an instrument, such as the Spiegel relaskop, should be used.

Table 8–2 gives sample tree data needed to compute the volume, V, of a number of trees, or of individual trees, by height accumulation. Very simply:

Table 8–2

Sample Tree Data for Computation of Volume by Height Accumulation by 2-Inch Taper Steps and 4-Foot Unit Heights

Dbh	Dob Taper Steps					Sum
	10	8	6	4	2	
9.5	1	3	4	2	0	10
7.7		1	5	2	0	8
10.5	1	5	3	2	0	11
L =	2	9	12	6	0	29
H =	2	11	23	29	29	94
H' =	2	13	36	65	94	210

$$V = A(\Sigma H') + B(\Sigma H) + C(\Sigma L) \qquad (8\text{–}10)$$

Volume coefficients, A, B, and C, for cubic feet are given in Table 8–3 for 2-inch taper steps, 4-foot unit heights, and mean dib/dob ratios. Grosen-

Table 8–3
Height-Accumulation Coefficients, A, B, and C, to Compute Cubic-Foot Volume by 2-Inch Taper Steps, 4-Foot Unit Heights, and Various Mean Dib/Dob Ratios

Mean Ratio Dib/Dob	Volume Coefficients for Cubic Feet		
	A	B	C
1.00*	0.175	0	0.0291
0.95	0.158	0	0.0263
0.90	0.141	0	0.0236
0.85	0.126	0	0.0210

*When computing volume outside bark, use coefficients for ratio of 1.00.
SOURCE: Grosenbaugh, 1954.

baugh (1954) also gives coefficients for 1-inch taper steps and 1-foot unit heights, coefficients for determination of board-foot volume, formulas to calculate coefficients for other cases, and the theory of height accumulation.

For the trees given in Table 8–2, the total cubic foot volume, inside bark, for a mean dib/dob ratio of 0.90 is:

$$V = 0.141(210) + 0(94) + 0.0236(29) = 30.3 \text{ cu. ft.}$$

Similarly, individual-tree cubic foot volume is:

$$V_{9.5} = 0.141(75) + 0(33) + 0.0236(10) = 10.8 \text{ cu. ft.}$$
$$V_{7.7} = 0.141(46) + 0(23) + 0.0236(8) = 6.7 \text{ cu. ft.}$$
$$V_{10.5} = 0.141(89) + 0(38) + 0.0236(11) = 12.8 \text{ cu. ft.}$$
$$\text{Total} \quad \overline{30.3} \text{ cu. ft.}$$

Enghardt and Derr (1963) found that computation of cubic volume of young even-aged stands of southern pine by height accumulation required less time and effort than conventional methods, and gave satisfactory accuracy for research purposes. Indeed, the potentialities of this unique system have been generally overlooked.

8–4. DIRECT DETERMINATION OF CUBIC VOLUME BY GRAPHICAL METHODS

The graphical method may be applied to the stump and stem taken together, or to any given section of the stem taken alone. To use the method one must have individual-tree taper measurements, that is, diameter measurements at intervals along the stem, perferably both inside and outside bark. It is most convenient to have measurements which were taken at regular intervals. However, if sufficient diameter measurements are taken so the taper of the tree is accurately depicted, the measurements may be taken at any chosen interval.

When suitable taper measurements have been obtained for a given tree, the cross-sectional area or diameter squared, both inside and outside bark, should be plotted over height on cross-section paper for each cross section for which measurements were taken. Then the points should be connected by smooth lines to give a profile which is analogous to that of one side of a longitudinal section taken through the center of the tree. A separate graph is prepared for each tree stem.

On the graph it is useful to label diameters at important points, such as top of stump, breast height, log ends, and the base of the merchantable or unused top, and to record pertinent information on species, locality, observers, date, and converting factor. Volumes for the entire stem, or for any of its sections, either inside or outside bark, may be obtained by measuring the required area on the graph and applying the converting factor as described in Chapter 7.

A special type of graph paper, called Forest Service Form 558a, is shown in Fig. 8–3. This form, which has been prepared specifically for graphical tree-volume determination, has several unique features:

1. Diameters can be plotted directly on the ordinate scale. (Note that, although the variable name on the ordinate scale is "diameter," the graduations are in terms of cross-sectional area. In other words, the spacings on the scale are in uniform cross-sectional area units. Thus, the spacings for the diameters become progressively greater as the diameters increase.)
2. Four different scales are given for diameter and four for height. Thus, one can select the combination that is best suited to the trees being graphed.
3. In the lower left-hand corner of the graph there is a tabular schedule of square inch-cubic foot conversion factors. The intersection, in this schedule, of lines that have been carried across the scales selected gives the converting factor to be used.

In using Forest Service Form 558a, the taper curve is plotted in the same manner as on ordinary cross-section paper, and the area obtained with a planimeter, or dot grid, as explained in Chapter 7.

8–5. DIRECT DETERMINATION OF CUBIC VOLUME BY DISPLACEMENT

The cubic volume of any part of a tree may be found by submerging it in a tank in which the water displacement can be accurately read. Such

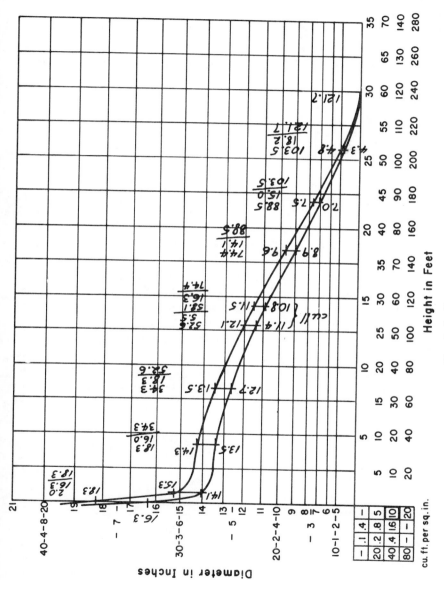

Fig. 8-3. Tree measurements.

a tank, termed a xylometer, affords the most accurate method of cubic volume determination. But to use the xylometer it is necessary to fell the tree and to cut it into sections that are small enough to handle, and small enough to fit into the tank. If total root, stump, stem, or crown volume is desired, the volumes of the individual pieces may be summed to give the desired total.

8–6. THE BARK FACTOR AND DETERMINATION OF BARK VOLUME

Average bark volume will run from ten to twenty per cent of unpeeled volume for most species. But we often need to know bark volume more accurately than this to determine peeled stem or log volume from unpeeled stem or log volume, the quantity of bark residue that will be left after the manufacturing process has been completed, and in cases where the bark has value, the quantity of bark available. We can, of course, compute unpeeled stem or log volume from outside bark diameter, peeled stem or log volume from inside bark diameter, and take the difference to secure a good estimate of bark volume. But the bark-factor method, which deserves more consideration than most foresters choose to give it, is easier to apply and gives sufficiently accurate results for most purposes. This method will now be discussed.

Bark thickness, which must be accurately determined to obtain reliable bark factors, may be determined as described in Section 3–3.2. The accuracy of bark measurements is increased if single-bark thickness is measured at two or more different points on a given cross-section of the stem, and the average single-bark thickness, b, computed. Then, diameter inside bark, d_u, may be computed from diameter outside bark, d, from equation: $d_u = d - 2b$. When d_u is plotted as a function of d, the relationship will be linear, or close to linear, with a Y-intercept of 0, or close to 0. (Figure 8–4 shows the relationship for white oak for the cross-section at breast height.) Consequently, it is reasonable to assume that the prediction equation for this relationship may be written in the general form $d_u = kd$. Since the regression coefficient, k, is normally determined at stump or breast height, we shall call it the *lower-stem bark factor*. Such bark factors range from 0.87 to 0.93, varying with species, age, and site. But since the major portion of the variation can be accounted for by species, it is reasonable and convenient to assume that the ratio will be constant for a given species. It is also convenient to assume that this bark factor will remain the same, for a given species, at all heights on the stem. Exceptions to this rule exist. For example, Johnson (1966) found that bark factors in the upper stem of young-growth Douglas fir trees are not the same as lower-stem bark factors, and so developed several equations to

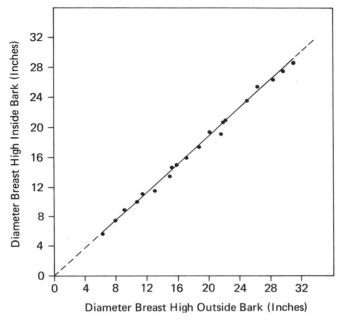

Fig. 8–4. Relationship between corresponding diameters inside and outside bark of white oak (see Table 8–4).

predict upper-stem bark factors, B_{us}. One of his equations may be written as follows:

$$B_{us} = [6194 - 2.6A + 3.2L + 2378(d_o/d) - 1545(d_o/d)^2 + 2533k]\ 10^{-4}$$

$$(8\text{–}11)$$

where:

A = tree age
L = height above ground of cross-section for which B_{us} is desired
d = diameter at breast height outside bark
d_o = diameter outside bark at cross-section for which B_{us} is desired
k = bark factor at stump height

The use of such equations is not, in this day of computers, limited because of computation time, but rather because of the time required to measure the independent variables. However, whether we assume that the bark factor is the same at all heights on the stem, or that the bark factor will be different at different heights on the stem, once the bark factor has been obtained, the method of using it to obtain bark volume is the same. We shall illustrate the method by assuming that k is the same at all heights on the stem. It will be apparent that the method would be quite time consuming if B_{us} were used.

An average value of k, to be reliable, should be based on twenty to fifty bark-thickness measurements and corresponding diameter-outside-bark measurements. By the method of least squares, k is determined so that the sum of squared deviations of the individual's d_u's (Y's) about the fitted regression line is a minimum. In this case, where we assume that when $X = 0$ then $Y = 0$, it is appropriate to use the following equation to determine k:

$$k = \frac{\Sigma \, dd_u}{\Sigma \, d^2}$$

When the variation of the dependent variable is proportional to the independent variable, as it generally is when d_u is plotted over d, Meyer (1953) has shown that the following formula will give the same results:

$$k = \frac{\Sigma \, d_u}{\Sigma \, d}$$

For the trees listed in Table 8–4 and plotted in Fig. 8–4, the first formula gives:

$$k = \frac{7179.62}{7628.93} = .941$$

The second formula gives:

$$k = \frac{341.7}{363.3} = .941$$

Agreement of these two formulas will not always be this good. But, for calculating k, the second formula will, for practical uses, always give satisfactory results.

The bark thickness, b, corresponding to an average value of k, can be determined as follows for any diameter, d:

$$b = \tfrac{1}{2}(d - d_u)$$

And since $d_u = kd$, then:

$$\begin{aligned} b &= \tfrac{1}{2}(d - kd) \\ &= \tfrac{1}{2}d(1 - k) \end{aligned} \qquad (8\text{--}12)$$

Thus, for a white oak cross-section of 14.0 inches in diameter, we may estimate the bark thickness to be:

$$\begin{aligned} b &= \tfrac{1}{2}(14.0)(1 - .941) \\ &= .413 \text{ inches} \end{aligned}$$

The average value of k can also be used to obtain cubic bark volume, V_b, and cubic volume inside bark, V_u, from cubic volume outside bark, V,

Table 8–4

Diameter and Bark Measurements of 20 White Oak Trees

	d	$2b$	d_u
	Dbh Outside Bark (inches)	**Double Bark Thickness (inches)**	**Dbh Inside Bark (inches)**
	30.8	2.2	28.6
	14.7	1.1	13.6
	24.8	1.2	23.6
	20.0	0.8	19.2
	21.7	1.1	20.6
	7.9	0.4	7.5
	15.8	1.1	14.7
	12.7	1.3	11.4
	18.6	1.0	17.6
	17.0	1.0	16.0
	26.1	0.8	25.3
	28.1	1.7	26.4
	10.6	0.6	10.0
	6.1	0.4	5.7
	29.4	1.6	27.8
	15.1	0.8	14.3
	21.5	2.3	19.2
	22.0	1.2	20.8
	11.4	0.7	10.7
	9.0	0.3	8.7
Sum	363.3	21.6	341.7

$$\Sigma d{\cdot}d_u = 7179.62$$
$$\Sigma d^2 = 7628.93$$

for a given stem section. If diameter outside bark at the middle of the section, d_m, diameter inside bark at the middle of the section, d_{mu}, and section length, L, are all in the same units, we have:

$$V = \frac{\pi d_m{}^2}{4}(L), \quad \text{and} \quad V_u = \frac{\pi d_{mu}{}^2}{4}(L)$$

And since:

$$d_{mu} = k d_m$$

then:

$$V_u = \frac{\pi}{4}(k d_m)^2(L) = k^2 V \tag{8–13}$$

Finally, since:

$$V_b = V - V_u$$
$$V_b = V(1 - k^2) \tag{8–14}$$

$$V_b \; (\%) = (1 - k^2)100 \qquad (8\text{--}15)$$

When V_u is determined by equation 8–13, it will be theoretically correct. However, V_b determined by equation 8–14 will be greater than the actual value. This is because V_b includes air spaces between the ridges of the bark. Indeed, a study by Chamberlain and Meyer (1950) shows that the difference in volume between stacked-peeled and stacked-unpeeled cordwood is, on the average, eighty per cent of the volume given by equation 8–14. One might not expect this result. But it comes about because in a stack of wood the ridges of the bark of one log will mesh with the ridges of another log, and because the weight of the logs will compress the bark. Thus, for practical purposes, we can rewrite equation 8–14 to give the bark volume of cordwood in stacks, V_{b_s}:

$$V_{b_s} = .8V(1 - k^2) \qquad (8\text{--}16)$$

8–7. METHODS OF STUDYING STEM FORM

There are wide variations in the form of the main stem of trees due to variations in the rates of diminution in diameter from the base to the tip. This diminution in diameter, known as taper, which is a fundamental reason for variation in volume, varies with species, diameter breast high, age, and site.

In a definitive study, Larson (1963) discussed the biological concept of stem form by a comprehensive review of the literature. In their studies of stem form, mensurationists have looked for pure expressions of stem form that are independent of diameter and height. But pure expressions have not been discovered; they are probably fictions. Nevertheless, the methods that have been developed for studying stem form have been useful. They may be considered under four headings: *form factors, form quotients, form point,* and *taper tables, curves, and formulas.*

8–7.1. Form Factors. A form factor is the ratio of tree volume to the volume of a geometrical solid, such as a cylinder, a cone, or a cone frustum, that has the same diameter and height as the tree. A form factor is different from other measures of form in that it can be calculated only after the volume of the tree is known. In formula form the form factor, f, is:

$$f = \frac{\text{Volume of tree}}{\text{Volume of geometrical solid of same diameter and height}} \qquad (8\text{--}17)$$

Early in the nineteenth century it was recognized that the form of tree stems approached that of the solids discussed in Section 8–3. But it was also recognized that there were many variations in form, and that a tree rarely was of the exact form of one of these solids. Thus, the form factor was conceived as a method of coordinating form and volume. That is to say, the main objective of the early work was to derive factors that would be independent of diameter and height, and by which the volume of standard geometrical solids could be multiplied to obtain the tree volume. For example, the ratio of the volumes of a paraboloid to a cylinder is 0.5 when the base diameter and the height of the two solids are equal; the volume of the paraboloid is obtained by multiplying the volume of the cylinder by 0.5.

The form factor that has been most commonly used may be expressed by the equation:

$$f = \frac{V}{gh} \qquad (8\text{--}18)$$

where:

V = tree volume in cubic units
g = cross-sectional area
h = height

This is termed a *cylindrical form factor* because the divisor is the volume of a cylinder.

The usefulness of form factors to estimate the volume of trees of variable form is limited. However, they find some use for rapid approximation of volume, and to obtain the volume of trees of little form variation. Belyea (1931) discussed form factors and their uses at some length.

8–7.2. Form Quotients. A form quotient is the ratio of a diameter measured at some height above breast height, such as one-half tree height, to diameter at breast height. In formula form the form quotient, q, is:

$$q = \frac{\text{diameter above breast height}}{\text{diameter at breast height}} \qquad (8\text{--}19)$$

Next to diameter breast high and height, form quotient is the most important variable that can be used to predict the volume of a tree stem. Thus, it may be used as the third independent variable in the construction of volume tables (see Chapter 9).

The original form quotient (Schiffel, 1899) took diameter at one-half total tree height, $d_{.5h}$, as the numerator, and diameter breast high, d, as the denominator. This was termed the *normal form quotient, q*:

$$q = \frac{d_{.5h}}{d} \qquad (8\text{--}20)$$

For this form quotient, as tree height decreases, the position of the upper diameter comes closer to the breast height point until, for a tree whose height is double breast height, they coincide. To eliminate this anomaly, Jonson (1910) changed the position of the upper diameter to a point halfway between the tip of the tree and breast height, $d_{½(h+4.5)}$, and called the ratio the *absolute form quotient*, q_a:

$$q_a = \frac{d_{½(h+4.5)}}{d} \tag{8–21}$$

The absolute form quotient is a better measure of stem form than the normal form quotient. However, it is not a pure expression of stem form. It is not independent of diameter and height, and varies within a given diameter–height class for a given species. For most species absolute form quotients diminish with increasing diameters and heights, varying between 0.60 and 0.80. (Absolute form quotient is 0.707 for a paraboloid, 0.500 for a cone, and 0.354 for a neiloid. These values hold irrespective of the diameter and height of the solid.)

In determining the normal or absolute form quotient, the two diameters may be taken either outside or inside bark. Although it is difficult to obtain an accurate upper-stem diameter inside bark, the ratio of the inside bark measurements is a better index of form than the outside bark measurements, because variable bark thicknesses do not then distort the ratio.

At this point it would be well to discuss the term *Form Class*. Originally the term was applied to a class, as in a frequency table, of absolute form quotients. For example, form classes with class intervals of 0.05 have often been laid out as follows: 0.575–0.625, 0.625–0.675, 0.675–0.725, and 0.725–0.775. The midpoints of these classes, 0.60, 0.65, 0.70, and 0.75, were used to name the classes, and a tree falling into a particular class was said to have the form quotient of the midpoint of the class. Tree-volume computations were classified by absolute form class as well as by diameter and height. Form class may be related to the density of the stand (Jonson, 1911) or to Form Point (Fogelberg, 1953), so it may be determined indirectly.

In North America the term form class has been used in a different sense. Girard (1933), in the course of work in the U.S. Forest Service, developed a form quotient for use as an independent variable in volume table construction. This measure, termed Girard Form Class, q_G, is the percentage ratio of diameter inside bark at the top of the first standard log to diameter breast high, outside bark. When 16-foot logs are taken as the standard:

$$q_G = \frac{d_{u17.3}}{d}(100) \tag{8–22}$$

This measure of form has three advantages over normal and absolute form quotients:

1. The top of the first log is close enough to the ground so that the diameter at that point may be accurately estimated or measured.

2. The reference diameter is near enongh to the ground to give a measure of butt swell.
3. Bark thickness is taken into account and its effect on taper partially eliminated.

As mentioned in Chapter 9, Girard Form Class is a useful form quotient that has been widely employed in United States forest practice.

Efforts to develop form quotients that can be computed from more accessible diameters have led to a number of form quotients of the type advocated by Maass (1939). Maass's form quotient is the ratio of the diameter at 2.3 meters above the ground to diameter at 1.3 meters above the ground. Unpublished studies by Miller (1952), however, of similar form quotients indicated that this quotient, whether measurements are inside or outside bark, is too variable for trees of the same species, diameter, and height to be of practical use.

8–7.3. Form Point. Form point is the percentage ratio of the height to the center of wind resistance on the tree, approximately at the center of gravity of the crown, to the total tree height.

It was hypothesized by Jonson (1912) that the development of the form of a tree stem, as exemplified by the absolute form quotient, depends upon the mechanical stresses to which the tree is subjected. These stresses come from the dead weight of the stem and crown, and the wind force. The wind force, it was concluded, is the most important stress, and "causes" the tree to "construct" its stem in such a way that the relative resistance to fracture or shearing will be the same at all points on the longitudinal axis of the stem. Thus, the main determinative of stem form is the focal point of wind force, or the point of greatest resistance to wind bending. Since the crown offers most of the resistance, it will be the location of the focal point of the wind force. Thus, the point where the wind resistance is the greatest is approximately at the center of gravity of the crown; it will vary with the size and shape of the crown. Except as they affect the size and shape of the crown, such tree characteristics as diameter, height, species, and age, and such things as the site factors, do not, so it was claimed, affect stem form. Form point, then, is the percentage ratio of the height of the center of wind resistance, approximately at the center of gravity of the crown, to total tree height. The greater the form point, the more nearly cylindrical will be the form of the tree.

In cases where the form point has been used, the average form points for the various diameter classes of a stand are obtained by sampling, and with these values as the independent variables, form classes are read from curves or tables (Fogelberg, 1953). Also, with the form point of an individual tree as the independent variable, the form class for an individual tree may be read from a curve or table.

It should be emphasized that the main value of the form point is to predict the absolute form quotient; there appears to be a good correlation between form quotient and form point. There are, however, some serious limitations to the use of form point. The focal point of wind resistance within the crown of any tree varies with the density of the crown and the position of the crown in the stand. Thus, the point is difficult to locate; two estimators will differ considerably on its selection.

8–7.4. Taper Tables, Curves, and Formulas. If sufficient measurements of diameter are taken at successive points along the stems of trees, one can prepare average taper tables which give a good picture of stem form. The ultimate purpose of all taper tables is to portray stem form in such a way that the data can be used in the calculation of stem volume or in the construction of volume tables. There are several ways of preparing taper tables (Chapman and Meyer, 1949), but the method of greatest utility is to average upper-log taper rates inside bark for standard log lengths according to diameter breast high and merchantable height in standard logs (Table 8–5).

Table 8–5
Average Upper-Log Taper Inside Bark (Inches) in 16-Foot Logs

Dbh (inches)	2-log tree 2d log	3-log tree 2d log	3d log	4-log tree 2d log	3d log	4th log
10	1.4	1.2	1.4			
12	1.6	1.3	1.5	1.1	1.4	1.9
14	1.7	1.4	1.6	1.2	1.5	2.0
16	1.9	1.5	1.7	1.2	1.6	2.1
18	2.0	1.6	1.8	1.3	1.7	2.2
20	2.1	1.7	1.9	1.4	1.8	2.4
22	2.2	1.8	2.0	1.4	2.0	2.5
24	2.3	1.8	2.2	1.5	2.2	2.6
26	2.4	1.9	2.3	1.5	2.3	2.7
28	2.5	1.9	2.5	1.6	2.4	2.8
30	2.6	2.0	2.6	1.7	2.5	3.0

SOURCE: Mesavage and Girard, 1946.

Since taper tables may be expressed in curve form, it is logical to express a taper curve by a mathematical function. And it is logical to use the formula to obtain the volume of the solid of revolution. Many formulas have been developed. But as Grosenbaugh (1966) said in his comprehensive study of stem form:

Many mensurationists have sought to discover a single simple two-variable function involving only a few parameters which could be used to specify the entire tree profile. Unfortunately, trees seem capable of assuming an infinite variety of shapes, and polynomials (or quotients of polynomials) with degree at least two greater than the observed number of inflections are needed to specify variously inflected forms. Furthermore, coefficients would vary from tree to tree in ways that could only be known after each tree has been completely measured. Thus, explicit analytic definition of tree form requires considerable computational effort, yet lacks generality. . . . Each tree must be regarded as an individual that must be completely measured, or else as a member of a definite population whose average form can only be estimated by complete measurement of other members of the population selected according to a valid sampling plan. . . . Hence, polynomial analysis may rationalize observed variation in form after measurement, but it does not promise more efficient estimation procedures.

Thus, it appears unwise to derive complicated relationships to characterize tree form. This notion is corroborated by Kozak and Smith (1966) who, after studying the multivariate techniques of Fries (1965) and Fries and Matern (1965), concluded that the use of simple functions, sorting, and graphical methods is adequate for many uses in operations and research.

9

Log Rules and Volume Tables

The methods that are described in this chapter involve the development of relationships to express the volume of a tree or log as a function of easily measured tree or log dimensions. These relationships, as expressed by formula, table, or graph, can be used to estimate the desired volume from the appropriate dimensions. The basic data for the development of many of the cubic volume relationships can be obtained by the methods described in Chapter 8.

9-1. ESTIMATION OF LOG VOLUMES

The estimated contents of logs, or cut sections, are commonly given in tables. Such log volume tables, termed *log rules*, are simply tabular statements of the estimated contents of logs of specified diameters and lengths. Although these tables may be prepared in any volume unit, they are commonly expressed in board feet, cubic feet, or cubic meters, or occasionally in standards. These units are defined in Chapter 7.

9-1.1. Board-Foot Log Rules. A board foot is a nominal volume unit. For example, if one visited a lumber yard to obtain a 1- by 12-inch ponderosa pine board 8 feet long, he would be given a ¾ by 11¼ inch board 8 feet long, and would be billed for 8 board feet; the volume would be computed from the nominal dimensions, not the exact dimensions.

Although there is an inexactness in the measurement of the board-foot volume of lumber, board-foot log rules showing the estimated number of board feet of lumber that can be sawed from logs of given lengths and diameters are frequently used to estimate the contents of logs and trees. This constitutes an attempt to estimate, before processing, the amount of lumber in logs and trees. Thus, we must distinguish between the measurement of the board-foot contents of sawn lumber, that is, *mill tally,* and the estimation of the board-foot contents of logs, that is, *log scale.* The board-foot mill tally, though not exact, is a well-defined unit; the board-foot log scale is an ambiguous unit. Thus, the amount of lumber sawed from any run of logs rarely agrees with the scale of the logs. This variation, O_v, may be expressed in board feet:

$$O_v \text{ (in board feet)} = \text{Mill Tally} - \text{Log Scale}$$

When O_v is positive, a mill has produced an *overrun;* when O_v is negative, a mill has produced an *underrun.*

Foresters, however, have typically expressed O_v as a percentage of log scale:

$$O_v \text{ (in per cent)} = \left(\frac{\text{Mill Tally} - \text{Log Scale}}{\text{Log Scale}}\right) 100$$

$$= \left[\left(\frac{\text{Mill Tally}}{\text{Log Scale}}\right) - 1\right] 100 \qquad (9\text{--}1)$$

where the ratio, $\dfrac{\text{Mill Tally}}{\text{Log Scale}}$, is the *overrun ratio,* that is, the number of board-feet mill tally per board-foot log scale.

The first board-foot log rule was used in New York State in 1825. Between 1825 and 1910 over 100 other log rules were devised. This is easy to understand. In those bygone days lumber was used mainly in the region in which it was manufactured—each region developed its own log rules. But, at best, log rules were inexact—many lumbermen thought they could construct better rules. Although log rules are still widely used in North America, today no more than twelve rules are employed.

In the construction of all known board-foot log rules, four basic methods have been used: (1) empirical mill studies, (2) drawing diagrams to scale, (3) mathematical formulas, and (4) combining existing log rules.

No matter what method is used, the yield of logs, V, in board feet, is estimated, in terms of lumber one-inch thick, from average small-end diameter inside bark, D, in inches, and log length, L, in feet.

9–1.2. Mill-Study Log Rules. In this method of constructing log rules a sample of logs is first measured on the log deck. Then, as each log is sawed, the boards are measured to determine the board-foot volume of the log. The log rule is prepared by relating board-foot yields, the dependent variable, with log diameters and lengths, the independent variables. The problem may be solved graphically or by method of least squares.

A rule of this type should give good estimates for mills that cut timber with peculiar characteristics, or for those that use specific milling methods. The method, however, has never been widely used. The Massachusetts log rule, one of the few rules constructed by this method that is still in use, was based on 1200 logs. It gives the volume in one-inch round-edged boards.

9–1.3. Diagram Log Rules. The procedure for the construction of a diagram log rule is simple:

1. Draw circles to scale to represent the small ends of logs of different diameters inside bark. Assume logs are cylinders of a specific length, such as 8 feet.
2. Use definite assumptions on saw kerf and shrinkage, and board width, and draw boards (rectangles) one-inch thick within the circles.
3. Compute the total board-foot contents for each log diameter.
4. Determine board-foot contents of other lengths by proportion.

When a diagram log rule is prepared, it will be found, for any given log length, that increases in volume, from one diameter to the next, will be slightly irregular. These irregularities may be eliminated by preparing a free-hand curve, or a regression equation, to predict volume from diameter for each length.

The *Scribner Log Rule*, the most widely used diagram log rule, was first published in 1846 by J. M. Scribner who based the rule on the following assumptions:

1. boards sawn will be one-inch thick and not less than 8-inches wide
2. loss from saw kerf and shrinkage will be one-quarter inch
3. logs are cylinders

Originally the rule was prepared for logs 12–48 inches in diameter, and the final smoothing of the values determined from the diagrams was omitted. Regression equations that smooth out the irregularities have been prepared, however, from the original Scribner Table (Bruce, 1925). For 16-foot logs the volume in board feet, V, in terms of diameter, D, is:

$$V = 0.79D^2 - 2D - 4 \qquad (9\text{--}2)$$

Since calculating machines were not generally available in the 19th century, scalers found the adding of long columns of figures laborious. Consequently, the Scribner rule was often converted into a *Decimal Rule* by dropping the units and rounding the values to the nearest ten board feet. Thus, 114 board feet was written 11, and 157 board feet was written 16.

Because the original Scribner rule did not give values for logs less than 12 inches in diameter, a number of lumber companies extrapolated to derive volumes for small logs. Finally, the Lufkin Rule Company prepared three tables using different assumptions to extend the rule to cover small logs. They published these as Decimal Rules, and called them the Scribner Decimal A Rule, the Scribner Decimal B Rule, and the Scribner Decimal C Rule. The Decimal C Rule is the only one of these rules still widely used.

There are other log rules based on diagrams. The best known are the Spaulding Rule, which is used on the Pacific Coast of the United States, and the Maine Rule, which is used in northeastern United States.

9–1.4. Mathematical Log Rules. To derive a mathematical log rule, a formula is developed, using definite assumptions on saw kerf, taper, and milling procedures, that gives the board-foot yield of logs in terms of their diameters and lengths. As will be seen, this is not a regression analysis.

The *Doyle Log Rule,* the oldest and most widely used mathematical log rule, was first published in 1825 by Edward Doyle. The rule states: "Deduct four inches from the diameter of the log, D, in inches, for slabbing, square one-quarter of the remainder, and multiply by the length of the log, L, in feet." As Herrick (1940) pointed out, when Doyle deducted four inches from the diameter of the log for slabbing, he was squaring the log. Then he calculated the board-foot contents of the squared log, or cant, as follows:

$$\frac{(D-4)(D-4)L}{12}$$

To allow for saw kerf and shrinkage, he reduced the volume of the cant by 25 per cent to obtain the final rule:

$$V = \frac{(D-4)^2 L}{12}(1.00 - 0.25) = \left(\frac{D-4}{4}\right)^2 L \qquad (9\text{–}3)$$

For 16-foot logs the *Doyle Rule of Thumb* is:

$$V = (D-4)^2 \qquad (9\text{–}4)$$

This points up the main reason this rule gained wide acceptance; it was genuinely simple, and could be easily applied.

When the Doyle Rule is applied to logs between 26 and 36 inches in diameter, it gives good results. When the rule is applied to large logs it gives an underrun; when applied to small logs it gives a high overrun. This comes about because the 4-inch slabbing allowance is inadequate for large logs and excessive for small logs. Despite these inaccuracies, the Doyle Rule is still widely used.

The *International Log Rule*, one of the most accurate mathematical log rules, was developed by Clark (1906). The derivation of the original rule is logical and simple. One first computes the board-foot contents of a 4-foot cylinder in terms of cylinder diameter, D, assuming the cylinder will produce lumber at the rate of 12 board feet per cubic foot:

$$\text{Solid board-foot contents of 4-foot cylinder} = \frac{\pi D^2}{4(144)}\,(4)(12) = 0.262D^2$$

To allow for saw kerf and shrinkage one assumes that, for each one-inch board cut, $\frac{1}{8}$th inch will be lost in saw kerf and $\frac{1}{16}$ inch in shrinkage:

$$\text{Lost from saw kerf and shrinkage} = \left(\frac{3/16}{1+3/16}\right)100 = 15.8\%$$

When reduced by 15.8 per cent, the volume of the 4-foot cylinder becomes:

$$0.262D^2(1.000 - 0.158) = 0.22D^2$$

Tests showed that losses from slabs and edgings constitute a ring-shaped zone around the outside of the log. The thickness of this collar, which Clark assumed to be about 0.7 inches, is approximately the same for all logs. Thus, if a 0.7-inch collar gives the correct allowance, a plank 2.12 inches thick and D inches wide will also give the correct deduction. In terms of cylinder diameter, D, in inches, the deduction is:

$$\frac{2.12(D)(4)}{12} = 0.71D$$

Thus, the net board-foot content of a 4-foot cylinder is:

$$V = 0.22D^2 - 0.71D \qquad (9\text{--}5)$$

To obtain the volume of logs over four feet long, a taper of one-half inch is allowed for each 4-foot log section. For instance, the formula for an 8-foot log becomes:

$$V = [.22D^2 - .71D] + [.22(D + \tfrac{1}{2})^2 - .71(D + \tfrac{1}{2})]$$
$$= .44D^2 - 1.20D - .3 \qquad (9\text{--}6)$$

The volume of sections less than 4-feet long is obtained by interpolation.

The original International Log Rule may be modified to give estimates for saw kerfs other than $\frac{1}{8}$th inch. For example, for a kerf of $\frac{1}{4}$th inch (shrinkage $\frac{1}{16}$th inch) the loss is:

$$\left(\frac{5/16}{1+5/16}\right)100 = 23.8\%$$

So the original rule may be converted to a $\frac{1}{4}$-inch rule by multiplying the values by the following factor:

$$\frac{1.000 - 0.238}{1.000 - 0.158} = 0.905$$

The factor to convert to a $\frac{7}{64}$-inch rule is 1.013; the factor to convert to a $\frac{3}{16}$-inch rule is 0.950.

The International Log Rule, or any other log rule, may be presented as a Decimal Rule. In fact, the U. S. Forest Service uses a $\frac{1}{4}$-inch International Decimal Rule.

Other formula rules, such as the British Columbia Rule, have been constructed, but they have never enjoyed the popularity of the Doyle and International Log Rules.

9–1.5. Combination Log Rules. Rules of this type were devised to meet specific conditions. For example, the *Doyle-Scribner Rule,* a combination of the Doyle and Scribner Rules, was prepared for use in defective and over-mature timber. Since the Doyle Rule gives an overrun for small logs, its values were used for diameters up to 28 inches. Since the Scribner Rule gives an overrun for large logs, its values were used for diameters 28 inches and over. Thus, the Doyle-Scribner Rule, which is still used by some private operators in the South, gives a consistently high overrun which is supposed to compensate for hidden defects.

The Scribner-Doyle Rule, exactly opposite to the Doyle-Scribner Rule, gives a consistently low overrun.

9–1.6. Comparison of Log Rules. Because different methods and assumptions are used in the construction of log rules, different rules give different results, none of which will necessarily agree with the mill tally for any given log (Table 9–1). This points out that the board-foot log scale, by any rule, is a unit of estimate rather than a unit of measure.

Table 9–1
Volume of 16-Foot Logs

Log Diameter (inches)	Mill Tally* (board feet)	Log Scale				
		Scribner	Maine	International—¼″ (board feet)	Doyle	Spaulding
6		18	20	20	4	
10	75	50	68	65	36	
14	145	114	142	135	100	114
18	229	213	232	230	196	216
22	382	334	363	355	324	341
26	578	500	507	500	484	488
30	665	657	706	675	676	656
34	862	800	900	870	900	845
38	1037	1068	1135	1095	1156	1064

*Average yield of logs sawed in an Indiana band mill.

9–1.7. Cubic Unit Log Rules. Rules may be prepared to give log volumes in cubic feet, or cubic meters, under bark, by average small-end diameter inside bark in inches or centimeters, and log length in feet or meters. They may also be prepared for average midpoint diameter inside bark (U. S. Forest Service, 1964). In either case it is logical to compute volume in four-foot sections, allowing one-half inch taper for each section; Smalian's, Huber's, and Newton's formulas are all applicable. Volume may be computed by the other methods described in Chapter 8.

Log rules may also be prepared to give the contents of logs in Hoppus feet or an assumed standard (Chapter 7).

9–2. APPLICATION OF LOG RULES—LOG SCALING

Scaling is the determination of the gross and net volumes of logs in board feet, cubic feet, cubic meters, or assumed standards.

9–2.1. Board-Foot Scaling. Logs are scaled in two phases: first, *gross scale* is determined, and then losses from defect are estimated and *net scale* calculated.

The determination of gross scale consists of measuring log length and diameter and determining the volume by a log rule. This is a simple procedure because the volume values for log rules are usually read from a *scale stick,* a flat stick that has board-foot volumes for different diameter values, and log lengths, printed on its faces.

A maximum scaling length of 20 feet is standard for the western regions of the United States; 16 feet is standard for the eastern regions. When logs exceed the maximum scaling length, they are scaled as two or more logs. If a log does not divide evenly, the butt section is assigned the longer length. The scaling diameter for the assumed point of separation can be estimated from the taper of the log. Although log lengths have been measured for many years in even feet, that is, 8, 10, 12, 14, and 16, there is a growing tendency to measure lengths, particularly of hardwoods, in both odd and even feet, that is 8, 9, 10, 11, and 12. In any case, an additional length, varying with logging conditions, but usually 3 or 4 inches, must be allowed for trimming. If a log does not have this allowance, it is normally reduced, for scaling, to the next lower unit length. If a log has "overtrim," it may be scaled, as a penalty, to the next higher unit length.

Most log rules call for diameter measurements inside bark, to the nearest inch, at the small end of the log. If a log is round, one measurement is enough. When a log is eccentric, as most logs are, the usual practice is to take a pair of measurements at right angles across the long and short axes of the log end and to average the results to obtain the scaling diameter.

To determine net scale one must deduct from gross scale the quantity of lumber, according to the log rule used, that will be lost due to defects. These deductions do not include material lost during manufacturing, or defects that affect the quality of the lumber. Rather, they include those defects that will reduce the volume of lumber.

Long experience and good judgment are required to estimate accurately defect deductions from outside evidence. Briefly, the deductible defects may be classified as:

1. Interior defects—any defect causing waste in lumber sawed from the interior section of the log, such as heart rot, butt rot, heart shake, pitch ring, heart check, pitch seam, or split.
2. Side defects—those defects which cause loss in lumber volume sawed from the outer sections of logs, including unsound sapwood, surface checking, borer holes, lightning or frost cracks, and fire scars.
3. Crook or sweep—crook is the abrupt deflection of a relatively short section of a log from the straight axis. Sweep is the overall bow, or deflection, of the axis of a log from a straight axis connecting the centers of the two end sections.

Many individual scalers have worked out their own procedures of estimating the volume of deductions. The beginner, however, should follow a standard procedure. For example, the following defect-deduction methods are approved for Forest Service scaling (U.S. Forest Service, 1964):

1. Squared-defect method, used for scaling most interior defects and some side defects;
2. Pie-cut method, used for scaling side defects such as deep fire scars, lightning scars, and frost cracks;
3. Diameter-deduction method, used for scaling side defects such as unsound sapwood and surface checking;
4. Length-deduction method, used for scaling crook and sweep defects, and side and interior defects that occur near the end of the log.

In all cases defect in the outer inch of the log can be ignored, since it will be lost in slabbing.

The *squared-defect method*, formerly termed the standard rule for deduction of defect, is the most widely used of the four methods of making deductions, and is, therefore, the only one of these methods that we shall discuss. It is based on the principle of diagraming, on the end of the log, the square or rectangle that will contain the entire defect. Then the length of the defect is estimated and the contents, in one-inch boards, of an imaginary timber with these dimensions is calculated. The volume of the imaginary timber is deducted from the gross scale of the log. For a log rule based on a saw kerf and shrinkage of ¼-inch (20 per cent of the volume is lost—80 per cent is recoverable), the formula to determine the defective portion is:

$$\text{Board-foot cull} = \frac{W'' \times T'' \times L'}{12} \frac{80}{100} = \frac{W'' \times T'' \times L'}{15} \quad (9\text{--}7)$$

where W'' and T'' are end dimensions of defect in inches plus an allowance for waste of 1-inch for each dimension, and L' is the length of the defect in feet. If a log rule with a different saw kerf is used, the denominator should be recalculated.

Grosenbaugh (1952a) has proposed a logical, and simpler, system of determining net scale. In this method the amount of lumber lost in defect is estimated by multiplying the gross scale by any log rule by the proportion of the log affected. The procedures for common defects can be summarized in five equations:

1. If defect affects an entire section of log:

$$P_d = \frac{l}{L} \quad (9\text{--}8)$$

2. If defect affects a wedge-shaped section of log:

$$P_d = \left(\frac{l}{L}\right)\left(\frac{\alpha}{360}\right) \quad (9\text{--}9)$$

3. If log has long sweep:

$$P_d = \frac{(S_w - 2)}{D} \quad (9\text{--}10)$$

4. If crook is present:

$$P_d = \left(\frac{l_d}{L}\right)\left(\frac{C}{D}\right) \quad (9\text{--}11)$$

5. If an interior defect can be enclosed in circle or ellipse:

$$P_d = \frac{(d_a + 1)(d_b + 1)}{(D - 1)^2}\left(\frac{l}{L}\right) \quad (9\text{--}12)$$

where:

P_d = proportion of gross scale lost due to defect
D = top diameter, inside bark, in inches
L = log length in feet
l = length of defect in feet
α = central angle of a wedge-shaped defect in degrees
S_w = departure in inches of a curved central axis from a straight axis connecting centers of two end areas
l_d = length of deflecting section in feet

C = maximum deflection in inches of the axis of a crook from straight axis of log

d_a = major axis of an elliptical interior defect

d_b = minor axis of an elliptical interior defect—if defect is circular, $d_a = d_b$

Again, in using these formulas, defect in the outer inch of the log can be ignored since it will be lost in slabbing.

9–2.2. Cubic-Foot Scaling. In cubic-foot scaling, log lengths and log diameters, and the consequent gross cubic volume, are determined as in board-foot scaling. But log lengths are usually rounded to the nearest foot above or below the actual measurement. In making deductions for defects, one deducts the total cubic volume of unmerchantable material; there is no deduction for saw kerf. Thus:

$$\text{Cubic-foot deduction} = \frac{W'' \times T'' \times L'}{144} \qquad (9\text{–}13)$$

where W'', T'', and L' are as in equation 9–7.

Log volumes in cubic feet can be converted to the unit of measure appropriate to each manufacturing plant with less uncertainty than in converting from board-feet log scale to board feet of lumber, or from board-feet log scale to square feet of veneer. The ratio of board-feet mill tally to cubic-feet log scale can be computed just as easily as the ratio of board-feet mill tally to board-feet log scale, that is, the overrun ratio, and it is more meaningful. Of course, the board foot–cubic foot ratio will differ from mill to mill just as the overrun ratio will differ, because both ratios depend upon the same factors (see Chapter 7).

9–2.3. Unmerchantable Logs. The definition of a cull, or unmerchantable, log is largely a local matter. Merchantability varies with species, economic conditions, and other factors. However, no matter what units are employed, specifications should give, for the merchantable log, the minimum length allowed, the minimum diameter allowed, and the minimum per cent of sound material left after deductions are made for cull. For example, a cull log might be defined as any log less than 8-feet long, less than 6 inches in diameter, or less than 50 per cent sound.

9–2.4. Sample Scaling. Under conditions where the scaling operation interferes with the movement of the logs, or where scaling costs are high, sample scaling should be considered. Sample scaling is generally feasible when: (1) logs are fairly homogeneous in species, volume, and value, (2) logs are concentrated in one place so they may be scaled efficiently, and (3) total number of logs is large.

Once one has decided to use sample scaling, he is faced with two basic questions: How many logs must be scaled to determine the total scale within limits of accuracy acceptable to both buyer and seller? How should the sample logs be selected?

The number of logs, n, to measure can be calculated from the formula applicable to a finite population:

$$n = \frac{CV^2 t^2 N}{Na^2 + CV^2 t^2} \qquad (9\text{--}14)$$

where:

CV = coefficient of variation expressed as a per cent

t = t-value corresponding to chosen probability

N = total number of logs in population

a = the desired standard error of mean expressed as a per cent of mean; that is, the level of accuracy desired

There are other formulas, adaptations of equation 9–14, to determine size of sample. For example, Gevorkiantz and Ochsner (1943) derived a formula to compute the proportion of the total number of logs to scale; Lynch (1954) prepared a set of guides that included a consideration of scaling costs.

An example will best illustrate the use of equation 9–14. Let us assume CV is 50 per cent for a lot of 10,000 logs, and the desired standard error is 3 per cent. Then if we let t be 2, giving approximately 20 to 1 odds that a chance discrepancy between the estimated and true scale will not exceed 3 per cent, we obtain:

$$n = \frac{50^2(2^2)(10,000)}{10,000(3^2) + 50^2(2^2)} = 1,000$$

The coefficient of variation may best be determined by taking a small preliminary sample. Gevorkiantz and Ochsner (1943) published a guide to determine an approximate value of CV^2 from the ratio of the range in volume to average volume. This approach offers little advantage, however, because a sample must be taken to compute the ratio.

A practical procedure to obtain the 1,000-log sample would be to scale every tenth log, that is, take a systematic sample. Of course, to obtain total volume every log must be counted since the total number of logs, N, is an estimate.

Random sampling may be used in sample log scaling, but systematic sampling is more easily applied. Furthermore, Lexen (1941) found no appreciable difference between the errors of systematic and random samples in scaling a large number of ponderosa pine and lodgepole pine logs. Although random sampling is required if one desires to calculate valid sampling errors, it is not essential if the sole purpose of sampling is to obtain an unbiased estimate of the average volume per log, and the total volume, for a given run of logs.

When logs are moved on or off trucks so rapidly that a scaler does not have time to obtain an accurate scale of individual logs, sample scaling, as described above, may not be feasible. Then the approach followed by Stage (1957) might be useful—prepare an equation to express truckload volume in terms of load dimensions. Stage's formula, based on measurements on forty-three truckloads of hemlock logs in Idaho, is:

$$V = \frac{L^{0.7012}C^{2.5237}}{3.5968N^{0.2289}} \qquad (9\text{--}15)$$

where:

V = truckload volume in board feet, Scribner
L = average length of load in feet
C = circumference of load in middle in feet
N = number of logs in load

The coefficient of determination, R^2, for this study was 0.68.

If a large number of truckloads is measured, it would be most convenient to solve the equation by computer. However, it is easy to solve the equation by putting it in logarithmic form.

A somewhat similar approach was followed by Row and Guttenberg (1966) when they prepared equations to predict board-foot volume of truckloads from load weight and number of logs (see Chapter 5).

9–3. CORD MEASURE

The cord unit, which is discussed in Section 7–3, has traditionally been applied to the measurement of firewood, pulpwood, excelsior wood, charcoal wood, and other relatively low-value products that are assembled in stacks.

In scaling a stack of wood one first records the length, the average of measurements taken on both sides of the stack, to the nearest foot. Then stack height is obtained by averaging measurements taken at intervals of about four feet. The height, which is reduced up to one inch per foot to compensate for settling and shrinkage, is recorded to the nearest inch. Finally, piece lengths are checked to see if they vary from the lengths specified in the sale or purchase contract (standard lengths for pulpwood cut in the United States are 4 feet, 5 feet, 5 feet 3 inches, and 8 feet 4 inches). If they do, the procedure given in the contract should be followed.

The volume in standard cords, V_c, of a stack of wood is calculated as follows:

$$V_c = \frac{L_s \times H_s \times L}{128} \qquad (9\text{--}16)$$

where:

L_s = stack length in feet
H_s = stack height in feet
L = stick length in feet

If stacks are piled on slopes, the length and height measurements should be taken at right angles to one another.

Since the above procedure gives gross cord volume, to obtain net cord volume deductions must be made for defective wood. The definitions of defects and the procedures of allowing for defects will vary from one organization to another. But in general deductions are made for *defective sticks* and for *loose piling*. Defective sticks include rotted sticks, burned sticks, undersized sticks, and peeled sticks with excessive bark adhering. Loose piling may occur when knots have been improperly trimmed, when excessively crooked wood is present, and when sticks have been carelessly piled.

When making deductions for defective sticks, the scaler examines each stick in a pile and notes which sticks will not meet specifications. These sticks are then culled by deducting the cubic space they occupy from the gross cubic space occupied by the pile—either a stick is acceptable or it is not acceptable. Deductions for loose piling are made by estimating the cubic space that would be occupied by sticks that could be included in the loose pile and subtracting this volume from the gross cubic space occupied by the pile.

The term "rough wood" is used to designate wood with bark in contrast to the term "peeled wood" which refers to wood with bark removed. It should be made clear in a sales contract whether wood is to be measured "rough" or "peeled." If the sale price is based on rough wood volume, then if peeled wood must be measured, volume must be increased 10 to 20 per cent, depending on bark thickness (see Section 8–6).

9–3.1. Determination of Solid Cubic-Foot Contents of Cordwood. It is often necessary to know the solid cubic-foot contents per cord. Although average converting factors, such as those given in Chapter 7, are often used, better factors are generally required. These can be determined by direct measurement or by photographic methods.

1. Direct measurement. The cubic volume of individual sticks, or of groups of sticks, can be determined by displacement (see Chapter 8). Also, the cubic volume of individual pieces can be computed by using Huber's, Smalian's, or Newton's formulas. In any case, when the cubic-foot space occupied by a pile is known, the ratio of solid cubic-foot volume to total cubic-foot volume can be calculated from the equation:

$$f = \frac{\text{solid cubic-foot volume of pile}}{\text{total cubic-foot volume of pile}} \tag{9–17}$$

The factor, f, multiplied by the space occupied by a cord, or by an entire pile, will give the solid cubic-foot contents of the volume of wood in question.

2. Photographic methods. The factor, f, can be estimated from photographs of the ends of sticks in a pile. One simply sets up, or holds, the camera at a convenient distance from the pile, say ten feet, with the optical axis of the lens perpendicular to the side of the pile. After a photograph is developed, a templet, consisting of about 16 systematically spaced pin holes per square inch at scale of 1:30, is placed over the photograph and the photograph perforated with a needle at each pin hole (Fig. 9–1). The photograph is then placed on a light table and the number of perforations falling in air spaces counted. Finally, f is computed as follows:

$$f = 1 - \frac{\text{(number of dots in air spaces)}}{\text{(total number of dots in grid)}} \qquad (9\text{–}18)$$

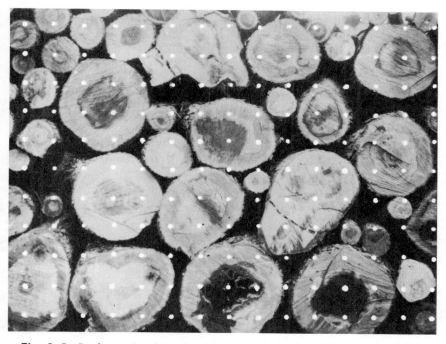

Fig. 9–1. Perforated polaroid photograph of portion of a truck load of low-quality hardwoods. Solid wood contents of this sample is 79 cubic feet per standard cord ($f = .62$). A 20 per cent photo sample of each load is sufficient to give ± 2.4 per cent accuracy at the 95 per cent confidence level (Garland, 1968).

Mountain (1949) shows how the method can be applied to any stack of wood with a 35 mm. camera. Garland (1968) shows how the method can be applied on truck loads with a polaroid camera to calculate solid wood contents so that truckers can be paid on the spot for solid wood hauled. For low quality hardwoods Garland's method was found to be better than weight scaling.

9–3.2. Determination of Cord Volume of Large Piles. Young (1954) has described a method of estimating the quantity of pulpwood in huge piles, as stored in the wood yards of pulp and paper companies. He used aerial photographs to prepare a contour map of the pulpwood piles and determined cross-sectional areas at successive contours by planimetering the map. Then, from the cross-sectional areas and contour intervals, he made estimates of the total space occupied by the pile. Of course, a contour map of a pile may also be prepared by ground survey methods. But, in either case, the space occupied by a pile is greater than the space occupied by an equal amount of stacked wood. Consequently, factors to reduce pile volume to cord volume must be developed. The above procedures are adaptations of the method used to estimate quantities of coal or earth in large piles.

9–4. ESTIMATION OF TREE VOLUMES

Tree volumes can be estimated from previously established relationships between some of the easily measured dimensions of a tree and its volume. Diameter, height, and form are the independent variables that are commonly used to determine the values of the dependent variable, tree volume. The final result of developing a relationship of this type is presented in the form of a *volume table*—a tabulated statement of tree volumes in cubic feet, cubic meters, board feet, cords, or other units, according to one or more of the previously mentioned tree dimensions.

9–4.1. Local Volume Tables. Local volume tables give tree volume in terms of diameter at breast height only. The term local is used because such tables are restricted to the local area for which the height–diameter relationship hidden in the table is relevant. Although local volume tables may be prepared from raw field data, that is, from volume and diameter measurements for a sample of trees, they are normally derived from standard volume tables (see Section 9–6). Table 9–2 shows a typical local volume table.

9–4.2 Standard Volume Tables. Standard volume tables give tree volume in terms of dbh and merchantable or total height. Tables of this type may be prepared for individual species, or groups of species, and specific localities. The applicability of a standard volume table, how-

Table 9–2
Example of a Local Volume Table
Yellow Poplar (*Liriodendron tulipifera*) in Stark County, Ohio
International Rule (¼-Inch Kerf)—Merchantable Stem to a
Variable Top Diameter

Dbh Outside Bark (Inches)	Volume per Tree (Board Feet)	Merchantable Length (Feet)	Basis in Trees (Number)
10	30	19.5	4
11	50	23	5
12	70	26.5	13
13	95	30	9
14	125	33	9
15	155	36.5	1
16	190	40	5
17	235	43	7
18	285	45.5	6
19	345	48	4
20	405	51	2
21	480	53.5	1
22	555	56	2
23	635	58	3
24	720	60	1
25	800	62	–
26	885	64	1
27	975	65.5	2
28	1065	67	1
29	1155	69	5
30	1245	70	9
31	1340	71.5	7
32	1435	72.5	7
33	1535	73.5	1
34	1630	74.5	1
35	1725	75	–
36	1825	76	–

Trees climbed and measured by personnel of Work Projects Administration Official Project 65-1-42-166 — the Ohio Woodland Survey. Measurements taken at 16-foot log lengths above a 2.0-foot stump height. Scaled as 16-foot logs, and additional shorter top logs; top sections less than 8 feet in length scaled as fractions of an 8-foot log. Basis, 107 trees.
Table prepared, in 1939, by curving volume of merchantable length over d.b.h.
Aggregate difference: Table is 0.8% low. Average percentage deviation of basic data from table, 19.4%.
SOURCE: Diller and Kellog, 1940.

ever, depends on the form of the trees to which it is applied rather than on species or locality; for each diameter–height class the form of the trees to which the table is applied should agree with the form of the trees from which the table was prepared. Table 9–3 shows a typical standard volume table.

9–4.3. Form Class Volume Tables. Form class volume tables give volume in terms of dbh, merchantable or total height, and some measure of form, such as Girard form class or absolute form quotient. Such tables come in sets with one table for each form class. The format of each table is similar to that of a standard volume table. Note that if a single form class table is chosen as representative of a stand, volume determinations may be in error because it is unlikely that all trees will be of the same form class. Furthermore, since form class varies with tree size, species, and site, it is unlikely that variations in form class will be random. Thus, it is difficult to obtain an accurate average form class for a stand. It is, therefore, undesirable to use a single form class table for any extensive area.

9–4.4. Descriptive Information to Accompany Volume Tables. A volume table should include descriptive information that will enable one to apply it correctly. This information includes the following:

1. Species, or species group, to which table is applicable, or locality in which table is applicable.
2. Definition of dependent variable, that is, volume, including unit in which volume is expressed.
3. Definition of independent variables, including stump height and top diameter limit, if merchantable height is used.
4. Author.
5. Date of preparation.
6. Number of trees on which table is based.
7. Extent of basic data.
8. Method of determining volumes of individual trees.
9. Method of construction.
10. Appropriate measures of accuracy.

Table 9–2 and Table 9–3 include these items.

The first three items in the above list should always be given. The remaining items are of less interest and are sometimes omitted. When measures of accuracy are given, they should be understood to be measures of accuracy of the table when it is applied to the data used in its construction. Such measures give no assurance that a volume table will apply to other trees. Thus, when an accurate estimate is required, a table should be checked against the measured volumes of a representative sample of trees obtained from the stands to be estimated (see Section 9–4.5).

Table 9-3

Example of a Standard Volume Table

Board Foot Volume, International ¼" Rule, for Red Oak (*Quercus rubra*) in Pennsylvania

Dbh (inches)	Merchantable Height—Number of 16-Foot Logs											
	½	1	1½	2	2½	3	3½	4	4½	5	5½	6
8	8	18	28	37	47	57						
9	11	23	35	48	60	73						
10	13	29	44	59	75	90	105	121				
11	17	35	54	72	91	109	128	146				
12	20	42	64	86	108	130	153	175	197			
13	24	50	76	102	127	153	179	205	231			
14	28	58	88	118	148	178	208	238	268	298	328	
15	33	67	102	136	170	205	239	274	308	343	377	
16	37	77	116	155	194	233	273	312	351	390	429	469
17		87	131	175	219	264	308	352	396	441	485	529
18		97	147	197	246	296	345	395	445	494	544	594
19		109	164	219	275	330	385	440	496	551	606	662
20		121	182	243	304	366	427	488	549	611	672	733
21			201	268	336	403	471	538	606	673	741	809
22			221	295	369	443	517	591	665	739	813	888
23			241	322	403	484	565	646	727	808	889	970
24			263	351	439	527	616	704	792	880	968	1057
25			285	381	477	572	668	764	860	955	1051	1147
26			309	412	516	619	723	826	930	1033	1137	1240
27				445	556	668	780	891	1003	1114	1226	1338
28				478	598	718	839	959	1079	1199	1319	1439
29				513	642	771	900	1028	1157	1286	1415	1544
30				549	687	825	962	1101	1239	1376	1514	1652
31					734	881	1028	1175	1323	1470	1617	1764
32					782	939	1096	1253	1409	1566	1723	1880
33					832	999	1165	1332	1499	1666	1833	1999
34					883	1060	1237	1414	1591	1768	1945	2122
35					936	1124	1311	1499	1686	1874	2062	2249
36					990	1189	1387	1586	1784	1983	2181	2380

Stump height, one foot. Top diameter, 8.0 inches, inside bark.

Block indicates extent of basic data. Basis, 210 trees.

Sample trees scaled as 16-foot logs; top section measured to nearest foot.

SOURCE: Bartoo and Hutnik, 1962.

Standard Error of regression coefficient = 0.00261

Proportion of Variation accounted for by the regression = 0.974

Tabular values derived from regression $V = -1.84 + 0.01914D^2H$

9–4.5. Checking Applicability of Volume Tables. In an applicability check one should compare the volume of sample trees with the estimated volume from the volume table to be checked. Three conditions should be observed in selecting sample trees:

1. Sample trees for a given species, or species group, should be distributed through the timber to which the volume table will be applied.
2. No sizes, types, or growing conditions should be unduly represented in the sample.
3. If a sample of cut-trees is used, this sample, if not representative of the timber, should be supplemented by a sample of standing trees. (Measurements on standing trees can be made by methods described in Chapter 3.)

Definite rules for measuring sample trees should be established. For example, the following rules are satisfactory for the eastern United States:

1. Diameters along the tree stem, inside and outside bark, should be taken at 8-foot intervals above a 1-foot stump, and at stump height, breast height, and merchantable height.
2. Diameter should be measured to nearest one-tenth inch and bark thickness to nearest one-twentieth inch.
3. Knots, swellings, and other abnormalities should be avoided at points of measurement by taking measurements above or below them.
4. Total or merchantable heights should be measured to nearest foot. Merchantable heights should be measured for utilization standards for the timber.

Table 9–4 illustrates how the comparison of measured and estimated volumes of sample trees should be made. For practical purposes, the aggregate difference of a test sample should not exceed $2CV/\sqrt{n}$, where CV is the coefficient of variation of the volume table being tested, and n is the number of trees used in the test. Since the coefficient of variation for the table tested in Table 9–4 is 15 per cent, the table is applicable without correction because:

$$\frac{2(15)}{\sqrt{62}} = 3.9\% > 1.0\%$$

If desired, checks may be made by diameter classes. And, of course, more complicated statistical tests, such as Chi Square, might be used. The above procedure, however, is generally satisfactory.

When a table is judged to be inapplicable, one should adjust the table, or obtain a better table. Practical methods of making adjustments are described by Gevorkiantz and Olsen (1955).

Table 9–4
Comparison of Measured and Estimated Volumes of Sample of Red Oak

Dbh Class (inches)	Sample Trees	Measured Volume	Estimated Volume*	Aggregate Difference
	(number)	(bd. ft.)	(bd. ft.)	(per cent)
13.0–15.9	14	2,010	2,045	−1.7
16.0–18.9	10	2,003	1,943	+3.1
19.0–21.9	9	3,041	3,106	−2.1
22.0–24.9	21	9,257	8,895	+4.1
25.0–27.9	4	2,084	2,223	−6.3
28.0–30.9	3	2,130	2,110	+0.9
31.0–33.9	0	—	—	—
34.0–36.9	1	870	860	+1.2
All classes	62	21,395	21,182	+1.0

*From volume table.
SOURCE: Gevorkiantz and Olsen, 1955.

9–5. CONSTRUCTION OF VOLUME TABLES

The principles of volume-table construction given by Cotta early in the 19th century are still valid:

> Tree volume is dependent upon diameter, height, and form. When the correct volume of a tree has been determined, it is valid for all other trees of the same diameter, height, and form.

Since the time of Cotta, hundreds of volume tables have been constructed and used. Numerous methods have been used to construct the tables. But since 1946 there has been a trend, particularly for hardwoods, to reduce the number of volume tables used by adopting *composite volume tables*, tables applicable to average timber, regardless of species. Indeed, where the same standards of utilization are employed, differences in tree volumes among species are often of no practical consequence. Excellent examples of composite volume tables are Herrick's (1946a) for hardwoods in Indiana, and Gevorkiantz and Olsen's (1955) for timber in the Lake States. These tables have been extensively tested and have been found to replace individual species tables, especially for the estimation of volume on large tracts. Adjustment factors can be used for individual species that vary from the average.

Why have so many volume tables been constructed? Why has so much research gone into the development of volume tables? The answer is that foresters have been looking for methods that are simple, objective, and accurate. Because trees are highly variable geometric solids, however, no single table, or set of tables, could possibly satisfy all of these conditions, regardless of the method of construction. Consequently, one by one the older methods of volume table construction have been abandoned. For example, the once popular harmonized-curve method (Chapman and Meyer, 1949), which requires large amounts of data to establish the relationships, and considerable judgment to fit the curves, is rarely used today. The alignment-chart method, another subjective method, has been generally discarded. Other discarded methods have been described by Spurr (1952). Today interest has focused on the use of mathematical functions, or models, to prepare volume tables. There is no advantage for the majority of foresters in using any other method.

9–5.1. Mathematical Models for Construction of Volume Tables. The equations given in Table 9–5 can serve as mathematical models for the construction of volume tables or as bases to develop other models.

Table 9–5
Tree Volume Equations

Local	Diameter-Volume	$V = aD^b$	(9–19)
Standard	Constant Form Factor	$V = bD^2H$	(9–20)
	Combined Variable	$V = a+bD^2H$	(9–21)
	Schumacher	$V = aD^bH^c$	(9–22)
Form Class	Short Cut	$V = a+bFD^2H$	(9–23)
	Form Diameter	$V = aD^bH^cD_u{}^d$	(9–24)

where:

$$V = \text{volume in cubic units or board feet}$$
$$D = \text{dbh}$$
$$D_u = \text{an upper-stem diameter}$$
$$H = \text{total or merchantable height}$$
$$F = \text{a measure of form (Girard form class or absolute form quotient)}$$
$$a, b, c, \text{ and } d = \text{constants}$$

The nature of equations 9–20 and 9–21, which both have combined variables, becomes clear when they are rewritten:

$$V = bX$$
$$V = a + bX$$

where:

$$X = D^2H$$

Both of these models are predicated on the assumption that when volume is plotted over X (that is, D^2H), the trend is linear. The constants, a and b, may be determined graphically, but the least squares solution is preferable. For equation 9–20 the line is forced through the origin; for equation 9–21 the Y-intercept is computed. The theory and details of the calculations can be found in any standard text on regression.

Equation 9–22, which was proposed by Schumacher and Hall (1933), is given in its non-linear form. Its logarithmic form, a form which has been utilized to fit non-linear tree volume equations, is:

$$\log V = \log a + b \log D + c \log H \qquad (9\text{--}25)$$

A logarithmic equation is more compatible with the homogeneity of variance assumption for regression. On the other hand, a bias is introduced in fitting the logarithmic equation and in recalculating the standard error in arithmetic units for comparison with non-logarithmic equations. But by using non-linear functions to estimate parameters, and by employing weighting methods to correct heterogeneous variance about the regression line, non-linear tree volume equations may be developed that retain the statistical advantages and overcome the shortcomings of the logarithmic equation. In fact, with the availability of computers, there appears to be little justification for the use of logarithmic models.

Moser and Beers (1969) give a method of utilizing equation 9–22 by non-linear regression. Since their procedure is one of the most feasible methods of volume-table construction, and since it is applicable to other non-linear functions, it will be discussed in more detail than the other methods.

To fit sample data to equation 9–22, it is necessary to estimate values of the parameters that minimize:

$$\sum_{i=1}^{n} \epsilon_i^2 = \sum_{i=1}^{n} (Y_i - \hat{a}D_i^{\hat{b}}H_i^{\hat{c}})^2 \qquad (9\text{--}26)$$

A rapid method of obtaining a convergent solution, which has been implemented as a SHARE program, is an algorithm developed by Marquardt (1963). Moser and Beers used a variant of this program with a weighting option to prepare a volume equation for northern red oak trees that gives merchantable cubic foot volume inside bark, V:

$$V = 0.003173D^{1.988825}H^{0.981921} \qquad (9\text{--}27)$$

The theory and details of weighted fitting of regression equations are part of standard regression theory. Gerrard (1966) and Cunia (1964), however, discuss weighted regression for volume-table construction. To solve the weighting problem, Moser and Beers (1969) grouped their data into D^2H classes and determined the volume variance for each class. Then, on plotting variance over D^2H they noted that variance was exponentially related to D^2H. Thus, the class variances, weighted by number of observations in each D^2H class, were fitted to derive the following variance function:

Table 9–6
Specimen of Comprehensive Tree Volume Tarif Table

Height–Dbh Access Table for Douglas Fir

Dbh	Total Height (Feet)				
	60	62	64	66	68
12.2	22.2	23.1	23.9	24.8	25.7
12.4	22.0	22.9	23.7	24.6	25.5
12.6	21.8	22.7	23.6	24.4	25.3
12.8	21.6	22.5	23.4	24.2	25.1
13.0	21.5	22.3	23.2	24.0	24.9
13.2	21.3	22.1	23.0	23.8	24.7
13.4	21.1	22.0	22.8	23.7	24.5
13.6	20.9	21.8	22.6	23.5	24.3
13.8	20.8	21.6	22.5	23.3	24.2
14.0	20.6	21.4	22.3	23.1	24.0
14.2	20.4	21.3	22.1	23.0	23.8
14.4	20.3	21.1	22.0	22.8	23.6
14.6	20.1	21.0	21.8	22.6	23.5

Instructions

1. Measure height and dbh of sample of trees representative of stand.

2. Look up tarif numbers of sample trees in appropriate *Height–Dbh Access Table* and average them. For example:

Height	Dbh	Tree Tarif No.
60	12.2	22.2
68	14.3	23.7
Etc.		—
	Mean =	24.5

3. In tarif book find tarif table with mean tarif number.

Table 9-6 (cont.)
Tarif Table No. 24.5

Top section — Volumes and Growth Multipliers

	Total Tree Volume				Volume to 4 Inch Top		Volume to 6 Inch Top					
	Including Top and Stump Cubic Feet		Including Top Only Cubic Feet		Cubic Feet		Cubic Feet		Bd Feet Scribner		Bd Feet Inter ¼"	
Dbh Inches	Vol A	GM A	Vol B	GM B	Vol C	GM C	Vol D	GM D	Vol E	GM E	Vol F	GM F
2	0.3	0.2	0.2	0.2	.	.	.	.	.	.	.	.
3	0.7	0.7	0.6	0.6	.	.	.	.	.	.	.	.
4	1.5	1.0	1.4	1.0	.	.	.	.	.	.	.	.
5	2.6	1.4	2.5	1.3	1.4	1.5	.	.	.	.	.	.
6	4.1	1.7	4.0	1.6	3.0	1.8	.	.	.	.	.	.
7	5.9	2.0	5.7	2.0	4.9	2.1	1.9	2.2	6	7.2	9	10.7
8	8.1	2.4	7.8	2.3	7.1	2.4	4.3	2.8	14	9.8	21	13.9
9	10.5	2.7	10.2	2.6	9.6	2.7	7.2	3.1	25	11.9	36	16.2
10	13.3	3.0	12.9	2.9	12.3	3.0	10.5	3.4	38	13.7	53	18.0

Bottom section — Ratios

	Total Tree Volume			Volume to 4 Inch Top		Volume to 6 Inch Top					
	Including Top and Stump	Including Top Only		Cubic Feet		Cubic Feet		Bd Feet Scribner		Bd Feet Inter ¼"	
Dbh	V/BA Ratio	V/BA Ratio	% of Vol A	V/BA Ratio	% of Vol B	V/BA Ratio	% of Vol C	V/BA Ratio	B/CU Ratio	V/BA Ratio	B/CU Ratio
2	9.3	8.3	89.0	.	.	.	.	.	.	.	.
3	12.5	11.6	92.5	.	.	.	.	.	.	.	.
4	16.3	15.4	94.4	.	.	.	.	.	.	.	.
5	19.0	18.1	95.5	9.7	51.0	.	.	.	.	.	.
6	20.7	19.9	96.1	14.9	71.9	.	.	.	.	.	.
7	22.0	21.2	96.4	18.1	82.1	6.8	37.7	21.1	3.1	32.0	4.7
8	23.0	22.2	96.6	20.1	87.6	12.3	61.1	40.6	3.3	59.9	4.9
9	23.7	23.0	96.7	21.5	90.7	16.3	75.6	56.8	3.5	81.5	5.0
10	24.3	23.6	96.7	22.5	92.6	19.1	84.6	69.6	3.6	97.5	5.1

This tarif table gives volume in cubic feet for entire tree and volume in cubic feet and board feet to various merchantable limits. Volume/basal area ratios for horizontal point sampling, and growth multipliers (GM) to determine growth are also given. The letters, A, B, C, etc., that follow Vol and GM are used for convenient identification of columns.
SOURCE: Turnbull and Hoyer, 1965.

$$s_i{}^2 = 0.62359e^{0.11082(D_i{}^2H_i/1000)} \qquad (9\text{--}28)$$

Weights were calculated from this equation as the inverse of the variances ($w_i = 1/s_i{}^2$) for the appropriate heights and diameters.

Moser and Beers (1969) found that the coefficients obtained in fitting the red oak data to equation 9–22 are different from those obtained by least squares fit of the logarithmic transformation, and the weighted non-linear equation gives a smaller index of fit (Furnival, 1961).

The coefficients for equation 9–19, a local volume table, may be calculated in a manner analogous to the calculation of the coefficients for equation 9–22. Further, the utilization of equations 9–23 and 9–24, form class volume tables, offers no great computational obstacles. However, Behre (1935) and Smith, Ker, and Csizmazia (1961) concluded that no practical advantage is gained from the use of a measure of form in addition to dbh and height.

9–6. DERIVATION OF LOCAL VOLUME TABLE FROM STANDARD VOLUME TABLE

A local volume table may be derived from a standard volume table by "localizing" the heights by dbh classes. The procedure is simple:

1. Measure the heights and dbh's of a sample of trees representative of those to which the local volume table will be applied. Record dbh to nearest tenth of an inch, and height to the nearest even foot.
2. Prepare a curve of height over dbh by the freehand method.
3. Read average heights to nearest even foot from the curve for each dbh class (usually two-inch classes).
4. Interpolate from the standard volume table the volume of the tree of average height for each dbh class, or if a standard volume equation is available, substitute the appropriate values in the equation and compute volume for each dbh class.

9–7. TREE-VOLUME TARIF TABLES

The term "tarif," which is Arabic in origin, means tabulated information. In continental Europe the term has been applied for years to volume table systems that provide, directly or indirectly, a convenient means of obtaining a local volume table for a given stand (Garay, 1961).

British tarifs (Hummel, 1955), which have been quite successful, stimulated the preparation of "Comprehensive Tree-Volume Tarif Tables" by Turnbull, Little, and Hoyer (1963). This clever system, which is summarized in Table 9–6, merits wider consideration in all types of inventories. It requires no curve fitting to obtain a local volume table; it provides a convenient method of converting from one unit of measure to another, or from one merchantable limit to another; to determine average annual volume increment per tree in any desired unit of volume and merchantable limit, one simply multiplies the average annual diameter increment in inches by the growth multiplier, GM.

9–8. VOLUME DISTRIBUTION IN INDIVIDUAL TREES

A knowledge of volume distribution over the tree stem can be used to improve volume estimates, and to aid in estimating volume losses from defects.

Table 9–7, and Fig. 9–2, which was derived from the table, illustrate two useful methods of expressing volume distribution. Although the per-

Table 9–7
Average Distribution of Tree Volume by Logs According to Log Position

Usable Length (16-foot logs)	Per Cent of Total Tree Volume in Each Log, by Position					
	1st	2nd	3rd	4th	5th	6th
1	100					
2	58	42				
3	42	33	25			
4	34	29	22	15		
5	29	25	21	15	10	
6	24	23	20	16	11	6

SOURCE: Mesavage and Girard, 1946.

centages vary slightly with tree diameter and unit of volume, they may be used without serious error for merchantable trees of all sizes that are measured in cubic or board-foot volume. Note that Fig. 9–2, which is basically for 16-foot logs, provides a satisfactory guide when heights are measured in 8- or 12-foot lengths.

Mathematical models (Honer, 1965) may also be used to express volume distribution as a ratio of volume to a given height to total volume.

9–9. ESTIMATING CULL IN TREES

In most timber types it takes years for a cruiser or timber estimator to gain a thorough knowledge of *woods cull*—defective butts and defective sections that will be cut out in the woods—and *mill cull*—defective material that will be cut out at the mill. For cruisers with this knowledge graphs, such as Fig. 9–2, provide convenient guides. For example, say for a tree that contains three 16-foot logs, it is judged by an experienced cruiser that 4 feet of the butt must be removed, and an 8-foot

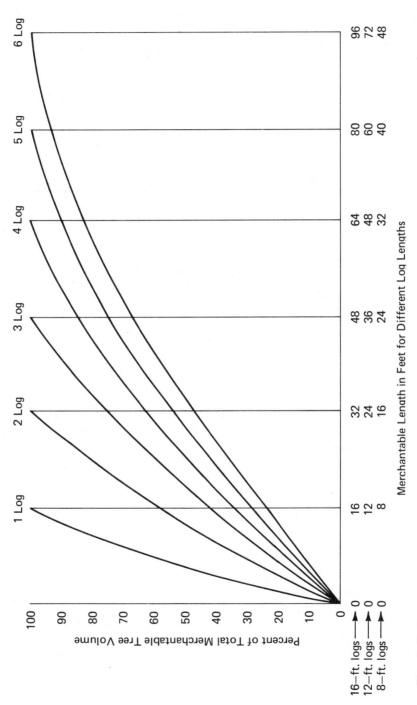

Fig. 9-2. Percentage of total merchantable volume at various heights for trees of different merchantable lengths (derived from Table 9-7).

section between 32 and 40 feet on the merchantable stem must be cut out. The cull, then, will be 12 per cent $(12 - 0)$ for the defective butt, and 13 per cent $(88 - 75)$ for the defective section, or 25 per cent for the tree.

Since many cruisers do not have the experience to estimate cull in the above manner, cull is often estimated by placing trees in cull classes that give, on the basis of visible defects, the percentage deductions to apply to gross volume (Zillgitt, 1946; Zillgitt and Gevorkiantz, 1946). But whatever method is used, a cull per cent applicable to a species, or species group, in a stand is normally determined by estimating the cull of a sample of 40 to 50 trees of the species, or species group. Then:

$$\text{Cull per cent} = \left(\frac{\text{cull volume of sample}}{\text{gross volume of sample}}\right) 100 \qquad (9\text{--}29)$$

This percentage is applied to all trees of the species, or species group, in the stand.

10

Grading Forest Products

Grading is the process of grouping something that is produced by nature or made by industry into classes or grades that reflect characteristics of quality or worth. In forestry, grading systems find numerous applications: Christmas trees, nursery stock, poles, piling, ties, shingles, cooperage lumber, veneer, logs, and trees are graded by qualities of interest to consumers; forest sites are ranked by timber producing capacity; wildlands are rated by recreational potential; and so on. This chapter treats the grading of forest products—principally logs and trees. Chapter 17 covers site quality and similar quality classifications.

10–1. QUANTIFICATION OF LOG AND TREE QUALITY

A unique characteristic of log and tree quality is that it may be measured as a continuous variable on an interval scale (although this is not commonly done) as well as a discrete variable on an ordinal scale. Therefore, it is enlightening to speak of "quantification of log and tree quality" (Ware, 1964) rather than simply of "log and tree grades," since the phrase "quantification of quality" infers alternative methods of expressing quality.

10–1.1. Problems in Quantifying Log and Tree Quality. Log and tree quality quantification systems must be intimately related to the quality of the products to be produced from any run of logs. Therefore, quality must be defined in terms of some derived product, preferably the product that gives maximum value for given logs. But there are problems since many trees are best suited for a mixture of derived products—lumber, veneer, and pulp. Even a log best suited for lumber will produce several grades, no grade being produced in the same quantity. Furthermore, the proportion of grades will vary with mill practices, mill efficiency, and markets. The same is true for a veneer log. Not only will the price differ with grades of lumber or veneer, but also with species, time, region, and market conditions. The problem in developing quality standards for logs and trees is that we must know the quality standards of the derived products.

For some derived products uniform specifications are not accepted throughout industry. For example, the diversity of specifications for hardwood veneer has greatly retarded the development of quality quantifiers for hardwood veneer logs. Also, the quality specifications may be unstable; from time to time there may be changes in the derived-product quality specifications that necessitate changes in the log and tree quality quantifiers. An example of this is the change that was recently made in the lumber grading rules for some of the western softwoods of the United States. Since such changes will continue in the face of technological advances and increasing competition from substitute materials, there is need to develop quality quantification systems that are adaptable to change.

Another problem arises in selecting variables to predict quality. A good system for quantifying quality is one for which the quality being quantified is highly correlated with log or tree characteristics that can be determined objectively. But quantifying quality in advance of manufacture is difficult because many of the characteristics that affect the quality of the derived products cannot be seen in the trees or logs. A list of some of the variables that can be used to predict quality will illustrate the problem: log or tree size, log or tree form, knots, stain and decay, wood density, compression wood, and spiral grain. Except for size there are difficulties in measuring or numerating the variables in this list. More research is needed to learn how to assess their influence on quality and to find other variables, perhaps ones related to genetic and environmental factors, that are correlated with log and tree quality.

The difficulty of analyzing the complex relationships between numerous timber characteristics and quality has also been a problem. The availability of electronic computers, however, should eliminate this problem.

10–1.2. Systems of Quantifying Log and Tree Quality. To quantify log or tree quality we must select suitable characteristics; the independent variables to predict quality and the dependent variable. Quality for logs or trees may be in terms of one or all of the following:

1. Value in dollars.
2. A single number, called *Quality Index*, that expresses the value of

the lumber in a log or tree as a percentage of the value of an equal volume of lumber of a base lumber grade (Herrick, 1946*b*).

3. Distribution of volume by quality classes of derived product.

One might think that through a multiple regression analysis equations could be developed to predict log or tree quality. Indeed, if suitable equations could be developed, forest inventory sampling designs could be employed that would include double sampling for quality; for each job an equation could be developed to estimate tree quality. Foresters, however, have been unable to develop suitable regression equations to quantify quality. Linear regression models that use variables such as log or tree size, knots, decay, and so on, account only for a marginal portion of the total variance of log or tree quality, however we desire to quantify quality. But even such linear regression analyses may be useful; the order of importance of the independent variables can be determined, and the variables best correlated with quality can be selected for log or tree grading systems. Before developing directly useful regression equations, however, more knowledge is needed on the variables that are related to quality, and the regression models identified that will adequately express the relationship between these variables and quality.

Essentially all systems used today for quantifying *log quality* place logs in broad classes or grades, the limits of which are defined by the surface characteristics on logs. A good example is the U.S. Forest Service's standard hardwood log grades (Vaughan, Wollin, McDonald, and Bulgrin, 1966), the first widely used log grades. The overall work plan for developing such log grades, as well as hardwood bolt grades, is covered in a U.S. Forest Products Laboratory Report (1958). Although there are some differences in details, softwood log grades have been developed along the same lines (Campbell, 1964).

Since trees are composites of logs, and since in the quantification of quality foresters have been preoccupied with log grades, foresters have used log grades in the following ways to develop tree grades:

1. Base tree grade on the grade of a 16-foot butt log, or of the best 12- or 14-foot section of the 16-foot butt log. (For example, say logs are separated into three grades, No. 1, No. 2, and No. 3. Then Grade A, Grade B, and Grade C trees might be trees with No. 1, No. 2, and No. 3 butt logs, respectively.) (Meteer, 1966).

2. Use the grades of all the logs in the tree. (For example, a two-log tree with a No. 1 butt log and a No. 3 second log would be a Grade 1–3 tree.) (Guttenberg and Reynolds, 1953.)

3. Base tree grade on the unweighted average of the grades of the standard length logs in the tree. (For example, a tree with two No. 1 logs and one No. 2 log, would have a tree grade of $\frac{4}{3}$ or 1.33.) (Herrick, 1956.)

The first practice, the one most commonly used, is simple, but the variation in the grades of the upper logs, from one tree to another, reduces its precision in predicting tree quality below that obtained in predicting log quality. A consideration of the other two methods reveals why they have been little used; they require an excessive amount of time to determine tree grade, unless very simple grading rules are used. Furthermore, the second method gives an excessive number of tree grades. But whatever method is used, tables may be developed that give tree quality (in terms of Quality Index, lumber grade yields, or log grade yields) by species, tree diameter, and tree height for each tree grade.

10–2. LOG GRADING SYSTEMS

Since a great variety of derived products come from the many species of logs cut, a great variety of log grades have been developed. These grading rules are constantly in the process of improvement and readjustment. Hence, it is inadvisable to give anything more than a sample of the grades here. For exact information readers are referred to the current edition of the grading rules of the species of interest.

The ability to identify defects is essential for grading logs. Lockard, Putnam, and Carpenter (1963) and Shigo and Larson (1969) have prepared handbooks on identification of grade defects in hardwoods. Campbell (1962) has prepared a similar guide for southern pines; Jackson (1962) one for ponderosa pine and sugar pine. Handbooks of this type should be used in conjunction with the appropriate log grading rules.

10–2.1. U. S. Forest Products Laboratory Hardwood Log Grading System.
This widely known system illustrates the requirements and complications of a good log grading system, whether it be for hardwoods or softwoods.

Originally the Forest Products Laboratory set up three broad log-use classes for hardwood logs: Factory Class, Construction Class, and Local-Use Class. In 1964 specifications were established for a Veneer-Use Class (Northeastern Forest Experiment Station, 1965). The four use classes may be defined as follows:

1. Factory Class—Logs falling in this class are divided into Grade 1, Grade 2, and Grade 3. Grading is based on the assumption that logs will be cut into lumber that will be graded by the rules of the National Hardwood Lumber Association for standard lumber. This is the most important use class.
2. Construction Class—This class is not separated into grades. A log of this class is graded on the assumption that it will be sawed into ties, timbers, and other products that are to be used for structural and weight-bearing purposes.
3. Local-Use Class—This class is not separated into grades. The

class is a catch-all for logs that do not qualify for the other classes. The main requirement is that logs qualify within limits of merchantability, a factor largely determined locally.

4. Veneer Class—This class includes logs that have potential value for veneer. At present there are no uniform U. S. Forest Service veneer grades. There are, however, numerous local veneer-log grade specifications such as those published by the Northern Hardwood and Pine Manufacturer's Association, Green Bay, Wisconsin. But the diversity of specifications for hardwood veneer has retarded the development of standard veneer-log grades.

It should be understood that the value of a log in one use class furnishes little clue to the value of a log in another use class. Therefore, it would be difficult to select the class into which to place a log, if all utilization possibilities were open. For most operators, however, the business situation determines the use class into which the logs should be put.

The standard specifications for the three grades of the important Factory Class are summarized in Fig. 10–1. Since most hardwood factory lumber is graded on the basis of the percentage of the board surface that will yield clear areas of specified sizes, the size and number of clear cuttings, as determined by position of grade defects, is of prime importance in determining grade of hardwood factory lumber logs. Other grading factors are position of log in tree, log diameter, log length, sweep, cull, and end defects.

10–2.2. Comparison of U. S. Forest Products Laboratory System with Other Hardwood Log Grading Systems. Before effectively employing the Forest Products Laboratory grades they must be studied at length and then applied for several weeks. Consequently, simplified hardwood log grading schemes have been developed that can be effectively employed with less preparation. Although the general basis of almost all hardwood log grading systems is the Forest Products Laboratory System, a number of wood-using industries, trade associations and universities have drawn up hardwood log grade specifications. The purpose of these systems is to provide:

1. A sound basis for establishing log selling prices or purchase prices.
2. An up-to-date estimate of derived-product grade yields of logs.
3. A chance to check quality production of mill against established standards.

Not all log grading systems will accomplish all of these things. Grade yield information is lacking for many "local" log grading systems, and grade yield information is inadequate or out of date for other "local" log grading systems.

The Purdue System, which is typical of the systems that have grown

Grading Factors		Log Grades							
		F1			F2				F3
Position in tree		Butts only	Butts & uppers		Butts & uppers				Butts & uppers
Diameter, scaling, inches		[1]13–15	16–19	20+	[2]11	12+			8+
Length without trim, feet		10+			10+	8–9	10–11	12+	8+
Clear cuttings[3] on each 3 best faces	Lenth, min., feet	7	5	3	3	3	3	3	2
	Number, maximum	2	2	2	2	2	2	3	No limit
	Fraction of log length required in clear cutting[4]	5/6	5/6	5/6	2/3	3/4	2/3	2/3	1/2
Sweep and crook allowance (maximum) in percent gross volume	For logs with less than 1/4 of end in sound defects	15%			30%				50%
	For logs with more than 1/4 of end in sound defects	10%			20%				35%
Total scaling deduction including sweep and crook		[5]40%			[6]50%				50%
End defects:	See instructions, Forest Products Laboratory, 1966								

[1] Ash and basswood butts can be 12 inches if otherwise meeting requirements for small No. 1's.
[2] Ten-inch logs of all species can be No. 2 if otherwise meeting requirements for small No. 1's.
[3] A clear cutting is a portion of a face free of defects, extending the width of the face.
[4] See table 46.
[5] Otherwise No. 1 logs with 41-60% deductions can be No. 2.
[6] Otherwise No. 2 logs with 51-60% deductions can be No. 3.

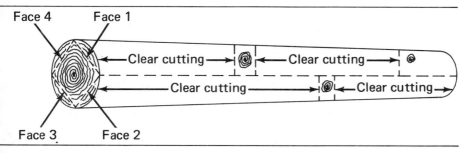

Face 4   Face 1

Face 3   Face 2

Fig. 10–1. Forest Service standard specifications for hardwood factory lumber logs (Forest Products Laboratory, 1966).

out of the Forest Products Laboratory System will illustrate the nature of the grades that have evolved from the Forest Products Laboratory grades. The simpler Purdue System does not recognize use classes; it applies to any sawlog, regardless of the end use of the material it contains. Basically, however, the system is best for hardwood factory logs. Compared to the Forest Products Laboratory grades for factory logs, the Purdue grades are extremely simple and are based on fewer rules and no exceptions. They are outlined in Fig. 10–2. The Purdue System is not as precise and does

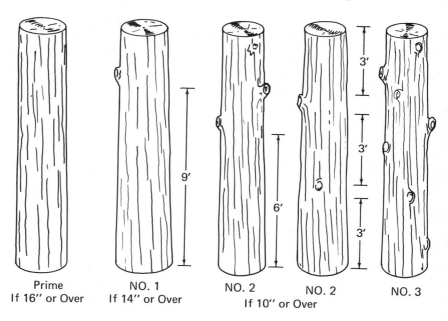

GRADE SPECIFICATIONS

Prime — At least 90 per cent surface clear on three visible faces in one section (A face is any one-quarter of the log surface). Must be 16 inches or more in diameter inside bark at the small end.

No. 1 — At least 75 per cent surface clear on three visible faces in one section. Must be at least 14 inches in diameter inside bark at the small end.

No. 2 — At least 50 per cent surface clear on three visible faces in two sections, neither of which is less than three feet long. Must be at least 10 inches in diameter inside bark at the small end.

No. 3 — Will not meet No. 2 specifications.

Fig. 10–2. Purdue specifications for hardwood sawlogs (Herrick, 1955).

not predict log value as accurately as the Forest Products Laboratory System (Walters and Herrick, 1956), but it can be applied at about half the cost (6 to 25 cents per thousand board feet versus 15 to 55 cents).

10–2.3. Softwood Log Grading Systems. There is no single system of softwood log grades that applies to a wide range of species as does the Forest Products Laboratory Hardwood Log grading system. The great variety of derived products that come from the many species of softwood logs has led to the development of numerous grade specifications. However, the majority of softwood logs fall into two use classes: yard lumber and veneer. Since most softwood lumber and most softwood veneer is graded on the assumption that the entire piece will be used, number of grade defects determines grade of softwood yard lumber logs and veneer logs. Other grading factors are log diameter, log length, sweep, and cull.

Grading bureaus have promulgated log grading rules for most of the important timber species of the western United States. Although grade yield information is lacking for a number of log grades used for certain species, the U. S. Forest Service is making efforts to remedy this situation for the more important species. In addition, the Forest Service has developed systems for grading southern pine logs (Campbell, 1964) and for grading logs in standing trees (Gaines, 1962; Lane, 1964).

10–3. APPLICATION OF LOG AND TREE GRADES

To obtain volume by log grades when scaling logs it is simply a matter of recording the additional grade variable and tabulating volume by species and log grades (and log diameter, if diameter is important to determine value). Where logs are bought and sold by grade, one can use the current market prices of logs of recognized grades to determine value.

If suitable tree grades are available, quality estimation in forest inventories requires collecting the additional grade variable. Using point sampling, line sampling or fixed-size plot sampling one can easily devise tally forms to record the data, whether all or only a sub-sample of trees are graded.

Beers and Miller (1964) describe an efficient horizontal point sampling system to obtain volume by species and log grades. However, if data are needed by log size as well as log grade, point or line sampling may be inefficient, unless used in conjunction with a fixed-size plot sampling system. Then logs can be graded on fixed-area plots taken at every nth sampling point. Through this double sampling procedure the per cent of the various log grades by log diameters that can be recovered is determined and applied to the volume data obtained in the main inventory. Of course, fixed-size plots may be used to obtain all the required information. In addition to collecting the usual data, the field crew might grade the logs in every merchantable tree on all plots. More practical procedures, however, would be to grade logs only on every fifth plot, or at some other interval, or on specially designated smaller plots that fall within the main plots. The higher the value of the timber, the greater the percentage of the trees that should be graded.

When log grades must be used to determine the quality of standing timber, simplification which includes only characteristics that can be recognized in standing trees should be developed. This is necessary because most log grading systems require a more detailed inspection of the logs than is practical on standing trees in the field. The log grading system shown in Fig. 10–2 is an example of a system which can be applied to standing timber.

11

Forest Inventory

11–1. INTRODUCTION

Most forest inventories in the past and present have been and continue to be timber estimates. In this sense a forest inventory is an attempt to describe the quantity and quality of forest trees and many of the characteristics of the land area upon which the trees are growing. With the increasing importance of forest areas for non-wood values such as recreation, watershed management, wildlife, or possible conversion to other land uses, the concept of a forest inventory must now be widened. When non-wood values are important, then these other characteristics of the forest and the land upon which it is situated, will have to be observed, measured where possible, and the resulting data analyzed (Ffolliott and Worley, 1965). In some cases, a forest inventory will seek only wood or timber quantities and qualities, in other cases both timber and non-timber information will be required and, with growing frequency, only non-timber information may be sought. The information needed for an evaluation of non-timber values associated with the forest and forest land will sometimes require different or additional observations and measurements. In many cases, a great deal of the information usually obtained in an inventory for timber can also be used for evaluating other forest values.

The following discussion of forest inventory will concentrate primarily on timber values, but the student should always recognize the frequent need for other forest information. In those cases when non-timber information is required, it is essential that specialists in these allied fields work cooperatively in planning and executing the inventory.

To obtain information for a forest inventory it is necessary to make a number of measurements of the trees which compose the forest and additional observations regarding the land upon which the forest is situated. These measurements may be taken in the forest itself or on aerial photographs. The specific measurements will depend on the kind of information required and may vary on different inventories. These measurements can be taken for the entire area of a forest and all the trees thereon. In this case it is called a complete or 100 per cent tally or inventory. When the measurements are taken on sample portions of the forest it is called a sampling inventory.

The terms "cruise" in North America and "enumeration" in other English-speaking areas have been frequently used instead of inventory. Unless defined differently, they are considered synonymous with the term inventory.

11–2. RELATIVE EMPHASIS OF THE ELEMENTS OF A FOREST INVENTORY

A complete forest inventory for timber evaluation provides a number of elements of information. Briefly, these basic elements are: a description of the forested area including ownership and accessibility; estimates of parameters of quantity in the standing trees such as volume or weight; and estimates of growth and drain. Additional kinds of information on timber character may also be included. These may include information on wildlife, areas of recreational and tourist interest, soil and land use capabilities and watershed values. In any specific inventory, the emphasis on, or elimination of, one or more of these elements may occur depending upon the objective of the forest inventory.

It is difficult, if not impossible, to try to list all the individual reasons for which forest inventories are carried out. The basic way in which inventories differ is in the greater or lesser emphasis which is placed on the various elements included in the previously given definition. There are not a series of unique inventories for different purposes, but a flexible continuum with varying emphasis on the individual elements. For example, inventories of private forest holdings may require more detailed information on volume by species, size classes, precise stand location, and road facilities than would be needed for a general appraisal of the total forest area or volume on a national or regional basis. Obviously, inventories basic to management decisions require information on stand growth and drain, whereas an inventory simply to prepare a logging plan would not need these data but, on the other hand, would place greater emphasis on topography, drainage patterns, and transportation system for use in drawing up an extraction scheme. Simply for illustrative purposes and not to be considered in any sense complete, one could prepare a list of some types of inventories and show the emphasis that could be placed on the various inventory elements. Table 11–1 indicates the varying relative emphasis for the kinds of inventories chosen as examples. The priority classes assigned to the various elements are not hard and fast but are subjective in nature. Therefore, one could debate the relative priorities given. It is not the exact priority which is important in studying this table but rather the principle of varying emphasis of consistent elements.

The types of inventories shown in Table 11–1 are to be considered only as general classes. Inventories for many other specific purposes will certainly occur. When other kinds of inventories are needed, it is worthwhile early in planning to make a general assessment of the relative emphasis to be placed on the inventory, elements to help in the later, more specific, details of inventory design.

11–3. QUANTITY RELATIONSHIPS IN FOREST INVENTORY

The main objective for a forest inventory of timber values is to present estimates of the quantity of timber in a forest according to a series of classifications such as species, sizes, qualities, etc.

When an expression of quantity of a tree or stand, such as volume or weight is required, it means that a procedure must be followed which will permit an estimate to be made of such quantity in the standing trees. Since it is impossible to measure directly quantities such as volume or weight of standing trees, some relationship between directly measurable tree or stand characteristics and the quantity expression must be utilized.

If one assesses all the relationships and procedures for expressing tree or stand quantity based on directly measurable characteristics which have been developed, it becomes apparent that they may be classified as follows:

A. Direct determination of individual tree or stand quantities from detailed field measurements of the trees or stand in question utilizing formulas or graphic procedures:
  1. Detailed measurements on *individual trees* in the field followed by the calculation of the contents of each tree by formulas or graphic procedures.
  2. Field measurements of *average stand characteristics* and their employment in a formula for direct estimation.
B. Estimation of the quantities in trees or stands utilizing general relationships previously derived from other trees or stands:
  1. Measurements of convenient dimensions of *trees* followed by quantity estimation using previously calculated relationships.
    a. In the field—measuring tree dimensions: dbh, basal area, height, form;

Table 11-1
Relative Emphasis of the Elements of a Forest Inventory

Examples of Typical Kind of Inventories	\multicolumn{8}{Forest Areas}

Examples of Typical Kind of Inventories	Area Estimates	Topographic Description	Ownership Pattern	Accessibility and Transportation Facilities	Volume or Other Parameter Estimation	Growth Estimation	Drain Estimation	Other Information for Recreation, Watershed, Possible Other Land Uses, Wildlife, etc.
National forest industry	II	II	II	II	II	II	II	II
Working plan surveys	I	II	II	II	II	I	I	II
Reconnaissance forest surveys	II	III	II	II	II	II	II	
Logging plan survey	II	I	III	II or III	II or III	III	III	III
Basic information for forest industry feasibility study	II		III	I	I	III	III	
Basic data for stumpage appraisal		II				I	I	II
Land use study	II	II	III	I	I	II	II	III
Recreation study	II	III	I	I	II	II	III	I
Watershed study	I	I	II	II	II	II	II	I

Priority classes

I — very important, needed in detail (or according to detailed stand classes)
II — general estimate
III — little emphasis or can be eliminated

178

      b. On areial photographs—photo images of tree dimensions; crown diameter, tree height.
2. Measurement of convenient dimensions of *stands* followed by quantity estimation using previously calculated relationships.
      a. In the field—measuring stand dimensions of average dbh, total basal area, height, form, age, number of trees.
      b. On aerial photographs—measuring photo images of stand characteristics: crown closure, number of trees, stand height, average crown diameter.

Category A includes those procedures which estimate directly the quantity of timber from a series of detailed measurements of the trees or sections thereof in a stand of timber. It pertains especially to estimates of cubic volumes. For example, detailed diameter measurements may be taken at known intervals along the stem of trees and the volume calculated from a formula for the cubic contents of a solid. In most past forest inventory work this procedure has been considered too slow and it has not been utilized in estimation of volumes of the tallied trees. This procedure is of prime importance in obtaining the basic data for the quantity relationships shown under Category B.1. and holds promise of greater application in forest inventory work with the improvement of dendrometers and the use of electronic computers.

Category B includes the commonly employed procedures which utilize directly and conveniently measured trees or stand characteristics as a basis for estimating tree or stand quantity. For example, the volume or weight of a tree may be obtained by measuring its dbh, height, and form in the field and then looking up its corresponding volume or weight as listed in a table. Of course, the table is a convenient expression of a previously derived relationship between easily measured tree dimensions and quantity, which may have taken much time and effort to develop. The basic data for a relationship of this type often require the detailed and time-consuming measurements and calculations necessary under Category A. This same procedure can be utilized with aerial photographs; but the tree dimensions will be those which are measurable on an aerial photograph. Other procedures have also been devised which require measurements of overall stand characteristics such as height, average diameter, basal area, form, etc. The timber quantity per unit area can then be read in a table according to the measured stand characteristics. Note well that this procedure also presupposes previously calculated relationships.

In the planning of a forest inventory for timber volume estimates a decision must be taken as to which of the several alternatives will be used for converting directly measurable tree dimensions to volume estimates. As in all the various phases of inventory planning a comparison of the time and costs involved in using the several alternatives must enter into the decision process. These must, of course, be considered in relation to the accuracy and detail of the information which can be obtained from the possible procedures.

11–3.1. Volume Table Approach. Of the various approaches discussed above, the relationship which has been most widely used in forest inventory work is that described under B.1.a. and most concisely expressed as the *volume table approach*. It is worth pointing out that the same approach could be used for estimating weight. In the following description, volume is mentioned since it is more commonly used.

The volume table approach has been so widely used and will continue to be so since its employment reduces the amount of time required in the field for individual tree measurements. Using this approach a few easily and directly observable dimensions of a tree are measured and the tree's volume is then estimated from a general relationship between these dimensions and volume. Thus, the limiting factor in the employment of this approach is the applicability of appropriate volume tables, or lacking previously prepared information, the feasibility of preparing new tables. (See Chapter 9 for a discussion of volume tables and their preparations.)

If volume tables are available, their suitability for the timber to be inventoried should be checked to see if the volumes indicated in the table agree with those actually found in the trees. It is extremely risky to accept a volume table prepared for some other locality or species simply because it is available. Doing so may introduce an error into the volume estimate that will invalidate all other work no matter how carefully it has been executed.

When no volume tables are available, consideration should be given to their construction (see Section 9–5). The preparation of volume tables can be a costly procedure since it requires the collection of basic data consisting of the measurements of the dimensions of a series of sample trees, the calculation or determination of the volumes of these trees, and the development of an equation or graphic relationship between tree dimensions and volume.

In considering the employment of volume tables it is important to be aware of the specifications used in their construction. This means a careful scrutiny of details such as volume units, minimum dbh, stump height, type of height measurement such as total or merchantable, and the minimum top diameter to which volume is measured. It should be obvious that the specifications of existing tables will strongly influence the volume specifications to be adopted in an inventory. If volume specifications are desired for an inventory other than those available in existing tables, it may be possible to convert these tables by appropriate corrections. If this proves impossible or not practical, it may well mean that new tables will have to be constructed or a volume relationship other than provided by a volume table used.

Although the volume table approach has been widely used, it has disadvantages which have stimulated consideration of methods for directly estimating the volumes of individual trees. The disadvantages of the volume table approach may be summarized as:

1. Any individual tree may not have the same height, diameter, and form characteristics as those used in the construction of the volume table employed.
2. Volume tables are constructed for specific units of measurement and utilization standards, and it is often impossible or unwieldy to try to change these specifications.
3. Any errors in the volume tables are incorporated into the estimate and in most cases no assessment of their magnitude is included.

11–3.2. Direct Volume Estimation of Individual Trees.

Direct estimation of the volume of any tree from its own unique dimensions will give a closer value than relying on volume tables. In addition, volume to whatever utilization limits and for any chosen units can be calculated from the basic measurements. This procedure is of no value if one wishes to estimate weight, since some kind of indirect relationship must be used for this parameter.

Direct measurement of the dimensions of a tree including the diameter at various points along the stem has long been used for determining the volumes of individual trees for special studies such as obtaining the basic data for volume regressions. To obtain upper-stem diameter measurements has required either climbing the tree or measuring with an optical instrument which permits the observer to remain on the ground at a distance from the tree. The expense and time required to obtain these measurements and the subsequent calculation of volumes are many times greater than required for an estimate of a tree's volume using a volume table. For this reason forest inventories have not often employed direct individual tree measurement and volume determination. However, recent improvements of dendrometers (see Chapter 3) and the preparations of programs to process the resulting measurements have demonstrated the feasibility of this approach (Grosenbaugh, 1954, 1964; Enghardt and Derr, 1963; and Mesavage, 1965a). An inventory will then depend on fewer but more carefully measured sample plots and trees and the usually unassessed contribution of volume tables to the total error of estimate will also be eliminated. In addition, a greater variety of volume estimates for a forest can be obtained than would be obtainable from volume tables by changing utilization limits as desired.

11–3.3. Volumes from the "Variable Plot Method." The generally utilized adaptation of p.p.s. sampling, frequently referred to as the "variable plot," Bitterlich, or point sampling method, gives a direct estimate of the basal area per unit land area. This basal area can then be used to estimate volume by employing a relationship between basal area and volume per unit land area. Short-cut procedures permit volume estimates to be made without the necessity of first estimating basal area. This application of p.p.s. sampling permits many modifications and variations in inventory work. For example, instead of using the system to estimate basal area, those trees selected at a point may be measured for dbh, height, etc., as in conventional fixed-area sampling and volumes obtained from a volume table. In this case the main difference between point sampling and conventional plot sampling is that the former does not require the establishment of plot boundaries and selects trees to be included in the sample proportional to their basal area. Other p.p.s. sampling techniques such as horizontal line sampling, vertical point sampling and vertical line sampling can also be used in volume estimation. These procedures are described in Chapter 14.

11–3.4. Stand Volume from Basal Area, Height, and Form Factor. Estimation of the volume of a stand can be made from measurements considered representative of the entire stand rather than by the summation of the volume of individual trees. The objective is to make a stand estimate rapidly without the necessity of measuring all or a sample of the trees for obtaining their volume. Volumes obtained in this way are useful if an overall volume estimate, not broken down into species, size, or quality classes is needed. It is especially useful for reconnaissance-type inventories. The procedure is less useful when detailed information regarding the forest is required.

The direct determination procedure previously mentioned as item **2** under Category A has been frequently used in approximate inventory work. To give but one example, the directly measured stand characteristics per unit land area such as average stand height $(\bar{h})$, basal area (g), and tree form, expressed as a form factor (f), can be put in the equation:

$$v = (\bar{h})(g)(f) \qquad (11\text{–}1)$$

for a direct estimation of the cubic volume per unit area (v). Note the assumption that the total stand volume is equal to the volume of a cylinder whose cross-sectional area is the basal area of the stand, whose height is average stand height, and whose volume is then reduced by a factor expressing the average departure of tree form from a cylinder.

Basal area and average stand heights can be obtained from individual tree measurements, but the advantages of a stand approach are lost.

With the use of sampling with probability proportional to size, basal area and average stand heights càn be obtained from angle counts without individual tree measurements (see Chapter 14).

11–3.5. Stand Volume Equations. The procedure shown as item 2 of Category B is another variation of the stand volume approach. In this case, the volume of a stand can be related to directly measurable stand characteristics by regression analysis in a manner similar to that discussed for individual trees. As discussed in Chapter 9, stand volume tables can then be prepared and used in an analogous manner to individual tree volume tables. Similar relationships could also be developed for weight estimation. Using this approach, it is necessary to make measurements of certain stand characteristics such as basal area, height, and age. Then the volume of the stand can be looked up in the previously prepared table.

Equations have also been prepared for indirect stand volume estimation from aerial photographs. The stand characteristics of crown density, crown closure, or crown diameter have been substituted for basal area which cannot be directly estimated on the aerial photographs (Hanks and Thomson, 1964; Pope, 1962; Moessner, 1962).

11–3.6. Stand Volume from Tree of Mean Volume. Another stand volume approach estimates the volume of a stand by determining the tree of average volume and multiplying by the number of trees in the stand. The difficulty with this procedure lies in determining what is the tree of average volume. In practice, the tree of mean basal area for a stand is first determined. The volume of a tree of this size can then be estimated from a basal area-volume relationship. The linear regression of the volume of individual trees on their respective basal area is called the *volume line*. A comprehensive treatment of this type of relationship can be obtained from Hummel (1953, 1955); Jolly (1951), and Assman (1943). From a volume-line relationship, the volume of the tree of mean basal area can be estimated.

A refinement of this procedure which increases its accuracy is obtained by dividing the stand into diameter classes and determining the tree of mean basal area within each class. The volumes for the individual classes are then obtained by multiplying by the number of trees in the respective classes. A summation of volumes for the classes yields the stand volume.

11–4. THE NEED FOR ADEQUATE PLANNING

Although the reasons for carrying out inventories may vary, there is a unity in their planning and execution regardless of the diverse ends to which the resultant information may be directed. Errors in planning can result in a wastage of time and money. Especially damaging may be the omission of essential data needed for management decisions. Equally serious, errors in the inventory results may lead to erroneous subsequent decisions.

In the planning of any forest inventory there are a number of items which must always be considered. The word *considered* is used instead of *included* for good reason. Not all of the items always have the same emphasis nor need to be included in all inventories. But for planning purposes they should always be considered and, if found not applicable, then eliminated. These items are shown below in a summarized check list. The order in which these items are presented is not rigid and may be modified although for the majority of cases the sequence is logical.

1. What the inventory is expected to show
2. Time and funds available
3. Possibilities of standardization or combination with other inventory data
4. Forest classfication system
5. Inventory sampling design including possibility of repeated or continuous forest inventory
6. Use of aerial photography
7. Maps
8. Quantity relationships
9. Personnel and training
10. Logistical support
11. Field measurements and recording forms
12. Calculation and compilation

Prior to the planning process all existing available information concerning the forest area should be compiled and studied. This should include any past surveys, reports, maps, or photographs. Reconnaissance trips to the field prove useful in learning the forest types and are essential if photo-interpretation is contemplated as a part of the inventory procedure. It is also desirable to gain at least a rough idea of the character of the timber, its range of quantities per unit area, and an idea of its variability. Information on the transportation system present in the form of railroads, roads, rivers, and trails is important as it can influence the method of travel and field procedures.

A detailed discussion of planning for forest inventories is given by Husch (1970). Only a brief consideration of the most important points is given here.

11–5. DECISIONS ON REQUIRED INFORMATION

The initial stage of planning should consist of deciding what kind of information the inventory will provide. A basic tenet that should be followed insofar as possible, is that all the people concerned with the inventory work or the use to which the final report will be put, have detailed discussions or reach agreement before proceeding to subsequent planning stages. Description of the stand parameters, units of measurements, and the desired precision for the estimates should be included. It is worth emphasizing here that, in planning an inventory, it is essential to decide on the allowable error and the specified probability early in the planning process (see Section 12–4). This should be decided upon after considering for what the information will be used. One should not blindly utilize some conventionally accepted error or probability merely from custom. Rather, the precision decided on should be sufficient for the use of the information. Greater precision than required means a waste of money. In arriving at a decision, one must keep in mind the economic importance of the forest area and its accessibility in terms of topography and the transportation system, the funds available, and the management decisions which will be based on the inventory information.

In this planning stage, the outlines of the tables which will appear in the final report should be prepared. Table outlines should include all titles, column headings, class limits, measurement units, and whatever other categories may be utilized to indicate inventory results. This is a task that cannot be postponed until after the data have been amassed since all subsequent inventory work is dependent on the decisions made at this time.

In too many cases, this very important initial stage has been entirely neglected in planning an inventory. Far too frequently, inventory planning consists of deciding on the number and distribution of sample units followed by making the specified measurements at great expense. A mass of data is gathered and then thoughts turn to what information can be extracted and in what form to present it. Often complaints are voiced by those wanting to utilize the inventory data that they are in an inconvenient form, that something has been left out, or that excess information has been included. The proper procedure should be exactly the reverse, i.e., the kind and form of the final results should be decided on first and then the inventory procedures designed to provide the information required.

11–6. AREAS

A most important consideration in any inventory program is the determination of areas in forest land, non-forest land, and any of the other classifications recognized. The boundaries of the areas to be included in the inventory should be delimited and where possible indicated on maps or aerial photographs. If possible, natural boundaries such as roads, rivers, or other topographic features should be used so that boundaries can be recognized in the field or on aerial photographs. It is a poor balance of effort to spend much time on tree or plot measurements without equally reliable information on the area to which these measurements relate. Subdivisions of the total area into units of convenient size should also be made. These subdivisions may be based on existing boundaries such as administrative units or topographic features or, if needed, artificial subdivisions may be made. The purpose of the subdivision is to show the inventory information for existing and needed subdivisions and also to permit easier control and execution of the inventory work.

On some inventories, information in respect to the distribution of different forms of ownership of a forest area may be needed when ownership has an effect upon management or forestry development.

11-7. FOREST AND OTHER LAND USE CLASSIFICATIONS

A standard system for forest classification, and if needed, for other land uses, should be adopted which will permit subdivision into classes or strata. This classification should include definitions of forest and non-forest lands, operable and non-operable forests, and any other classes based on species composition and utility which are needed for forest management. If land uses other than for timber production are under study, the necessary classifications must be formulated with their definitions.

A classification system is essential to an inventory for timber estimation or other related forest information to permit the subdivision of a heterogeneous forest into smaller, more easily comprehensible, and homogeneous units. This subdivision or stratification will permit more efficient sampling and allow the preparation of maps showing the different forest and land use conditions necessary for managing the forest areas.

Classification can be carried out on the ground, in the course of field work, or from aerial photographs. Classification in the field was utilized before the development of aerial photo-interpretation and photogrammetric techniques and is still required in cases where aerial photographs are not available. This kind of classification has the disadvantage of not presenting information of forest and land use classes and stratification prior to field work. Classification from photo-interpretation is desirable and should be utilized whenever possible since it permits prior stratification, is more rapid and, in many cases, more accurate than field classification. If classification from photos is combined with field checking, then even greater accuracy can be achieved.

Classification system for forest and other land use must be based on previously selected characteristics or criteria. The criteria to be employed will depend on whether classification is to be carried out in the field or from aerial photographs. If aerial photographs are employed, the classification scheme must be based on those characteristics which are recognizable and measurable on the photo. For example, forest classification from photographs can be done based on vegetative cover type, stand height, crown density or cover, and derived categories such as volume classes.

If the number of criteria chosen are few, then the resulting classification will be of a general nature; if the number of criteria are many, a more detailed and numerous subdivision will result. In the design of a classification scheme the minimum size area to be recognized should be established. When aerial photographs are employed the scale of the photography will influence this minimum area. Small-scale photography will require larger minimum areas than can be classified on larger scale photographs.

In formulating a forest classification system one must recognize that a forest is more than an amorphous commingling of trees and other vegetation occupying an area of land. A forest is composed of many groups of trees or stands which have some unifying characteristics. Classification systems are then built upon the use of those characteristics which can be recognized in the forest. The following characteristics have proven most useful and practical and should be considered in formulating a forest classification system. The classification system which is finally devised will use some or all of these characteristics in combination and detail commensurate with the purpose of the classification. If an inventory is needed for intensive management, a more detailed system will be required than information for a reconnaissance-type inventory.

1. *Composition*—Groups of trees or stands having certain recognizable species composition form forest types which are needed for forest management. Forest-type designation is probably the most widely used basis for forest inventory classification.
2. *Size*—A forest area can be subdivided into classes according to the sizes of trees found in its various stands. Classification can be based on tree height (especially useful in aerial photographic interpretation) tree diameter, age, and volume.
3. *Density*—Classes may be established based on crown closure percentages (utilizing aerial photographs), basal area, and number of trees per unit land area.
4. *Site*—A forest area may be subdivided into site classes according to its quality or productivity for growing forests.

In addition to the criteria of classification mentioned above, forest land can also be classified according to its operability or has been more frequently, but less logically, expressed as its "accessibility." Operability here means the relative economic feasibility of managing a forest area or extracting the timber involved. Operability or "accessibility" cannot be considered simply in the physical sense of being able to reach a forest area. It must be considered as a combination of physical difficulties with their attendant costs as compared to the value or return obtainable from the forest area. If operable forests can first be delimited, then forest inventory can be concentrated on these areas, leaving the less operable lands for lower intensity surveys, thus reducing the overall cost of the inventory.

Knowledge of the management status of forest lands is often valuable information, especially in the formulation of national and regional forest policy. A classification system which describes the intensity or kind of forest management practiced can be established, e.g., unmanaged, extensively managed, and intensively managed.

A classification system to express the ownership pattern of forest land often is of value. Classes can include designation such as public lands and subdivisions of national, state, municipal, etc., and various categories of private ownership.

11–8. PARAMETERS TO EXPRESS QUANTITY OF TIMBER AND NON-TIMBER INFORMATION

When timber is the primary interest of an inventory, this requires the choice of parameters which express amount of wood material. In some cases, there are additional valuable, non-timber products which may be evaluated; for example, bamboo, bark, and nuts. Further non-timber information is frequently required as a part of the inventory objective. This may include such items as evaluation of forest areas for recreational or wildlife use, soil studies for agricultural evaluation, and watershed studies.

An inventory for timber evaluation is concerned with quantitative expression of the amount of usable raw material in a forest and its location. The raw material may be the amount of timber suitable for sawlogs, veneer logs, pulpwood, fuelwood, or any of the uses to which the cellulose or other yields produced by a forest may be destined. The most common parameters to describe timber quantities are frequencies of trees according to species and some type of size class, and volume in any of the numerous units. There is no reason why other stand parameters, such as weight or bole surface area cannot be used. Whatever the parameter chosen, a clear definition of its meaning is essential. Thus, for volume, specifications should state if it is gross or net, over or under bark, and the merchantability units. Merchantibility units refer to the portion of a stand or tree which is considered commercially usable. Decisions must be made on those specifications which limit merchantibility. This means minimum dbh, lengths of trunks or logs, and a definition of limit of merchantability in the upper stem of the tree. A decision must be also made on whether or not unmerchantable portions of trees or stands should be included in, shown separately, or eliminated from inventory estimates.

Consideration should be given to estimating the total as well as merchantable volume. Merchantable volume is defined by limits which can change because of technological developments or price fluctuations. If these changes occur it is easier to make new merchantable volume estimates from total volume figures rather than attempt to convert merchantable volumes based on other limits.

The units which will be used to express the quantities to be measured should be chosen. Thus, if volume of timber is the expression of quantity, units such as board foot, cubic foot, cubic meter, hoppus foot, etc., should be chosen. Further, the units for all other measurements in the inventory should be selected. Wherever possible, the metric system for all measurements is to be recommended. In those countries where other measurement systems must be used, it would be advantageous to indicate also the inventory results according to the metric system.

Measurements or quantitative expressions are almost invariably shown in terms of size classes in the interest of summarizing and consolidating information. Decisions should be made on size classes and limits for each measurement as: dbh, height, form, volume, number of trees per unit area, or any other parameters.

Frequency data showing numbers of trees according to such classification systems as species, dbh, or height classes are commonly recorded and presented in the form of stand tables. An example is given in Table 11–2. Stand tables can be on a unit area basis, such as per acre or hectare, or by the total area of the stand. A stand table is useful in depicting the stand structure or distribution of sizes and species in a stand.

Volume is the most common inventory measure of timber quantity. Any of the volume units, such as board feet, cubic feet, cubic meters, etc., can be used. Volume information for a stand can be presented as total or per unit area figures for the entire stand, by species, or according to species and tree sizes, in stock tables. A stock table is a counterpart to stand table but shows volume information rather than tree frequencies. Table 11–3 is an example of a stock table on a per acre basis. For brevity, stand and stock information can be combined into one table.

Volume estimates which include both sound and defective wood material are called gross estimates. If the volume of defective or cull material is deducted from the gross estimate, a net estimate results.

With the gradual conversion to the use of weight for scaling pulpwood, estimating the weight of pulpwood stands will become a necessary inventory task. The usefulness of this stand characteristic depends on the development of relationships of stand weight to directly measurable charac-

Table 11–2
Example of a Total Stand Table

Species and number of stems according to dbh for the 10-inch class and up, for 518 acres of hardwood type of a 640-acre tract in northern New York.

Dbh (inches)	Sugar Maple	Beech	Yellow Birch	Hemlock	Red Spruce	Total
10	304	1018	160	15	1503	3000
12	752	1973	350	47	1149	4271
14	1279	1970	446	15	428	4138
16	1602	1429	461	5	98	3595
18	1662	1035	430		15	3142
20	1148	562	415			2125
22	827	159	498			1484
24	420	77	364			861
26	241	21	256			518
28	47		208			255
30	26		150			176
32			110			110
34			36			36
36			20			20
38			15			15
Total	8308	8244	3919	82	3193	23746

Table 11–3
Example of an Average Acre Stock Table

Data from 20.8 acres of pitch pine type in Central New Hampshire

Dbh (inches)	Pitch Pine	Balsam Fir	Red Spruce	White Pine	Red Pine	Red Maple	White Birch	Amer. Elm	Total
				Cubic Feet Per Acre					
6	17.6	2.5	5.0	3.9		14.5	4.3		39.6
7	37.9	4.0	4.0			12.9			67.0
8	27.6	22.4							50.0
9	25.5	20.1	13.4			13.4	7.6		80.0
10	60.8	18.8	18.8	27.0		10.6			136.0
11	40.2		13.3	13.3			14.0		80.8
12	48.0	16.4						14.1	78.5
13	61.3	17.6							78.9
14	17.4				18.4				35.8
15	21.8								21.8
16	82.3							18.1	100.4
17									
18	158.8								158.8
19									
20	37.7								37.7
Total	636.9	101.8	54.5	44.2	18.4	51.4	25.9	32.2	965.3

teristics such as tree diameter and height. Just as volume relationships have been prepared in the form of volume tables, similar relationships can be developed for weight.

11–9. GROWTH AND DRAIN

Since a forest is not a static, inanimate storehouse, but a living changing complex, provision must be made for estimates of growth and drain so that knowledge of the forest resource can be kept up to date over a period of time. When growth estimates are needed a decision must be made whether estimates will be obtained from a single inventory using some prediction procedure based on increment cores or if a system of repeated inventories at periodic intervals will be used (see Chapters 12 and 16).

On certain inventories, it may be necessary to estimate the quantity of timber which is cut from a forest and that which is destroyed by natural enemies. The sum of all quantities removed on an annual or periodic basis is called drain. The losses due to natural enemies are of two kinds: namely, those which occur because of normal mortality, and those caused by occasional disasters or catastrophes such as forest fires, epidemics of diseases or insects, and typhoons.

11–10. MAPS

Maps are important in forest inventory work both as an essential part of the final results and in executing the inventory. To be complete, the statistical information provided in the results of an inventory must be supplemented by maps. It means little to know the quantity of timber or have information on the characteristics of a forest area unless they can be related to location on the ground by a map. Maps are also extremely useful in the execution of a forest inventory for such purposes as planning the acquisition of aerial photography, distributing field sampling units, assisting in field travel and sampling unit establishment, and as a base upon which to delineate forest and land use conditions.

Both supplementing existing maps and preparing new ones are best done using aerial photogrammetric and photo-interpretation techniques. Maps for inventories of small areas can also be prepared using only field procedures if aerial photographs are not available or the cost of their acquisition is excessive in comparison to obtaining needed maps from field procedures. Mosaics and orthophotographs, described in Section 13–2, can supplement or substitute for conventional maps.

In summary, any mapping program for a forest inventory depends on what kind of information must be included as a part of the final results and what is needed for executing the inventory, balanced against the cost entailed.

11–11. EFFECT OF TIME AND FUNDS AVAILABLE

The question of time and funds available is a vital, and in many cases, controlling aspect in inventory planning. The main factors influencing the cost of a forest inventory are the type of information required, the standard of precision, the total size of the area to be surveyed, and the minimum size of the unit areas in the forest for which estimates are required.

Basic general information on the areas of the important forest types or classes is relatively inexpensive as much of the data can be obtained from aerial photographs. As more detailed information on forest ownerships and on the quantities of standing timber become necessary the cost of the inventory increases. Information on growth and drain is technically the most difficult and frequently the most expensive phase of a forest inventory.

The standard of precision desired greatly influences costs. Since costs rise with increasing precision, careful judgment must be exercised in determining the required level for the different elements of an inventory.

Costs per unit area will decrease as the size of the inventory area increases. The minimum size of the unit of land area within the forest for which independent estimates are to be prepared will also influence costs. It may be possible to prepare estimates for units of 10,000 hectares of forest land to an acceptable precision for a small expenditure per hectare. If, however, it is desired to make an independent estimate for each 100-hectare block within the forest with the same precision, the cost per hectare will be many times greater. Estimates based on large unit areas are usually sufficient for regional or national management planning purposes while estimates of small unit areas are necessary for intensive forest management.

Each possible inventory design will have a certain total cost and the design chosen should be that one which will yield the desired information with an acceptable limit of error for the lowest cost.

The principal items in a design which will affect the cost are personnel, vehicles, and other transport together with maintenance and fuel, office space, equipment and supplies, instruments and field equipment, aerial photographs and data processing.

The time available for an inventory must also be kept in mind. Sometimes it may be necessary to have results of lower precision available in a short time rather than expending a longer period for more precise estimates.

11–12. INVENTORY DESIGN

The design of a forest inventory is an art in which the knowledge and experience of the inventory specialist is combined to prepare a methodology which will yield the required information. There must be latitude to meet the variety of forest, topographic, economic, and transportation conditions encountered. The design need be limited only by the ingenuity of the designer and the statistical and cost requirements. For a discussion of the possibility of standardization in planning forest inventories see Husch (1966).

The required forest inventory information, namely, areas, quantities, and characteristics of timber, growth, and drain and any non-timber estimates, can be obtained by observations and measurements in the field, on aerial photographs, or by a combination procedure from both sources. By far the most useful and practical approach is a combined procedure in which aerial photographs are used for forest classification or stratification, mapping, and frequently area determination, while ground work is employed for detailed information about forest conditions and timber quantities and qualities. It is possible to prepare a forest inventory design utilizing only field work, but it is less efficient and is not recommended if aerial photographs can be obtained. It is also possible, under some circumstances, to design a forest inventory based entirely on aerial photographic interpretation and measurements. In most cases, this is not satisfactory since the amount of information and the detail obtainable directly from aerial photographs are limited. Only rough approximations of timber quantity, species, quality, and sizes can be obtained directly from aerial photographs. The utility of this aproach is also limited by the quality of photos, availability of such aids as aerial photographic volume tables, techniques for distinguishing species, and experience and skill of photo-interpreters.

Detailed discussions regarding sampling designs for use in forest inventories are covered in Chapter 12.

11–13. FIELD MEASUREMENT PLANNING

There is wide latitude and flexibility in the size and organization of field crews depending on the sampling procedures designed, forest condition, labor conditions, and in many cases, tradition. Inventory work in temperate zone forests generally utilizes small-sized crews often of one or two men. Small crew organization has evolved since accessibility is often easy due to abundant roads, relatively easy travel in the forest, and the existence of highly trained technicians. Inventories in tropical areas usually require bigger crews for several reasons. Dense vegetation often requires cutting paths for crew movements to establish plot boundaries or to get lines of sight to individual trees. Crew members usually have less technical training and are assigned single, specific tasks resulting in a large crew to carry out a series of measurements. In tropical forests, plot sizes are larger and often complete tallies are taken for extensive areas. Custom in some tropical areas necessitates a big crew since individual workers will only agree to execute certain tasks. Additionally, in remote regions, especially in tropical areas without vehicular access, a field crew may require a large number of laborers to move field and camping equipment. Whatever the crew size and assignment of tasks, it is essential that specific and clear instructions be given to each crew member so that he knows precisely what are his tasks and responsibilities.

Although individual inventories differ in their specifications, a basic principle in planning all forest inventory work is that a complete set of written instructions be prepared before field work starts. To minimize later changes in instructions, procedures for field work should be tested prior to incorporating them into the operating procedures. In preparing instructions, efforts should be made to eliminate the exercise of individual judgment in where and how to take measurements. For example, plot location procedures should not permit field crews to exercise subjective choice of position or permission to move a plot to a more accessible position or seemingly more "typical" stand. The aim should be to standardize completely all work so that the quality and reliability of the measurements will be the best possible, and equal regardless of which individual happens to do the work. The occurrence of mistakes or non-random errors must be held to the absolute minimum.

In planning for field work, decisions should be made on the kind of instruments to be used for each of the required measurements. It is best to settle upon a standard set of instruments and have all field measurements made with the standard instruments. The use of several kinds of instruments to make the same type measurement should be avoided. To avoid systematic errors, the chosen instruments should be periodically checked to see that they are in adjustment.

Decisions should be made on the precision to be used for each of the measurements required. Thus, tree diameters at breast high (dbh) may be required to the nearest centimeter, inch, tenth of centimeter, etc. The finest reading required for each measurement should then be included in directions for the use of each of the field crews' instruments.

It is essential that inventory field work include a checking procedure. Using plot, strips, or point sampling this means that a certain percentage of these sampling units are subject to a remeasurement after their original measurements. The results of this measurement are checked against the original results to see if the work meets the required standards. If appreciable differences occur in plot boundaries, trees tallied, individual tree measurement, etc., the causes of the differences should be immediately resolved before proceeding with further work. The checking procedure should be designed so that crews are not aware of where or when their work will be checked. Field checking of this kind may seem an excessive expense and unproductive, but it is a worthwhile investment which will result in more reliable final estimates.

There is no standard form or tally sheet for recording field observations of measurements. The design of a form depends upon the information to be gathered and to a large extent the way this information will then be processed. Rather than attempt to present examples of field forms, it would be more useful to mention a few fundamentals which are basic to the design and use of the field form.

The design of a field form should be preceded by the following planning stages:

1. decisions on required information;
2. the preparation of the format of tables to show the expected results of an inventory;
3. decisions on the required field measurements.

Once the field forms are designed, they should be field tested to see if they perform satisfactorily. If not, they should be modified and further tested until suitable, after which they can then be put into operational use. Even here it will occasionally prove necessary to further modify the form if experience indicates it can be improved.

Field forms can be designed using any of the four approaches described in Section 2–4. To supplement this description, a few points especially related to field forms for forest inventory are shown here:

1. *Field forms for recording observations without concern for subsequent calculations.* An example of one possible form for field measurements of diameter, height, and species for use in a volume inventory is shown in Fig. 11–1. Note that diameter and height classes are designated. For a volume inventory using local volume tables, only diameter need be recorded for the several species. A simpler type of form would then suffice since it would be unnecessary to segregate the tally by height classes.
2. *Field forms permitting subsequent calculations and recording results.* As an example, a field form of the preceding type can be designed so that space is available for entering the volumes for each of the diameter and height classes and for totals. This keeps the derived values and the original data together. The disadvantage is the large amount of space required to allow entering the derived values.

The cumulative volume tally sheet (Macon and Gevorkiantz, 1942;

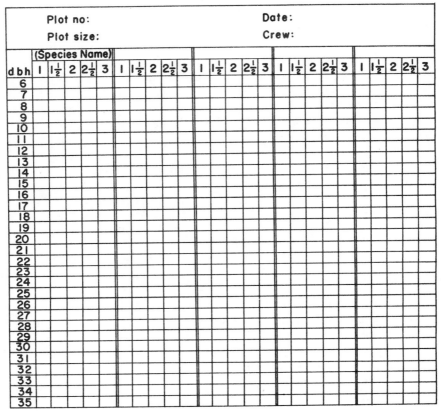

The numbers, I, I½, etc., refer to the number of 16-foot logs.

Tally can be kept by a dot system as follows:

1	.	6	⌐.
2	:	7	⊓
3	∴	8	⊔
4	::	9	⊠
5	⌊:	10	⊠

Fig. 11–1. Example of tally sheet for field measurements of dbh height, and species.

Miller, 1949) is a form of the type which allows the automatic conversion of diameter and height measurements to volume and simultaneously shows current totals. For each diameter and height class a series of volumes are printed on the tally form, as shown in Table 11–4. The first volume figure in a class represents the volume of a single tree of the specified diameter and height. The

Table 11-4
Cumulative Board-Foot Volume Tally Sheet by DBH and Number of 16-Foot Logs

Volumes per acre in hundreds of board feet, Doyle Scale, based on Lake States composite volume tables.[1]

Dbh (Inches)	Number of Logs	Cumulative Board-Foot Volumes											Total
12	1	~~1~~	~~3~~	~~4~~	~~6~~	~~7~~	~~8~~	10	12	13	14	16	
	2	~~2~~	~~5~~	~~7~~	9	12	14	16	18	21	23	25	16
14	1	~~2~~	~~5~~	~~7~~	~~10~~	12	15	17	20	22	24	27	
	2	~~4~~	~~8~~	12	16	20	24	28	32	36	40	43	18
16	1	~~4~~	~~7~~	~~11~~	14	18	21	25	28	32	36	39	
	2	~~8~~	12	18	24	30	36	42	48	54	60	67	
	3	8	16	24	32	40	49	57	65	73	81	89	17
18	1	~~5~~	~~10~~	15	20	25	30	35	40	45	50	54	
	2	8	16	25	33	41	50	58	66	74	82	91	
	3	~~11~~	22	34	45	56	67	78	90	101	112	123	21
20	1	~~8~~	13	20	26	32	39	46	52	58	65	72	
	2	~~11~~	22	33	44	55	66	77	88	99	110	132	
	3	15	30	45	59	74	89	104	119	134	148	163	17

Volume per acre.................. 8.9M

[1] The trees crossed out represent the tally in a 1/5-acre plot.

second volume figure represents two trees, the third figure three trees, etc., within the height and diameter class. Trees are tallied by successively crossing out these figures in the height and diameter categories in which the tree falls. At the completion of a tally on a sample area, the last figure in each height and diameter class represents the respective total volumes. The plot total is the sum of these volumes. The volumes shown in Table 11–4 are on a per acre basis for tally on a .2-acre plot. Cumulative tally sheets can be made up for any volume table and unit desired. It is difficult to keep a separate tally by individual species on these cumulative forms. The problem can be solved if a composite volume table for all species is used.

3. *Field forms for subsequent transfer of data to machine input device.* The majority of forest inventories use recording forms of this type. They have the advantage of a durable, easily read record of field observations and, with proper design, minimize the work of transferring field observations to computer input devices.

4. *Field forms on machine input devices.* Inventory field forms can be printed directly on mark sensing or prescored cards as shown in Fig. 2–2. Although the step of transferring field observations to

machine input device is eliminated, the disadvantages described in Section 2–4 often preclude the use of these forms in forest inventory work.

It is worth pointing out that the set of instructions prepared for guiding measurement procedures and recording the resultant data should include the use of the field forms. A brief description should be given covering the entry of data in each column of the form.

11–14. CALCULATION AND COMPILATION

Plans for calculation and compilation of photo-interpretation data and field measurements should preferably be made well in advance of starting work. The most satisfactory sequence is to plan for calculation and compilation concurrently with planning the design for obtaining the necessary observations. It is illogical and inefficient to postpone consideration of compilation procedures until data are obtained. In addition, foreknowledge of the calculation and compilation procedures can have an influence on the data to be collected. An illustrative example is the precision with which dbh measurements might be required in the field if volume tables will be used later in compilation work. Thus, there would be little point in measuring diameters to a tenth of a centimeter if the volume tables indicate volumes by full centimeter dbh classes.

The statistical formulas to be used for estimating means, totals, and standard errors should be decided upon early in the planning process. It is worthwhile to check the use of these with some simulated data, especially to work out the optimum sequence of computational steps for their employment. The computational work of a forest inventory can be carried out at three levels of sophistication: (1) by hand or with desk-type calculators; (2) using punched cards with sorting and computational systems; and (3) with electronic computers. In terms of complexity and equipment needed the first is the simplest and requires the least costly apparatus. However, this does not necessarily mean it will be the cheapest. The second and third levels require increasingly complex and costly equipment but nevertheless they actually may be more economical to use. Which to employ depends on the size of the inventory, funds, and equipment or services available. For a discussion of data processing procedures see Chapter 2.

12

Sampling in Forest Inventory

12–1. INTRODUCTION

For large forest areas it is impractical to measure all trees to determine the characteristics of the timber because the time and cost required are excessive in relation to the value and usefulness of the information obtained. A more efficient way is to use sampling, which can provide the necessary information at a much lower cost and greater speed. Another advantage, often unrecognized, is that a sampling procedure may produce more reliable results than a complete tally. Since only a portion of the forest is measured in the form of sampling units, greater care can be exercised in the fewer required measurements, supervision can be improved, fewer but better trained personnel suffice, and the probable number of non-sampling errors will be reduced. In addition, the idea of precision is constantly in the forefront at all stages in a sampling inventory whereas a complete tally may give the delusion of the acquisition of information without error.

This chapter and Chapters 13 and 14 are concerned with the application of sampling theory and techniques to forest resource evaluation. For a basic treatment of sampling theory and technique, the reader is referred to Kish (1965); Cochran (1963); Yates (1960); Sukhatme (1954); Hansen, Hurwitz, and Madow (1953); and Deming (1950).

12–2. SAMPLING TERMINOLOGY IN FOREST INVENTORY

In forest inventory work, sampling consists of measuring portions of a population (the forest and its characteristics), and, from the measured sampling units, obtaining estimates that are considered representative of the parent population. The sampling units may be stands, compartments, administrative units, fixed area plots, or strips or sampling points. The total aggregate of these sampling units constitutes the population. The group of sampling units chosen for measurement constitutes the sample. For purposes of selecting the sampling units, a "frame" can be prepared which can be a diagram or list of all the possible sampling units in the population.

12–3. ERRORS IN FOREST INVENTORY

All forest inventories are subject to errors which can be grouped into two classes: sampling errors and non-sampling errors. Taken together, they make up the total error of the estimate. This total error is the difference between the estimate taken from a sample and the true population value. If no non-sampling errors are present, then the total error is equivalent to the sampling error.

12–3.1. Precision and Accuracy in Forest Inventory. The precision of a forest inventory based on sampling is indicated by the size of the sampling error and excludes the effects of biases. Accuracy of an inventory refers to the size of the total error and, thus, includes the effects of biases. Estimates from a precise inventory would have a small sampling error. Estimates from an accurate inventory would have to be both precise and have little or no bias. Thus, we could have a precise inventory which was not accurate if the results contained a large bias.

In forest inventory, as in any sampling procedure, we are really primarily concerned with the accuracy of an estimate. (See Sayn-Wittgenstein, 1965.) However, we most often speak of precision simply because it is easier to measure. We try to achieve accuracy by designing an inventory for the maximum or stipulated precision and by eliminating or reducing bias to a minimum.

12–3.2. Sampling Errors. Sampling errors result from the fact that the sample is only a portion of the population and may not produce values identical to the population parameter. Assuming that no non-sampling errors exist, the difference between the sample estimate and the population value is measured by the standard error of the estimate. This standard error is a measure of the expected size of the sampling error and is often expressed as a percentage of the estimated mean when it is called the sampling error in per cent. In designing a sample forest inventory, one should decide upon a precision desired for the estimate. This desired precision is usually expressed as the acceptable sampling error in per cent. The lower the standard error, the higher the precision. The sampling error in forest inventory work depends on the size of the sample, the variability of the individual sampling units of the forest, and the sampling procedure used. Using one of the probability sampling procedures, the size of the sample can be estimated which will yield the required sampling error.

The sampling error for the estimate of the total quantity from a forest inventory would have to consider both the sampling errors of the quantity estimate, such as mean volume per unit area, and of the estimate of the total area. If the area is known exactly or its sampling error is unimportant, then the estimate of the total quantity would be this area multiplied times the mean volume and its standard error. If both area and volume were estimates with sampling errors, the total volume would be:

$$x\bar{v} \pm \sqrt{x^2 s_{\bar{v}}^2 + \bar{v}^2 s_x^2} \qquad (12\text{--}1)$$

where:

x = estimate of the total area
$\bar{v}$ = estimate of the mean volume per unit area
$s_{\bar{v}}^2$ = variance of the mean volume per unit area
s_x^2 = variance of the estimate of total area

12–3.3. Non-Sampling Errors. Non-sampling errors may contribute importantly to the total error of estimate of an inventory, even to the extent of being greater than the sampling error. Frequently, the accuracy of a forest inventory is considered entirely indicated by the size of the standard error without considering the fact that unmeasured, non-sampling errors may also have contributed substantially. Precautions should be taken to minimize the possibility of these kinds of errors since, once they occur, they are difficult to detect, assess, and eliminate. Note that non-sampling errors can occur for both complete tallies and for sampling inventories.

The non-sampling errors in forest inventory can arise from numerous causes, such as mistakes in the location of sampling units, mistakes in making measurements or in recording observations, faulty methods of compilation, and calculation mistakes.

These errors can be regarded as of two general types, depending upon how they arise (excluding occasional gross mistakes due to carelessness):

1. Measurment errors occurring randomly;
2. Consistent errors causing a bias.

If measurement errors occur randomly, one can expect their mean to approach zero. If the mean of the population of errors is not zero, a bias is introduced.

12–4. CONFIDENCE LIMITS AND THE RELIABLE MINIMUM ESTIMATE

Forest inventory estimates can be expressed as a range, with an associated probability, called a confidence interval. The confidence interval, bounded by confidence limits, describes the range in which the population parameter is expected to occur at a given probability. The upper and lower limits to a confidence interval, CI, for the mean, $\bar{x}$, are found from its standard error as:

$$CI = \bar{x} \pm ts_{\bar{x}} \qquad (12\text{--}2)$$

The value of t for a chosen probability level can be found from "Student's" distribution using $n - 1$ degrees of freedom, where n is the size of the sample.

Instead of expressing the estimate of the quantity of timber from an inventory by a mean and its confidence interval, an analogous expression called the Reliable Minimum Estimate (RME) is often used (Dawkins, 1957). The RME expresses the minimum quantity expected to be present with an associated probability level. It is often the case that a management decision (e.g., whether or not to log an area) is dependent on there being a minimum quantity of timber available. The usual analysis of inventory data will show an estimated mean and its standard error from which the probability of finding a required minimum quantity can be determined. Note that this will always be in the form of a probability statement.

To calculate the RME it is necessary to first have the mean and its standard error. The expression of the RME is then:

$$\text{RME} = \bar{x} - ts_{\bar{x}} \qquad (12\text{--}3)$$

This appears the same as the lower limit of the confidence interval. However, the value of t for the probability level is obtained only from the negative side of the symmetrical distribution. In using a table of t values where the sign is ignored, the appropriate value would be obtained using the column for double the probability level required. Thus, the t value for a probability level of .05 would be read under the column headed .10 recognizing the appropriate degrees of freedom. As an example, suppose the inventory has shown the following estimate:

Mean volume per hectare = 120.0 cubic meters

$s_{\bar{x}}$ =   20.0 cubic meters

Number of sampling units =   20

What is the RME at a probability of .05? At this probability the value of t with 19 degrees of freedom as read under the column headed .10 is 1.729

$$RME = 120.0 -   1.729(20.0)$$
$$= 120.0 - 34.6$$
$$= 85.4$$

This means that the expected volume per hectare is not less than 85.4 cubic meters unless a 1 in 20 chance has occurred.

12–5. SAMPLING DESIGN

The sampling design to meet inventory objectives is determined by the kind of sampling units, their size and shape if on an area basis, the number to be employed, and the manner of selection and resultant distribution over the forest area, followed by the procedures for measurements in the selected units and the analysis of the resulting data. The designer of a forest inventory has wide latitude in formulating the design by varying the specifications for each of the above mentioned elements to yield a desired degree of precision at a minimum or specified cost.

Sampling designs using fixed-area sampling units date back to the 19th century in Europe. They are still very commonly used although sampling with varying probability, especially point sampling, has been increasingly employed in recent years. The designs discussed in this chapter can be used with any chosen sampling unit, plot, strip, or sampling point or line.

It is essential to understand that there is no one inventory design which can be universally applied. The design to use is the end product of a series of considerations, each having an influence on how the sampling will be carried out. The factors that influence the design are:

1. Information required and its desired precision.
2. Composition of the forest and its variability.
3. Topography and accessibility to and within the forest.
4. Availability of personnel and level of skill.
5. Time and money available for the work.
6. Availability of aerial photographs or maps.
7. Designer's knowledge of statistics and sampling theory.

The details of an inventory sampling design can vary widely and it is impossible to describe all the infinite variations. However, the majority of the many variations can be grouped into several general categories. The discussion of sampling design presented in this chapter should be viewed as an introductory treatment dealing with the simpler cases. More sophisticated designs can be prepared by specialists but are beyond the province of this introductory presentation.

We can consider basic inventory designs in the following categories:

A. *Probability sampling*
 1. Simple random sampling
 2. Stratified random sampling
 3. Multistage sampling
 4. Multiphase sampling
 5. Sampling with varying probabilities
B. *Non-random sampling*
 1. Selective sampling
 2. Systematic sampling

In probability sampling, the probability of selecting any sampling unit is known prior to the actual chance drawing. This probability is greater than zero and may be equal for all units at all times or it may vary as the sampling proceeds. Frequently, in forest inventory work, the probabilities are not known but are assumed to be equal. This is referred to as an equal-chance selection method.

In non-random sampling the units which constitute the sample are not chosen by the laws of chance, but by personal judgment or systematically.

Sampling on successive occasions is a means of determining changes which have taken place over a period of time and can employ any of the basic inventory designs.

12–6. SIZE AND SHAPE OF FIXED-AREA SAMPLING UNITS

If the sampling unit to be used in a forest inventory is of a fixed area, it is necessary to specify its size and shape. Sampling units of this type are called plots or strips depending on their dimensions. The term "plot" is loosely applied to sampling units of small area and diverse shapes, such as square, rectangular, or circular. A strip is a special case of a rectangular plot whose length dimension is many times its width.

Unbiased estimates of timber volume and other stand parameters can be obtained from any plot size or shape although the precision and cost of the survey may vary significantly. Small sampling units are frequently more efficient than larger ones. For a given intensity of sampling (percentage of an area actually tallied) small sampling units tend to increase the precision since the number of independent sampling units is larger. However, the size of the most efficient unit will also be influenced by the variability of the forest. Small sampling units taken in forests of variable composition will result in a high coefficient of variation and larger sampling units will be more desirable. In heterogeneous forests, as are often found in tropical regions, small sampling units may result in a large number of sampling units having no measurable trees and the application of normal distribution theory may be inappropriate (Heinsdijk, 1965).

The larger the plot size for a given intensity, the fewer the number of plots and the smaller the time and cost for traveling and establishing plots. However, the tallying time per plot will be greater. Where travel is difficult, as in remote tropical areas, the question of travel time to plots assumes paramount importance.

In summary, the ultimate choice of the size of a sampling unit must be based on a consideration of both cost and desired precision. This is expressed by the relative efficiency of different-sized plots. Efficiency in this sense is measured by:

$$E = \frac{(se)_1{}^2 t_1}{(se)_2{}^2 t_2} \qquad (12\text{--}4)$$

where:

$(se)_1$ = standard error in per cent for one plot size or shape used as the basis for comparison

$(se)_2$ = standard error in per cent for the other plot size or shape to be compared

t_1 = cost or time for base plot size or shape

t_2 = cost or time for compared plot size or shape

Solving the equation gives the efficiency of plot size or shape two, relative to plot size or shape one. If E is less than 1, then plot one is more efficient than plot two. If E is greater than 1, plot two is the more efficient. The optimum plot size or shape will be that which is more efficient.

Procedures for investigating optimum plot sizes are given by Mesavage and Grosenbaugh (1956), Tardif (1965), and O'Regan and Arvanitis (1966).

In North America the most commonly used plot sizes for mature or near mature timber are .20 to .25 acre. Chacko (1962) has summarized the most commonly used plot sizes in several countries and his results are reproduced in Table 12–1. In tropical areas, larger plots have proven more useful due to greater heterogeneity of the forest. The guiding principle in the choice of plot size should be to have a plot large enough to include a representative number of trees, but small enough so that the time required for measurement is not excessive. Spurr (1952) recommends that the plot size should be large enough to include at least twenty

Table 12–1
Plot Sizes Used in Forest Inventories in Selected Countries

Country	Type of Inventory	Plot Size Hectare	Acre
England	National Survey	.04	.1
U.S.A.	Saw-timber[1]	.08	.2
	Pole-timber[2]	.04	.1
	Sapling	.004	.01
Sweden	National Survey	.0138	.03
Finland	National Forest Survey	.1	.25
Japan	Timber	.05–.20	.12–.50
Canada	Timber	.08–.10	.20–.25
Germany	Timber	.01–.05	.02–.12

[1] Saw-timber—all softwoods 9.0 inches dbh and up; hardwoods 11.0 inches dbh and up.
[2] Pole-timber—softwoods from 5.0 to 8.9 inches dbh; hardwoods 5.0 to 10.0 inches dbh.
SOURCE: Chacko, 1962.

measurable trees. For dense stands of small-sized trees, plots should be small, while for widely spaced stands of larger timber, plots must be larger.

A commonly used practice is to establish a series of concentric plots of different sizes at each sampling location and to tally trees within specified size classes on each plot. The intent is to reduce the plot area for small-sized trees and increase it for large-sized trees, with the objective of tallying approximately equal numbers of trees in several size classes.

Plots can assume any shape. Circular plots have been most widely used. A study by Johnson and Hixon (1952) has shown that a rectangular .3-acre plot (66 by 198 feet or 1 by 3 chains) was the most efficient size and shape in old-growth Douglas fir. Osborne (1946) had pointed out earlier that theoretically a rectangular plot with the long axis at right angles to the contours should be the most efficient since the plots would tend to cross the range of timber conditions. Kulow (1966) found in his investigations that plot shape did not affect the size of the sampling error. He found that the characteristics of plot shape that would influence a decision were the ease of establishment and the length of the plot perimeter. Circular plots have the advantage that a single dimension, the radius, can be used to define the perimeter. The dimensions of commonly used sample plots are given in Appendix Table A–5.

12–7. SIMPLE RANDOM SAMPLING

Simple random sampling is the fundamental selection method and all other sampling procedures are really modifications whose intent is to achieve greater economy or precision. Simple random sampling requires that there be an equal chance of selecting all possible combinations of the n sampling units from the population. The selection of each sampling unit must be free from deliberate choice and must be completely independent of the selection of all other units.

Using simple random sampling, the entire forest area is treated as a single population. If fixed-area sampling units are used, the entire forest area is considered as being composed of these spatial units which we can designate as N. If sampling points are used, the size of N can be considered infinite. From this population, a sample of n sampling units with equal probability of selection is then randomly chosen.

Unrestricted random sampling in forest inventory yields an unbiased estimate of the population mean and the necessary information to assess the sampling error but has the following disadvantages:

1. The requirement of devising a system for randomly selecting the plots or points.
2. The difficulties of locating widely dispersed field positions of selected sampling units.
3. Time-consuming and expensive non-productive traveling time between units.
4. The possibility of an uneven distribution of sampling units resulting in uneven sampling of the population.

Instead of using plots or points, the sampling unit may be the strip. For recording purposes, the strip may be subdivided into smaller recording units. It is important to remember that the entire strip is still considered as the ultimate sampling unit and is the basis for determining the number of degrees of freedom.

An advantage of a continuous strip over plots or points is that a tally is taken for the entire strip traversed so that there is no unproductive walking time between sampling units. Strips have a disadvantage in that the number of sampling units and resulting number of degrees of freedom is small. Compared to plot sampling of equal intensity, in strip sampling the size of the sampling unit is larger and the number of sampling units smaller. The larger size sampling unit results in a reduction in the variability but this advantage is counteracted by the smaller number of sampling units. For this reason the sampling error of a strip sampling design is usually larger than for plot sampling, assuming the same sampling intensity.

Forest inventory using random sampling requires aerial photographs or a map to establish a frame from which to draw the sample randomly. Figure 12–1 shows the simple case of a square or rectangular-shaped forest which can be subdivided perfectly in N sampling units of fixed area. After the number, n, of sampling units is decided upon, they are chosen from the frame using any of the usual procedures for random selection.

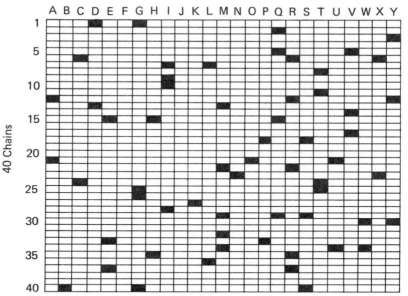

(a) Using plots. Forest area of 200 acres divided into 1000 sampling units of
     .2-acre (2 X 1 chain). Sixty plots randomly chosen.

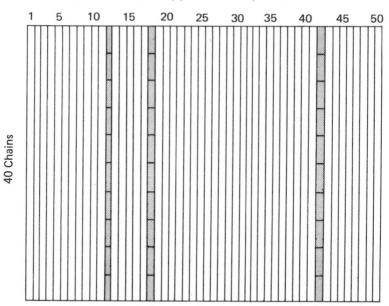

(b) Using strips. Forest area of 200 acres divided into 50 strips 1-chain wide
     and 40 chains long (4 acres). Three strips randomly selected with record-
     ing units of 4 X 1 chains.

Fig. 12–1. Simple random sampling.

The selection can be with or without replacement. If sampling with replacement is followed, there is a possibility of the same sampling unit being selected again and the population can be considered infinite. For large finite populations, the calculation of means and standard errors can be done as though dealing with an infinite population since the finite correction factor, $\dfrac{N-n}{N}$, approaches unity. Most sampling with fixed area plots or strips in forest inventory is done without replacement. Using sampling points, the population is infinite and the sampling is carried out with replacement.

The analysis of the resulting data from the sampling units is summarized below. Note that the formulas are applicable whether dealing with plots, strips, or sampling points. It is worth pointing out that separate tallies for each sampling unit in a forest inventory must be recorded in order to calculate the sampling errors. Given:

n = number of sampling units measured

N = total number of sampling units in the forest

X_i = the quantity X measured on the ith sampling unit

$\bar{x}$ = the mean of X per sampling unit; an estimate of the population mean

s = standard deviation of the sample

$s_{\bar{x}}$ = standard error of the mean

x = the estimated total of X for the population

Then:

$$\bar{x} = \frac{\sum\limits_{i=1}^{n} X_i}{n} \tag{12-5}$$

$$s^2 = \frac{\sum\limits_{i=1}^{n} (X_i - \bar{x})^2}{n-1} \tag{12-6}$$

or:

$$s^2 = \frac{n \sum\limits_{i=1}^{n} X_i^2 - \left(\sum\limits_{i=1}^{n} X_i\right)^2}{n(n-1)} \tag{12-7}$$

$$s_{\bar{x}}^2 = \frac{s^2}{n}\left(\frac{N-n}{N}\right) \tag{12-8}$$

(For an infinite population, the finite correction factor would be omitted.)

The estimate of the population total is then:

$$x = N\bar{x} \tag{12-9}$$

The number of sampling units needed to yield an estimate of the mean with a specified allowable error and probability can be calculated from:

$$n = \frac{Nt^2s^2}{N(AE)^2 + t^2s^2} \qquad (12\text{--}10)$$

For an infinite population:

$$n = \frac{t^2s^2}{(AE)^2} \qquad (12\text{--}11)$$

Expressing the standard deviation and allowable error in percentages:

$$n = \frac{Nt^2(cv)^2}{N(AE\%)^2 + t^2(cv)^2} \qquad (12\text{--}12)$$

For an infinite population:

$$n = \frac{t^2(cv)^2}{(AE\%)^2} \qquad (12\text{--}13)$$

where:

cv = coefficient of variation
AE = allowable standard error in units of X
$AE\%$ = allowable sampling error in per cent

Note that in the formulas, s and cv refer to the standard deviation and coefficient of variation of a preliminary sample taken to give an indication of the variability of the population. The AE is an arbitrarily chosen level and the t value depends on the required probability and degrees of freedom. The t value should be looked up in Student's t distribution with $n - 1$ degrees of freedom, where n refers to the number of sampling units in the preliminary sample. Of course, to be correct, n should be the number of sampling units which is being sought. However, since this is unknown, the n of the preliminary sample can be used. Note that the actual probability level for the indicated number of sampling units will consequently change. If a preliminary sample has not been taken and if the expected sample size is large (over 30), the t values for an infinite number of degree of freedom may be used.

In case the amount of money for a survey is fixed, the number of sampling units must be determined within this restriction. If the total cost or amount of money for a survey is given as c, then:

$$c = c_o + nc_1 \qquad (12\text{--}14)$$

where:

c_o = overhead cost of a survey including planning, organization, analysis, and compilation
c_1 = cost per sampling unit
n = number of sampling units

The number of sampling units is indicated as:

$$n = \frac{c - c_o}{c_1} \qquad (12\text{--}15)$$

If preliminary information on the mean and variance of the population is known from experience or a preliminary sample, it is then possible to estimate what precision can be obtained with this cost and sample size.

12–7.1. Ratio and Regression Estimation. When the forest to be sampled, using fixed-area units, is irregular in form, the possibility exists of having fractional plots or irregular length strips. This is illustrated in Fig. 12–2. (The problem in relation to sampling points is discussed in Chap-

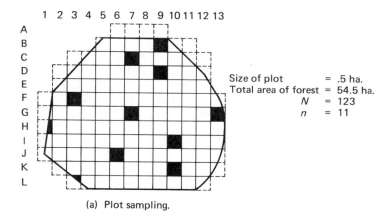

Size of plot   = .5 ha.
Total area of forest = 54.5 ha.
N = 123
n = 11

(a) Plot sampling.

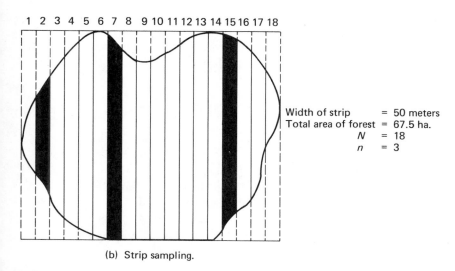

Width of strip   = 50 meters
Total area of forest = 67.5 ha.
N = 18
n = 3

(b) Strip sampling.

Fig. 12–2. Simple random sampling of irregularly shaped forest areas.

ter 14.) Situations of this type arise very frequently in actual application. Note that to meet the requirement of sampling units of equal size, it has become necessary in Fig. 12–2 to sketch imaginary boundaries to enclose the irregular boundaries of the actual forests. The area within each boundary has been divided into equal-sized sampling units. Some of the plots and strips fall entirely in the forest and others include both the forest area and a zone beyond. For this reason, it is necessary to measure two variables for each plot or strip; the area in the sampling unit actually in the forest area and the quantity of timber on this area. The mean volume per unit area for the forest must then be calculated using the ratio or regression methods of estimation.

In the majority of cases involving plot sampling, the ratio or regression procedures have been bypassed in the interests of simplifying field work, saving time and reducing the later calculations. Thus, if a plot falls so that it straddles a forest or stratum boundary, instead of measuring both the area and quantities of that portion of the unit in the forest, a number of other, questionable procedures have been used. These involve moving the plots so that they fall entirely within or without the forest or assigning them to the stratum in which the center point falls. To avoid the possibility of bias arising from these procedures, the ratio or regression methods are recommended.

When the ratio estimation procedure is employed, the sample should consist of thirty or more sampling units so that the inherent bias of the method becomes negligible. In addition, the method is only truly applicable when the linear relationship, as shown by a regression line, between the two variables, timber quantity and area per sampling unit, passes through the origin. When the linear regression does not pass through the origin (i.e., volume per unit can be zero when plot area is non-zero), the regression method of estimation is preferable.

RATIO ESTIMATION

Given:

V_i = the quantity measured on the ith sampling unit

X_i = the area of the ith sampling unit

$\bar{v}$ = the mean of the observed V_i on the selected sampling units

$\bar{x}$ = the mean area of the sampling units selected

$\bar{r}$ = estimate of the mean quantity per unit area

v = estimate of the total quantity (e.g., volume) of the forest

X = known total area of the forest

Then:

$$\bar{r} = \frac{\dfrac{\sum\limits_{i=1}^{n} V_i}{n}}{\dfrac{\sum\limits_{i=1}^{n} X_i}{n}} = \frac{\sum\limits_{i=1}^{n} V_i}{\sum\limits_{i=1}^{n} X_i} \tag{12-16}$$

$$v = X\bar{r} \tag{12-17}$$

If the area is known without any sampling error, then the variance of the total estimate of quantity is:

$$s_v{}^2 = X^2 s_{\bar{r}}{}^2 \tag{12-18}$$

If the total area of the forest is an estimate, x, and has a sampling error, then the variance is:

$$s_v{}^2 = x^2 s_{\bar{r}}{}^2 + \bar{r}^2 s_x{}^2 \tag{12-19}$$

where:

$s_v{}^2$ = variance of the total quantity
$s_{\bar{r}}{}^2$ = variance of the ratio $\bar{r}$
$s_x{}^2$ = variance of the total area estimate

$$s_{\bar{r}}{}^2 = \left(\frac{N-n}{N}\right)\frac{s^2}{n} \tag{12-20}$$

where:

$$s^2 = \frac{\bar{r}^2}{n-1}\left(\frac{\sum\limits_{i=1}^{n} V_i{}^2}{\bar{v}^2} + \frac{\sum\limits_{i=1}^{n} X_i{}^2}{\bar{v}^2} - \frac{2\sum\limits_{i=1}^{n} V_i X_i}{\bar{v}\bar{x}}\right) \tag{12-21}$$

The number of sampling units for a given precision can be estimated by solving equation 12–20 for n and using a preliminary estimate of s^2. Student's t can be incorporated to vary the probability level.

REGRESSION ESTIMATION

Using this method, an estimate of the mean volume on the sampling units is adjusted by means of a regression coefficient. The regression coefficient indicates the average change in volume per unit change in area between the sampling units in the sample and the population. The total size of the forest area and the total number of sampling units in the population and their average size must be known.

Given:

X_i, V_i, X, v, and $\bar{v}$ are as defined for ratio estimation
b = regression coefficient

$\bar{v}_{\text{reg}}$ = adjusted estimate of the mean volume per sampling unit in the population

$\overline{X}$ = the mean area per sampling unit in the population

$\bar{x}_n$ = the mean area of the sampling units selected

$$\bar{v}_{\text{reg}} = \bar{v} + b(\overline{X} - \bar{x}_n) \tag{12–22}$$

$$b = \frac{\sum\limits_{i=1}^{n} X_i V_i - \dfrac{\sum\limits_{i=1}^{n} X_i \sum\limits_{i=1}^{n} V_i}{n}}{\sum\limits_{i=1}^{n} X_i^2 - \dfrac{\left(\sum\limits_{i=1}^{n} X_i\right)^2}{n}} \tag{12–23}$$

The estimate of the mean volume per unit area, $\bar{r}_{\text{reg}}$, is:

$$\bar{r}_{\text{reg}} = \frac{\bar{v}_{\text{reg}}}{\overline{X}} \tag{12–24}$$

The estimate of the variance of the regression, $s_{\bar{v}_{\text{reg}}}^2$, is:

$$s_{\bar{v}_{\text{reg}}}^2 = \frac{s^2}{n}\left(\frac{N-n}{N}\right) \tag{12–25}$$

where:

$$s^2 = \frac{1}{n-2}\left\{\left[\sum_{i=1}^{n} V_i^2 - \frac{\left(\sum\limits_{i=1}^{n} V_i\right)^2}{n}\right] - b\left[\sum_{i=1}^{n} V_i X_i - \frac{\sum\limits_{i=1}^{n} V_i \sum\limits_{i=1}^{n} X_i}{n}\right]\right\} \tag{12–26}$$

The estimate of the variance of the volume per unit area, s_{reg}^2, is:

$$s_{\text{reg}}^2 = \frac{s_{\bar{v}_{\text{reg}}}^2}{\overline{X}^2} \tag{12–27}$$

The estimate of the total volume of the population, v, is:

$$v = \bar{r}_{\text{reg}} X$$

or:

$$v = \bar{v}_{\text{reg}} N \tag{12–28}$$

and its variance is:

$$s_v^2 = X^2 s_{\text{reg}}^2 \tag{12–29}$$

12–8. STRATIFIED RANDOM SAMPLING

In many cases a heterogeneous forest may be broken down by stratification into subdivisions called strata.

In forest inventory work the purpose of stratification is to reduce the variation within the forest subdivisions and increase the precision of the population estimate.

Stratified random sampling in forest inventory has the following advantages over simple random sampling:

1. Separate estimates of the means and variances can be made for each of the forest subdivisions.
2. For a given sampling intensity, stratification often yields more precise estimates of the forest parameters than does a simple random sample of the same size. This will be achieved if the established strata result in greater homogeneity of the sampling units within a stratum than for the population as a whole.

On the other hand, the disadvantages of stratification are that the size of each stratum must be known or at least a reasonable estimate be available; and sampling units must be taken in each stratum if an estimate for that stratum is needed.

Stratification is achieved by subdividing the forest area into strata on the basis of some criterion such as topographic features, forest types, density classes, volume, height, age, site, etc., classes. If possible, the basis of stratification should be the same characteristic which will be estimated by the sampling procedure. Thus, if volume per unit area is the parameter to be estimated, it is desirable to stratify the forest area on the basis of volume classes. Aerial photographs are of tremendous assistance in stratification for forest inventory. In fact, it is safe to say that aside from mapping, the greatest use so far for aerial photographs in forest inventory has been precisely for this purpose.

The different strata into which a forest may be divided can be irregular in shape, of varying sizes, and of different importance. Stratification permits the sampling intensity and precision to be varied for the several strata.

An arbitrary form of stratification is often used in sampling large forest areas where there is little basis for some kind of natural subdivision. This often occurs in inventories of large, tropical forest areas where maps or photographs are not available or where photo-interpretation reveals little basis for stratification. In this case, the forest can be broken into uniform-sized squares or rectangles even though it is known that the resulting blocks may not contain homogeneous subpopulations. But it is reasonable to assume greater homogeneity within a smaller block than in the larger, entire forest.

Within each of the M strata into which the forest is divided, a number of sampling units are randomly chosen. Figure 12–3 shows a forest broken down into three strata of fixed-area sampling units, all of the same size.

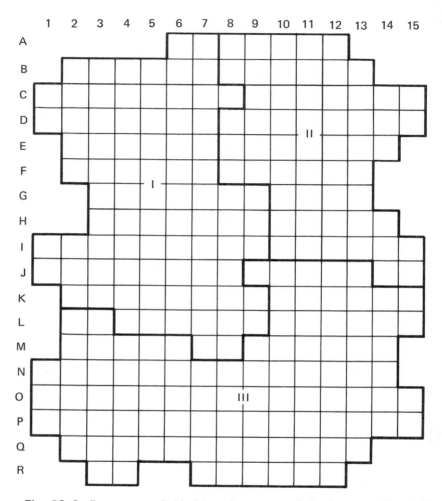

Fig. 12–3. Forest area divided into three unequal-sized strata. All sampling units are .5 acre.

The analysis of the data obtained from stratified random sampling is summarized below for the situation where the plots or strips are all of a uniform size as illustrated by Fig. 12–3.

Given:

M = number of strata in the population

n = total number of sampling units measured for all strata

n_j = total number of sampling units measured in the jth stratum

N = total number of sampling units in the population

N_j = total number of sampling units in the jth stratum

X_{ij} = the quantity X measured on the ith sampling unit of the jth stratum

$\bar{x}_j$ = the mean of X for the jth stratum

$\bar{x}$ = the estimated mean of X for the population

P_j = proportion of the total forest area in the jth stratum $= \dfrac{N_j}{N}$

x = estimated value of X for the population

$s_j{}^2$ = the variance of X for the jth stratum

$s_{\bar{x}}{}^2$ = estimated variance of the mean for the population

$s_x{}^2$ = estimated variance of x

The estimate of the mean per stratum is:

$$\bar{x}_j = \frac{\sum\limits_{i=1}^{n} X_{ij}}{n_j} \tag{12-30}$$

The estimate of the mean for the population is:

$$\bar{x} = \frac{\sum\limits_{j=1}^{M} N_j \bar{x}_j}{N} = \sum_{j=1}^{M} P_j \bar{x}_j \tag{12-31}$$

The estimate of the total for X for the entire population is:

$$x = \sum_{j=1}^{M} N_j \bar{x}_j$$

or:

$$x = N\bar{x} \tag{12-32}$$

The variance for each stratum in the population, $s_j{}^2$, is calculated as described for simple random sampling. The variance of the mean for the population is then calculated from:

$$s_{\bar{x}}{}^2 = \frac{1}{N^2} \sum_{j=1}^{M} \left[\frac{N_j{}^2 s_j{}^2}{n_j} \left(\frac{N_j - n_j}{N_j} \right) \right] \tag{12-33}$$

If the population consists of strata sufficiently large that the finite correction factor is insignificant or information is available on the relative sizes of the strata, then we can estimate the variance from:

$$s_{\bar{x}}{}^2 = \sum_{j=1}^{M} P_j{}^2 \frac{s_j{}^2}{n_j} \tag{12-34}$$

The standard error of the total estimate of x is then:

$$s_x{}^2 = N^2 s_{\bar{x}}{}^2 \tag{12-35}$$

The n_j sampling units actually chosen and measured per stratum should not be used to estimate the relative size of a stratum. Proportions in the strata should be estimated *a priori* to the actual sampling.

12–8.1. Estimation of Number of Sampling Units. To estimate the number of sampling units needed, it is necessary to have preliminary information on the variability of the strata in the population, and to choose an allowable error and probability level similar to that described for simple random sampling. With this information, the intensity of sampling can be estimated. The total number of sampling units can then be allocated to the different strata either by proportional or optimum allocation.

In proportional allocation, the number of sampling units in a stratum, out of the total sample, is in proportion to the area of the stratum. In optimum allocation, the number of sampling units per stratum is proportional to the standard error of the stratum weighted by area. Optimum allocation will give the smallest standard error for a stratified population when a given total of sampling units are taken. If we wish to get the most precise estimate of the population mean for the expenditure of money, then optimum allocation should be used. The allocation can be done either if the costs of sampling units in all strata are equal or if they differ.

Using proportional allocation, advance knowledge of the variability in the several strata is desirable to determine the total sample size. Where no information on the variability of the individual strata is available, it is necessary to estimate the total sample size for the entire population as though simple random sampling was being employed.

Using proportional allocation, the determination of sample size, n, for a given precision when information on variability per strata is available is:

$$n = \frac{t^2 \sum\limits_{j=1}^{M} p_j s_j{}^2}{(AE)^2 + \dfrac{t^2 \sum\limits_{j=1}^{M} p_j s_j{}^2}{N}} \qquad (12\text{--}36)$$

and:

$$n_j = p_j n \qquad (12\text{--}37)$$

If the population can be considered infinite, then:

$$n = \frac{t^2 \sum\limits_{j=1}^{M} p_j s_j{}^2}{(AE)^2} \qquad (12\text{--}38)$$

Using optimum allocation, the determination of sample size, n, with specified precision is shown below for the simplest case when costs per sampling unit are the same in all strata. The sampling intensity is changed in each stratum, according to its variability, to achieve a given precision with the smallest possible number of sampling units.

$$n = \frac{t^2 \left(\sum_{j=1}^{M} p_j s_j \right)^2}{(AE)^2 + \dfrac{t^2 \sum\limits_{j=1}^{M} p_j s_j^2}{N}} \qquad (12\text{--}39)$$

(for a finite population)

and:

$$n_j = \frac{p_j s_j}{\sum\limits_{j=1}^{M} p_j s_j} \, n \qquad (12\text{--}40)$$

If the population can be considered infinite, then:

$$n = \frac{t^2 \left(\sum_{j=1}^{M} p_j s_j \right)^2}{(AE)^2} \qquad (12\text{--}41)$$

For the determination of sample size by optimum allocation when the costs per sampling unit vary per stratum, or if the total cost of the inventory is fixed, the student is referred to Cochran (1963).

Frequently, the use of stratified random sampling may result in the boundary lines of strata passing through the uniform sampling units near strata boundaries, resulting in varying areas tallied. This is analogous to the situation, described in Section 12–7.1, for simple random sampling. When this occurs, ratio estimation or regression procedures as described by Cochran (1963) and Loetsch and Haller (1964) should be used.

12–9. MULTISTAGE SAMPLING

In multistage sampling, a population consists of a list of sampling units (primary stage), each of which is made up of smaller units (second stage), which in turn could be made up of still smaller units (third stage). A random sample would be chosen from the primary units. A random subsample of the secondary units would then be taken in each of the selected primary units, and the procedure would be continued to the desired stage. This procedure is called multistage sampling in general. Two-stage sampling, the commonest application, which is discussed in this chapter, indicates the sampling stops at the secondary stage. For example, a forest to be inventoried might consist of numerous compartments that could be considered the primary units in a sampling design. Plots chosen in the selected compartments would then form the secondary units. Similarly, an inventory design using plots on randomly chosen lines or strips is a form of two-stage sampling. Another frequently used two-stage sampling design in forest inventory employs groups of plots or sampling points at randomly chosen locations.

Multistage sampling in forest inventory is not restricted to fixed-area sampling units but can also be employed with variable plot procedures. Thus, a series of primary locations could be randomly chosen in a forest and, at each location, a number of secondary points chosen for selection of trees using the variable plot procedure. In all cases the group of secondary units selected within each of the primary units can be referred to as a cluster.

Multistage sampling has the principal advantage of concentrating the measurement work close to the locations of the chosen primary sampling units, rather than spreading it over the entire forest area to be inventoried. This is of advantage when it is difficult and costly to locate and get to the ultimate sampling unit, while it is comparatively easy and cheap to select and reach the first-stage unit. In these cases it is advantageous to·reduce the unproductive and costly expenditure of time between secondary sampling units. Another advantage of two-stage sampling is the likely reduction in non-sampling errors by closer supervision and control of field work when sampling units are concentrated in fewer locations. Two-stage sampling frequently yields estimates of a required precision at lower costs than for mono-stage sampling.

To permit the calculation of unbiased estimates of means and standard errors, random selection of sampling units at all stages should be used. It would also be possible to select primary units such as forest compartments with probability proportional to their sizes and then choose secondary units on a random basis.

Frequent use is made of systematic selection in two-stage sampling (see Section 12–12). A common design employed in forest inventory utilizes randomly chosen primary sampling units but then systematically selects the secondary units within them. Examples are random lines or geometric figures with systematic plot locations or clusters of plots in a fixed pattern around a randomly located point. Fixed clusters of this type do not permit a valid measure of within-cluster variation. However a valid estimate of the sampling error may be·calculated on the variation between first-stage units. The entire cluster would have to be considered as the ultimate sampling unit. In many instances analyses are carried out as though the systematically sampled cluster consisted of randomly chosen plots with the knowledge that the estimate of within-cluster variation may well be biased.

In two-stage sampling, m sampling units are selected from the M primary units of the population as a first stage. From each of the selected m units, n secondary units are then chosen from the population of N secondary units within each primary sampling unit. Note that if all M primary units are selected, the design is equivalent to stratified random sampling.

The most common cases encountered using two-stage sampling in forest inventory are:

1. All primaries of equal size containing equal numbers of secondaries of uniform size—see Fig. 12-4 (a).
2. Primaries of unequal sizes containing varying numbers of secondary units of uniform size—see Fig. 12-4 (b).
3. Primaries of unequal size, containing varying numbers of secondary units of variable size—see Fig. 12-4 (c).

Case 3 frequently occurs in forest inventory since uniform-sized primary units falling on forest or strata boundaries will be divided. The analysis requires the use of ratio estimation.

Only case 1 will be discussed here. The student is referred to Cochran (1963) for analyses of cases 2 and 3. The formulas for estimates of the means, total, and their variances are shown below:

where:

M = total number of primary sampling units in the population
N = the number of secondary units per primary, equal for all primaries
m = the number of primary units in the sample
n = the number of secondary units per primary in the sample, equal for all primaries
X_{ij} = the quantity, e.g., volume, measured on the ith secondary unit in the jth primary
$\bar{x}_j$ = the estimate of the mean of X for the jth primary unit
x_j = the estimate of the total of X for the jth primary unit
x = the estimate of the total of X for the entire forest
$\bar{x}$ = the estimate of the mean of X for the entire forest
$s_{\bar{x}}^2$ = estimate of the variance of the mean for the entire forest
s_X^2 = estimate of the variance of the total for the entire forest

The estimate of the population mean is:

$$\bar{x} = \frac{1}{mn} \sum_{j=1}^{m} \sum_{i=1}^{n} X_{ij} \qquad (12\text{--}42)$$

The estimate of the variance of the mean is:

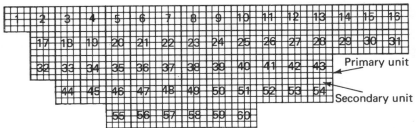

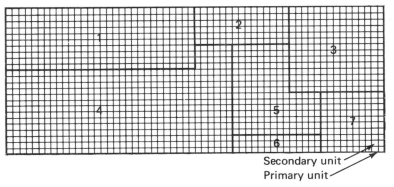

(a) Equal-sized primary units containing equal numbers of secondaries of uniform size.

(b) Unequal-sized primaries containing varying numbers of secondary units of uniform size.

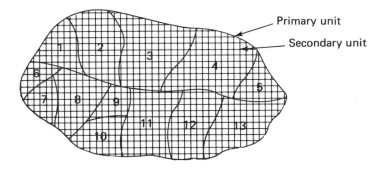

(c) Unequal-sized primary units containing varying numbers of secondary units of variable size.

Fig. 12–4. Division of forest area into primary units for two-stage sampling.

$$s_{\bar{x}}^2 = \left(1 - \frac{m}{M}\right)\frac{s_B^2}{m} + \left(1 - \frac{mn}{MN}\right)\frac{s_W^2}{mn} \qquad (12\text{--}43)$$

where:

s_B^2 = estimate of the variance between the means of the secondary sampling units within primaries

s_W^2 = estimate of the variance within the groups of secondary sampling units

The values for these estimates can be most easily obtained from an analysis of variance as follows:

Source of variation	DF	Sum of Squares	Mean Square
Between primaries	$m - 1$	SS_{between}	$\dfrac{SS_{\text{between}}}{m - 1} = s_b^2 = s_W^2 + ns_B^2$
Within primaries	$m(n - 1)$	SS_{within}	$\dfrac{SS_{\text{within}}}{m(n - 1)} = s_W^2$
Total	$mn - 1$	SS_{total}	

Therefore:

$$s_B^2 = \frac{s_b^2 - s_W^2}{n} = \frac{s_W^2 + ns_B^2 - s_W^2}{n} \qquad (12\text{--}44)$$

The sums of squares for the analysis of variance table can be found as follows:

$$SS_{\text{between}} = \frac{\sum\limits_{j=1}^{m}\left(\sum\limits_{i=1}^{n} X_{ij}\right)^2}{n} - \frac{\left(\sum\limits_{j=1}^{m}\sum\limits_{i=1}^{n} X_{ij}\right)^2}{nm} \qquad (12\text{--}45)$$

$$SS_{\text{within}} = \sum\limits_{j=1}^{m}\sum\limits_{i=1}^{n} X_{ij}^2 - \frac{\sum\limits_{j=1}^{m}\left(\sum\limits_{i=1}^{n} X_{ij}\right)^2}{n} \qquad (12\text{--}46)$$

When the number of primary units in the population is large, the formula for the variance of the mean can be reduced to:

$$s_{\bar{x}}^2 = \frac{s_b^2}{mn} = \frac{s_B^2}{m} + \frac{s_W^2}{mn} \qquad (12\text{--}47)$$

Then:

$$x_j = \frac{N}{n}\sum\limits_{i=1}^{n} X_{ij} \qquad (12\text{--}48)$$

$$x = \frac{M}{m}\sum\limits_{j=1}^{m} x_j \qquad (12\text{--}49)$$

$$s_X{}^2 = M^2 N^2 s_{\bar{x}}{}^2 \tag{12-50}$$

Estimates of the numbers of sampling units at the two stages can be made as shown below:

$$n = \sqrt{\frac{c_1}{c_2} \frac{s_W{}^2}{s_B{}^2}} \tag{12-51}$$

where:

n = optimum number of secondary units per primary
c_1 = cost of establishing a primary unit
c_2 = additional cost of establishing and measuring a secondary unit

$s_W{}^2$ and $s_B{}^2$ = estimates from a preliminary sample

Then:

$$m = \frac{t^2 \left(s_B{}^2 + \dfrac{s_W{}^2}{n} \right)}{(AE)^2 + \dfrac{1}{M} \left(s_B{}^2 + \dfrac{s_W{}^2}{N} \right)} \tag{12-52}$$

or, for an infinite population:

$$m = t^2 \frac{\left(s_B{}^2 + \dfrac{s_W{}^2}{n} \right)}{(AE)^2} \tag{12-53}$$

where:

m = the number of primary units required for an estimate of the mean with a given precision
AE = a chosen allowable error
t = Student's t for a chosen probability level

We can estimate the number of primary units required to obtain optimum precision when we have a fixed total amount of money available for the inventory. It is first necessary to estimate the optimum number of secondary units per primary as above. Then the number of primary units which should be taken is:

$$m = \frac{c}{c_1 + n c_2} \tag{12-54}$$

12–10. MULTIPHASE SAMPLING

Multiphase sampling finds numerous applications in forest inventory. The most used adaptation, which will be covered here, utilizes two phases and is often referred to as double sampling.

In double sampling an estimate of one variable is obtained by utilizing its relationship to another. The method is of most interest when information on the principal variable is costly and difficult to obtain, whereas the secondary and related variable can be more easily and cheaply observed. Thus, the aim of double sampling is to reduce the number of measurements of the costly variable without sacrificing precision of the estimate.

The general procedure in double sampling is that in a first phase a large random sample is taken of a secondary or auxiliary variable, X, which will yield a precise estimate of its population mean or total. In a second phase, a random subsample is taken from the previous sample and on these sampling units measurements are taken of the principal variable, Y. Note that the first and second phases are mutually dependent since the measurements in the secondary phase are taken from a portion of the sampling units of the first phase. Thus we have a small sample on which both the auxiliary and principal variables, X and Y, have been measured. With these data a regression can be developed between the two variables which can be utilized with the large sample of the auxiliary variable to make an estimate of the mean and total for the principal variable.

The relationship of Y and X may have one of numerous forms. For illustrative purposes a simple linear relationship will be demonstrated. However, it is well to bear in mind that in many instances a curvilinear relationship may be required.

An example of double sampling in forest inventory is the procedure using a combination of aerial photographic interpretation and field plots. The first phase of sampling consists of estimating the volumes on aerial photographs of a large number of relatively inexpensive sampling units employing photo-interpretation and measurement techniques. In the second phase, a subsample of these plots is selected and visited in the field for direct determination of their volumes. This subsample is much smaller since field plots are more expensive than photo plots. A regression is then prepared between field-plot volumes and photo-plot volumes permitting a corrected volume estimate to be made for the large, inexpensive sample of the first phase.

In double sampling the corrected estimate is obtained from a regression of the form:

$$\bar{y}_{\text{reg}} = \bar{y}_m + b(\bar{x}_n - \bar{x}_m) \tag{12-55}$$

where:

$\bar{y}_{\text{reg}}$ = regression estimate of the mean of Y (principal variable) from double sampling

$\bar{y}_m$ = estimate of the mean of Y from the second, small sample

$\bar{x}_n$ = estimate of the mean of X (auxiliary variable) from the first, large sample

$\bar{x}_m$ = estimate of the mean of X from the second, small sample

b = the linear regression coefficient

n = number of sampling units in the first, large sample

m = number of sampling units in the second, small sample

The regression coefficient is calculated from:

$$b = \frac{\sum_{i=1}^{m} (X_i - \bar{x}_m)(Y_i - \bar{y}_m)}{\sum_{i=1}^{m} (X_i - \bar{x}_m)^2} = \frac{\sum_{i=1}^{m} X_i Y_i - \dfrac{\sum_{i=1}^{m} X_i \sum_{i=1}^{m} Y_i}{m}}{\sum_{i=1}^{m} X_i^2 - \dfrac{\left(\sum_{i=1}^{m} X_i\right)^2}{m}} \qquad (12\text{--}56)$$

where:

X_i = the quantity X measured on the ith sampling unit of the second, small sample

Y_i = the quantity Y measured on the ith sampling unit of the second, small sample

The estimate of the variance of the regression estimate is then:

$$s_{\bar{y}\text{reg}}^2 = \frac{s_{y\cdot x}^2}{m} + \frac{s_{y\cdot x}^2(\bar{x}_n - \bar{x}_m)^2}{\sum_{i=1}^{m} (X_i - \bar{x}_m)^2} + \frac{s_y^2 - s_{y\cdot x}^2}{n} \qquad (12\text{--}57)$$

For finite populations the correction factor can be applied and in this case the first two terms of the expression are multiplied by $1 - \dfrac{m}{M}$ and the last term by $1 - \dfrac{n}{N}$. N represents the total number of sampling units in the first phase of double sampling (large sample).

The values for insertion in the formula for the variance are calculated from:

$$s_{y\cdot x}^2 = \frac{\sum_{i=1}^{m} (Y_i - \bar{y}_m)^2 - b^2 \sum_{i=1}^{m} (X_i - \bar{x}_m)^2}{m - 2} \qquad (12\text{--}58)$$

$$s_y^2 = \frac{\sum_{i=1}^{m} (Y_i - \bar{y}_m)^2}{m - 1} = \frac{\sum_{i=1}^{m} Y_i^2 - \dfrac{\left(\sum_{i=1}^{m} Y_i\right)^2}{m}}{m - 1} \qquad (12\text{--}59)$$

Frequently, the middle term in equation 12–57 is dropped under the assumption that the difference between $\bar{x}_n$ and $\bar{x}_m$ is negligible. Using this assumption, Loetsch and Haller (1964) show a procedure for estimating the optimum number of sampling units in the two phases.

Double sampling can also be carried out using ratio estimates, remembering that the ratio estimate is a conditioned regression in which the relationship between the two variables, X and Y, is such that a zero value of X means a zero value of Y (Cochran, 1963).

12–11. SAMPLING WITH VARYING PROBABILITIES

Forest inventory sampling with unequal probability of selection for the sampling units has become increasingly important in recent years. Indeed, some recent advances in forest inventory are based precisely on the application of sampling theory with varying probabilities of selection. The "Bitterlich" or "variable plot" method and the procedure called "three-P," or sampling with probability proportional to prediction, discussed in Chapter 14, are applications of this aspect of sampling theory.

The sampling units which constitute a population are often of unequal size in forest inventory work. For example, a forest area may consist of variable-sized compartments or stands which can be designated as the sampling units. Similarly, if the trees on a forest area are considered the sampling units, evidently there will be a range in their sizes as could be expressed by dbh, basal area, height, etc. When the sampling units are of unequal size, selecting the sample with probability proportional to the size of the units (often called p.p.s. sampling) will give more efficient estimates in terms of smaller standard errors. The methodology of sampling with probability proportional to size is covered in Chapter 14.

The size charcteristic of the sampling unit affecting the probability of selection may be the same parameter under investigation or it may be different. As an example of different variables, the volume of timber may be the required estimate for a forest composed of varying-sized compartments in which the probability of selecting a compartment will be proportional to its area. Basal area estimation by the horizontal point sampling method is an example of the variable to be estimated and the size characteristic determining probability of selection being the same.

It should be apparent that *a priori* knowledge of the sizes of the sampling units is necessary for a determination of the probabilities of selection of each unit. In the example of a forest of varying-sized compartments, the area of each compartment would have to be known. In the variable plot method, the size of each possible sampling unit, the tree, and its probability of selection is known by determining it on the ground.

After the selection of sampling units is made, then the parameter to be investigated is measured on the selected units. Thus, after several compartments of varying sizes had been selected from a forest based on their areas to form the sample, then the volumes of timber on each would be observed. In horizontal point sampling, if the tree is selected its measurement is taken, if rejected it is passed by. For basal area determination the measurement reduces merely to a count of the trees. For estimation of other tree characteristics, additional measurements would be required.

12–12. NON-RANDOM SAMPLING

In forest inventory work, two applications of non-random sampling can be utilized: selective and systematic sampling.

12–12.1. Selective Sampling. Selective sampling consists of choosing samples according to the subjective judgment of the observer. The observer may have a set of rules as a guide as to what kind of sample he should select. Within the framework of these rules, he then selects what appears to him to be a good sample. Selected sampling may give good approximations of population parameters, but there are several deficiencies weighing against its employment. Human choice is too often prejudiced and colored by individual opinion with the result that estimates are likely to be biased. In addition, selected samples will not yield a measure of the reliability of the estimate since probability theory is based on the laws of chance. Selective sampling has been used at times in timber volume estimation, especially prior to a recognition of the application of sampling theory to forest inventory. For example, the timber estimator would reconnoiter a forest area and select what appeared to him to be one or more unit areas of average stand conditions. The measurement of these units would then be considered representative of the entire tract.

12–12.2. Systematic Sampling. In systematic sampling, the sampling units are spaced at fixed intervals throughout the population. Forest inventories using a systematic sampling design have advantages which explain their frequent use. They provide good estimates of population means and totals by spreading the sample over the entire population. They are usually faster and cheaper to execute than designs based on probability sampling since the choice of sampling units is mechanical and uniform, eliminating the need for a random selection process. Travel between successive sampling units is easier since fixed directional bearings are followed and the resulting travel time consumed is usually less than that required for locating randomly selected units. The size of the population need not be known since every unit occurring at a fixed interval is chosen after an initial point has been selected. The sampling then continues until no further sampling units are found. In addition, mapping can be carried out concurrently on the ground since the field party traverses the area in a systematic gridiron pattern. In forest inventory work the systematic distribution of sampling units can be used with fixed-area plots or strips and also in locating the sampling points or lines in the variable plot application of p.p.s. sampling.

Since the units for a systematic sample are fixed at some regular interval, there will be a fixed set of possible samples. If a sampling interval,

k, is chosen, there will be k possible samples. For the mean of a systematic sample to be an unbiased estimate some form of random choice must be incorporated into the sampling process. The only randomization possible is the selection of one of the fixed sets of systematic samples. Which set chosen will depend on the selection of the initial sampling unit in the population.

The initial sampling unit can be randomly chosen out of the entire population of units or it may be randomly selected from the first k units in the population. In either case, once the first unit is chosen all following units will be selected at intervals of k units.

Many forest inventories use another starting procedure in the interest of simplicity, with the assumption that any bias in the resulting estimate of the mean will be negligible. Thus the start of a set of systematically distributed sampling units is frequently established at some easily accessible arbitrarily chosen point in the forest.

12–12.3. Sampling Error for a Systematic Inventory. If the total population of sampling units in a forest were randomly distributed, exhibiting no pattern of variation, then a systematic sample would be equivalent to a random sample, and the random sampling formulas would be applicable for estimating the sampling error. The failure of a systematic distribution of sampling units to satisfy requirements of randomness is especially the case when working with biological populations as in sampling a forest for an inventory. In biological populations the components are rarely, if ever, arranged completely independently of each other but, rather, show a systematic or periodic variation from place to place. If sampling units are systematically selected, then variation in the observed values may no longer be ascribable to randomness if the interval between sampling units happens to coincide with the pattern of population variation.

The larger the forest area inventoried, the greater is the amount of variation that can be expected and the more likelihood that a systematic sample will give a better estimate of the mean than a completely random sample. Even for a stratified population, a systematic sample will probably yield a better estimate of the mean if the strata are large and with considerable variation. As the homogeneity of the defined strata increases, the estimates from a random and systematic sample will tend to agree.

Fundamentally, the reason a systematic sample will not yield a valid estimate of the sampling error is that variance computations require a minimum of two randomly selected sampling units. A systematic sample (the entire set of units) really consists of a single selection from the population. The sampling interval, k, divides the population in k clusters or sets of n sampling units and then only one of these clusters constitutes the sample.

Various methods to approximate the sampling error of a systematic sample have been devised. The systematic sample of equidistant sampling units can be considered as a simple or unstratified random sample and the sampling error computed as for a random sample. Osborne (1942) has shown that the sampling error computed in this way estimates the maximum sampling error which may considerably overestimate the actual sampling error. A simple and useful procedure to approximate more closely the true sampling error is the method of successive differences described in the following sections. For other procedures the student is referred to Yates (1946, 1948, and 1949), Finney (1947, 1948, 1950, and 1953) and Meyer (1956). However, it remains that there is no satisfactory and valid method for estimating the sampling error of a systematic sample.

Shiue (1960) has proposed a method of systematic sampling which maintains the advantages of systematic sampling and also provides a means of validly estimating the sampling error. With this method, several systematic samples are taken, with the initial sampling unit chosen randomly for each start. Using a line plot procedure, the first sample of systematically located plots constitutes the first cluster. Another systematic sample would be the second cluster, etc. Based on these clusters, estimates of the mean plot volume and its sampling error can be computed. To avoid a large t value and to maintain a small confidence interval for a given probability level, at least five random starts should be used.

12–12.4. Systematic Strip Sampling. Using strips as the sampling unit, the systematic distribution is accomplished by first dividing the forest area into N strips of uniform size. Sampling units would then be taken at intervals of every k^{th} strip to form the sample of n strips. Figure 12–5 shows a forest area divided into 50 strips of uniform length. The selection of n strips at a sampling interval of k strips can be carried out in two ways:

1. A random selection of a number from 1 to N can be made and the corresponding strip chosen as the initial sampling unit. Sampling units at the interval, k, are then taken in both directions from this initial strip. A practical way of carrying this out is to select some random number between 1 and N, divide by the interval, k, and obtain the remainder of the division. This remainder will have the value between 1 and k. Then select the strip with this number as the first sampling unit. All subsequent strips at intervals of k are then selected.
2. Randomly select a number between 1 and k for the first strip. All subsequent strips are taken at intervals of k strips.

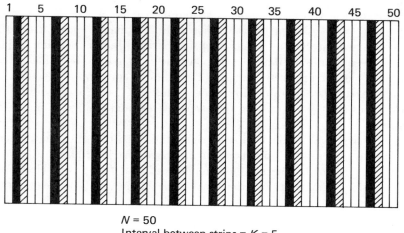

$N = 50$
Interval between strips $= K = 5$

Methods for selecting systematic sample:

1) Random number chosen between 1 and $N = 38$

$$\frac{38}{5} = 7\frac{3}{5}$$

Start at strip equivalent to remainder 3, and every fifth strip chosen thereafter. Indicated by crosshatching.

2) Random number chosen between 1 and $K = 2$.
Start at strip 2 and every fifth strip chosen thereafter. Indicated by shading.

Fig. 12–5. Forest area divided into strips for systematic strip inventory.

Both procedures will yield the same probable number of systematic samples. The first procedure will yield an unbiased estimate of the mean, whereas the second procedure may give a slightly biased result if the value of N is not an exact multiple of k. The first procedure should be used if possible. The second procedure, however, must be used if the size of the population is not known, as may occur in sampling a forest where no map is available.

It will be more often the case that the forest is irregular in shape rather than square or rectangular. If the area is then divided into strips of equal width, the strips will differ in length and consequently in their areas. Thus, the possible systematic samples which could be obtained by taking every k^{th} strip may differ in size. Zenger (1964) has described a method which draws a systematic sample in such a way that the probability of selection of a strip is proportional to its length.

Applying strip sampling, the field party starts from a base line, or one side of the tract, and runs a straight strip on a campass bearing across the tract stopping at the other side. The party then offsets the predetermined interval and runs back to the base line or boundary. The procedure continues until all the strips in the sample have been measured. The timber occurring on the strips is tallied and represents the sample of the entire stand. Separate tally sheets may be kept for the different forest types or stand classes so that separate estimates may be made for them.

It is desirable to orient strips at right angles to the drainage pattern in order to increase the likelihood of having the strip transect all stand conditions. In North America the common width of strip is one chain (66 feet) or less. The width of the strip and the interval between strips determine the intensity or percentage of the total area tallied. The intensity of a systematic strip design is expressed by:

$$P = (W/D) \ 100 \qquad (12\text{–}60)$$

where:

P = intensity of inventory in per cent
W = width of strip in a given unit
D = distance between strips in same units as W

The intensity of a systematic design using 1-chain wide strips spaced at intervals of 10 chains is then $\frac{1}{10}$ (100) = 10 per cent. For a given intensity, narrow strips at closer spacing will give more uniform distribution and better coverage of the stand area than fewer strips that are wider but more distantly spaced, although the cost will be greater.

When the strips are all of equal size, the estimate of the population mean is often calculated from equation 12–5 and the sampling error from equation 12–8 under the assumption that the strips constitute a random sample.

A method of approximating the actual sampling error utilizes the differences between pairs of successive sampling units. Since there are n strips, there will be $n - 1$ differences. The estimate of the variance of the mean is then given by:

$$s_{\bar{x}}^2 = \frac{\sum\limits_{i=1}^{n-1} (X_{i+1} - X_i)^2}{2n(n-1)} \left(\frac{N-n}{N} \right)$$

$$= \frac{(X_2 - X_1)^2 + (X_3 - X_2)^2 + (X_4 - X_3)^2 + \ldots + (X_n - X_{n-1})^2}{2n(n-1)}$$

$$\left(\frac{N-n}{N} \right) \qquad (12\text{–}61)$$

If the sampling units are not of equal size as would occur in a strip sample of an irregular-shaped forest area, the ratio method of estimation can be used. Thus, an estimate of the area of each sampling unit, X_i, and the observation, such as volume, on the units, V_i, are required to obtain the ratio estimate as described in Section 12–7. An estimate of the variance of the ratio estimate, $\bar{r}$, is given by:

$$s_{\bar{r}}^2 = \frac{N - n}{2Nn(n - 1)\bar{x}^2}$$

$$\left[\sum_{i=1}^{n-1} (V_{i+1} - V_i)^2 - 2\bar{r} \sum_{i=1}^{n-1} (V_{i+1} - V_i)(X_{i+1} - X_i) \right.$$

$$\left. + \bar{r}^2 \sum_{i=1}^{n-1} (X_{i+1} - X_i)^2 \right] \quad (12\text{--}62)$$

12–12.5. Systematic Plot Sampling. If sampling units such as plots or points are used, the sample is systematic in two dimensions, i.e., the sampling units are at the chosen interval, k, in the two directions normal to each other. The following discussion pertains to systematic sampling with fixed area plots. A discussion of the distribution of sampling points is given in Chapter 14. As with the strip method, there is a fixed possible number of samples which is determined by the sampling interval chosen. Figure 12–6, illustrating a systematic distribution of plots, shows a rectangular area made up of 60 vertical columns and 40 horizontal rows forming a population of 2,400 fixed-area units. If we choose a sampling interval of $k = 10$ in each direction, there will be $(10)(10) = 100$ possible independent samples. The selection of sample plots at a sampling interval of k can be carried out in a manner analogous to those described for the strip method. The only difference is that there are two dimensions instead of one.

1. A random selection of a number from 1 to the total number of columns is first made. The same procedure is followed for a random selection of one of the rows. The two random numbers indicate the coordinates of the starting point for the sample grid.
2. Starting at one corner of the tract, a random selection is made from the first k by k grid. All subsequent sample plots are then taken at the consistent interval of k in both directions.

The more common case will be a forest of irregular shape as shown in Fig. 12–7. The first method of selecting a sample requires establishing an imaginary boundary to completely enclose the area. The initial unit can then be chosen in a fashion similar to that used for Fig. 12–7. Since the number of columns and rows are not exact multiples of the sampling interval, the size of a sample will vary depending on the initial point chosen and the shape of the tract. In this case, 19 sample plots form the

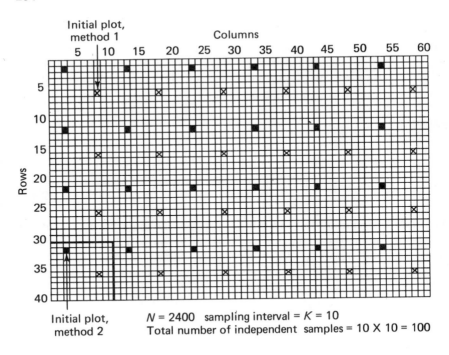

$N = 2400$ sampling interval $= K = 10$
Total number of independent samples $= 10 \times 10 = 100$

Methods for selecting systematic sample:
   1) Random selection for column = 28
      $\frac{28}{10} = 2 \frac{8}{10}$. The remainder is 8, therefore start at column 8

      Random selection for row = 16.
      $\frac{16}{10} = 1 \frac{6}{10}$. The remainder is 6, therefore start at row 6.

      The 24 sampling units are indicated by x's.

   2) Choosing the lower lefthand 10 by 10 grid, one of the 100 sampling
      units is randomly selected. The 24 sampling units are indicated by
      shading.

Fig. 12–6. Systematic distribution of equi-spaced plots for forest inventory.

sample. Using the other method of selecting the sample, we can arbitrarily choose the lower left-hand corner of the tract and out of the first 10 by 10 square randomly select one unit. All subsequent units will then be selected at the k by k interval resulting in $n = 18$.

When sampling units are spaced on an equidistant grid, the calculation of mean, total, and their standard errors is often carried out as though the units were randomly chosen. Loetsch and Haller (1964) demonstrate

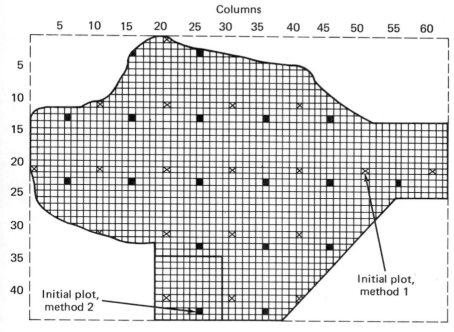

Sampling interval = K = 10
Total number of independent samples = 10 × 10 = 100

Methods for selecting systematic sample:
1) By selecting random numbers the initial plot is column 51, row 21. All subsequent plots are taken at intervals of 10 in both directions. The 19 sampling units are indicated by X's.

2) Choosing the lower left hand 10 by 10 grid, the sampling unit at column 26, row 43 is randomly selected. The 18 sampling units are indicated by shading.

Fig. 12–7. Systematic distribution of equi-spaced plots for forest inventory of irregularly shaped area.

that taking the sum of the squared differences between successive sampling units of one of the two axes of the grid will yield a closer approximation of the true standard error. Thus, in Fig. 12–7, the differences between successive sampling units within columns 6, 16, 21, 31, 36, 41, 46, 51, and 56 would be taken. For each line of sampling plots, j, the sum of the squared differences is:

$$\sum_{i=1}^{n_j-1} (X_{(i+1)j} - X_{ij})^2$$

The approximation of the variance for all M lines of sample plots is then:

$$s_{\bar{x}}^2 = \frac{\sum\limits_{j=1}^{M} \sum\limits_{i=1}^{n_j-1} (X_{(i+1)j} - X_{ij})^2}{2n(n_j - 1)} \qquad (12\text{–}63)$$

For small samples the result should be multiplied by the finite correction factor $\left(\dfrac{N - n}{N}\right)$

For practical reasons, the equidistant spacing of sampling units is often dropped, resulting in the interval between lines being greater than between units. If this modification is used with fixed-area sampling units, the method is called line plot sampling. Numerous possible line plot distributions can be devised, depending on the size of the plot, distance between plots on a line, and the distance between lines. A line plot design can be drawn up using the following relationships:

$$Ap = PA \qquad (12\text{–}64)$$

$$n = Ap/a \qquad (12\text{–}65)$$

$$P = a/BL \qquad (12\text{–}66)$$

where:

A = total stand area
Ap = area of stand tallied
P = intensity of inventory as a decimal
a = area per plot in square units of B and L
n = number of plots
B = spacing between plots on a line in a given unit
L = spacing between lines in same units as B

For a 5 per-cent inventory using .2-acre plots and choosing a 10-chain spacing between lines, the distance between plots is:

$$B = a/PL = \frac{.2(43560)}{(.05)(10)(66)} = 264 \text{ feet} = 4 \text{ chains}$$

The design is shown in Fig. 12–8.

In the analysis of the resulting data, the standard error of the mean is often computed using a single degree of freedom for each of the plots. This can be done with some justification with a systematic sample on an equispaced grid. But with an uneven distribution of sampling units, the rationale for assuming each plot as an independent selection diminishes. A more tenable assumption is to treat the line of sampling units as a single unit and assume randomness only between the lines. If the number of units per line varies, the ratio estimation procedure can then be used. It is also possible to treat the sample as a two-stage design with the line

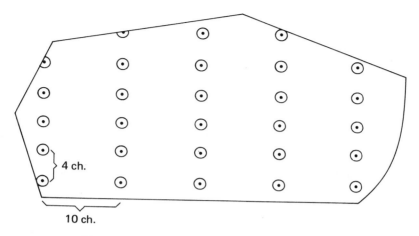

Five per cent line plot inventory using .2-acre
plots spaced 4 chains apart on lines 10 chains
apart.

Fig. 12–8. Systematic line plot inventory.

of units forming the primary unit and the units on lines comprising the
secondary units. It is worth remembering, however, that in this case
neither the primary nor secondary units have been randomly selected as
is required in two-stage sampling.

12–13. REPEATED SAMPLING IN FOREST INVENTORY

Repeated sampling (or sampling on successive occasions) in forest inventory has three objectives:

1. To estimate quantities and characteristics of the forest present at
   the first inventory.
2. To estimate quantities and characteristics of the forest present at
   the second inventory.
3. To estimate the changes in the forest during the intervening period.

The repetitive process can be continued and at the occasion of all subsequent inventories the previous inventory becomes the first and the new
inventory is the second.

Repeated sampling can be carried out in any of the four ways illustrated in Fig. 12–9 and described below. Of the four approaches, the third
—successive sampling with partial replacement—is the most efficient.

12–13.1. New Sample Drawn at Each Inventory. As shown in Fig.
12–9 (a), sampling units at occasion 2 are different from those at occa-

n_1 = sample at first inventory

n_2 = sample at second inventory

n_3 = m sampling units measured at both inventories (matched)

u = sampling units taken only at first inventory (unmatched)

n = sampling units taken only at second inventory (unmatched)

n_2 can be greater than, less than, or equal to n_1

$n_3 = 0$

(a) New sample drawn at each occasion.

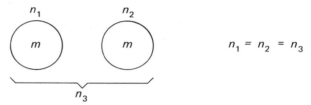

$n_1 = n_2 = n_3$

(b) Same sample remeasured on succeeding occasions.

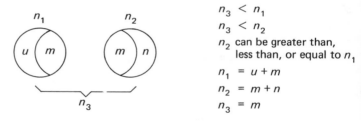

$n_3 < n_1$

$n_3 < n_2$

n_2 can be greater than, less than, or equal to n_1

$n_1 = u + m$

$n_2 = m + n$

$n_3 = m$

(c) Successive sampling with partial replacement.

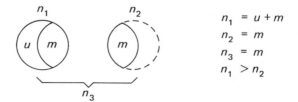

$n_1 = u + m$

$n_2 = m$

$n_3 = m$

$n_1 > n_2$

(d) Second sample a subsample of the first.

Fig. 12–9. Types of repeated sampling.

sion 1. The means, totals, and standard errors would be calculated separately as described in Section 12–7. The estimation of the change or growth would be the difference in the means for the two inventories. The estimate of the variance of this difference, s_d^2, is:

$$s_d^2 = \frac{s_x^2}{n_1} + \frac{s_y^2}{n_2} \tag{12–67}$$

where:

s_x^2 = variance at first inventory
s_y^2 = variance at second inventory
n_1 and n_2 = number of sampling units at first and second inventories

12–13.2. Same Sample Remeasured at Succeeding Occasions. The sampling units taken at the first inventory are remeasured at the second and all succeeding inventories as shown in Fig. 12–9 (b). This is the concept of permanent sample plots and the basis of the Continuous Forest Inventory (CFI) system developed in North America. The estimates of the means, totals, and standard errors at each inventory again would be found as for two separate inventories. Similarly, the differences between the means for each inventory would indicate the changes in the forest. However, since the same sampling units are taken on both occasions, then the standard error of the difference would be calculated for paired plots as:

$$s_d^2 = \frac{s_x^2 + s_y^2 - 2r_{xy}s_x s_y}{n} \tag{12–68}$$

The greater the correlation as expressed by r_{xy} between X and Y, the measurements at the first and second inventory, the greater the reduction in the variance. The correlation can be expected to be large for short periods. However, it has been demonstrated by Hool and Beers (1964) that the correlation may remain surprisingly high, even for a 15-year remeasurement interval.

12–13.3. Successive Sampling with Partial Replacement. At the second inventory, a portion of the initial sampling units are remeasured and new ones are taken as shown in Fig. 12–9 (c).

A detailed account of the development and application of this procedure to forest inventory is given by Ware and Cunia (1962), Cunia (1965), and Frayer (1966). Only a brief summary is presented here and the student is referred to the abovementioned references for an explanation of the statistical theory.

At the initial and second inventories, there are two kinds of sampling units as shown in Fig. 12–9 (c). They are:

u = sampling units measured only at the first inventory
m = sampling units measured at the first and second inventories
n = sampling units measured only at the second inventory.

From observations on these sampling units the quantities present at each inventory and the growth over the period can be calculated. Estimates at the initial inventory utilize data from all the u and m units measured. From the m units a relationship can be established between sampling unit volumes found at the initial and second inventories. A regression can then be determined and used to estimate the volumes of the u units at the second inventory and the volumes of the n units as they were at the initial inventory. As a result there are volume estimates for all units, some from direct measurement and others from a regression. The value of this procedure is that volume and growth estimates and their variances are obtained from all units, both temporary and permanent.

12–13.4. Sample at Second Inventory—Subsample of First.

At the second inventory a portion of the sampling units taken at the first inventory is remeasured as shown in Fig. 12–9 (d).

The estimate of the mean at the first inventory uses the data from the u and m units. At the second inventory, measurements are only taken on the m units. From these m units a relationship is again established between the volumes found on units measured at both the first and second inventories. The mean volume at the second inventory is then determined using the data from the n_1 units in a regression based on this relationship.

The growth over the inventory period is expressed as the difference between the overall mean at the initial inventory and the regression estimate for the second inventory.

13

Aerial Photographs in Forest Inventory Sampling

13–1. INTRODUCTION

Aerial photography is an extremely important tool in forest inventory and, whenever possible, it should be employed. The great advantages which can be gained in forest classification, mapping, area estimation, distribution of field sampling units, estimates of stand characteristics, and assistance in planning access by using aerial photographs should always be kept in mind in forest inventory planning. Inventory work can be carried out without the use of aerial photographs, but it will usually be less efficient and will restrict the inventory planner in designing his procedures. There is no single method of employing aerial photographs in forest inventory work. The forester has wide latitude in incorporating photo-interpretative and photogrammetric techniques into an inventory design.

The most common approach has been to utilize aerial photographs to prestratify a forest and then sample the various strata on the ground for detailed information. In addition to stratification, photo-interpretation and photogrammetric techniques have been developed which, in essence, permit the forester to sample the forest using the photographic images of the trees rather than the trees themselves on the ground. The photographic images do not provide the same amount of detail or accuracy of measurement that is attainable in the field, but the advantages of speed and lower cost may offset the approximate nature of the estimates, especially where a high order of accuracy is not essential.

The highlights of these techniques are covered briefly in this chapter. No attempt will be made here to explain the fundamentals of aerial photogrammetry and photo-interpretation or their application to forestry. The student is referred to the following references on this specialized subject: Manual of Photogrammetry (1966), Manual of Photographic Interpretation (1960), Manual of Color Aerial Photography (1967), Loetsch and Haller (1964), Spurr (1960), and Avery (1968).

13-2. FOREST CLASSIFICATION AND MAPPING

Aerial photo-interpretative and photogrammetric techniques provide excellent means for the preparation of planimetric, topographic, and forest stand maps rapidly, accurately, and cheaply. Maps of forest stands are a vital part of any inventory. The boundaries of forest types and other stand-condition classes can be delineated with greater ease and accuracy, within broad limits, from the stereoscopic examination of aerial photographs that can be done on the ground. Broad classifications, such as forest or non-forest, and coniferous, deciduous, or mixed forests, can easily be recognized with little training. Detailed classifications, such as forest types, can often be recognized from the pictorial elements of the photograph by more skilled photo-interpreters. Differences in the tone, texture, shadow, and outline make this a relatively easy task. It is usually not possible to identify species except under special circumstances as when large areas of pure stands occur or a particular species has some special characteristic, such as the tone, texture, or shape of its crown, or color, when color photographs are used, which distinguishes it from surrounding species. With the improvements in color photography, photo-interpretation of previously unrecognizable forest types and, in some cases, species identification has become feasible (Manual of Color Aerial Photography, 1967; Cooper and Smith, 1966; Aldrich, 1966).

Forest areas can also be subdivided by aerial photographic interpretation into stand classifications of height, relative age, or density. The correct identification of forest types or condition classes is largely dependent on the individual skill and experience of the photo-interpreter. A forester familiar with a region can recognize stand or vegetation characteristics, not only by the pictorial elements but also by the forest site.

A recently developed photogrammetric procedure which produces an "orthophotograph" holds considerable promise as an alternative to some of the older mapping techniques. An orthophotograph is a photographic representation of a portion of the earth's surface in an orthographic projection. It is produced by converting vertical perspective aerial photographs to the equivalent of orthographic photographs. The instrument which performs this conversion is called an orthophotoscope. The resulting orthophotographs can be treated as true maps showing planimetric information. It is often convenient to join the orthophotographs into an orthophotographic mosaic. A great advantage of the orthophotograph is that it not only contains the wealth of detail of a photograph but also has the positional accuracy of a map. Orthophotographs usually do not include contours as shown on topographic maps, but this feature can be shown if required.

Mosaics are worth mentioning here even though they are not truly maps. The conventional mosaic is an assemblage of portions of aerial photographs which have been matched together to form a continuous photographic representation of a part of the earth's surface. Because photographs are perspective views, the resulting assemblage incorporates the resulting image displacements and scale variation. However, a mosaic may serve as an excellent substitute for a map when its deficiencies are recognized or are of little importance.

13–3. AREA DETERMINATION

The areas of forest stands can be determined directly from aerial photographs or maps prepared from the photographs. This necessitates the delineation of the boundaries of the stands on the photographs or on the maps. Conventional methods, such as planimetering, weighing, grid counts, etc., covered in Chapter 6, can then be used to measure the areas. More accurate determinations will be obtained from maps rather than photographs since photographic scale variation and image displacements are eliminated or reduced in the preparation of maps. However, where the required accuracy of area determination is not too high and where the effect of scale change and image displacement on the photographs is not pronounced, acceptable area estimates can be made directly from the aerial photographs by treating them as equivalent to a map.

A second method of area estimation from aerial photographs utilizes sampling instead of total stand area determination. Sampling techniques for area estimation directly from aerial photographs are faster and cheaper for large forest tracts or where maps have not been previously prepared, because it is not necessary to delineate the boundaries of the forest area and its subdivisions on the photograph or show them on a map. Sampling for area determination can be accomplished by establishing a number of sampling units directly on the photographs showing the forest area and its strata. Sampling units may be plots or transect lines, either in a random or systematic distribution. Area determination from plot sampling is the most practical and the following section describes the procedure. For a discussion of area determination by transect sampling, see Loetsch and Haller (1964).

13–3.1. Areas by Plot Sampling. Using this procedure, a number of small sample plots are distributed on the photographs which cover the entire area under investigation. Each plot is then classified as falling in one of the previously defined strata or forest classes. Actually, a distribution of points is used, but it is often difficult to recognize forest conditions on a point and for this reason the classification is usually based on a small area or plot surrounding each point. Photographic plots will vary in size depending on the sample area on the ground which is considered necessary to define forest conditions. In North America this has often been .2-acre (.081 hectare) which at the commonly used scales of 1:10,000 to 1:20,000 results in a photographic plot of from .126 to .063 inch (3.2 to 1.6 millimeters).

The photographic plots are located in the central portion of each photograph, often referred to as the "effective area" to avoid sampling the same area twice. The effective area of a photograph depends on the overlap and sidelap of photographs in a flight line and for adjacent strips, Avery and Meyer (1962) define it as: "For any aerial photograph that is one of a series in a flight strip, that central part of the photograph delimited by the bisectors of overlaps with adjacent photographs." The definition can be extended for the photographs in adjacent flight lines. For simplicity, a systematic distribution of the sample plots is often used, although this may result in biased area determinations where large differences in elevation of the terrain occur. Scale variations will cause an oversampling for portions of a photograph showing terrain at higher elevations than the principal point and undersampling for areas at lower elevations. Several procedures have been proposed to eliminate this source of error but the most practical one consists of establishing the systematic grid and then correcting the area estimates based on a check of scale variation. If only one point per photograph is used as may occur in a very extensive survey, it can be placed at the nadir, or for practical purposes, at the principal point. This will minimize the effects of relief displacement and related scale change since image displacement is eliminated or small at the nadir and principal points.

A systematic distribution of plots has been found more practical than a random distribution and will usually give good estimates of the proportions. As a systematic sample, however, it will not yield valid estimates of the sampling error. Nevertheless, randomness is frequently assumed and a sampling error calculated. Similarly, the number of systematic sample plots for a required precision is often estimated from the random sampling formulas. One way of determining a valid sampling error is to take repeated systematic samples with random starts. This will yield repeated values of the proportion and can be used to estimate a mean and its variance.

The most convenient way of establishing a systematic distribution of plots is by placing a dot grid of transparent plastic over the photograph. Ideally, it should be positioned at random, although this is often abandoned in favor of a fixed position for convenience. All dots are considered the center of a small plot of fixed area and assigned to the appropriate forest class. The area in any class can then be found from the relationship:

$$\frac{\text{area in a stand class}}{\text{total area sampled}} = \frac{\text{number of plots in the stand class}}{\text{total number of plots for all classes}}$$

or:

$$\frac{a}{A} = \frac{n}{N} = p$$

and:

$$a = \frac{n}{N} A = pA \tag{13-1}$$

Since the total area must be known, the method provides a means of estimating proportions in the stand classes. The number of photo sample plots required for estimates of the areas in the various stand classes with a required precision may be found from:

$$n = \frac{pqt^2}{s_p{}^2} \tag{13-2}$$

where:

p = a preliminary estimate of the proportion of the area in a stand class or stratum

$q = 1 - p$

t = t value corresponding to the chosen probability level

s_p = a chosen allowable sampling error expressed as a decimal

For example, the number of photographic plots needed to estimate the percentage of an area in a given stratum with a probability of .95 and an allowable error of 1 per cent and roughly estimated as occupying 60 per cent of the total area is:

$$n = \frac{(.60)(.40)(1.96)^2}{(0.1)^2} = 9216$$

The number of photographic plots for each stand class should be calculated separately. The largest number of plots for any class should be used since this number should meet or exceed the sampling requirements for any class.

The actual sampling error of the proportion in any class can be determined after the photographic classification from:

$$s_p{}^2 = \frac{pq}{n-1} \qquad (13\text{--}3)$$

No finite correction factor is used since the number of possible points which could be selected is infinite.

A check of the photographic estimates should be made in the field and an adjustment carried out to correct for incorrect classification. The procedure is described in the following Section 13–4.

If the total area or area of a stratum covered by aerial photographs is unknown, it may be estimated by calculating the area represented by each point of a uniformly spaced grid. This area factor can be determined from the spacing between points and the scale of the photographs. The total number of points multiplied by the area factor will give an estimate of the total area.

13–4. ERRORS IN AERIAL PHOTOGRAPHIC AREA ESTIMATES

The sampling techniques for area estimates from aerial photographs yield estimates that may have errors due to incorrect photo-interpretation and photographic scale variation and image displacements due to topographic relief. Furthermore, these sources of error may occur simultaneously. When incorrect photo-interpretation has occurred, a photographic plot may be assigned to the wrong stratum. Using transects, the position of a boundary line intersection on a transect may be incorrectly located or a portion of a transect with correctly positioned boundaries may be assigned to the wrong stratum.

Topographic relief will affect area estimates from photographic plots or transects causing an overestimation of areas above a datum and an underestimation for areas at lower elevations than the datum. If there is little difference in elevation on a photograph or if image displacements are small, then this source of error is of minor importance.

To assess the effects of, and make adjustments for, photo-interpretation errors, scale change and relief displacement require field checking of a portion of the photo-interpretation results.

A plot sampling technique lends itself readily to field checking and adjustment and for this reason has been preferred in most inventory work. When the transect technique is used, field checking is more complicated unless the transect lines radiate from the nadir points of the photographs.

A detailed presentation of procedures for checking and adjustment of area estimates in inventory work using aerial photographs is given by Loetsch and Haller (1964). Only a brief discussion of checking and adjustment for errors in photo-interpretation using the plot sampling technique is given here. A check can be made by visiting at least thirty of the photographic plots for each stratum to determine if the photo plots were correctly assigned to the established strata. Usually, some of the plots will prove to have been incorrectly classified on the photographs, resulting in errors in the area estimates. The photographic area estimates must then be adjusted. As an example, suppose estimates of 50,000, 20,000, 10,000, and 5,000 acres had been made for the four stand classes A, B, C, and D of an area of 85,000 acres. A field check of 150, 60, 30, and 30 plots in these stand classes was carried out. The results of the check are summarized in Table 13–1.

Table 13–1
Results of Field Check

Stand class	N_j Number of photo plots	P_j Proportion of photo plots	n_j Number of plots field checked	n_{ji} Check plots in stand class				P_{ji} Proportion of check plots in stand class			
				A	B	C	D	A P_{j1}	B P_{j2}	C P_{j3}	D P_{j4}
A	11,800	.59	150	120	15	10	5	.80	.10	.07	.03
B	4,600	.23	60	3	55	2	1	.05	.92	.03	.00
C	2,400	.12	30	2	2	25	1	.07	.07	.83	.03
D	1,200	.06	30	0	2	2	26	.00	.07	.07	.86
M	20,000	1.00									

Using stand class A as an example, the adjusted proportion is calculated as follows:

$$p_A = \sum_{j=A}^{D} p_j p_{j1} \qquad (13\text{–}4)$$

Note that p_{j1} means the proportions of the other stand classes that are actually in stand class A.

Inserting the values from the table in the formula:

$$p_A = (.59)(.80) + (.23)(.05) + (.12)(.07) + (.06)(.00)$$
$$= .49$$

and the area in stand class A is:

$$area_A = (.49)(85,000) = 41,650 \text{ acres}$$

The adjustment would then be carried out similarly for the other stand classes.

The variance of the adjusted proportion for stand class A can then be calculated from the formula:

$$s_{p_A}{}^2 = p_j{}^2 \frac{p_{j1}(1 - p_{j1})}{n_j} + \frac{p_j p_{j1}{}^2 - (p_j p_{j1})^2}{N} \tag{13-5}$$

The variance of the adjusted proportion of stand class A can be calculated using Table 13–2.

Table 13–2

Calculations for Variance of Adjusted Proportions of Stand Classes

Stand class	P_j Proportion of photo plots	n_j	$P_j^2 \dfrac{P_{j_1}(1 - P_{j_1})}{n_j}$	$P_j P_{j_1}$	$P_j P_{j_1}^2$
A	.59	150	$(.59)^2 \dfrac{(.80)(.20)}{150} = .000371$	$(.59)(.80) = .4720$	.377600
B	.23	60	$(.23)^2 \dfrac{(.05)(.95)}{60} = .000042$	$(.23)(.05) = .0115$	.000575
C	.12	30	$(.12)^2 \dfrac{(.07)(.93)}{30} = .000031$	$(.12)(.07) = .0084$	.000588
D	.06	20	$(.06)^2 \dfrac{(.00)(1.00)}{20} = .000000$	$(.06)(.00) = .0000$	.000000
M	1.00	260	.000444	.4919	.378763

$$s_{p_A}{}^2 = .000444 + \frac{.378763 - (.4919)^2}{20,000}$$
$$= .000450$$
$$s_{p_A} = .021$$

The error of the area estimate adjusted for interpretation errors is:

$$(.021)(85,000) = 1,785 \text{ acres}$$

Similar calculations would be required for each of the other stand classes.

13–5. VOLUME ESTIMATES FROM AERIAL PHOTOGRAPHS

Three methods have been developed for making volume estimates directly from aerial photographs: individual tree volume estimation, stand volume estimation from stand measurement, and volumes from ocular comparisons with photographs of stands of known volume.

With these methods, sample plots are first located on the aerial photographs. Using the individual tree volume method, the height and crown diameter are measured and corresponding gross volumes read from a photographic volume table (see Chapter 9). The compilation of volumes on the plot is then analogous to ground inventory procedures. Using a stand volume approach, the average stand height, average crown diameter, and crown closure percentages can be measured on the photographic sample plots, and gross stand volumes per unit area can be read directly from a photographic stand volume table.

Rough, direct stand volume estimates can be made by examining the photographic appearance of a stand and comparing it to photographs or stereograms of stands of known volumes. A stereogram is a fixed pair or portion of a pair of photographs properly oriented for stereoscopic viewing. Selected plots in various timber types can be chosen on aerial photographs and a reference file of stereograms prepared to cover as wide a range of forest conditions as desired. These plots are then measured on the ground and detailed stand information is compiled. The volume of a stand appearing on an aerial photograph is then assumed to be the same as the volume for the stand on the stereogram to which it is most similar.

Direct photographic volume estimates have several important limitations. The estimate includes only trees whose crowns are visible in the photographs, possibly missing the volumes of trees in the understory. It is often difficult to recognize individual tree crowns and to measure tree heights, especially on photographs at small scales and for closed stands. The accuracy of measurement and photo-interpretation is also dependent on the skill and experience of the photo-interpreter. In addition, for commonly used scales of approximately 1:10,000 or smaller, no information on species, size, distribution, or amount of defect can be obtained from photographic volume estimates. With photographs of these scales, aerial photographic volume estimates cannot attain the accuracy of ground inventories. Recent tests on the use of large-scale 70 mm. photography, both color and black and white, taken from low-flying helicopters, have shown that in some cases species identification is possible, and individual tree variables such as height, crown diameter, and even dbh can be reliably measured (Aldrich, 1966; Lyons, 1966; Sayn-Wittgenstein and Aldred, 1967). Tree volume estimation directly from aerial photographs at these scales is considerably improved, but it is safe to say that, for detailed volume estimates and observations on quality, defects, and merchantable heights, direct field observations are essential. The advantages of direct photographic methods lie in their speed and economy. When the sacrifice of detail or accuracy of an estimate is acceptable, as in reconnaissance work, aerial photographic volume estimates can be satisfactory. Direct photographic volume estimates are also useful in providing preliminary information for calculating the number of field sampling units needed for ground inventory and as a basis for stratification into volume classes.

Improved photographic estimates are possible if relationships between photographic and ground volume estimates are prepared using double sampling as described in Section 12–10. These relationships can be developed by making estimates on photographs and checking them against field determinations for the same sampling units.

13–6. COMBINED AERIAL PHOTOGRAPHIC AND FIELD INVENTORIES

Combined inventory designs utilize the best aspects of both ground and photographic techniques. Sampling is controlled by information obtained directly from the aerial photographs, but volume estimates are obtained from measurements on field plots or sampling points.

Aerial photographs used in a combined inventory permit rapid and accurate stratification and area estimation. Stereoscopic examination of the photographs while in the field can be of great help in identifying previously chosen ground positions. Photographs can also be effective in facilitating crew movements by providing knowledge of the terrain.

Field sampling units are measured in much the same manner as for conventional ground techniques, although occasionally some additional measurements may be taken to check photographic measurements or photo-interpretation results.

One extensively used combined inventory design utilizes photographic plot sampling for area estimates followed by field sampling of a portion of these plot locations for volume estimation. To use this design, aerial photography should be available of a quality which will permit interpretation and identification of the categories of the chosen land and forest classification system. The accessibility of an area should permit visiting scattered sampling units in the field without an excessive amount of time spent on travel. Consequently, this design may be inappropriate in an area of no roads or rivers or where helicopter landing is impossible. The design is especially useful in inventory work of large forest areas where the field sampling intensity must be kept low.

The estimates of total volume based on this inventory design will have a combined error made up of the contribution from the standard errors of the area estimates and volume estimates. The formulas for a combined stratified sampling design, assuming both photographic and field sampling units are randomly selected, are presented here. In actual practice, the requirement of randomness is often neglected in favor of a more easily applied systematic procedure. Thus, a systematic grid of photographic sampling points is used and the number of required field sampling units is taken at some fixed interval from the photographic points.

The combined standard error of the estimated mean quantity per sampling unit for the jth stratum is:

$$s_{\bar{x}_j}{}^2 = \frac{p_j s_j{}^2}{n_j} + \frac{p\bar{x}_j{}^2 - (p_j \bar{x}_j)^2}{k} \tag{13-6}$$

and for the population:

$$s_{\bar{x}}{}^2 = \sum_{j=1}^{M} \frac{p_j{}^2 s_j{}^2}{n_j} + \frac{1}{k}\left[\sum_{j=1}^{M} p_j \bar{x}_j{}^2 - \left(\sum_{j=1}^{M} p_j \bar{x}_j \right)^2 \right] \tag{13-7}$$

in which:

$$s_j{}^2 = \frac{\sum\limits_{i=1}^{n_j} X_{ij}{}^2 - \left(\dfrac{\sum\limits_{i=1}^{n_j} X_{ij}}{n_j} \right)^2}{n_j - 1} \tag{13-8}$$

where:

p_j = proportion of the area in the jth stratum from photo-interpretation
n_j = number of field sampling units in the jth stratum
k = number of photo sampling units

All other symbols are the same as defined in Section 12–8.
The variance of the estimates of the population total is then:

$$s_x{}^2 = N^2 s_{\bar{x}}{}^2 \tag{13-9}$$

When fixed area sample plots are used, then:

$$N = \frac{\text{total area in population}}{\text{size of a field plot}}$$

When a "variable plot" estimate has been made, then N is the number of multiples of the size of the land unit area, e.g., acre or hectare.

As described in the Manual of Photographic Interpretation (1960), the number of photographic and field sampling units for a required precision can be estimated if preliminary information is available on the proportional areas of the strata, variability in the forest, and cost of photo and field sampling units.

The total number of field sampling units can be estimated from:

$$n = \frac{\left(\sum\limits_{j=1}^{M} p_j s_j \right)^2 \sqrt{c_f} + \left(\sum\limits_{j=1}^{M} p_j s_j \right) \sqrt{\sum\limits_{j=1}^{M} p_j \bar{x}_j{}^2 - \left(\sum\limits_{j=1}^{M} p_j \bar{x}_j \right)} \sqrt{c_p}}{\sqrt{c_f}\, s_{\bar{x}}{}^2} \tag{13-10}$$

where:

n = total number of field sampling units required

M = number of strata in the population

p_j = preliminary estimate of proportion of the forest in the jth stratum

s_j = preliminary estimate of the standard deviation in the jth stratum

$\bar{x}_j$ = preliminary estimate of the mean of the quantity per sampling unit in the jth stratum

$s_{\bar{x}}^2$ = acceptable variance of the mean quantity per sampling unit

c_f = cost of a sampling unit in the forest

c_p = cost of a photo-interpretation sampling unit

The estimated required number of field sampling units per stratum using optimal allocation is:

$$n_j = \frac{p_j s_j}{\sum\limits_{j=1}^{M} p_j s_j} \, n \qquad (13\text{--}11)$$

The estimated total number of photographic sampling units can be found from:

$$k = \frac{\sqrt{\sum\limits_{j=1}^{M} p_j \bar{x}_j^2 - \left(\sum\limits_{j=1}^{M} p_j \bar{x}_j\right)^2} \, \sqrt{c_f}}{\left(\sum\limits_{j=1}^{M} p_j s_j\right) \sqrt{c_p}} \, n \qquad (13\text{--}12)$$

13–7. RECENT DEVELOPMENTS IN AERIAL FOREST PHOTOGRAPHY

New photographic techniques and materials which can be useful to forest inventory work are in the process of development or have already been put into limited use. The principal developments are:

13–7.1. Use of Large-Scale Photography. The possibility of using aerial photographs of large scale for forest photo-interpretation has been considered for many years and an early study was reported by Rogers (1952). His investigation showed little advantage was gained from scales greater than 1:5,000. Interest has recently revived in the possibilities afforded by large-scale stereoscopic photography taken from low-flying helicopters (Aldrich, 1966). Stereoscopic coverage at large scales (greater than 1:3,000) can be obtained for sample locations while complete coverage at smaller conventional scales (greater than 1:10,000) is obtained by standard aerial photography using fixed-wing aircraft. Investigations have shown that accurate measurements can be made of tree height, crown width, stand density, and, in some cases, tree dbh (Kippen and Sayn-Wittgenstein, 1964). Principal interest has centered on the use of 70 mm. cameras for this large-scale photography. Recent studies have concentrated on mounting two of these cameras on a fixed beam under a helicopter (Lyons, 1964; 1966). Accurate determination of the elevation of the helicopter is obtained using a radar altimeter recently developed in Canada. The objective of these studies is to make practical an inventory design in which cheap photo plots could be substituted for more expensive ground plots to obtain an estimate of stand volume. Thus, one would take a sample of photo plots at a large scale and obtain, photogrammetrically, individual tree measurements. The volumes of these trees would then be estimated from aerial photo volume tables.

13–7.2. Aerial Remote Sensing. Remote sensing in general terms is the detection of objects by some sensing technique which is distant from the object of interest. Conventional aerial photography, thus, is a form of remote sensing. Other kinds of remote sensing techniques under investigation which may prove of value to forestry are heat and infrared detectors and radar. The development of space vehicles also provides a platform for these sensing devices much as an aircraft provides a camera station for present day aerial photography.

Photography from earth-orbiting space vehicles should be of value in the mapping of large forest regions since these photographs can provide a synoptic view of large areas of the earth's surface. However, for detailed photo-interpretation and measurements, conventional aerial photography is still superior. Heat, infrared, and radar detectors can be of value since they can be used at night and when the weather is too poor for ordinary aerial photography. This can be of great advantage in securing information about forest areas in tropical regions where it is extremely difficult to obtain conventional aerial photographs due to cloud cover. For further discussion, the reader is referred to Heller (1965), Hirsch (1965), Parker and Wolff (1965), Badgley and Vest (1966), and Wilson (1967).

13–7.3. Color Aerial Photography. Color aerial photography using prints or transparencies has now reached the stage where it is no longer a curiosity and can be considered for routine employment in forest inventory work. Several types of color film such as natural or real, false color, spectrozonal, etc., are available in which different kinds of vegetation can be distinguished by their variations in color. Color is still expensive since the film, processing, and prints, if required, cost more than for black and white photography. References of interest on the subject include the Manual of Color Aerial Photography (1967), Cooper and Smith (1966), and Mott (1966).

13–7.4. Automating Photo-Interpretation. Combining improvements in aerial photography electronics and optics, it is possible to execute automatically some aspects of photo-interpretation. Langley (1965) has shown how land use and forest types can be automatically interpreted and recorded by detecting differences in a light intensity on color film using a microdensitometer scanning device.

14

Inventory Using
Sampling with
Varying Probabilities

14–1. INTRODUCTION

In the discussion of stratified sampling (Chapter 12), the advantages of sampling more intensively in the larger strata were evident. In stratified sampling the techniques of proportional and optimum allocation of sample units are used to assure that those strata comprising large portions of the population are also represented to the same extent in the sample. Samplers use another general technique to assure adequate representation of the larger components of the population; rather than adjust the number of sample units to locate in each group, the probability of selecting that group (or individual) is modified so that the larger or more valuable population components are given an increased chance of being selected for the sample.

Pioneer work on the subject of sampling with varying probabilities, or as it is called in classical sampling literature, "sampling with probability proportional to size," (p.p.s. sampling) was done by Hansen and Hurwitz (1943), and later thoroughly described by Hansen et al. (1953). Foresters made use of this general concept without realizing it upon the introduction of "angle-count cruising" by Bitterlich (1947). This was not recognized, however, as a type of p.p.s. sampling until pointed out by Grosenbaugh (1955).

In recent years several useful variations of the variable-probability-sampling notion have come to the fore. In a discussion of the advantages of sampling with unequal (i.e., varying) probabilities, Grosenbaugh (1967) classifies the major types of such sampling as:

1. list sampling (probability of sampling a previously listed item is made proportional to a listed quantity associated with the item)
2. 3P sampling (probability proportional to prediction)
3. p.p.s. sampling (probability proportional to size)

This chapter follows Grosenbaugh's classification, although the reader is cautioned to note that "p.p.s. sampling" as it is universally known and referred to in classical sampling literature is thus made a subdivision of sampling with varying probabilities. Therefore, p.p.s. sampling should, for present purposes, be thought of in both the broad and narrow sense— in the broad sense as a concept of sampling synonymous with sampling with varying probabilities, and in the narrow sense as a type of forest sampling where individual tree selection is made proportional to some measurable element of tree size. It will become evident that both "list sampling" and 3P sampling embody concepts commonly associated with p.p.s. sampling in the broad sense.

14–2. LIST SAMPLING (WITH VARYING PROBABILITIES)

List sampling with varying probabilities can be applied where the listed items are individual elements having different sizes, or where the listed items are clusters having different numbers of elements, or some other appropriate expression of size. In the usual forestry context we can think of individual trees as the elements, and compartments or stands as clusters. This type of variable probability sampling applied to individual listed trees is usually impractical, because of the necessity of listing each element prior to sampling. Therefore, we shall discuss the technique for compartments (cluster of trees) having varying, but known, areas.

The sampling method is carried out first by listing the compartments in any order, along with their measure of size, say area. A sample size is decided upon, and sampling (with replacement) is performed in such a way as to give the larger compartments a greater chance of being selected. The selected compartments are then visited and measurements taken on the variable of interest. The analysis of the data, subsequently shown, yields unbiased estimates of means, totals, and their variances.

To illustrate the procedure, consider a forest made up of compartments having areas designated by X_i. We want to choose n compartments with selection probability proportional to X_i and measure the variable Y_i on each of the chosen compartments. We must first list the compartments as shown in Table 14–1, obtaining a column of cumulative areas in the

Table 14–1
List of Compartments and Individual and Cumulative Areas for Use in List Sampling with Varying Probabilities

Compartment	Area in Acres (X_i)	Cumulative Total of X_i	Associated Numbers
1	25	25	1–25
2	10	35	26–35
3	30	65	36–65
4	28	93	66–93
5	15	108	94–108
6	30	138	109–138
7	38	176	139–176
8	51	227	177–227
9	40	267	228–267
10	12	279	268–279
11	60	339	280–339
12	80	419	340–419
Total:	419		

process. It is also helpful to show a column of associated numbers which indicates the set of consecutive integers from the one above the previous cumulative total to and including the cumulative total of the compartment in question.

If we decide that $n = 5$, then 5 random numbers are appropriately drawn from the range of integers 1 through 419, the total area of the compartments. A compartment is chosen as part of the sample if the random number falls within the interval indicated in the column of associated numbers. Thus, the following might be chosen:

Random numbers drawn	Compartments chosen
153	7
052	3
414	12
283	11
177	8

After the compartments are visited and measurements taken regarding the variable of interest, Y_i, the estimate of the mean value of Y per unit area is:

$$\bar{r} = \frac{1}{n} \sum_{i=1}^{n} \frac{Y_i}{X_i}$$

$$= \frac{1}{n} \sum_{i=1}^{n} r_i \qquad (14\text{--}1)$$

where:

Y_i = the quantity measured on the ith compartment, e.g., total compartment volume

X_i = size of the ith compartment, e.g., compartment area

n = number of compartments chosen

$\bar{r}$ = mean value of Y per unit value of X, e.g., mean volume per acre (hectare)

r_i = ratio of Y_i to X_i

The variance of $\bar{r}$ can be estimated from:

$$s_{\bar{r}}^2 = \frac{\sum\limits_{i=1}^{n} r_i^2 - \dfrac{\left(\sum\limits_{i=1}^{n} r_i\right)^2}{n}}{n(n-1)} \qquad (14\text{--}2)$$

The estimate of the total Y for the population, then, is:

$$\hat{y} = \bar{r}X \qquad (14\text{--}3)$$

with estimated variance:

$$s_{\hat{y}}^2 = s_{\bar{r}}^2 X^2 \qquad (14\text{--}4)$$

where:

$\hat{y}$ = estimate of the total Y

X = the total of X_i for the entire population

Instead of a complete tally within each compartment as implied above, a more practical procedure would be to take a subsample of secondary sampling units within each of the chosen compartments. Subsampling is more fully discussed in Section 12–9.

More sophisticated designs making use of list sampling with varying probabilities are also possible. For example, we can combine it with stratified sampling where a large forest is divided into managements units (strata) based on political subdivision, overstory pattern, topography, etc. Within each of the management units a series of compartments of varying sizes may be listed and list sampling performed to select the desired number of compartments, and, as noted before, rather than completely measuring a compartment, subsampling within the compartment would lead to a more practical design.

14–3. 3P SAMPLING

The necessity of listing the units prior to sampling acts as a severe deterrent to list sampling in many forestry applications, especially those where individual trees are the potentially listed items. Grosenbaugh (1963a), making use of a principle similar to that proposed by Lahiri (1951) to overcome the prior listing requirement, proposed a type of sampling which utilizes the p.p.s. concept but the element of size concerned is (in the usual application) the timber cruiser's on-the-spot estimate of tree volume. The name put forth by Grosenbaugh for this technique is "3P sampling" which should be interpreted as "sampling with probability proportional to prediction."

The purpose in the present treatment of 3P sampling is to make the reader aware of the general concept and application of the method. For details, reference should be made to the works of Grosenbaugh (especially 1963a, 1964, 1965, and 1967).

This type of sampling has been applied exclusively to timber sales where each tree in the population (all the marked trees) is assessed for a "crude" prediction of volume or value and a subsample of these trees is selected for more detailed measurements. For this purpose it appears to be very efficient.

Before listing the steps in a simplified application of 3P sampling it is perhaps best to dwell on the basic sampling concept which leads to the name "probability proportional to prediction." The analogy given by Mesavage (1965b) is convenient for this purpose:

> . . . suppose we have 20 cards numbered one to twenty. If we stipulate that the predicted volume of a sample tree must be equal to or greater than the number on a card subsequently drawn at random, a tree with a prediction of 1 would have only 1 chance in 20 to qualify [as a sample tree to be carefully measured for volume], whereas one with a predicted volume of 15 would have 15 chances in 20. The probability of selection is thus seen to be proportional to prediction . . .

The steps in conducting a 3P sampling for the purpose of estimating the total volume of timber marked for sale might be as follows:

1. Designate a sample size, n, the number of trees to be carefully measured for volume.

   This can be determined by applying formulas involving estimates of coefficient of variation and desired precision or by use of a crude guide such as Mesavage (1965b) indicates on a large timber sale —for trained cruisers 100 or so trees are usually sufficient for an accuracy of 1.5 per cent, and, for inexperienced cruisers, approximately 200 trees are needed to achieve the same accuracy. It is worth noting here that it is the consistency (precision) of the cruiser's estimates which leads to high accuracy using 3P, and individual or volume table bias is of little consequence. Thus, the experienced cruiser, though possibly biased, is probably less erratic in his estimates than the beginner and, therefore, likely to have a more efficient sample.

2. Estimate the sum of volumes for the N trees making up the sale. Thus:

$$\hat{x} = \text{estimated} \sum_{i=1}^{N} X_i$$

where:

X_i = the cruiser's *estimate* of tree volume (this can also be an entry from a volume table utilizing the cruiser's estimate or measurement of tree diameter and possibly height)

Note that X, the actual sum of estimated volumes is *known* only after the inventory is completed.

3. Designate the maximum individual tree volume expected as K. Thus:

$$K = \text{maximum } X_i$$

K, then, is used as the upper limit of the set of integers running from 1 through K, which will act as the means by which each tree will be checked for qualification as a sample tree to be measured in detail.

4. Adjust the set of integers to insure obtaining close to the sample size desired. That is, define:

$$n = \frac{\hat{x}}{K + Z} \tag{14–5}$$

where:

n = expected sample size
$\hat{x}$ = estimate of the total volume of all trees
Z = the number of "rejection symbols" to be randomly mixed with the set of integers 1 through K

Thus, if we decide on $n = 200$ and if $\hat{x} = 240{,}000$ bd. ft. and maximum tree volume $K = 1{,}000$ bd. ft., Z must be 200, otherwise we would likely obtain 240 sample trees rather than the desired 200.

5. Visit each of the N trees comprising the sale. At each tree:

   a. estimate directly or indirectly using a volume table the tree volume (or value), X_i
   b. record the estimate
   c. draw a number (or symbol) at random from the set of integers 1 through K having the Z interspersed rejection symbols. A

special device invented and described by Mesavage (1967) facilitates this operation.

6. If the random integer drawn is *less than or equal to* the volume estimate, X_i, measure the tree for accurate volume determination. This volume is then recorded as Y_i, the actual volume of the ith tree. In Grosenbaugh's (1965) 3P program (THRP), the volume calculations (based on measurements using the Barr and Stroud dendrometer) as well as steps 8 and 9 are done by computer subsequent to the field work.

7. If the random integer drawn is *greater than* the estimate, X_i, or if instead of a number a rejection symbol is drawn, nothing more is required from the tree and the crew moves on to the next marked or to-be-marked tree.

8. After completion of the inventory the total volume of the N marked trees can be estimated from the formula:

$$\hat{y} = X \left(\frac{\sum\limits_{i=1}^{n} \dfrac{Y_i}{X_i}}{n} \right) \qquad (14\text{--}6)$$

where:

$$X = \sum_{i=1}^{N} X_i$$

In words, then, the estimated total marked volume is equal to the sum of the estimates of tree volume obtained from the complete population times the average ratio of actual to estimated volume, obtained from the n sample trees.

At the completion of the inventory one should have approximately the sample size, n, originally prescribed, but minor variations are possible because of vagaries associated with random numbers in the selection procedure.

9. The variance of the estimate, $\hat{y}$, can be estimated, although it is pointed out by Ware (1967) that no exact expression for the true variance exists and that the following equation is suggested by Grosenbaugh:

$$s_{\hat{y}}^2 = \frac{\sum\limits_{i=1}^{n} \left(\dfrac{Y_i X}{X_i} - \hat{y} \right)^2}{n(n-1)} \qquad (14\text{--}7)$$

Other approximations for the variance have been proposed but it appears that unanimity on a recommended "best approach or formula" has not been reached.

14-4. P.P.S. SAMPLING (POINT AND LINE SAMPLING)

Beginning with the work of Bitterlich (1947) through that of Keen (1950) and Grosenbaugh (1952b, 1958) the concept known variously as "angle count cruising," "plotless cruising," "point sampling," and "variable plot cruising," has earned a valuable place in the forester's tool kit. Probably no single forestry technique has been described so often, as indicated by the excellent bibliographies by Thomson and Deitschman (1959), and by Labau (1967). Numerous articles have focused on the topic "why point sampling works," and it is evident that there is no "one way" to develop the workings of the technique. One of the more traditional discussions of Bitterlich's angle count cruising (or, more definitively, "horizontal point sampling") would proceed as in the following section.

14–4.1. Fundamental Concept of Horizontal Point Sampling. In the application of horizontal point sampling, a series of sampling points is chosen much as one would select plot centers for fixed-size plots. The observer occupies each sampling point, sights with an angle-gauge (an instrument designed to "project" a horizontal angle of some arbitary size) at breast height on every tree visible from the point, and tallies all trees that are greater than the projected angle of the gauge. Figure 14–1

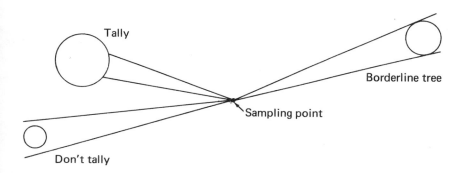

Fig. 14–1. Selection of trees in point-sampling.

illustrates the procedure. The circles represent the cross-sections of trees at breast height, and the lines indicate the angle projected from the sampling point. Any variables associated with the selected trees may be measured, just as in the case of fixed-size plots, but the unique feature of horizontal point sampling is that *no tree measurements* are needed to obtain an unbiased estimate of basal area per acre (hectare) from that sampling point. The number of trees counted which are larger than the projected angle, multiplied by a constant factor, dependent only on the size of the angle, yields the basal area per acre (hectare) estimate. Thus, it will be shown that each qualifying tree (i.e., each tree larger than the projected angle), regardless of its dbh represents the same basal area per acre.

In order to show this, it is helpful to refer to Fig. 14–2, where two trees are depicted at locations where the gauge angle is precisely tangent to the breast height cross-section, and to keep the following in mind:

1. The angle gauge is projecting a fixed horizontal angle, θ.
2. At any sampling point a series of concentric circular plots is established (conceptually), a different plot radius being associated with every *different* tree diameter.
3. The radius of each concentric plot is determined by each different

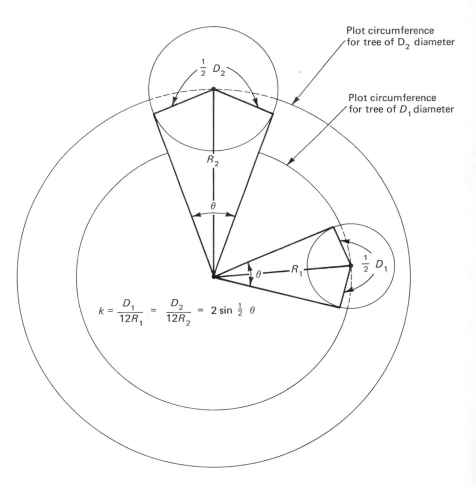

Fig. 14–2. Gauge constant $k = \dfrac{D}{12R}$, where D is tree diameter in inches and R is plot radius in feet.

tree diameter and is not influenced by the actual spatial location of the tree; therefore, for the purpose of development, all trees can be considered in the "borderline" condition as shown in Fig. 14–2.

4. At the borderline condition, the ratio of tree diameter to plot radius is a constant. Thus, for a given gauge angle, θ, tree diameter in inches, D, and plot radius in feet, R, we can define this "gauge constant," k, to be:[1]

$$k = \frac{D}{12R} = 2 \sin \frac{\theta}{2} \qquad (14\text{–}8)$$

(Note that the only function of the 12 in this formula is to maintain the same units in numerator and denominator.)

The basal area per acre represented by each qualifying tree, F, can now be shown to be not dependent on tree diameter:

F = (Basal area for the tree) (factor to convert to an acre basis)

$$= BA_i \; \frac{\text{area of one acre}}{\text{plot area for the } i^{\text{th}} \text{ tree}}$$

$$= \frac{\pi D_i^2}{4(144)} \cdot \frac{43560}{\pi R_i^2}$$

$$= 10890 \left(\frac{D_i}{12R_i} \right)^2$$

$$= 10890 \, k^2 \qquad (14\text{–}9)$$

It should be clear now that we can choose a gauge constant, k, such that $10890 \, k^2$ is some convenient number. Therefore, in practice we will first choose a specific value of F, and so fix the ratio of $\frac{D_i}{12R_i}$ which, as a consequence, implies a different plot radius for every different tree diameter. Now, all trees of the same diameter that are located less than their "plot-radius distance" from a given sampling point will be "on the plot" and their basal areas can be converted to an acre basis. For example, if a gauge angle is used for which $k = 0.0303$, then for each tree greater than the projected angle:

[1] In the usual metric units D is in centimeters, R is in meters; therefore:

$$k = \frac{D}{100R} = 2 \sin \frac{\theta}{2}$$

and the basal area in square meters per hectare, F, is:

$$F = \frac{\pi D_i^2}{40,000} \cdot \frac{10,000}{\pi R_i^2} = \frac{D_i^2}{4R_i^2} = 2500 \, k^2$$

$$F = 10890 \, k^2$$
$$= 10890(0.0303)^2$$
$$= 10.0 \text{ square feet per acre}^2$$

Although we might now develop horizontal point sampling in detail, it is more illuminating to approach the subject from a basic viewpoint so that other useful forms of p.p.s. sampling closely allied to horizontal point sampling can be understood and used. To do this, we will develop the logic from fixed-area plots of one size through concentric fixed-area plots of several sizes to point and line sampling, where there are many sizes of "plots" used at each sample location.

14–4.2. A Classification Scheme. To explain the operation of p.p.s. sampling in forest inventory it is convenient to refer to one-size fixed-area plot sampling as *monareal* plot sampling, two-size concentric fixed-area plot sampling as *biareal,* three-sizes as *triareal,* and, therefore, point and line sampling in general as *polyareal plot sampling.*

In monareal plot sampling the same size circular or rectangular (square or strip) plot is used for all trees. Then, all trees are measured on a number of monareal plots (such as one-fifth acre circular plots or one-chain wide strips) which comprise a known portion of the area inventoried. A class of trees, in particular, diameter and height classes, can expect to be sampled in proportion to the frequency of trees in the given class. Thus, in many inventories, small diameter and small height classes will be sampled more intensively than large diameter and large height classes, because, in most stands, there are more small trees than large trees.

We may, of course, modify monareal plot sampling so we will get fewer small trees, but still an adequate sample, and a more desirable sample of large trees by using two sizes of concentric circular plots, or two widths of strips. We could, for example, use one-tenth acre circular plots for trees under 14 inches in diameter, and one-fifth acre circular plots for trees 14 inches and over. If we desired to use strips, we could, in an analogous fashion use two widths of strips, or, on the other hand, we could let the plot size be dependent on total or merchantable tree height rather than tree diameter. For example, we could use one-tenth acre circular plots for trees under 30 feet in total height, and one-fifth acre circular plots for trees 30 feet and over, or, if we preferred rectangular plots, we could use one-half chain wide strips for trees under 30 feet in total height, and one-chain wide strips for trees 30 feet and over.

In triareal plot sampling, for which we should obtain a more desirable sample of trees in three broad classes, we might, for example, use a one-tenth acre circular plot for trees under 12 inches in diameter, a one-

---

[2] A metric system example would be to choose $k = 0.028284$, leading to $F = 2500(0.028284)^2 = 2.0$ square meters per hectare.

seventh acre circular plot for trees 12 to 16 inches in diameter, and a one-fifth acre circular plot for trees 16 inches and over in diameter. And, of course, all the alternatives of biareal plot sampling are possible for triareal plot sampling.

When this line of thought is taken to its logical conclusion, it is seen that a different size of circular or rectangular plot can be specified for each different tree diameter or tree height resulting in polyareal plot sampling. But, until Bitterlich (1947) first wrote about the use of the horizontal angle gauge to estimate stand basal area per unit of land area, serious consideration was not given to the application of this concept. Indeed, few foresters felt it was practical even to use biareal or triareal plot sampling. Few foresters saw the implications and practicality of polyareal plot sampling until Grosenbaugh (1952b, 1955, 1958) pointed out that an angle gauge could be used to select sample trees with probability proportional to some element of size, and postulated the theory of point sampling to obtain unbiased estimates of frequency, volume, growth, value, height, etc., per acre from measurements of such p.p.s. sample trees.

Both the work of Bitterlich and that of Grosenbaugh were landmarks. They both displayed flashes of originality seldom seen. The original concept of angle count cruising is unquestionably traced back to Bitterlich; however, the works of Grosenbaugh, although they emphasized horizontal point sampling, covered the entire theory of p.p.s. sampling as the basis of what we have called polyareal plot sampling. Hirata (1955) was the first to employ the vertical angle gauge in vertical point sampling to estimate mean squared height, and Strand (1957) the first to describe horizontal and vertical line sampling.

Line sampling theory, with which most foresters are unfamiliar, is but an extension or analogy of point sampling theory. Thus, it is desirable to discuss the theory of all polyareal plot systems at one time; that is, to use Grosenbaugh's specific terminology, to discuss the following systems together: horizontal point sampling, horizontal line sampling, vertical point sampling, and vertical line sampling.

To get a clear picture of all the polyareal plot sampling systems, it is well first to review monareal plot sampling. This can best be done by a study of Figs. 14–3 (a) and 14–3 (b). In Fig. 14–3 (a) a monareal circular plot is drawn around a plot center. It is obvious which trees are to be measured. Then, in Fig. 14–3 (b) monareal circular plots are drawn with each tree as a center. In this case we are saying that each tree has a plot associated with it and that the plots are all of the same size. But no matter whether we think in terms of plots centered on points or plots centered on trees, we shall select the same trees for measurement. One may think of rectangular plots in the same manner.

The selection of trees using horizontal point sampling is illustrated in

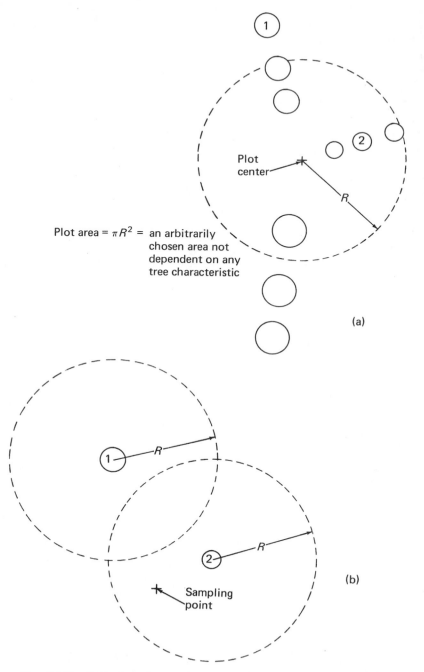

Fig. 14–3. Selection of trees in monareal plot sampling using (a) the point-centered concept, and (b) the tree-centered concept. Tree number 2 qualifies, tree number 1 does not.

Figs. 14–4 (a) and 14–4 (b). These two figures demonstrate that (1) plot size varies with tree size, (2) either the point-centered or tree-centered concept will result in the same trees being selected, and (3) a tree's associated plot size is determined by a borderline tree of its size, although a tree may be in (I), borderline (B), or out (O), depending on its distance from the sampling point.

The remaining forms of polyareal plot sampling are illustrated in Figs. 14–5, 14–6, and 14–7, and, although only the point- or line-centered concept is shown, one should realize that the tree-centered approach is equally appropriate. Furthermore, it should be evident that in the two horizontal systems tree selection is accomplished by projecting a small horizontal angle, and in the two vertical systems tree selection is accomplished by projecting a large vertical angle.

In the next section we shall discuss the basic theory of all polyareal systems. To understand this discussion it is essential to refer to Figs. 14–4 to 14–7 and to remember that:

1. In *horizonal point sampling* the plot associated with any given tree is circular and its area (or radius squared) is a linear function of tree diameter squared.
2. In *horizontal line sampling* the plot associated with any given tree is rectangular and its area (or width) is a linear function of tree diameter.
3. In *vertical point sampling* the plot associated with any given tree is circular and its area (or radius squared) is a linear function of tree height squared.
4. In *vertical line sampling* the plot associated with any given tree is rectangular and its area (or width) is a linear function of tree height.

14–4.3. General Theory of Polyareal Plot Sampling. Assuming it is decided to employ one of the p.p.s. systems in a specific forest inventory, how are the necessary formulas, and ultimately, the numerical values developed for field application and data summarization?

Before the steps leading to these formulas are listed we will describe a system of terminology and symbolism that will greatly facilitate the development. To introduce the proposed terminology, an example from monareal plot sampling will be used.

It is clear that each tree tallied on a one-fifth acre plot represents $\dfrac{1}{1/5}$ or 5 trees per acre. Furthermore, a 12-inch, one-log tree with a volume of 40 board feet represents $40\left(\dfrac{1}{1/5}\right) = 200$ board feet per acre, or $12\left(\dfrac{1}{1/5}\right) = 60$ inches of diameter per acre. Thus the ratio, 1/(plot area

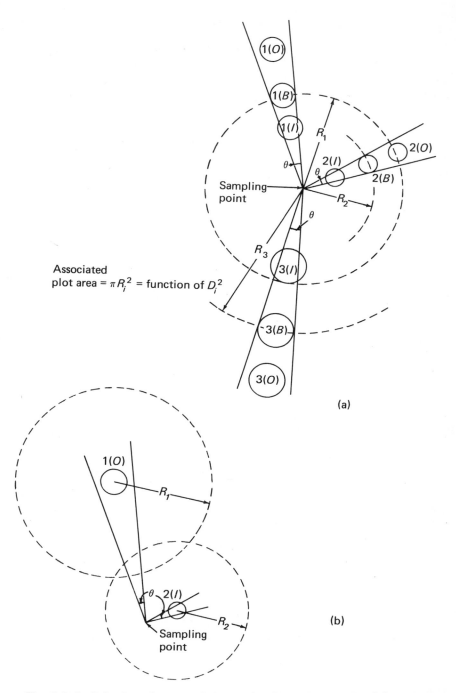

Fig. 14–4. Selection of trees in horizontal point sampling using (a) the point-centered concept, and (b) the tree-centered concept. Tree number 2 (*I*) qualifies, tree number 1 (*O*) does not.

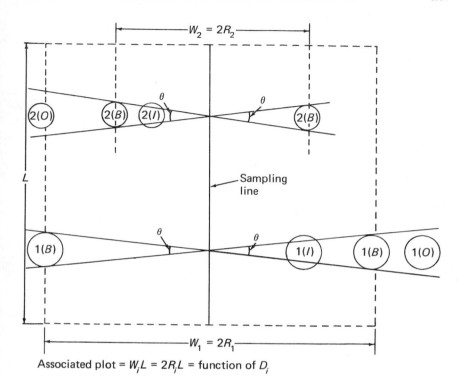

Associated plot = $W_iL = 2R_iL$ = function of D_i

Fig. 14–5. Selection of trees in horizontal line sampling using the line-centered concept.

in acres), is a *per acre conversion factor* and can be called the *tree factor* since it specifies the number of trees *per acre* represented by each tree on the plot. For any given plot size the tree factor is constant and easy to employ. Thus, it never has been necessary to label the per acre contribution of volume (e.g., 200 board feet) or the per acre contribution of diameter (e.g., 60 inches). However, by analogy these can be called the *volume factor* and the *diameter factor*, respectively, since they represent the number of board feet per acre and the number of inches of diameter per acre represented by each tree on the plot.

On the other hand, when dealing with polyareal plot sampling, the per acre conversion factor (tree factor) is not constant but is dependent upon tree size; it, therefore, will be found helpful to use specific factor names, and to assign symbols and develop formulas for them. When applied to polyareal plot sampling, the "factor terminology" then leads to:

"tree factor" —the number of trees per acre (hectare) represented by each tree tallied,

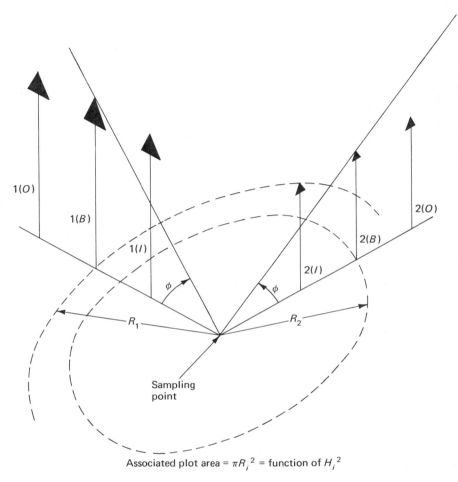

Associated plot area = πR_i^2 = function of H_i^2

Fig. 14–6. Selection of trees in vertical point sampling using the point-centered concept.

  "basal area factor"—the number of units of basal area per acre (hectare) represented by each tree tallied,
  "volume factor" —the number of units of volume per acre (hectare) represented by each tree tallied,
  "height factor" —the number of units of height per acre (hectare) represented by each tree tallied,
  etc.

A table of "standard symbolism" is given in Table 14–2. The system was developed with a conscious effort to employ terms that have been com-

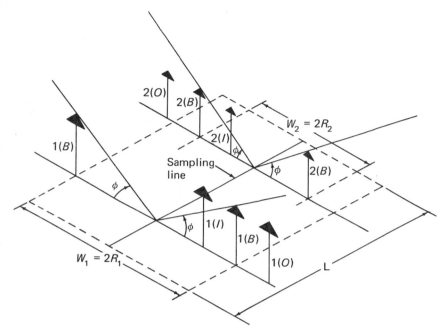

Associated plot area = $W_i L = 2R_i L$ = function of H_i

Fig. 14–7. Selection of trees in vertical line sampling using the line-centered concept.

monly used. For example, the letter "F" was used to symbolize the "horizontal factors" and the letter "Z" to symbolize the "vertical factors." Furthermore, the following "rules" were employed in the development of this symbolism:

1. Use the term "factor" to imply a certain number of units per acre (hectare) represented by each tree tallied for any tree characteristic.
2. Use capital letters for point sampling factors, and lower case letters for line sampling factors.
3. Use a lower-case subscript to indicate the tree characteristic involved (volume, diameter, circumference, etc.) if any tree dimensions are needed to obtain the actual value of the factor.
4. Use no subscript when no tree dimensions are needed to obtain the actual value of the factor. Thus, the four unsubscripted factors "characterize" the four types of polyareal sampling. For example, F = basal area per acre (hectare) represented by each tree tallied, characterizes horizontal point sampling.

Table 14-2
Useful Symbolism for the Application of Polyareal Plot Sampling[a]

Item To Be Symbolized	Type of Polyareal Sampling				Units Represented by Each Tree Tallied	
	Horizontal		Vertical		English System	Metric System
	Point	Line	Point	Line		
Tree factor[b]	F_t	f_t	Z_t	z_t	number trees per acre	number trees per hectare
Basal area factor	F	f_b	Z_b	z_b	square feet per acre	square meters per hectare
Diameter factor	F_d	f	Z_d	z_d	inches or feet per acre	centimeters or meters per hectare
Quadratic height factor	F_{qh}	f_{qh}	Z	z_{qh}	feet squared per acre	meters squared per hectare
Height factor	F_h	f_h	Z_h	z	feet per acre	meters per hectare
Volume factor	F_v	f_v	Z_v	z_v	board feet, cubic feet, cords, or tons per acre	cubic meters or kilograms per hectare
Circumference factor	F_c	f_c	Z_c	z_c	inches or feet per acre	centimeters or meters per hectare
Bole surface area factor	F_s	f_s	Z_s	z_s	square feet per acre	square meters per hectare
Gauge constant	k	k	q	q		
Gauge angle	θ	θ	ϕ	ϕ		
Distance multiplier	HDM	HDM	VDM	VDM		
"Plot" radius	R		R		feet	meters
"Plot" length		L		L	chains	number of 20-meter lengths
"Plot" width		$W=2R$		$W=2R$ feet		meters
Expansion constant	E					

[a]Horizontal point:　probability proportional to (diameter)^2
　Horizontal line:　probability proportional to diameter
　Vertical point:　probability proportional to (height)^2
　Vertical line:　probability proportional to height
[b]Tree factor　　　　= the number of trees per acre (hectare) represented by each tree tallied
　Basal area factor = the number of square feet per acre (square meters per hectare) represented by each tree tallied, etc.

Returning now to the basic question: For a given system how does one develop formulas so that each different "factor" can be expressed in terms of tree characteristics?

Regardless of the type of polyareal plot sampling under consideration, there are only three steps needed to develop any factor. They are:

1. Obtain the associated plot area in terms of the appropriate tree characteristic (that is, diameter for horizonal sampling, height for vertical sampling).

Example: In horizontal point sampling, any tree of diameter, D_i, and plot radius, R_i, will have the following plot area in square feet:[3]

$$\text{plot area} = \pi R_i{}^2$$
$$= \pi \left(\frac{D_i}{12k}\right)^2$$

where:

k = gauge constant = $\dfrac{D}{12R}$ = ratio of tree diameter in inches to plot radius in inches

2. Obtain the "tree factor" (that is, the per acre conversion factor, or number of trees per acre represented by each tree tallied) by dividing the associated plot area into the square-foot area of one acre (square-meter area of one hectare in the metric system). Example: In horizontal point sampling, when we express area in square feet, the tree factor will be:[4]

$$\text{tree factor} = F_t = \frac{43560}{\text{associated plot area}}$$
$$= \frac{43560}{\pi \left(\dfrac{D_i}{12k}\right)^2}$$
$$= \frac{43560(144k^2)}{\pi D_i{}^2}$$

and dividing both numerator and denominator by (4×144), we get:

$$F_t = \frac{(43560/4)k^2}{\pi D_i{}^2/(4 \times 144)} = \frac{10890\ k^2}{.005454\ D_i{}^2}$$

[3] In metric units, plot area in square meters = $\pi R_i{}^2 = \pi \left(\dfrac{D_i}{100k}\right)^2$, where $k = \dfrac{D}{100R}$, the ratio of tree diameter in centimeters to plot radius in centimeters.

[4] Using metric units:

$$F_t = \frac{10,000}{\pi \left(\dfrac{D_i}{100k}\right)^2} = \frac{10,000k^2}{\pi \left(\dfrac{D_i}{100}\right)^2}$$

and if numerator and denominator are divided by 4 we have:

$$F_t = \frac{2500k^2}{.00007854D_i{}^2}$$

Therefore, since $F = 2500k^2$ and $.00007854D_i{}^2$ equals tree basal area in square meters

$$F_t = \frac{F}{BA_i}.$$

And, finally, since the horizontal point basal area factor, F, equals $10890k^2$, and $.005454D_i^2$ equals tree basal area, BA_i, $F_t = \dfrac{F}{BA_i}$.

3. Obtain any other factor for the system under consideration by multiplying the appropriate tree characteristic by the tree factor and simplifying.

Example: In horizontal point sampling:[5]

$$\text{basal area factor} = F = (\text{tree } BA)\,(\text{tree factor})$$

$$F = BA_i \left(\frac{10890k^2}{BA_i}\right)$$

$$= 10890k^2$$

$$\text{volume factor} = F_v = (\text{tree volume})\,(\text{tree factor})$$

$$F_v = V_i \left(\frac{F}{BA_i}\right)$$

$$\text{diameter factor} = F_d = (\text{tree diameter})\,(\text{tree factor})$$

$$F_d = D_i \left(\frac{F}{BA_i}\right)$$

$$= D_i \left(\frac{F}{.005454\,D_i^2}\right)$$

$$= \frac{F}{.005454\,D_i}$$

and since the constant, $\dfrac{F}{005454}$, occurs quite often, we shall call it the expansion constant, E. Then:

$$F_d = \frac{E}{D_i}$$

$$\text{circumference factor} = F_c = (\text{tree circumference})\,(\text{tree factor})$$

$$F_c = C_i \left(\frac{F}{BA_i}\right)$$

$$= \pi D_i \left(\frac{F}{.005454\,D_i^2}\right)$$

$$= \frac{576F}{D_i}$$

[5] In the metric system:

$$F = BA_i\,(\text{tree factor}) = BA_i \left(\frac{2500k^2}{BA_i}\right) = 2500k^2$$

$$F_d = D_i \left(\frac{2500k^2}{BA_i}\right) = D_i \left(\frac{F}{.00007854D_i^2}\right) = \frac{F}{.00007854D_i} = \frac{E}{D_i}$$

where:

$$E = \frac{F}{.00007854}, \text{ etc.}$$

This simple procedure will lead to all the "factor" formulas given in Table 14–3(a)—English system—or Table 14–3(b)—metric system—for polyareal plot sampling.

The great utility of these formulas is that they indicate the use of simple field procedures to estimate certain stand parameters: in fact, it is frequently possible to eliminate the need to measure certain tree dimensions with no loss in accuracy.

A few examples will illustrate the possibilities.[6]

Example A. To estimate basal area per acre, even though individual tree basal area depends on tree diameter, if *horizontal point sampling* is used, basal area per acre is a constant for each tree which qualifies. Specifically, since $F = 10890k^2$, if $k = \frac{1}{33} = .030303$, $F = \dfrac{10890}{1089} = 10$ square feet per acre.

Example B. To estimate the sum of circumferences per acre, even though individual tree circumference depends on tree diameter, if *horizontal line sampling* is used, the sum of circumference per acre is a constant for each tree which qualifies. Specifically:

$$f_c = C_i(f_t)$$

$$= \pi D_i \left(\frac{3960k}{D_i}\right)$$

$$= 3960\pi k$$

Thus, if $k = \frac{1}{33}$, $f_c = 3960\pi(\frac{1}{33}) = 377$ inches of circumference per acre.

Example C. (This example illustrates a very powerful general approach for estimation of stand volume.) It will be noted in Table 14–3 that the horizontal point volume factor is $F_v = V_i (F_t)$, which may also be written $F_v = V_i\left(\dfrac{F}{BA_i}\right)$. If we are willing to accept the assumption that individual tree volume can be estimated by the linear regression estimate $V_i = bD_i^2H_i$, where b is the regression coefficient properly derived for the local timber, then:

$$F_v = bD_i^2H_i \left(\frac{F}{.005454\, D_i^2}\right)$$

$$= \left(\frac{bF}{.005454}\right) H_i = bEH_i$$

Thus, if we use a basal area factor, F, of 10, and a tree volume equation such as $V = .01914D^2H$, the volume factor becomes:

$$F_v = \frac{0.01914(10)}{.005454} H_i$$

$$= 35.09H_i$$

[6] Similar examples can be developed using the metric system.

Table 14-3(a)
Equations for Obtaining Common Factors and Constants* – English Units

Item	Type of Polyareal Plot Sampling			
	Horizontal		Vertical	
	Point	Line	Point	Line
Gauge constant	$k = \dfrac{D}{12R} = 2\sin\dfrac{\theta}{2}$		$q = \dfrac{H}{R} = \tan\phi$	
Plot radius or half-width (feet)	$R = \dfrac{D}{12k} = \dfrac{33\sqrt{10}\,D}{12\sqrt{F}}$	$R = \dfrac{D}{12k} = \dfrac{330\,D}{f}$	$R = \dfrac{H}{q} = \dfrac{66\sqrt{10}\,H}{\sqrt{\pi Z}}$	$R = \dfrac{H}{q} = \dfrac{330H}{z}$
Associated plot area (sq. ft.)	$\text{Area} = \pi R^2$ $= \pi\left(\dfrac{D}{12k}\right)^2$	$\text{Area} = 66L\,(2R)$ $= \dfrac{11\,LD}{k}$	$\text{Area} = \pi R^2$ $= \pi H^2\cot^2\phi$	$\text{Area} = 66L\,(2R)$ $= 132\,LH\cot\phi$
Tree factor (trees per acre)	$F_t = \dfrac{43560}{\text{Area}}$ $= \dfrac{10890\,k^2}{.005454\,D_i^2}$ $= \dfrac{F}{BA_i} = \dfrac{E}{D_i^2}$	$f_t = \dfrac{43560}{\text{Area}}$ $= \dfrac{3960\,k}{D_i}$ ** $= \dfrac{f}{D_i}$	$Z_t = \dfrac{43560}{\text{Area}}$ $= \dfrac{43560\,q^2}{\pi H_i^2}$ $= \dfrac{Z}{H_i^2}$	$z_t = \dfrac{43560}{\text{Area}}$ $= \dfrac{330\,q}{H_i}$ ** $= \dfrac{z}{H_i}$
Basal area factor (sq. ft. per acre)	$F = BA_i\,(F_t)$ $= 10890\,k^2$	$f_b = BA_i\,(f_t)$ $= 6.875\,\pi k D_i$	$Z_b = BA_i\,(Z_t)$	$z_b = BA_i\,(z_t)$
Diameter factor (in. per acre)	$F_d = D_i\,(F_t)$ $= \dfrac{E}{D_i}$	$f = D_i\,(f_t)$ $= 3960\,k$	$Z_d = D_i\,(Z_t)$	$z_d = D_i\,(z_t)$
Quadratic height factor (ft. squared per acre)	$F_{qh} = H_i^2\,(F_t)$	$f_{qh} = H_i^2\,(f_t)$	$Z = H_i^2\,(Z_t)$ $= \dfrac{43560}{\pi}\,q^2$	$z_{qh} = H_i^2\,(z_t)$ $= H_i\,330\,q$

Height factor (ft. per acre)	$F_h = H_i (F_t)$	$f_h = H_i (f_t)$	$Z_h = H_i (Z_t)$ $= \dfrac{43560}{\pi H_i} q^2$	$z = H_i (z_t)$ $= 330 q$
Volume factor (cubic or weight units per acre)	$F_v = V_i (F_t)$ $= b D_i^2 H_i (F_t)$ $= b H_i E$	$f_v = V_i (f_t)$	$Z_v = V_i (Z_t)$	$z_v = V_i (z_t)$
Circumference factor (in. per acre)	$F_c = C_i (F_t)$ $= \dfrac{576 F}{D_i}$	$f_c = C_i (f_t)$ $= 3960 \pi k$	$Z_c = C_i (Z_t)$	$z_c = C_i (z_t)$
Bole surface area factor (sq. units per acre)		$f_s = b C_i H_i (f_t)$ $= b H_i\, 3960\, \pi k$		$z_s = b C_i H_i (z_t)$ $= b D_i\, 330\, q$
Expansion constant	$E = \dfrac{F}{.005454}$ $= F(183.352)$			
Distance multiplier	$HDM = \dfrac{33\sqrt{10}}{12\sqrt{F}} = \dfrac{1}{12 k}$	$HDM = \dfrac{330}{f} = \dfrac{1}{12 k}$	$VDM = \dfrac{66\sqrt{10}}{\sqrt{\pi Z}} = \dfrac{1}{q}$	$VDM = \dfrac{300}{z} = \dfrac{1}{q}$

* D_i = diameter in inches
BA_i = basal area in square feet
H_i = height in feet
C_i = circumference in inches
V_i = volume in any desired unit for the ith tree
** f_t and z_t calculated on assumption that L = 1 chain

Table 14–3(b)

Equations for Obtaining Common Factors and Constants* — Metric Units

Item	Type of Polyareal Plot Sampling			
	Horizontal		Vertical	
	Point	Line	Point	Line
Gauge constant	$k = \dfrac{D}{100R} = 2\sin\dfrac{\theta}{2}$		$q = \dfrac{H}{R} = \tan\phi$	
Plot radius or half-width (meters)	$R = \dfrac{D}{100k} = \dfrac{D}{2\sqrt{F}}$	$R = \dfrac{D}{100k} = \dfrac{250\,D}{f}$	$R = \dfrac{H}{q} = \dfrac{100H}{\sqrt{\pi Z}}$	$R = \dfrac{H}{q} = \dfrac{250H}{z}$
Associated plot area (sq. meters)	Area $= \pi R^2$ $= \pi\left(\dfrac{D}{100k}\right)^2$	Area $= 20L(2R)$ $= \dfrac{LD}{2.5k}$	Area $= \pi R^2$ $= \pi H^2\cot^2\phi$	Area $= 20L(2R)$ $= 40LH\cot\phi$
Tree factor (trees per hectare)	$F_t = \dfrac{10000}{\text{Area}}$ $= \dfrac{2500\,k^2}{.00007854\,D_i^2}$** $= \dfrac{F}{BA_i} = \dfrac{E}{D_i^2}$	$f_t = \dfrac{10000}{\text{Area}}$ $= \dfrac{25000\,k}{D_i}$** $= \dfrac{f}{D_i}$	$Z_t = \dfrac{10000}{\text{Area}}$ $= \dfrac{10000\,q^2}{\pi H_i^2}$ $= \dfrac{Z}{H_i^2}$	$z_t = \dfrac{10000}{\text{Area}}$ $= \dfrac{250\,q}{H_i}$** $= \dfrac{z}{H_i}$
Basal area factor (sq. meters per hectare)	$F = BA_i(F_t)$ $= 2500\,k^2$	$f_b = BA_i(f_t)$ $= .625\,\pi k D_i$	$Z_b = BA_i(Z_t)$	$z_b = BA_i(z_t)$
Diameter factor (cm. per hectare)	$F_d = D_i(F_t)$ $= \dfrac{E}{D_i}$	$f = D_i(f_t)$ $= 25000\,k$	$z_d = D_i(Z_t)$	$z_d = D_i(z_t)$
Quadratic height factor (meters squared per hectare)	$F_{qh} = H_i^2(F_t)$	$f_{qh} = H_i^2(f_t)$	$Z = H_i^2(Z_t)$ $= \dfrac{10000\,q^2}{\pi}$	$z_{qh} = H_i^2(z_t)$ $= H_i 250q$

Height factor (meters per hectare)	$F_h = H_i(F_t)$	$f_h = H_i(f_t)$	$Z_h = H_i(Z_t)$ $= \dfrac{Z}{H_i}$	$z = H_i(z_t)$ $= 250q$
Volume factor (cubic or weight units per hectare)	$F_v = V_i(F_t)$ $= bD_i^2 H_i(F_t)$ $= bH_iE$	$f_v = V_i(f_t)$	$Z_v = V_i(Z_t)$	$z_v = V_i(z_t)$ $= bD_i^2 H_i(z_t)$ $= bD_i^2\, 250q$
Circumference factor (cm. per hectare)	$F_c = C_i(F_t)$ $= \dfrac{40000F}{D_i}$	$f_c = C_i(f_t)$ $= 25000\pi k$	$Z_c = C_i(Z_t)$	$z_c = C_i(z_t)$
Surface area factor (sq. units per hectare)		$f_s = bC_iH_i(f_t)$ $= bH_i 25000\pi k$		$z_s = bC_iH_i(z_t)$ $= bD_i\, 250q$
Expansion constant	$E = \dfrac{F}{.00007854}$ $= F(12732.37)$			
Distance multiplier	$HDM = \dfrac{1}{2\sqrt{F}} = \dfrac{1}{100k}$	$HDM = \dfrac{250}{f} = \dfrac{1}{100k}$	$VDM = \dfrac{100}{\sqrt{\pi Z}} = \dfrac{1}{q}$	$VDM = \dfrac{250}{z} = \dfrac{1}{q}$

* D_i = diameter in centimeters
BA_i = basal area in square meters
H_i = height in meters
C_i = circumference in centimeters
V_i = volume in any desired unit for the ith tree
** f_t and z_t calculated on the assumption that L = no. of 20 meter lengths

This means that tree diameter can be ignored in the field tally. Furthermore, every foot of height, in this case merchantable height, in a tree which qualifies represents 35.09 board feet of volume per acre. And so every 16-foot log represents 16 times 35.09 or 561 board feet per acre.

Example C is the theoretical foundation of the commonly used practice of assuming that "a one-log (16-foot logs) qualifying tree represents 600 board feet per acre, a two-log qualifying tree represents 1200 board feet per acre, and so on," as discussed by Miller (1963). This type of inventory has been termed "point sampling with diameter obviation" (Beers, 1964).

Careful study of Table 14–3(a) or Table 14–3(b) will show that there is a degree of circularity involved and that to derive certain of the formulas it is helpful to make use of relations derived separately from the table. For example, in developing the horizontal point sampling tree factor (see example under step 2 of "three steps to develop any factor"), in order to obtain the relation between the tree factor, F_t, and the basal area factor, F, it is necessary to make use of the relation $F = 10890k^2$ which was derived earlier. Of course, F is the "characteristic factor" for horizontal point sampling. Similarly, each other type of polyareal plot sampling has a "characteristic factor" and this factor has a simple relation to the appropriate gauge constant. These relationships, shown in Table 14–4, should be memorized or kept close at hand for ready reference.

Let us point out that if the inventory is such that individual tree measurements of diameter and height must be recorded, and if the data are to be processed by computer, there is little advantage in poring over Table 14–3 in search of short-cut solutions. The general summarization formulas shown in Table 14–5 are all that one needs.

Table 14–4
Basic Relationships for Polyareal Plot Sampling

Type of Sampling	Characteristic Factor Name	Symbol	Equation Relating Characteristic Factor and Gauge Constant[a] Using English Units	Using Metric Units
Horizontal point	Basal Area Factor	F	$F = 10890k^2$	$F = 2500k^2$
Horizontal line	Diameter factor	f	$f = 3960k = 12\sqrt{10F}$	$f = 2500k = 500\sqrt{F}$
Vertical point	Quadratic height factor	Z	$Z = \dfrac{43560}{\pi}q^2$	$Z = \dfrac{10000}{\pi}q^2$
Vertical line	Height factor	z	$z = 330q = \dfrac{\sqrt{10\pi Z}}{2}$	$z = 250q = 2.5\sqrt{\pi Z}$

[a]For horizontal sampling $k = 2\sin\dfrac{\theta}{2}$ and for vertical sampling $q = \tan\phi$, where θ and ϕ represent respectively the horizontal and vertical gauge angles in degrees.

Table 14-5
Summarization Equations for Use in Polyareal Plot Sampling

A. An estimate of a per-acre (hectare)characteristic, X_i, assuming m trees at *one point* (point sampling) or along a line segment *one chain* (20 meters in metric system) in length (line sampling) can be obtained from the following summarization equations, where $X_1, X_2, \ldots X_m$ represent the individual tree values for the characteristic being estimated:

1. Horizontal point sampling:

$$X_i = X_1 \left(\frac{F}{BA_1} \right) + X_2 \left(\frac{F}{BA_2} \right) + \ldots + X_m \left(\frac{F}{BA_m} \right)$$

where:
  F = basal area factor
  $BA_1, BA_2, \ldots, BA_m$ = basal area observed on individual trees

2. Horizontal line sampling:

$$X_i = X_1 \left(\frac{f}{D_1} \right) + X_2 \left(\frac{f}{D_2} \right) + \ldots + X_m \left(\frac{f}{D_m} \right)$$

where:
  f = diameter factor
  $D_1, D_2, \ldots, D_m$ = diameter observed on individual trees

3. Vertical point sampling:

$$X_i = X_1 \left(\frac{Z}{H_1^2} \right) + X_2 \left(\frac{Z}{H_2^2} \right) + \ldots + X_m \left(\frac{Z}{H_m^2} \right)$$

where:
  Z = quadratic height factor
  $H_1^2, H_2^2, \ldots, H_m^2$ = squared height observed on individual trees

4. Vertical line sampling:

$$X_i = X_1 \left(\frac{z}{H_1} \right) + X_2 \left(\frac{z}{H_2} \right) + \ldots + X_m \left(\frac{z}{H_m} \right)$$

where:
  z = height factor
  $H_1, H_2, \ldots, H_m$ = height observed on individual trees

B. Therefore, an *average* per-acre (hectare) estimate obtained from n points visited in a sample can be calculated by dividing the sum of the n sample estimates, ΣX_i by n. For line sampling the total length of line (in chains or in number of 20 meter units) is used instead of n.

14-4.4. Angle Gauges for Horizontal Sampling. For horizontal point or horizontal line sampling one needs an angle gauge which will accurately "project" a small horizontal angle, generally under five degrees. A tree which appears larger than the projected angle is considered "in," and a tree which appears smaller than the projected angle is considered "out."

Basically, there are two different ways of "projecting" the angle:

1. By prolonging two lines of sight from the eye through two points whose lateral separation, w, is fixed, and which are both in the same horizontal plane and at the same fixed distance, L, from the eye—Fig. 14–8 (a).
2. By deviating the light rays from the tree through a fixed angle— Fig. 14–8 (b).

Types of Instruments. Instruments based on the first principle include the stick-type angle gauge, the Panama angle gauge, and the Spiegel relaskop. To construct a stick-type angle gauge, a device which clearly

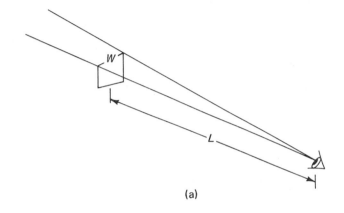

(a)

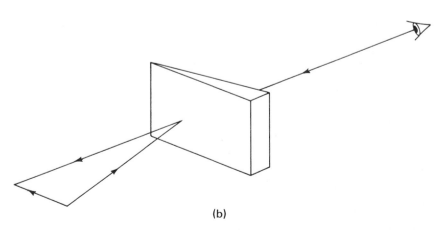

(b)

Fig. 14–8. Projecting a horizontal angle (a) by prolonging two lines of sight, and (b) by deviating the light rays through a fixed angle.

illustrates the principle behind all of these instruments, one simply provides a "stick" with a peep sight to position the eye, and a crossarm of predetermined width which is placed on the stick at a predetermined distance from the peep sight. To determine the width of the crossarm one must know the gauge constant, k, for the basal area factor, F, to be used, and make a decision on stick length, L. Then crossarm width, w, will be: $w = kL$.

The Spiegel relaskop uses the same basic principle. Instead of using a stick on which to position the crossarm, the Spiegel relaskop utilizes the principle of the *reflector sight* to image the scale (crossarm), which is on a wheel only a few inches from the eye, at a suitable viewing distance.

The thin prism or optical wedge is the only instrument of the second type which has been used by foresters. Briefly, a prism is a device made of optical glass or plastic in which the two surfaces are inclined at some angle, A (the refraction angle), so that the deviation produced by the first surface is further increased by the second. The chromatic dispersion is also increased. However, chromatic dispersion is not a cause of appreciable error unless a telescopic device is used in conjunction with the prism.

The cruising prisms which foresters have used in horizontal point sampling generally have a refracting angle of less than six degrees. Such prisms are made in square, rectangular, and round shapes.

The effect of "projecting" a fixed angle with a thin prism is shown in Fig. 14–9. In the figure the ray which is tangent to points a, b, and c on the sides of the tree to the observer's right is refracted to E. Thus, when an observer at E sights through the prism to points a, b, and c, he will see these points as if they were at a', b', and c'. Of course, all visible points on each tree cross-section will be displaced so each cross-section will ap-

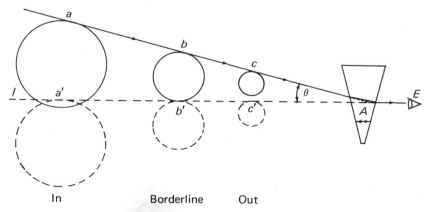

In   Borderline   Out

Fig. 14–9. Representation of image deflection using a prism (cross-section through prism and trees).

pear to be displaced as shown in the drawing. To use the prism as a gauge the observer looks *through* the prism at the right side of the trees—that is, at points a, b, and c, Fig. 14–9, and, at the same time, *over* the prism at the left side of the trees on the line of sight to I. He notes if the right side is, or is not, refracted past the left side. The actual "picture" that will be obtained when a round prism is used is shown in Fig. 14–10. Similar "pictures" are obtained with rectangular prisms.

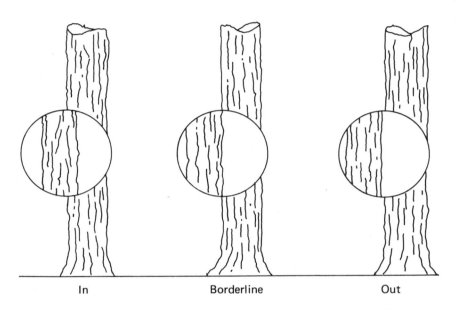

In	Borderline	Out

Fig. 14–10. Representation of image deflection using a prism (the picture as seen by the observer when using a round prism).

Although the thin prism is the only commonly used horizontal angle gauge based on the second principle, it is quite possible to deviate the light rays from the tree through a fixed angle by using either mirrors or right-angle prisms. Compared to the thin prism, such a device would be expensive, cumbersome, and probably difficult to use. On the other hand, this instrument would be free of chromatic dispersion, a condition that appears to be difficult, or expensive, to eliminate with the thin prism. Until magnification is required for horizontal angle gauging, the elimination of chromatic dispersion is unimportant.

Modification of the Angle Gauge. Since the determination of forest stand parameters is on a horizontal land area basis, the projected angle used must be corrected if the terrain is not level. Specifically, the gauge constant, k, must be reduced to a value, k_r, where $k_r = k$ (cos S), and where S is the slope angle in degrees.

For angle gauges based on the principle of projecting a horizontal angle by prolonging two lines of sight, as in Fig. 14–8 (a), slope correction can be achieved by reducing the crossarm width, w, to the value w_r, where $w_r = w$ (cos S), or increasing stick length, L, to the value L_r, where $L_r = L/$cos S. Employing both of these concepts, Robinson (1969) describes a very useful slope-correcting variable basal area factor stick-type gauge. The Spiegel relaskop uses an ingenious method of varying "crossarm" width. It has a "strip" scale that varies in width directly as the cosine of the slope angle. This scale, which is mounted on a weighted wheel, is seen "projected" on the target (the tree) and rotates by gravity to the appropriate position as the line of sight is raised or lowered.

Slope correction can be achieved when the thin prism is used by rotating the prism in a plane perpendicular to the line of sight through an angle equal to the slope angle. Such rotation properly reduces the gauge angle. The practical utility of this fortuitous relationship will not be discussed further except to point out that by prism rotation one can change the basal area factor very conveniently. For example, a prism having a basal area factor of 10.2 can be changed to one with a factor of 10.0 by rotating it perpendicular to the line of sight through an angle of 14 per cent:

$$\text{Since } k_r = k(\cos S) \tag{14–10}$$

$$\text{leading to } F_{\text{res}} \cong F(\cos^2 C) \tag{14–11}$$

$$\cos C \cong \sqrt{\frac{F_{\text{res}}}{F}} = \sqrt{\frac{10}{10.2}} \tag{14–12}$$

$$\cong \sqrt{.9803922} = .99015$$

$$\text{therefore, } C \cong 8°3' \text{ or } 14 \text{ per cent}$$

where:

k_r = resultant gauge constant after rotation
k = gauge constant of unrotated prism
C = angle of rotation
F = basal area factor (unrotated prism)
F_{res} = resultant basal area factor after rotation

Table G–9 in Beers and Miller (1966) can be used to avoid the calculations.

An additional rotation is required for slope correction which is not directly additive to the basic rotation. Although detailed discussion is beyond the present scope, it is worth noting that the following relationship has been found (see Beers and Miller, 1964):

$$\cos T = \cos S (\cos C) \tag{14–13}$$

where T is the total rotation in degrees required to correct for a slope of S degrees as well as to modify the gauge angle to a desired F_{res} by rotating the prism through the angle C in degrees. Angle C is found as described in the previous paragraph.

14–4.5. Angle Gauges for Vertical Sampling. For vertical point or vertical line sampling one needs an angle gauge which will accurately "project" a large vertical angle. A tree which appears larger than the projected angle is considered "in," and a tree which appears smaller than the projected angle is considered "out."

If ϕ is the vertical gauge angle in degrees, then, as Fig. 14–11 shows, ϕ must be corrected for slope. But even though the vertical angle changes on slope sights, the vertical gauge constant, $q = H/R$, does not change. Thus, one will project the correct vertical angle under all conditions if a device is used that maintains a constant ratio between a fixed vertical distance, H, and a fixed horizontal distance, R.

Rough plans for an instrument for vertical angle gauging are shown in Fig. 14–12. This device consists of a horizontal arm of length, R, mounted perpendicular to a movable vertical arm. A peep sight is mounted on the horizontal arm to position the eye, and two sighting marks are placed on the vertical arm to delimit distance H. In a device of this type, the gauge constant, $q = H/R$, is held constant.

Although several instruments similar to this have been built, e.g., conometer by Hirata (1955), and Jukohscope by Kaibara (1957), there appears to be little advantage in using such special instruments. Any clinometer which has a per cent scale can be used efficiently for vertical gauging as explained below.

Since the correct vertical gauge angle is projected so long as the gauge constant, q, is held constant, it follows that the correct gauge angle is projected when:

1. The tangent of the gauge angle (in a right triangle) equals q. Thus, in Fig. 14–11(a), $\tan \phi = q$.
2. The sum of the tangents of the angles sighted above and below the horizontal equals q. Thus, in Fig. 14–11(b), $\tan A + \tan B = q$.
3. The difference between the tangents of the two angles sighted above the horizontal equals q. Thus, in Fig. 14–11(c), $\tan A - \tan B = q$.

Since a per cent slope is the natural tangent of the vertical angle multiplied by 100, it follows that if we multiply the gauge constant, q, by 100, it will be expressed in per cent. Consequently, such instruments (clinometers) as the Abney level and the Haga altimeter, if they have a per cent scale, can be used to check trees to see if they are larger than, or smaller than, the projected vertical angle. Figure 14–13 reveals that one need remember only two simple rules to identify qualifying trees:

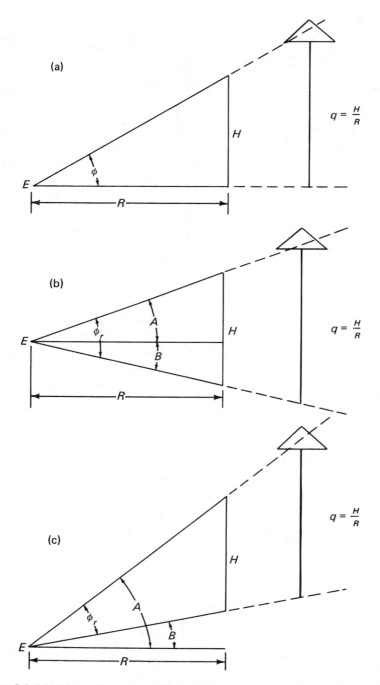

Fig. 14–11. When the ratio, H/R, is held constant, the correct vertical angle will be "projected." In (a) ϕ is the vertical gauge angle; in (b) and (c) ϕ_r is the slope-corrected vertical gauge angle.

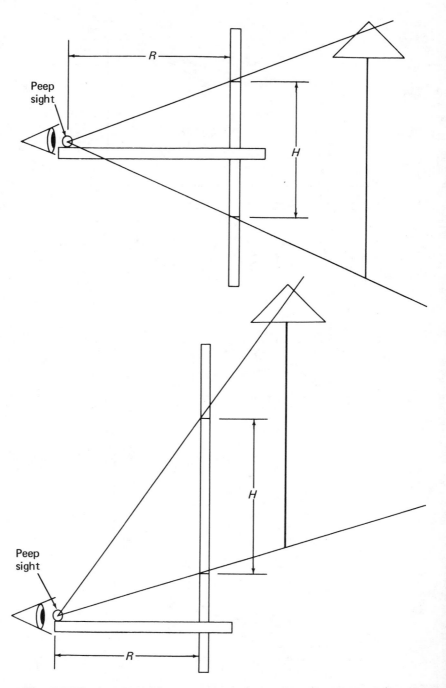

Fig. 14–12. Instrument for vertical angle gauging. The ratio, H/R, is held constant in all positions of the horizontal arm.

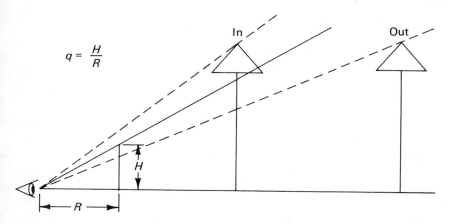

$$q = \frac{H}{R}$$

Fig. 14-13. A tree is "IN" if the per cent reading for the tree is greater than 100q. A tree is "OUT" if the per cent reading for the tree is less than 100q.

1. A tree will be "in" if the per cent readings, summed or subtracted as appropriate, to the tip and base of a tree (or to the merchantable limit and stump height) is *greater than* 100 times the gauge constant, q.
2. A tree will be "out" if the per cent readings, summed or subtracted as appropriate, to the tip and base of a tree (or to the merchantable limit and stump height) is *less than* 100 times the gauge constant, q.

To take a specific example, assume we have decided to use a vertical angle for gauging total height for which q is 1. Thus, 100q will be 100. Now, if we obtain a reading (with a per cent Abney level) of +67 to the tip of a tree and a reading of −40 to the base of the tree, the tree will be "in" because 107 (that is 67 + 40) is greater than 100. Then, on another tree, if the readings to the tree base and tip are +15 and +63, the tree will be out because 48 (that is 63 − 15) is less than 100.

There is little question that vertical sampling, in particular, vertical line sampling, is a potentially powerful forest sampling method. Initial trials have shown that it can be efficiently applied. However, additional experience will be required to fully demonstrate its usefulness as a practical inventory technique.

14-5. TALLY METHODS AND DATA SUMMARY

There is a variety of basic tally and processing methods for point and line sampling. But it is always possible for the forester to develop useful variations of the basic systems. Our purpose in this section is to describe briefly certain fundamental principles.

14–5.1. Principles. The form that the field tally will take depends primarily upon the following conditions: (1) the manner in which the data are to be processed—by hand, desk calculator, or computer; (2) whether or not a sampling error is to be calculated; (3) the type of p.p.s. sampling to be employed; (4) the nature of answers needed—volume, basal area, etc.; and (5) the number and type of classification variables to be employed—species, diameter class, grade, etc.

If the inventory is to be computer processed, the field tally is straightforward; generally, every qualifying sample tree is measured and described with regard to location (point or line) number, tree number, species, dbh, height, grade, form class, product class, vigor class, crown class, management potential class, or a subset thereof. In the design of the tally sheet, if porta-punch cards are not used, care should be taken to facilitate subsequent keypunching. The reduction of field measurements to the desired estimates of stand parameters is accomplished by the computer program, making use of processing formulas such as those noted in Table 14–5.

If sampling errors of the desired parameter estimates are to be calculated, the individual tree information must be kept separate by locations, that is by points or lines. In the computer processing case described in the previous paragraph this is routine since the identity of the point or line is usually maintained. In the common dot-dash tally system, however, a supplementary tally is ordinarily necessary to make valid estimates of the sampling error. Because of the extra time and effort involved, such a supplementary tally is frequently overlooked. The conscientious forester, however, is well advised to develop a convenient system to accomplish such a tally, for without a sampling error calculation his estimate is of unknown reliability. Examples of a supplementary tally and the calculation of the sampling error are given by Beers and Miller (1964).

The inventory planner who has elected to use a dot-dash tally system will usually do so for the reason of expediency, for only by such a tally will the tree information be sorted into the appropriate classes (species, dbh, grade, etc.) *as the tally is made*. Therefore, at the conclusion of the inventory, making use of a desk calculator, the estimates of the pertinent stand characteristics already broken down by classes are available within hours, or even minutes.

14–5.2. Use of the Factor Concept. Adoption of the "factor concept" described in Section 14–4.3 makes possible the universal application of the following "guides" for the data reduction to a great range of dot-dash tally systems. These guides are: (1) every tallied tree has one volume factor, tree factor, basal area factor, height factor, etc., associated with it; (2) an estimate of the average volume, average number of trees, average basal area, average height, etc., *per acre* (or *hectare*) for any specified breakdown (species class, dbh class, grade, grade within species, etc.) can be obtained by:

1. determining the sum of the appropriate "factor" over all trees in that breakdown, and
2. dividing by the number of points (point sampling) or number of line segments (line sampling) visited.

14–5.3. Volume-Basal Area Ratios. It is perhaps appropriate at this point to make reference to a general method of data reduction in horizontal point sampling which makes use of volume-basal area ratios (V-BAR), as described by Dilworth and Bell (1968). This approach represents an alternative to the method employing the "factor concept," which we have followed in this text because of the greater generality evident when all forms of point and line sampling are considered.

In the V-BAR approach, tree volume tables are converted to V-BAR tables by dividing each cell in the volume table by the basal area corresponding to each cell. In this way one obtains a table which shows, for a range of tree sizes, the number of units of volume per unit of basal area on an individual tree basis. In horizontal point sampling, then, the volume per acre (hectare) at a point can be found by multiplying the basal area factor times the count of qualifying trees times the sum of the V-BAR's of these trees.

Tables of V-BAR's and tables of volume factors, for horizontal point sampling can readily be derived from one another as follows:

$$F_v = \text{tree volume} \left(\frac{F}{\text{tree basal area}} \right)$$

$$= \left(\frac{\text{tree volume}}{\text{tree basal area}} \right) F$$

$$F_v = (\text{V-BAR}) F \qquad (14\text{–}14)$$

therefore:

$$\text{V-BAR} = \frac{F_v}{F} \qquad (14\text{–}15)$$

where:

F_v = volume factor
F = basal area factor
V-BAR = volume-basal area ratio on an individual tree basis

15

Growth of the Tree

15–1. INTRODUCTION

The most important growth phenomenon in forestry is the growth of individual trees and stands. This chapter will deal with the growth of individual trees; Chapter 16 will deal with the growth of stands.

Tree growth consists of elongation and thickening of roots, stems, and branches. Growth causes trees to change in weight and volume (size), and form (shape). Linear growth of all parts of a tree results from the activities of the primary meristem; diameter growth from the activities of the secondary meristem, or cambium, which produces new wood and bark between the old wood and bark. Total and merchantable height growth, diameter growth at breast height, and diameter growth at points up the stem are elements of tree growth most commonly measured by mensurationists—from these elements, volume or weight growth of sections of the stem, or of the entire stem, may be determined. Root and branch growth is also measured in certain cases.

15–1.1. Growth as an Ecological Expression. Tree growth is influenced by the genetic capabilities of a species interacting with the environment. Environmental influences include *climatic factors*—air temperature, precipitation, wind, and insolation; *soil factors*—soil, physical and chemical characteristics, moisture, and microorganisms; *topographic characteristics* —slope, elevation, and aspect; and *competition*—influences of other trees, lesser vegetation, and animals. The sum of all these environmental factors is expressed as *site quality*, although *competition* is of less importance than the other factors since it is transient and can be changed by silvicultural treatments. When a site has favorable growing conditions, it is considered "good." When a site has inhibitive growing conditions, it is considered "poor." Because the environmental conditions favorable for one tree species may be unfavorable for another tree species, site quality must be considered by individual species. Extremes exist that provide absolute limits for all species as exemplified by timber lines on mountains and in polar regions. But since site quality is an effect best expressed by the average reaction of the trees on an area of land, it is more readily measured for stands than for individual trees. Measures of site quality are, therefore, discussed in Chapter 17.

15–1.2. Methods of Expressing Tree and Stand Growth. The increase in a tree (or stand) dimension should be qualified by the period of time during which the increment occurred. The period may be a day, a month, a year, a decade, etc. When the period is a year, the increase, termed *current annual increment* (c.a.i.), is the difference between the dimensions measured at the beginning and at the end of the year's growth. Since it is difficult to measure some characteristics, such as volume, for a single year, the average annual growth for a period of years, termed *periodic annual increment* (p.a.i.), is often used in place of c.a.i. This is found by obtaining the difference between the dimensions measured at the beginning and at the end of the period, say five or ten years, and dividing by the number of years in the period. If the difference is not divided by the number of years, it is termed *periodic increment*. The average annual increase to any age, termed *mean annual increment* (m.a.i.), is found by dividing the cumulative size by the age.

These increment measures are applicable to individual trees (or stands) for any measurable growth characteristic. However, they have been most commonly applied to the volume growth of stands.

15–2. GROWTH CURVES

When the size of an organism (e.g., volume, weight, diameter, or height for a tree) is plotted over its age, the curve so defined is commonly called the growth curve—Fig. 15–1 (a). Such curves, characteristically S- or sigmoid-shaped, show the cumulative size at any age. Thus, they are more descriptively termed *cumulative growth curves*. A true growth curve, which shows increment at any age, results from plotting increment over age—Fig. 15–1 (b).

The S-shaped form of the cumulative growth curve is evident for individual cells, tissues, and organs, and for individual plants and animals for the full life span. Also, the pattern of growth for short growing periods, such as a growing season, tends to follow the S-shaped curve.

Although the exact form of the cumulative growth curve will change

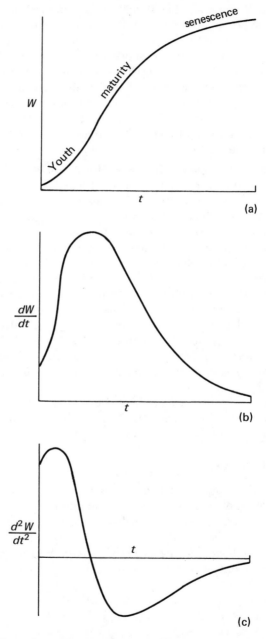

Fig. 15–1. The curve of cumulative growth is shown in (a); growth rate in (b); and acceleration in (c). (W = size; t = age.)

when the tree dimension (height, diameter, basal area, volume, or weight) plotted over age is changed, the cumulative growth curve has characteristics that hold for all dimensions of a tree. With this in mind an insight into tree growth can be obtained by studying Fig. 15-1 (a), and the derived curves, Fig. 15-1 (b) and Fig. 15-1 (c). During youth the growth rate increases rapidly to a maximum at the point of inflection in the cumulative growth curve, and the acceleration first increases and then drops to zero at the point of inflection in the cumulative growth curve. During maturity and senescence the growth rate decreases with related changes in acceleration.

Curves of current annual increment, periodic annual increment, and mean annual increment may also be derived from a cumulative growth curve by computing increments from sizes read from the cumulative growth curve at chosen ages, and plotting the increments over age. Figure 15-2 shows curves of p.a.i. and m.a.i. that were derived from a cumulative height-growth curve. From this figure it is seen that m.a.i. culminates when it equals p.a.i. (this is also true when m.a.i. equals c.a.i.). A formal proof of this could be given, but the reason is obvious; m.a.i. will lag behind p.a.i., if it is smaller than p.a.i. When p.a.i. drops below m.a.i., m.a.i. must decrease; it, therefore, reaches its maximum when equal to p.a.i.

It should be noted that c.a.i. could be found analytically as the first derivative, if cumulative growth is expressible as an equation.

Finally, in working with growth curves, one should realize that each species, perhaps each tree, dispenses a time of its own making. This physiological time varies from one tree species to another, and from one stage of development to another. In a sense, then, it is true that a twenty-year-old aspen is older than a twenty-year-old Douglas fir; the aspen develops more rapidly than the Douglas fir.

15-3. HEIGHT AND DIAMETER GROWTH

Characteristically, a cumulative growth curve of height over age for trees shows a juvenile period of less than a decade, a long maturing period when the trend is nearly linear, and a leveling off in old age. A cumulative growth curve of diameter over age shows much the same trend; there is, however, more of a tendency toward curvilinearity during the period of maturity. Since diameter is usually measured at breast height, d.b.h. cannot be measured until a tree is over 4.5 feet tall. Consequently, some of the early growth is over before measurement begins—curves of d.b.h. over age may not reflect some of the early youth portion.

Past height and diameter growth of individual trees may be determined (1) from repeated measurements of total size at the beginning and

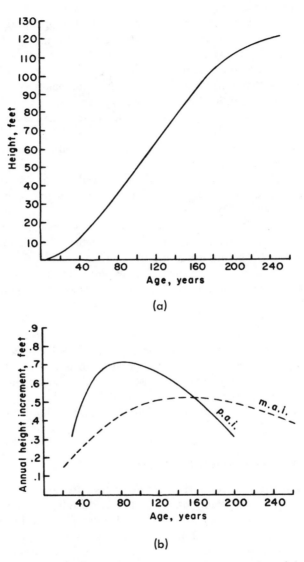

Fig. 15–2. The cumulative height growth curve is shown in (a); the curves of periodic annual height growth (p.a.i.) and mean annual height growth (m.a.i.) are shown in (b); (p.a.i. and m.a.i. curves derived from cumulative height growth curve).

at the end of specified growing periods, and (2) from increment measurements of past growth.

15–3.1. Repeated Measurements. Height growth of an individual tree can be obtained by measuring the total (or merchantable) height of a standing tree at the initiation and at the cessation of a specified growing period, and taking the difference. Tree heights up to seventy-five feet can be accurately and precisely determined with telescopic measuring poles that can be purchased from forestry and engineering supply companies. However, for measuring heights over thirty feet, poles are slow and cumbersome; then it is more convenient to use a transit or some other precise tripod-mounted instrument that gives height indirectly. Repeated measurements of trees with hand-held hypsometers generally do not give sufficiently precise increment measurements.

Diameter growth of an individual tree can be obtained by measuring the diameter at the beginning and at the end of a specified period, and taking the difference. Since annual diameter increment is small, when instruments such as calipers and diameter tapes are used, measurements are frequently taken at intervals of several years. However, for short periods, even for a day, diameter growth can be obtained with more precise instruments (see Chapter 3).

15–3.2. Increment Measurements. Increment measurements of past height growth can be made quickly if a reference point is marked on a tree, or on a pole by the tree. Past increment for intervals during a growing season, for a growing season, or for a specified period may be measured from this reference point. Also, past height increment may be determined by stem analysis (Section 15–5). And for species for which the internodal lengths on the stem indicate a year's growth, past height growth may be determined by measuring internodal lengths.

In regions where tree growth has a seasonal or annual growth pattern, past diameter increment can be obtained from increment borings or cross-sectional cuts. Borings or cross-sections can be secured at any point along the stem. However, diameter increment is most often determined at breast height from increment borings. But, when dealing with high-quality trees, it may be advisable to bore at stump height to eliminate damage in the butt log. Meyer (1953) explained how to convert growth at stump height to growth at breast height.

Average radial growth may be determined from several increment cores taken at breast height, but usually only one core is taken. This core should be extracted halfway between the long and short diameters at breast height. The length of the core depends on the past period for which growth is desired. If growth for the life of the tree is needed, the boring should reach the pith; if growth for a past period is needed as the basis of growth predictions, the boring should include the number of rings in the period, usually five or ten years.

When a core of no more than 0.75 inches is satisfactory, an increment hammer may be used (Bickerstaff, 1948). This device is used like an ordinary hammer. The tree is struck at right angles to the stem surface, the tool removed from the tree, and the core ejected with a plunger.

If increment cores are taken to the office for study, each core should be labeled in the field and placed in a suitable container to avoid breakage. A grooved board with cover makes a convenient carrier. Large drinking straws make excellent holders for individual cores. Cores can be measured in the office with greater accuracy than in the field by techniques that utilize a low-power microscope. However, when the core length is needed only to the nearest .05 inches, as is often the case, field measurements made with a 10X hand lens are sufficiently accurate.

15–4. HEIGHT-DIAMETER CURVES

If two variables are each correlated with a common variable, they will appear to be correlated with each other. Since both tree height and tree diameter are correlated with age, height appears to be correlated with diameter. Such height curves, which are often plotted as free-hand curves, particularly for preparing local volume tables, appear to have a relation that can be expressed by a mathematical function. Since the curve form may vary from one forest stand to another, several functions have been developed:

1. $H = 4.5 + bD - cD^2$ (Trorey, 1932)
2. $H = 4.5 + h(1 - e^{-aD})$ (Meyer, 1940)
3. $\log H = a + b \log D$ (Stoffels and Van Soest, 1953)
4. $H = a + b \log D$ (Henricksen, 1950)

where:

H = total height in feet
D = d.b.h. in inches
e = base of natural logarithms
a,b,c = constants

The parabolic equation, $H = 4.5 + bD - cD^2$, can be used to describe the height-diameter relationships of many forest stands. However, if one desires to use a mathematical function to describe the height-diameter relationship for a particular stand, he should test to see which function is most applicable.

15–5. STEM ANALYSIS

A record of the past growth of a tree may be obtained by a stem analysis. Such a study shows how a tree grew in height and diameter and how it changed in form as it increased in size. In making a stem analysis one counts and measures the growth rings on stem cross-sections at different heights above the ground. Measurements may be taken on a standing tree by using an increment borer, if the tree is not too big or the wood too hard. It is more convenient and more accurate, however, to obtain the measurements from cut cross-sections.

The procedure for making a stem analysis on cut cross-sections is simple:

1. Fell tree and cut stem into sections of desired lengths.
2. Determine and record species, d.b.h., total height, years to attain stump height, and total age.
3. Measure and record the height of the stump, length of each section, and length of tip.
4. Measure and record average diameter at top of each section.
5. Find an average radius on each cross-section and draw a line along it with a soft pencil.
6. Along each average radius count the annual rings from the cambium inward, marking the beginning of each tenth ring, or other desired period. Record the total number of rings at each cross-section.
7. From the center of each cross-section, measure outward toward the cambium along the average radius, recording the distance from the center of each tenth ring, or to other desired ring count. The fractional part of a decade, or other desired period, will be measured and recorded first.

Table 15–1 shows how the measurements should be recorded, and Table 15–2 how the height measurements should be summarized. Note that lengths are normally recorded to the nearest foot, diameters are recorded to the nearest one-tenth inch, and radii are recorded to the nearest one-twentieth inch.

In Fig. 15–3 the data from Tables 15–1 and 15–2 are presented in graphic form. Diameters at each level are first plotted against height. Diameters representing the same ages are then connected to form a series of taper curves for specified ages. The terminal position of each curve is estimated from the curve of height over age (prepared from Table 15–2), as indicated for the 14-year taper curve.

Table 15–1
Measurements for Stem Analysis of a 34-Year Old Red Oak

Species __Red Oak__ DBH __10.2″__ Total Height __54′__

Years to attain stump height __2__ Total Age __34__

Date __March 2, 1968__ Measured by __CIM__

Section No.	Length (feet)	Top Dib (inches)	No. of Rings at Top	Distance Along Average Radius from Heart to Each 10th Ring-Inches (inches)*									
				1	2	3	4	5	6	7	8	9	10
1 stump	1	10.3	32	0.65	2.50	3.80	5.15						
2	16	8.7	24	1.30	3.00	4.35							
3	16	6.0	17	1.65	3.00								
4	14	2.7	9	1.35									
5	7	0	0										

*Double these values to give average diameters when plotting taper curves.

Table 15–2
Height Summary for Stem Analysis of a 34-Year Old Red Oak

	Section No.				
	1	2	3	4	5
Length (feet)	1	16	16	14	7
Height above ground of top of section (feet)	1	17	33	47	54
Ring count top of section	32	24	17	9	0
Years to grow section	2	8	7	8	9
Years to attain height at top of section	2	10	17	25	34

15–6. AREAL AND VOLUME GROWTH

Besides height and diameter growth, areal growth (basal area and bole surface area) and volume, or weight, growth may be of interest. Although the cumulative growth curves for both areal growth and volume growth are typically S-shaped, the exact form of the curves is variable.

Basal area growth may be estimated from periodic measurements of d.b.h. Bole surface area growth may be estimated by calculating surface

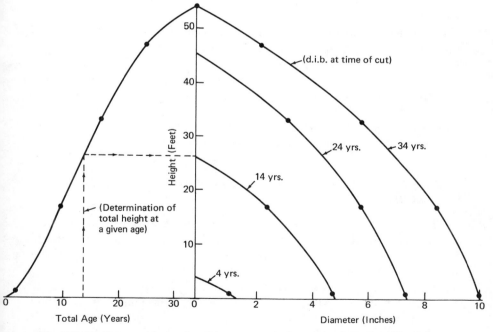

Fig. 15–3. Stem analysis of a 34-year-old red oak; taper curves by 10-year intervals.

area and surface area growth from periodic measurements of stem diameters at predetermined intervals along the stem. And volume growth, the most important growth determination, may be estimated by taking periodic measurements of d.b.h., d.b.h. and height, or d.b.h., height, and form, and determining volumes at beginning and end of period from a local, standard, or form-class volume table, as appropriate, and taking the difference. Of course, stem analysis may be used to obtain the required measurements, and graphical methods to determine the volumes.

Baker (1960) has called attention to a simple formula that permits rapid field computation of current annual volume increment of individual trees. The formula is:

$$I = \frac{D \times H \times W}{100} \qquad (15\text{--}1)$$

where:

I = current annual volume increment in cubic feet
D = diameter at breast height inside bark
H = total height in feet
W = width of last complete ring in inches

Note that this formula permits rapid determination of gross annual volume increment of the initial volume per acre from individual tree determinations.

Board feet or cords are not good measures of volume growth because of fundamental limitations (see Chapter 7). Thus, growth estimates in board feet or cords are best made by converting cubic growth estimates into these units. And although weight growth has never received much attention, procedures for estimation of weight growth are not difficult. As Hirai (1950) found, weight and volume increments of individual trees are almost parallel in their patterns. Therefore, procedures for weight growth estimation are analogous to procedures for volume growth estimation.

15–7. EFFECTS OF TRANSIENT ENVIRONMENTAL INFLUENCES ON GROWTH

The environmental factors that affect the growth of trees may be *stable* or *transient*. Stable factors—soil texture, slope, aspect, and soil nutrient level—do not change appreciably during the life of a tree. Transient factors—fluctuations in climate and competition between organisms—change cyclically or erratically during the life of a tree.

If past growth is used as a basis for growth predictions, it is important to recognize the magnitude of the effect of the transient factors. When stand competition is altered by cutting, growth will be affected; the changes for a given time are readily related to the cutting. When there are climatic variations, they also affect growth. These fluctuations, however, are not so recognizable, and are not as easy to segregate from the total growth response. Yet, it may be necessary to estimate and evaluate the growth variation due to climatic changes. For example, if the effect on a tree or stand of a release cutting were under investigation, the periodic volume growth before and after the cutting could be used as the measure of the growth response, except that part of the response may be due to variations in climate as well as to a decrease in competition.

An adjustment can be made when it is necessary to eliminate the effect of climatic variations on growth. Meyer (1942) devised a procedure for adjusting diameter growth data to eliminate these effects. This procedure consists of plotting annual increments for individual trees, or averages for several trees, over time and fitting a trend line to the points. The deviations from the trend line for individual years can then be expressed as percentages of the trend line values, and can be assumed to be related to changes in weather conditions. Thus, growth estimates for a period of years may be increased or decreased by the magnitude of the average per cent deviation for the period. Since the variation in growth due to climate decreases as the length of the growth period increases, most growth measurements are made for periods of five years or more.

15–8. GROWTH PERCENTAGE

Growth percentage is a means of expressing the increment of any tree parameter in relation to the total size of the parameter at the initiation of growth. Although growth percentage is most frequently used for volume and basal area growth, it is applicable to any parameter.

In terms of *simple interest,* growth per cent, p_i, is:

$$p_i = \frac{s_n - s_o}{ns_o} (100) \qquad (15\text{–}2)$$

where:

s_o = size of parameter at beginning of growth period
s_n = size of parameter at end of growth period
n = number of units of time in growth period

In this formula, average growth per unit of time is expressed as a percentage of the initial size, s_o. To illustrate, if the present volume of a tree is 400 board feet, and the volume ten years ago was 300 board feet:

$$p_i = \frac{400 - 300}{10(300)} (100) = 3.3\%$$

In terms of *compound interest,* growth per cent, p, is:

$$p = \left(\sqrt[n]{\frac{s_n}{s_o}} - 1 \right) 100 \qquad (15\text{-}3)$$

In this form, p may be computed by logarithms. But when compound interest tables are available, a more convenient form of the formula is as follows:

$$(1 + p)^n = \frac{s_n}{s_o} \qquad (15\text{-}4)$$

The compound interest rate for the previously mentioned tree is then:

$$(1 + p)^n = \frac{400}{300} = 1.333$$

$$p = 2.9\%$$

The compound interest rate is based on the premise that the increment for each unit of time is accumulated, resulting in an increasing value of s_o. Thus, as the period increases the simple and compound interest rates will diverge more and more. For short periods, however, they will be almost the same.

To avoid the use of compound interest tables, Pressler based a simple rate of interest on the average value for the period, $(s_n + s_o)/2$, which has the effect of reducing the rate to near the compound interest rate. *Pressler's growth per cent, p_p, is:*

$$p_p = \left(\frac{s_n - s_o}{s_n + s_o} \right) \frac{200}{n} \qquad (15\text{-}5)$$

For the previous example:

$$p_p = \left(\frac{400 - 300}{400 + 300} \right) \frac{200}{10} = 2.86\%$$

It is essential to remember that growth percentages are ratios between increment and initial size. Thus, percentages change as the amount of increment and the base upon which it accrued changes. As trees grow the base of the percentage constantly increases, and the growth percentage declines even though the absolute increment may be constant or even increasing slightly. In early life the growth percentage for a tree is at its highest because the base of the ratio is small; the percentage falls as the size of the tree increases. Although young trees may grow at compound rates for limited periods, growth per cent is generally an unsafe tool to predict tree or stand growth, because of the uncertainty in extrapolating growth per cent curves.

15–9. DETERMINATION OF GROWTH FROM INCREMENT CORES

Diameter growth is normally desired at breast height. And although most increment borings are made at breast height, growth measurements made at stump height may be converted to growth at breast height (Meyer, 1953).

Increment borings should be taken from trees on sample plots or sample points. For example, if one used ⅕-acre plots on a cruise, he might lay out ¹⁄₂₀-acre plots within selected ⅕-acre plots (say one in four) and bore trees on the ¹⁄₂₀-acre plots. If one used horizontal point sampling ($F = 10$), he might use a forty-factor gauge at selected points to choose trees to bore. For each species or species group studied, a reliable estimate of average diameter increment by diameter classes can be obtained from a representative sample of about 100 increment measurements.

A word of warning: Boring one, two, or any predetermined number of trees per plot, rather than sampling as explained in the previous paragraph, will result in an overestimation of growth because in open stands the sample will represent a larger proportion of the trees than in dense stands—trees in open stands grow faster than trees in dense stands.

A form for recording the field data is shown in Table 15–3. This table indicates the recommended degree of accuracy of measurements and calculations. Generally only columns 1, 2, 3, 4, and 6 are completed in the field. The core to determine past ten-years radial wood growth should be extracted halfway between the long and short diameters.

The constant, K, the average ratio of diameter outside bark to diameter inside bark, is the inverse of the ratio used to calculate bark volume (Section 8–6). Thus, the equation of the straight line expressing diameter outside bark, d, as a function of diameter inside bark, d_u, is:

$$d = Kd_u \tag{15–6}$$

K varies by species and, to some extent, by locality.

Average values of K are calculated as follows:

$$K = \frac{\Sigma\, d}{\Sigma\, d_u}$$

Thus, for the trees listed in Table 15–3, $K = 1.10$.

The calculations for columns 5, 7, and 10 in Table 15–3 are self-explanatory. To calculate column 8, that is, past diameter at breast height outside bark, d_p, past diameter at breast height inside bark, d_{u_p}, is multiplied by K (equation 15–6). To calculate column 9, that is, periodic diameter increment outside bark, i, the past ten-years radial wood growth, L, is doubled and multiplied by K. This is true because if, in a given period, $2L$ inches of wood are laid on a given past diameter inside bark,

Table 15-3
Determination of Diameter Growth from Increment Cores

(1) Tree No.	(2) Species	(3) Present dbh ob (d)	(4) Double bark ($2b$)	(5) Present dbh ib (d_u)	(6) Past 10-yrs. radial wood growth (L)	(7) Past dbh ib (d_{up})	(8) Past dbh ob (d_p)	(9) Periodic dbh ob increment (i)	(10) Periodic Annual dbh ob increment ($i/10$)
					(in inches)				
1	Hd. Map.	16.2	1.4	14.8	1.32	12.2	13.4	2.90	0.290
2	Hd. Map.	12.6	1.1	11.5	0.75	10.0	11.0	1.65	0.165
3	Hd. Map.	10.4	1.0	9.4	0.80	7.8	8.6	1.76	0.176
4	Hd. Map.	12.2	1.1	11.1	1.08	8.9	9.8	2.38	0.238
.		.	.	.	.	.	.	.	.
.		.	.	.	.	.	.	.	.
100	Hd. Map.	17.8	1.6	16.2	1.04	14.1	15.5	2.29	0.229
Totals:		1285.0	117.0	1168.0	98.70	970.6	1068.0	217.14	21.714
Averages:		12.85	1.17	11.68	0.987	9.71	10.68	2.171	.2171

where:

$d_u = d - 2b$

$d_{up} = d_u - 2L$

$d_p = K(d_{up})$

$i = K(2L)$

Data is normally averaged by diameter classes. Averages for columns 5, 7, 8, 9, and 10 can be computed from the averages for columns 3, 4, and 6, and the constant K, without computing the individual values in the columns.

$K = 1285/1168 = 1.10$

d_{u_p}, in terms of present diameter inside bark, d_u, past diameter inside bark will be:

$$d_{u_p} = d_u - 2L$$

and

$$2L = d_u - d_{u_p}$$

And, if in a given period, i inches of wood and bark are laid on a given past diameter outside bark, d_p, in terms of present diameter outside bark, d, past diameter outside bark will be:

$$d_p = d - i \qquad (15\text{--}7)$$

and:

$$
\begin{aligned}
i &= d - d_p \\
&= K(d_u) - K(d_{u_p}) \\
&= K(d_u - d_{u_p}) \\
&= K(2L) \qquad (15\text{--}8)
\end{aligned}
$$

Table 15–3 makes it convenient to plot periodic or periodic annual diameter growth over present diameter outside bark, or over past diameter outside bark, and thus obtain average diameter growth by diameter classes. When the trend of the curve can be represented by a straight line, the curve can easily be fitted by the method of least squares. However, if the trend of the curve is not linear, it may be difficult to find a mathematical function to express the curve form. When a mathematical function cannot be found, a free-hand curve can be fitted to the data.

Whether one plots diameter growth over present diameter outside bark or over past diameter outside bark, the final growth determinations will generally be about the same. However, the second alternative, which assumes that trees of a given diameter will have the same average diameter growth that trees of that diameter had in the past, is preferred to the first alternative, which assumes that future average diameter growth will equal past average diameter growth.

If data are available to predict the trend of diameter growth, average diameter growth may be raised or lowered to fit the trend. This, however, is usually an unnecessary refinement.

16

Stand Growth

16–1. TYPES OF STAND GROWTH

The structure of a stand, that is, the distribution of trees by diameter classes, changes from year to year because of the growth, death, and cutting of trees. Thus, many problems of stand growth are best understood by considering a stand as a population of trees, and by studying the changes in the structure of this population. For example, consider an even-aged stand that has been measured at two successive inventories, ten years apart (Fig. 16–1). If the periodic diameter growth of all trees was two inches, the periodic growth of this stand would be characterized by a displacement of the diameter distribution two inches to the right. The difference between the two inventory volumes represents the gross growth of the volume present at the first inventory. This is depicted in Fig. 16–1, if one omits ingrowth, and disregards mortality and cut.

The importance of *ingrowth, mortality,* and *cut* in any expression of stand growth is illustrated in Fig. 16–1. But, before more precise presentation is considered, these important terms must be clearly defined. Although volume is the forest parameter stressed in the following definitions, the terms are equally appropriate if another characteristic such as basal area is considered.

Ingrowth is the number or volume of trees periodically growing into measurable size. (There will normally be ingrowth between any two successive inventories, particularly when measurements are made above a minimum diameter, such as six or eight inches. The volume of the ingrowth may be fifty per cent or more of total cubic volume growth, and will be variable from one period to another.)

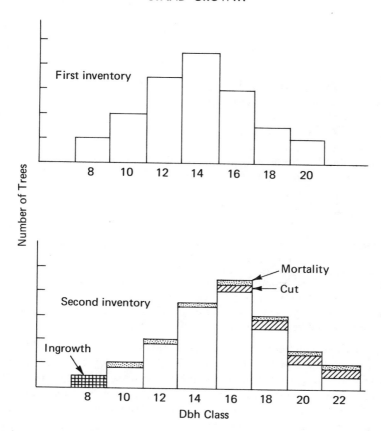

Fig. 16–1. Schematic representation of the changes in stand structure of an even-aged stand due to growth over a 10-year period (Beers, 1962).

Mortality is the number or volume of trees periodically rendered unusable through natural causes such as old age, competition, insects, diseases, wind, and ice. (Mortality may be insignificant to catastrophic, and may occur at any time during a growth period.)

Cut is the number or volume of trees periodically felled or salvaged, whether removed from the forest or not. (A cut may be light, medium. or heavy, and may occur at any time during the period.)

With the above definitions in mind, the generally accepted growth terms (Beers, 1962) can be defined by equations:

$$G_g = V_2 + M + C - I - V_1 \tag{16–1}$$

$$G_{g+i} = V_2 + M + C - V_1 \tag{16–2}$$

$$G_n = V_2 + C - I - V_1 \tag{16–3}$$

$$G_{n+i} = V_2 + C - V_1 \qquad (16\text{--}4)$$

$$G_d = V_2 - V_1 \qquad (16\text{--}5)$$

where:

G_g = gross growth of initial volume
G_{g+i} = gross growth including ingrowth
G_n = net growth of initial volume
G_{n+i} = net growth including ingrowth
G_d = net increase
V_1 = stand volume at beginning of growth period
V_2 = stand volume at end of growth period
M = mortality volume
C = cut volume
I = ingrowth volume

It should be noted that in the above equations *mortality* and *cut* may be defined in two different ways:

1. M and C represent the volume of M and C trees at the time of their death or cutting, or
2. M and C represent the volume of M and C trees at the time of the first inventory—that is, the initial volume of M and C trees.

The method of inventory generally dictates the most applicable definition of mortality and cut. For example, in inventory systems where the trees are not numbered, it is necessary to measure mortality trees at the time of the second inventory, which amounts to measuring them at the time of death, and to measure cut trees at the time of cutting. Under these conditions definition 1 would apply, and computations of growth that included M and C would then include growth put on by trees that died or were cut during the period between inventories.

If the inventory system utilizes numbered trees, as most continuous forest inventory (CFI) procedures do, one can use the initial volume of cut and mortality trees and avoid measuring cut trees at the time of cutting. Under these conditions, definition 2 would apply, and computations of growth that included M and C would not include growth put on by trees that died or were cut during the period between inventories. Of course, if numbered trees are used, cut trees may be measured at the time of cutting, and mortality trees at the second inventory, but this practice, which is seldom followed, requires extra care and "bookkeeping."

When gross growth of initial volume (equation 16–1) is computed using definition 2 for M and C, it includes only the growth on the trees that survived the period. Then it is often called *survivor growth*. When gross growth of initial volume is computed using definition 1 for M and C, it includes growth on trees that later died or were cut. Then it is often called *accretion*. (Note that growth on trees that later died or were cut may be an important component if cutting or mortality has been heavy, or if the interval between the inventories is long.) Marquis and Beers (1969) recommended that "the terms *survivor growth* and *accretion* be used where appropriate, and that *gross growth of initial volume* be considered a general term applicable only when either of these precise terms is not appropriate."

There is little advantage to use additional terms to qualify the growth terms expressed by equations 16–2 to 16–5. When these formulas are used, however, one must understand which definition is used for M and C.

16–1.1. Applications to Modern Continuous Forest Inventory.

Equations 16–1 to 16–5 apply when tree volumes are first totaled and the resulting sums manipulated. But if we use the modern CFI approach and begin at the tree level, it is desirable to apply the following equations to calculate the various types of growth:

$$G_g = V_{s_2} - V_{s_1} \tag{16–6}$$

$$G_{g+i} = G_g + I \tag{16–7}$$

$$G_n = G_g - M \tag{16–8}$$

$$G_{n+i} = G_g + I - M \tag{16–9}$$

$$G_d = G_g + I - M - C \tag{16–10}$$

where:

G_g, G_{g+i}, G_n, G_{n+i}, and G_d are as defined in Section 16–1

V_{s_1} = initial volume of survivor trees, that is, live trees measured at both inventories

V_{s_2} = final volume of survivor trees, that is, live trees measured at both inventories

M = initial volume of mortality trees

C = initial volume of cut trees

I = final volume of ingrowth trees

Since M and C represent the initial volume of mortality and cut trees, gross growth of initial volume, G_g, is correctly termed survivor growth. With this in mind, let us study Table 16–1 to illustrate the differences between equations 16–1 to 16–5 and equations 16–6 to 16–10.

If the volume totals from Table 16–1 are used, the net growth including ingrowth is obtained from equation 16–4:

$$G_{n+i} = V_2 + C - V_1 = 749.3 + 241.4 - 744.4 = 246.3$$

Neither mortality volume nor ingrowth volume enters into the calculation.

Table 16–1

Growth Data from a 1/5-Acre Permanent Sample Plot—Growth Period: 10 Years

Tree number	Tree status[1]	Sound Volume of						Net growth
		First inventory	Second inventory	Survivor growth	Mortality	Cut	Ingrowth	
		Board feet						
1	20	62.1	—	—	62.1	—	—	−62.1
2	24	81.3	—	—	—	81.3	—	—
3	24	66.8	—	—	—	66.8	—	—
4	22	42.4	62.3	19.9	—	—	—	19.9
5	22	63.3	122.5	59.2	—	—	—	59.2
6	22	106.0	163.8	57.8	—	—	—	57.8
7	12	—	34.6	—	—	—	34.6	34.6
8	24	93.3	—	—	—	93.3	—	—
9	22	82.0	119.8	37.8	—	—	—	37.8
10	22	147.2	246.3	99.1	—	—	—	99.1
Plot totals		744.4	749.3	273.8	62.1	241.4	34.6	246.3
Symbol		V_1	V_2	G_g	M	C	I	G_{n+i}

[1] Tree status as used here defines the class of tree from a growth-contribution standpoint. Status at each inventory is coded as follows: 0 = not present, 1 = pulpwood size, 2 = sawlog size, 3 = cull, 4 = cut. By combining the tree classes at successive inventories, then 20 = sawlog mortality, 24 = sawlog cut, 22 = sawlog survivor tree, 12 = sawlog ingrowth from pulpwood size, etc.
SOURCE: Beers, 1962.

But if the growth per tree is first calculated, then the net growth including ingrowth is obtained from equation 16–9:

$$G_{n+i} = G_g + I - M = 273.8 + 34.6 - 62.1 = 246.3$$

Or in an approach that typifies the modern CFI procedure, G_{n+i} may be obtained by totaling the last column in Table 16–1, where cut trees were not entered.

It should be clear that the other growth terms may be computed by the alternate formulas, and that the same results will be obtained by consistent use of either equations 16–1 to 16–5 or equations 16–6 to 16–10.

It will be noted that Table 16–1 uses the term *sound volume*. This is done to avoid the use of the terms net and gross when referring to tree or stand soundness, that is, amount of defect. This follows the suggestion of Meyer (1953) that tree or stand volume before defect deduction be termed *total* tree volume (rather than gross), and that tree or stand volume after defect deduction be termed *sound* tree volume (rather than net). Employing this terminology, we can have gross and net stand growth in terms of total or sound stand volume.

16–2. DIRECT ESTIMATION OF STAND GROWTH

Direct methods of estimating stand growth are based on an analysis of a given stand from measured variables. Indirect methods (Section 16–3) make use of yield or growth information that may be presented in tabular or equation form, and that is generally derived from stands other than the one being studied. Indirect methods are basically comparative. Direct methods are not comparative, although data may be used from other stands.

The important direct methods of estimating growth fall under two headings: *stand-table projection* and *total-stand projection*. In Sections 16–2.1 and 16–2.2 these methods will be discussed to illustrate the general techniques. H. A. Meyer (1942) and Spurr (1952) discuss other direct methods that may be of interest for certain purposes.

16–2.1. Stand-table Projection. To apply any stand-table projection method, the following data are needed:

1. Diameter growth information.
2. Present stand table.
3. Local volume table.
4. Information to calculate ingrowth.
5. Estimates of mortality.

Diameter growth information is most commonly obtained from increment borings (Section 15–9). However, excellent diameter growth information may be obtained from repeated measurements of permanent plots. In any case, there are three basic ways that diameter growth information may be applied to the present stand table in conjunction with a local volume table to obtain a growth estimate:

1. Assume that all trees in each diameter class are located at the class midpoint, and that all trees will grow at the average rate. Table 16–2 illustrates this approach:

Column 2 is obtained as explained in Section 15–9.
Column 3 = Column 1 + Column 2.
Column 4 gives the local volume table values for the diameters given in Column 3. The values may be read from a curve of volume over tree diameter (Column 6 over Column 1), or calculated by an appropriate volume equation.
Column 5 is obtained from inventory data.
Column 6 gives the local volume table values for the diameters given in Column 1.
Column 7 = Column 4 × Column 5.
Column 8 = Column 5 × Column 6.
Column 9 = Column 7 − Column 8.

Table 16-2

Calculation of 10-Year Predicted Volume Growth Per Acre, Assuming That All Trees in Each Diameter Class Are Located at the Class Midpoint, and That All Trees Will Grow at the Average Rate

(1)	(2)	(3)	(4)	(5)	(6)	(7)	(8)	(9)
Present dbh class	10-Year dbh increment	Future dbh	Future volume per tree	Present stand table	Present volume per tree	Future stock table	Present stock table	Volume production
(inches)	(inches)	(inches)	(cu.ft.)	(number)	(cu.ft.)	(cu.ft.)	(cu.ft.)	(cu.ft.)
6	2.02	8.02		41.73				
8	1.88	9.88		28.73				
10	1.74	11.74	17.0	21.73	12.5	369.4	271.6	97.8
12	1.60	13.60	24.2	17.33	18.4	419.4	318.9	100.5
14	1.46	15.46	31.9	12.87	25.6	410.6	329.5	81.1
16	1.32	17.32	40.7	9.47	34.2	385.4	323.9	61.5
18	1.18	19.18	50.1	8.27	44.1	414.3	364.7	49.6
20	1.04	21.04	62.3	5.00	55.6	311.5	278.0	33.5
22	0.90	22.90	75.3	3.47	68.5	261.3	237.7	23.6
24	0.76	24.76	89.8	2.87	83.5	257.7	239.6	18.1
26					100.1			
Total				151.47		2829.6	2363.9	465.7

Note that the sum of Column 9 equals the periodic gross growth of the initial volume. However, if the periodic diameter growth of the 8-inch diameter class had been over 2.00 inches, all trees in this class would have grown to measurable size, that is, to the 10-inch class, and would have been *ingrowth*. This, of course, would have increased volume production. Thus, results may be inconsistent if an attempt is made to include ingrowth. But when no attempt is made to determine ingrowth, the method gives good estimates of gross growth of the initial volume.

2. Assume trees in each diameter class are evenly distributed through the class, and each tree will grow at the average rate. Table 16–3 illustrates this approach. In this case a future stand table is predicted by first calculating the movement ratio, M, for each diameter class:

$$M = I/C$$

where:

I = periodic diameter increment
C = diameter class interval in same units as I

Thus, the movement ratio for the 12-inch diameter class (Table 16–3) is:

$$M = 1.60/2 = 0.80$$

Table 16–3
Calculation of 10-Year Predicted Volume Growth Per Acre, Assuming Trees in Each Diameter Class Are Evenly Distributed Through the Class, and Each Tree Will Grow at the Average Rate

(1)	(2)	(3)	(4)	(5)	(6)	(7)	(8)	(9)	(10)	(11)	(12)
						Number of trees moving					
Dbh class	10-Year dbh increment	Movement ratio	Present stand table	Volume per tree	Future stand table	0 classes	1 class	2 classes	Future stock table	Present stock table	Volume production
(inches)	(inches)	(M)	(number)	(cu.ft.)	(number)				(cu.ft.)	(cu.ft.)	(cu.ft.)
6	2.02	1.01	41.73				41.31	0.42			
8	1.88	0.94	28.73		43.03	1.72	27.01				
10	1.74	0.87	21.73	12.5	30.25	2.82	18.91		378.1	271.6	106.5
12	1.60	0.80	17.33	18.4	22.38	3.47	13.86		411.8	318.9	92.9
14	1.46	0.73	12.87	25.6	17.33	3.47	9.40		443.6	329.5	114.1
16	1.32	0.66	9.47	34.2	12.62	3.22	6.25		431.6	323.9	107.7
18	1.18	0.59	8.27	44.1	9.64	3.39	4.88		425.1	364.7	60.4
20	1.04	0.52	5.00	55.6	7.28	2.40	2.60		404.8	278.0	126.8
22	0.90	0.45	3.47	68.5	4.51	1.91	1.56		308.9	237.7	71.2
24	0.76	0.38	2.87	83.5	3.34	1.78	1.09		278.9	239.6	39.3
26				100.1	1.09				109.1		109.1
Total			151.47		151.47				3191.9	2363.9	828.0

The two digits to the right of the decimal point indicate the proportion of the trees in the class that will move one class more than indicated by the digit to the left of the decimal point. And so, for the 12-inch class, $0.80 \times 17.33 = 13.86$ trees move one class, and $0.20 \times 17.33 = 3.47$ trees move zero classes.

In Table 16–3 the movements for all classes are shown in Columns 7, 8, and 9, and the future stand table in Column 6. The arrows show how the trees are moved into the future stand. The method of computing Columns 10, 11, and 12 is identical to the method of computing Columns 7, 8, and 9 in Table 16–2.

Note that the sum of Column 12 in Table 16–3 equals the periodic gross growth including ingrowth, and that ingrowth is 27.43 trees $(0.42 + 27.01)$, or 343.9 cubic feet (27.43×12.5). This is a reasonable estimate of ingrowth.

3. *Recognize the actual position of trees in each diameter class and apply the diameter growth for individual trees in the class.* In this approach movement percentages are calculated by applying actual individual increments to individual tree diameters. A graphic solution (Wahlenberg, 1941) may be used, but a simple tabular solution is equally satisfactory, and lends itself to electronic data processing. For example, in Table 16–4 tree movement percentages are computed for the 8-inch diameter class for the data used in Tables 16–2 and 16–3. These percentages are applied to the present stand table to obtain number of trees moving. Other than for this, the future stand table and the future stock table are predicted as in Table 16–3.

Table 16–4
Determination of Tree Movement Percentages from
Raw Data for 8-Inch Diameter Class

Raw Data					Summary		
Dbh class	Present dbh	10-Year dbh increment	Future dbh	Classes move	Classes move	Trees moving	Trees moving
(inches)	(inches)	(inches)	(inches)	(number)	(number)	(number)	(per cent)
	7.1	1.5	8.6	0	0	3	30
	7.3	1.6	8.9	0	1	5	50
	7.4	1.5	8.9	0	2	2	20
	7.5	1.8	9.3	1	Total	10	100
8	7.9	2.5	10.4	1			
	8.1	1.6	9.7	1			
	8.3	1.8	10.1	1			
	8.5	2.6	11.1	2			
	8.7	1.7	10.4	1			
	8.9	2.2	11.1	2			

Ingrowth. As previously indicated, if the method depicted in Table 16–3 is used to predict growth, reasonable estimates of ingrowth may be determined by including, in the initial stand table, several diameter classes below the merchantable limit. If the method depicted in Table 16–2 is used, inconsistent estimates of ingrowth may be obtained by this procedure. In any case, estimates of ingrowth are unreliable for long prediction periods or for rapidly growing trees, because then the original tally may exclude trees that will be present in the future stand.

Mortality. Mortality, which was not considered in the preceding examples (Tables 16–2 and 16–3), may be accounted for by:

1. deducting predicted number of trees dying from each diameter class of the present stand table prior to projecting the present stand table, or
2. deducting predicted number of trees dying from each diameter class of the future stand table after projecting the present stand table, but before computing the future stock table.

In thrifty middle-aged stands, or in stands under intensive management, mortality will not be large and can be accurately predicted. In young stands and in old stands, mortality will often be great, and because of its erratic nature, cannot be accurately predicted. In any case allowances are made only for normal mortality resulting from old age, competition, insects, diseases, wind, etc. No allowance is made for catastrophic mortality resulting from fire, epidemics, great storms, etc.

Good information on mortality may be obtained from permanent sample plots. From such information for any given stand one can determine the relations between mortality and age, diameter, stand density, and species, and thus apply the mortality information to other stands. But when one desires to make a prediction by stand-table projection, he will often lack suitable permanent sample plot data. Then, mortality estimates must be obtained from a stand inspection that is normally made during the cruise. In the inspection, which is quite subjective, one estimates on plots, or points, the number of trees, by species and diameter classes, that died during some past period, say 10 years, or that will die during some future period. When the mortality information is summarized, it is expressed as percentages of the trees in each diameter class of the stand table.

A final word on stand-table projection: If accurate diameter growth information is used, any stand-table projection method will give an excellent estimate of gross growth of the initial basal area. Of course, basal area growth is an important component of volume growth. But so is height growth. Therefore, the determination of gross growth of the initial volume also depends on the stability, during the prediction period, of the height-diameter relationship for which the local volume table was constructed. It also assumes no change in form.

It has been demonstrated that the future height-diameter relationship will not necessarily be the same as the present height-diameter relationship (Chapman and Meyer, 1949). For large areas and for uneven-aged stands this change may be slight, but for small areas and for even-aged stands the change may be substantial, even for periods of ten to twenty years. But, except for abnormal conditions, form changes may be safely ignored for short periods.

Thus, stand-table projection will give good results for uneven-aged stands of immature timber that are understocked. Then mortality will be small and predictable, ingrowth may be accurately predicted, and the height-diameter relationships will change only slightly. In even-aged stands, young dense stands, and overmature stands, stand-table projection will often give inaccurate results because of the change in the height-diameter relationships, and the high and unpredictable mortality.

Although considerable emphasis is given to the prediction of diameter growth in stand-table projection, and although diameter growth predictions are usually quite accurate, height growth and mortality predictions are often crude. Therein lies the weak link of the method. Consequently, when height growth and mortality predictions are in question, it is a waste of time to give great attention to diameter growth. Then, a simpler system (Section 16–2.2) would save time and would give just as good results.

16–2.2. Total Stand Projection. A basic total stand projection method, termed the two-way method, was proposed by Spurr (1952). This method is based on the proposition that:

$$\frac{V_f}{V_p} \cong \frac{B_f \cdot H_f \cdot F_f}{B_p \cdot H_p \cdot F_p}$$

and

$$V_f \cong V_p \left(\frac{B_f \cdot H_f}{B_p \cdot H_p} \right) \tag{16–11}$$

where:

V_f = future average cubic foot volume per acre
B_f = future average basal area in square feet per acre
H_f = future average stand height in feet
F_f = future average stand form factor
V_p = present average cubic foot volume per acre
B_p = present average basal area in square feet per acre
H_p = present average stand height in feet
F_p = present average stand form factor

Since the present stand form factor, F_p, will remain essentially unchanged for ten to twenty years, the usual prediction period, F_p, will be approximately equal to F_f. Therefore, the stand form factors are canceled in equation 16–11. And so cubic foot volume growth per acre, I_V, which may be gross or net growth with or without ingrowth, depending on how B_f is determined, will be:

$$I_V = V_f - V_p = V_p \left(\frac{B_f \cdot H_f}{B_p \cdot H_p} - 1 \right) \qquad (16\text{–}12)$$

Present volume, V_p, may be determined by any desired inventory procedure. Present basal area, B_p, may be determined from diameter measurements of a sample of trees, but it is more efficient to use horizontal point sampling (see Chapter 14). Again, present average stand height, H_p, may be determined from height measurements of a sample of trees, but it is more efficient to use a combination of vertical line and fixed-size plot sampling.

The prediction of future basal area and future average stand height can be seen to be the key to the accuracy of the two-way method. Since basal area growth and height growth are relatively independent, and since the variables used to estimate one are not normally used to estimate the other, each is best estimated separately. Thus, the term "two-way method."

A convenient method of estimating basal area growth was developed by Spurr (1952). From information that may be collected during an inventory, gross growth of the initial basal area per acre, I_B, is estimated from the equation:

$$I_B = \frac{\Sigma \, X^2 (\Sigma \, d_u{}^2 - \Sigma \, d_{u_p}{}^2)}{183.3456 (\Sigma \, d_u{}^2)} \qquad (16\text{–}13)$$

where:

X = diameter breast height in inches, o.b., for all trees tallied in stand
d_u = present diameter breast height in inches, i.b., for trees sampled for increment cores
d_{u_p} = past diameter breast height in inches, i.b., for trees sampled for increment cores

Future basal area is determined by adding basal area growth to the present basal area.

Future basal area may also be predicted by utilizing increment cores and horizontal point sampling (Fender and Brock, 1963). At an appropriate number of points, a count is made of qualifying trees by the usual horizontal point-sampling procedures. Then one determines by increment cores the past periodic diameter growth of each nonqualifying-merchantable tree that might grow enough to qualify at the end of the growth period. Assuming that each tree will grow the same amount in the future as it did in the past, one makes an examination with the angle gauge to determine the number of trees that will qualify at the end of the period. The check to determine the future status of any tree is made by moving a calculated distance closer to the tree and regauging; if the tree appears "In" after moving closer to the tree, it is counted as a *status changer*. Specifically:

$$\text{Distance to move toward tree in feet} = \text{HDM}(2LK) \qquad (16\text{--}14)$$

Then, the future average basal area per acre in square feet, B_f, will be:

$$B_f = (C + C_s)F \qquad (16\text{--}15)$$

and:

$$I_B = C_s F \qquad (16\text{--}16)$$

where:

HDM = horizontal distance multiplier for tree in question (Table 14–3)

L = past periodic radial wood growth in inches

K = the average ratio of diameter outside bark to diameter inside bark (Section 15–9)

C = present average tree count per point as determined by horizontal point sampling

C_s = average number of trees per point changing status as determined by point-center extension

F = basal area factor (Table 14–3)

Future stand height for even-aged stands is best predicted from site index curves. The present stand age and height can be used to determine site index, and the expected height at the future age can be read from the site index curves. Future stand height for uneven-aged stands can be predicted from measurements of height growth on permanent sample plots.

In fully stocked, even-aged stands past the juvenile growth period, total basal area per acre tends to remain constant, and so net basal area growth per acre will be approximately zero. Therefore, in such stands volume growth is largely associated with height growth, and the accuracy of prediction depends mainly on an accurate height growth determination.

In uneven-aged stands where the large trees are periodically cut or are periodically dying, the average height of the stand remains fairly constant. In fact, present and future average stand heights, H_p and H_f, may be considered to be approximately equal. This means that volume growth in such stands is largely associated with basal area growth, and that equation 16–12 may be simplified by canceling H_p and H_f:

$$I_V = V_p \left(\frac{B_f}{B_p} - 1 \right) = \frac{V_p}{B_p} (B_f - B_p) = \left(\frac{V_p}{B_p} \right) I_B$$

And since $I_B = C_sF$:

$$I_V = \frac{V_p}{B_p} (C_sF) \tag{16-17}$$

where terms are as defined for equations 16–11, 16–12, and 16–16.

Equation 16–17 points up a convenient growth prediction method that should not be overlooked when it is applicable.

We have now discussed stands in which growth is associated mainly with height, and stands in which growth is associated mainly with basal area. However, in partially stocked even-aged stands, and in irregular or unmanaged uneven-aged stands, volume growth may be associated with both height and basal area growth. Then, care must be used to evaluate both height and basal area growth if the two-way method is used.

Finally, if one desires to determine net growth by the two-way method, mortality is deducted, in terms of basal area, from future basal area. Mortality estimates are made by the methods discussed in Section 16–2.1. If ingrowth estimates are desired, ingrowth is added, in terms of basal area, to the future basal area. Ingrowth estimates may also be made by the methods described in Section 16–2.1. However, the use of horizontal point sampling is more efficient. Then, each premerchantable tree that is "In" should be tallied as an ingrowth tree if:

$(d + 2LK) >$ (lower limit of smallest merchantable diameter class)

Then:

$$\text{Average basal area ingrowth per acre} = C_IF \tag{16-18}$$

where:

d = present diameter breast height in inches, o.b.
L, F, and K are as defined for equations 16–14 and 16–15
C_I = average number of qualifying-premerchantable trees per point that will become merchantable during growth period

16–3. INDIRECT ESTIMATION OF STAND GROWTH

In the indirect approach of estimating stand growth, it is assumed that the growth of a particular stand will follow a predictable pattern as established by a yield table, or a yield equation (Section 17–4).

16–3.1. Growth Prediction from Normal Even-aged Yield Tables.
To apply a normal yield table to determine growth, the site class and the density relative to the normal stand [1] must be determined for individual

---

[1] A *normal stand* is one in which all growing space is effectively occupied but having ample room for development of the crop trees. Synonym: *Fully stocked stand*.

stands that fall in different age classes, such as 10, 20, 30, or 40 years. To determine age, ring counts, or borings, at stump or breast height, of ten to fifteen dominant and codominant trees are averaged. Age at the cross-section of the ring count is generally satisfactory. It should be mentioned that it is possible to estimate the volume of even-aged stands from normal yield tables (Section 17–4.1) if age, site index, and density relative to the normal stand are known. However, such volume estimates are seldom made in American practice, because they are not as reliable as estimates obtained from a forest inventory. But the volume estimates from normal yield tables may be compared with the results of a forest inventory, and if the two values show reasonable agreement, the yield tables may be used for prediction of future growth. Very simply:

$$I_V = p(Y_f - Y_p) \qquad (16\text{–}19)$$

where:

I_V = volume growth per acre

p = ratio of actual stand volume to normal stand volume (Section 17–2.1)

Y_f = future volume per acre from normal yield table

Y_p = present volume per acre from normal yield table

For periods of ten to twenty years, a volume growth estimate by this method would give reasonable results. For longer periods changes in stocking must be considered to avoid serious errors.

As a rule, the stocking of a young understocked stand tends to increase, or to approach the normal stand condition, while the stocking of an abnormally dense stand tends to decrease. The best bases for reliable predictions of changes in stocking are repeated observations of permanent plots. Studies based on permanent sample plots have been reported by Briegleb (1942) for Douglas fir, W. H. Meyer (1933, 1942) for Douglas fir and loblolly pine, and Watt (1950) for eastern white pine.

If observational data are lacking, an approximation of changes in stocking can be made by using a formula developed by Gehrhardt (1930) and adapted for American usage by Duerr (1938).

To illustrate the application of a normal yield table to determine growth when the trend to normal stocking is considered, assume a 10-year growth estimate is desired for a 70-year-old Douglas fir stand with site index of 160. From the yield table for Douglas fir (McArdle, Meyer, and Bruce, 1949), the normal volumes for trees 7 inches in diameter and over are:

70 years = 11,900 cubic feet
80 years = 13,360 cubic feet

Further assume a recent inventory has shown the average volume of the stand 7 inches in diameter and over to be 8,920 cubic feet. The present stocking is thus $\left(\dfrac{8,920}{11,900}\right)$ 100 or 75 per cent of normal stocking. Assuming an increase in stocking of 4 per cent per decade, the predicted stocking at age 80 will be 75 + 4 or 79 per cent of normal stocking. The estimated net growth, I_V, for the next 10 years is therefore:

$$I_V = (13,360)0.79 - (11,900)0.75 = 1,629 \text{ cubic feet}$$

16–3.2. Derived Growth and Yield Functions. Moser and Hall (1969) point out that it is preferable to present growth and yield information in equation form because of the widespread use of digital computers and of modern statistical techniques. Further, modern innovations in forestry have created the need for dynamic growth and yield functions that can be revised periodically to incorporate results from new practices.

Growth and yield functions may be developed for even-aged, uneven-aged, or age-indeterminable stands.

The ideal data for growth and yield functions are complete chronological records of entire stands from establishment to harvest, termed a *real growth series* (Turnbull, 1963). But in traditional practice data have often been used from temporary plots covering a wide range of sites and ages. This is termed an *abstract growth series*. As a compromise between these two extremes, permanent plots may be established and remeasured at fixed intervals. This is termed an *approximated real growth series.* The approximated real growth series will approach the real growth series.

The best independent variables to predict growth, whether it be volume, basal area, or height growth, should be selected by an objective statistical analysis in which the variables are related singly, and in combination, with the dependent growth variable.

Growth is a function of many interacting stand-site factors that should be integrated over time. For even-aged stands the general form of the function at any given time might be:

Growth = f(species, density, age, site quality)

Density might be expressed by basal area per unit area, number of trees per unit area, or stand density index. Site quality is usually expressed by site index.

For uneven-aged stands the general form of the function at any given time might be:

Growth = f(species, density, site quality)

where neither the density or the site quality measures are related to age.

Moser and Hall (1969) have given an appropriate methodology for deriving growth and yield models for uneven-aged stands. They point out that site index and soil characteristics have been used to express site quality in growth functions for uneven-aged stands with inconclusive results. Thus, until the effect of site can be quantified, it is best to construct separate yield functions for discrete site quality classes.

16–4. PAST GROWTH FROM REPEATED MEASUREMENTS

The determination of growth by repeated inventories of permanent sample plots, or of entire woodlands, is one of the most logical methods of determining past growth. The data obtained from a series of periodic measurements give a complete historical record of stand growth. These data can be used for growth prediction, or to study the effects of cultural practices, insect attacks, weather, and other factors on growth.

The successful use of repeated measurements requires a well-designed scheme of taking measurements and of making calculations. These schemes generally fall under two headings: European *method of control* and American *continuous forest inventory system*. Both systems are designed to measure the growing stock at any given time and to give detailed estimates of growth. However, *continuous forest inventory* (CFI) is a more sophisticated management tool than the *method of control*. It provides a scientific study of individual trees and of their relationship to their immediate environment. It is an excellent channel for translating research into field practice.

One should realize that a crude estimate of net growth can be obtained by taking the difference between the volumes obtained on two successive temporary-sample-plot inventories of an area. Since the same sampling units are not measured in both inventories, however, the precision of the growth estimate will be somewhat poorer, and the accuracy of the growth estimate will be generally less, than when permanent sample plots are used. But, if the permanent sample plots are not representative of the forest, the growth estimate may be biased, even though its precision may be high.

The European method of control was first presented by Gurnaud in France in 1878. The American continuous forest inventory system, which evolved from the method of control, has its genesis in 1934 (Stott, 1968). In the evolutionary process a basically different method of growth analysis has evolved—field grouping of data versus maintaining individual tree records.

Growth and stocking estimates are obtained in the method of control by grouping trees in the field by diameter classes and species, and working up the data by simple techniques, not necessarily requiring the use of computers. Since the tree measurements are grouped, individual tree identity and location is lost. Thus, detailed summaries of growth and stocking, as obtained using CFI, are not possible.

Growth and stocking estimates are obtained in CFI by maintaining individual tree records and plot descriptions, and by making precise tree measurements in conformance to a detailed plan for computer analysis.

Although the method of control has been mainly used on woodlands where complete inventories are feasible, it is also applicable on large forests where permanent sample plots are used. And in some cases it would give the desired information at less cost than CFI. If on a large property, however, plots are small and numerous, it is more difficult to keep an accurate record of felled and dead trees with the method of control than with CFI.

16–4.1. Method of Control. The method of control depends on:

1. A well-defined procedure of measuring and remeasuring the diameters of standing trees.
2. Measuring and determining the volume of felled trees and mortality trees in the same manner as standing trees.
3. A simple method of determining ingrowth.
4. Use of permanent local volume tables (or tarifs).

Each time an inventory is taken, the diameter measurements must be made in the same manner. The point of measurement is marked by a two-inch horizontal mark made at breast height with paint or a bark scribe. On remeasurement the old mark is renewed. If calipers are used, the graduated beam is placed against the mark; only one measurement is normally made. But no matter what instrument is used, calipers or diameter tape, measurements are made at the height of the mark.

The diameters of cut trees and mortality trees are measured and recorded by diameter classes and species when the stand is marked for cutting, or if desired, the diameters of mortality trees may be measured at the time of an inventory; cut and mortality trees together constitute *trees removed*.

One should note that it is possible to measure accurately the volume of felled trees and to compare this volume with the volume table. Then:

$$q = \frac{\text{Actual Volume of Felled Trees}}{\text{Volume of Felled Trees from Volume Table}}$$

represents a correction factor that can be used for better estimation of volume of trees marked for cutting.

16–4.2. Determination of Diameter Increment by Diameter Classes by Method of Control. An ingenious method, developed by French foresters, makes it possible to obtain diameter increment by diameter classes by

326 FOREST MENSURATION Ch. 16

the method of control. An example will illustrate the method (Table 16–5).

Since the calculations must begin with the highest diameter class, this class is put at the top of Table 16–5. To start, let us postpone discussion of Columns 2 and 3 and turn to Columns 4 and 5, realizing that Columns 4 and 5 include the corrected figures to be used to compute diameter increment. Consider Column 4 the first inventory figures, and Column 5 the second inventory figures. Now, in the 32-inch class 0 trees were measured at the first inventory, and 1 tree was measured at the second inventory. Therefore, 1 tree rose from the 30- to the 32-inch class during the period between inventories. Since 1 tree moved out of the 30-inch class, this left 1 tree in the 30-inch class to be joined by 3 trees rising into the class, giving 4 trees at the second inventory. For a *specific class:*

$$\begin{pmatrix} \text{No. trees rising} \\ \text{into the class} \end{pmatrix} = \begin{pmatrix} \text{No. trees 2nd} \\ \text{inventory} \end{pmatrix}$$
$$- \begin{pmatrix} \text{No. trees 1st} \\ \text{inventory} \end{pmatrix} + \begin{pmatrix} \text{No. trees rising} \\ \text{out of the class} \end{pmatrix}$$

Note in Table 16–5 that 484 trees rose into the 10-inch class. This represents the ingrowth and equals the difference between the totals of Columns 4 and 5.

Double rising, Column 7, is the sum of trees rising out of a class and into a class. Thus, for the 32-inch class, $DR = 0 + 1 = 1$; for the 30-inch class, $DR = 1 + 3 = 4$, etc. Double effective, Column 8, is the sum of trees in the first and second inventories after correction for trees removed. Thus for the 32-inch class, $DE = 0 + 1 = 1$; for the 30-inch class, $DE = 2 + 4 = 6$, etc.

Column 9, DR/DE, is used to calculate the periodic diameter increment, I, given in Column 10:

$$I = \left(\frac{DR}{DE} \right) C \tag{16–20}$$

where:

C = width of diameter classes

Note that the average periodic diameter increment for all trees is obtained as follows:

$$\left(\frac{\Sigma DR}{\Sigma DE} \right) C$$

Periodic diameter increment is divided by the number of years in the period to obtain periodic annual diameter increment, Column 11.

H. A. Meyer (1942) gives proof of the method, and Beers (1963) empirically substantiates it.

Table 16-5

Calculation of Periodic Annual Diameter Increment by Diameter Classes by the Method of Control

(1) Dbh class (inches)	(2) Inventory Spring, 1949 (number)	(3) Trees removed (number)	(4) Inventory Spring, 1949 minus trees removed (number)	(5) Inventory Spring, 1959 (number)	(6) Trees rising (number)	(7) Double rising (number)	(8) Double effective (number)	(9) DR/DE	(10) Periodic diameter increment (inches)	(11) Periodic ann. dia. increment (inches)
32	0		0	1	0	1	1	1.000	2.00	0.200
30	2		2	4	1	4	6	.667	1.33	.133
28	3		3	0	3	3	3	1.000	2.00	.200
26	3	2	1	9	0	8	10	.800	1.60	.160
24	10	1	9	7	8	14	16	.875	1.75	.175
22	10	4	6	21	6	27	27	1.000	2.00	.200
20	23	4	19	39	21	62	58	1.069	2.14	.214
18	37	7	30	72	41	124	102	1.216	2.43	.243
16	73	5	68	169	83	267	237	1.127	2.25	.225
14	194	17	177	234	184	425	411	1.034	2.07	.207
12	249	9	240	379	241	621	619	1.003	2.01	.201
10	418	15	403	507	380	864	910	.949	1.90	.190
					484					
Total	1022	64	958	1442		2420	2400			

$$\frac{\Sigma DR}{\Sigma DE} = 1.008$$

Average = 2.02   0.202

No. trees ingrowth = 1442 − 958 = 484 (checks with last figure Col. 6). Trees were removed (Col. 3) immediately following the 1949 inventory. Data from 143 permanent sample plots of 1/5-acre located on Morgan-Monroe State Forest, Indiana. Sample area: 28.6 acres. Growth period: 10 years.

Diameter growth figures obtained in the above manner may be used in growth predictions in the same way as increment core data are used (Section 16–2.1). They are also valuable for silvicultural purposes.

16–4.3. Calculation of Diameter Increment in Presence of Cut and Mortality. In discussing Table 16–5 in Section 16–4.2, an explanation of how to handle trees removed by cutting or mortality was omitted. In the example, cutting, and a small amount of mortality, was assumed to take place immediately after the first inventory. Thus, the trees removed were subtracted from the first inventory to obtain Column 4. If cutting had taken place immediately before the second inventory, we would have added the trees removed to the second inventory. If cutting had taken place halfway through the period, we would have subtracted one-half of the trees removed from the first inventory, and added one-half of the trees removed to the second inventory. If cutting had taken place in the third year of a ten-year period, we would have subtracted seven-tenths of the trees removed from the first inventory and added three-tenths of the trees removed to the second inventory. In equation form:

$$\begin{pmatrix} \text{No. trees to} \\ \text{subtract from } i^{\text{th}} \\ \text{dia. class of 1st inv.} \end{pmatrix} = \left(\frac{\begin{pmatrix} \text{No. years from date} \\ \text{of removal to 2nd inv.} \end{pmatrix}}{(\text{No. years in period})} \right) \begin{pmatrix} \text{No. trees removed} \\ \text{in } i^{\text{th}} \text{ dia. class} \end{pmatrix}$$

$$\begin{pmatrix} \text{No. trees to add} \\ \text{to } i^{\text{th}} \text{ dia. class} \\ \text{of 2nd inv.} \end{pmatrix} = \left(\frac{\begin{pmatrix} \text{No. years from 1st inv.} \\ \text{to date of removal} \end{pmatrix}}{(\text{No. years in period})} \right) \begin{pmatrix} \text{No. trees removed} \\ \text{in } i^{\text{th}} \text{ dia. class} \end{pmatrix}$$

16–4.4. Determination of Volume Increment by Method of Control. Table 16–6 shows the calculation of volume growth by the method of control for the data used in Table 16–5. Once the columns are completed and totaled as shown in Table 16–6, the calculation of growth is simply a matter of applying the growth formulas from Section 16–1. For example:

$$G_{g+i} = V_2 + (M + C) - V_1$$
$$= 136988 + 8968 - 88286 = 57670$$

$$\text{Ingrowth (No. Trees)} = 1442 + 64 - 1022 = 484$$

And since it is assumed that all ingrowth trees move into the smallest measurable class, in this case the 10-inch class:

$$I = 484(30) = 14520 \text{ bd. ft.}$$

A different analysis will provide information on volume growth by diameter classes. The procedure is shown in Table 16–7 for the data used

Table 16–6
Calculation of Volume Growth by the Method of Control

(1)	(2)	(3)	(4)	(5)	(6)	(7)	(8)
Dbh class	Volume per tree	Inventory— Spring, 1949		Inventory— Spring, 1959		Cut and Mortality	
(inches)	(bd ft.)	Trees (number)	Volume (bd. ft.)	Trees (number)	Volume (bd. ft.)	Trees (number)	Volume (bd. ft.)
32	577	0		1	577		
30	538	2	1,076	4	2,152		
28	491	3	1,473	0			
26	442	3	1,326	9	3,978	2	884
24	386	10	3,860	7	2,702	1	386
22	329	10	3,290	21	6,909	4	1,316
20	273	23	6,279	39	10,647	4	1,092
18	217	37	8,029	72	15,624	7	1,519
16	161	73	11,753	169	27,209	5	805
14	112	194	21,728	234	26,208	17	1,904
12	68	249	16,932	379	25,772	9	612
10	30	418	12,540	507	15,210	15	450
Total		1,022	88,286	1,442	136,988	64	8,968

Type of Growth	Periodic (bd. ft.)		Periodic Annual (bd. ft.)	
	Total	Per acre	Total	Per acre
G_{g+i}	57,670	2,016	5,767	202
I	14,520	508	1,452	51
G_g	43,150	1,506	4,315	151
G_d	48,702	1,703	4,870	170

Symbols are defined in Section 16–1.
Total is for sample area of 28.6 acres.
Data from 143 permanent sample plots of 1/5-acre located on Morgan-Monroe State Forest, Indiana. Sample area: 28.6 acres. Growth period: 10 years.

in Table 16–5. Columns 2, 3, and 4 in Table 16–7 are determined exactly as Columns 4, 5, and 6 in Table 16–5. Column 6, volume difference per tree, is the difference between volumes for subsequent diameter classes; Column 7, volume increment, is the product of Columns 4 and 6. The total of Column 7 is accretion, G_g.

A careful study of Tables 16–6 and 16–7 will point up the value of the method of control as a management tool. The system permits continuous analysis and examination of the makeup of a stand—the results of different cutting and cultural practices may become clearer at each inventory.

Table 16–7
Calculation of Periodic Volume Growth by Diameter Classes
by the Method of Control

(1)	(2)	(3)	(4)	(5)	(6)	(7)
Dbh class	Inventory Spring, 1949 minus trees removed	Inventory Spring, 1959	Trees rising	Volume per tree	Volume difference per tree	Periodic volume increment
(inches)	(number)	(number)	(number)	(bd. ft.)	(bd. ft.)	(bd. ft.)
32	0	1		577		
			1		39	39
30	2	4		538		
			3		47	141
28	3	0		491		
			0		49	—
26	1	9		442		
			8		56	448
24	9	7		386		
			6		57	342
22	6	21		329		
			21		56	1,176
20	19	39		273		
			41		56	2,296
18	30	72		217		
			83		56	4,648
16	68	169		161		
			184		49	9,016
14	177	234		112		
			241		44	10,604
12	240	379		68		
			380		38	14,440
10	403	507		30		
			484			
Total	958	1,442				43,150

Data from 143 permanent sample plots of 1/5-acre located on Morgan-Monroe State Forest, Indiana. Sample area: 28.6 acres. Growth period: 10 years.

16–5. CONTINUOUS FOREST INVENTORY

To many foresters continuous forest inventory (CFI) implies making precise tree measurements on permanent plots in conformance to a detailed plan for computer analysis that requires individual tree and plot records. This concept, however, may be modified in various ways. But the plots always must represent the entire forest; cutting, mortality, growth, etc., on the plots should be representative of cutting, mortality, growth, etc., on the rest of the forest.

It should be understood that CFI will yield more than growth and volume information. It was designed as a means of periodically assessing change in the forest so that management would be alerted to the need for policy changes for the forest. However, the system will not necessarily give all data needed for continuing forest management. Because of the low sampling intensity of most CFI systems, temporary samples may be needed to supplement the permanent plot data.

An efficient CFI system cannot be designed without a clear understanding of the purposes of the system. Some of the purposes might be:

1. Provide volumes by species, tree grades, and size classes for the different timber types that are significant for differentiating products to be harvested.
2. Assess relative economic availability of trees and areas of varying qualities.
3. Provide growth information for the different timber types that will give a basis for calculating allowable cut.
4. Evaluate results of silvicultural practices, including planting, in terms of survival, quality, and growth of regeneration.
5. Evaluate need for timber stand improvement.
6. Provide a basis for determining areas to be planted, area of non-productive land, and ratio of mortality to cut.
7 Provide values, volumes and growth rates for depletion and other purposes in accounting for timberlands.

16–5.1. Planning Considerations for Continuous Forest Inventory. The use of stratification with optimum allocation is highly efficient for a single inventory. But since fire, wind damage, insect attacks, harvesting, and natural changes in species composition continually alter the strata, unstratified sampling is commonly employed in CFI to assess change.

Plots are commonly located in a square-grid pattern. However, random location of plots is feasible and is sometimes used. But in planning a CFI system the economy-minded forester might ask: If the total number of plot locations is reduced, and two or more plots are measured at each location instead of one plot, will the accuracy of results be reduced? Should all of the "permanent" plots be remeasured or should some be replaced by new ones? Or to put the same questions in statistical terms: Should we consider multistage sampling (Chapter 12)? Should we consider sampling with partial replacement of units (Chapter 12)?

There are cases where such modifications might improve the efficiency of the CFI system; each forest manager must answer the questions in light of his needs.

Circular plots of one-fifth or one-seventh of an acre are commonly used. Although permanent points may also be used, they are less desirable (Beers and Myers, 1965). A decision on the number of plots to use is difficult, because the sample must be applicable now and in the future, and large enough to estimate several forest parameters. But assuming a particular sampling system, and a desired degree of precision, the number of plots to use depends on the variability of the parameter being estimated and the area of the forest (Chapter 12). In practice, sampling intensities range from about 0.03 to 0.1 per cent. Within a given region, variability tends to increase as the size of the forest area increases, but not proportionately. Thus, the larger the area of the forest, the lower the sampling intensity needed for any desired precision.

Once a decision has been made on the number of plots to establish, and on the sampling system to use, plots can be efficiently located on a photo mosaic (or a map) by means of a transparent templet. To prepare the templet, a square-grid or random pattern of small holes is pricked into a transparent sheet. For example, when a 0.05 per cent sample is to be used on a square-grid pattern, the spacing, L, in chains, for one-fifth-acre plots would be:

$$L = \sqrt{\frac{10a}{p/100}} = \sqrt{\frac{10(0.2)}{0.05/100}} = 63.25 \text{ chains (4174 feet)}$$

where:

  a is plot size in acres
  p is per cent sample

If the photo mosaic on which the plots are to be located has a scale of 1:15840, the spacing of the holes on the templet will be 3.16 inches. The completed templet is randomly placed on the mosaic so as to cover the desired ownership, and plot locations are pricked through holes that fall within the ownership. Normally, the plot locations are transferred to 9 by 9 inch contact prints that may be taken into the field.

The usual procedure for each plot is to determine, from the photograph, an azimuth and a distance to the plot center from a permanent feature, such as a survey corner, road intersection, etc., that can be used to locate the plot for establishment and for remeasurement. This azimuth and distance is used by the field crew to locate the plot without bias. When a plot is first established, it is good practice to compare its photo and ground location, and to change the photo location if it does not agree with the ground location.

When a plot is established, its center is marked on the ground by an aluminum or treated-wood stake. The location of the stake should be carefully referenced by recording the azimuth and distance to two or more witness trees on the plot. All trees that are measured are numbered with paint or with metal tags and marked at the point of diameter breast height measurement with a short paint line.

Field data may be recorded on mark-sense cards or prescored cards

(Fig. 2–2), and transferred to permanent punch cards by machine methods. Or field data may be recorded on field-tally sheets, or on tape, and transferred to cards by a key-punch operator. The data are normally coded, even when recorded on tape.

Two-man crews are satisfactory for locating, measuring, and remeasuring CFI plots. And for every four or five crews there should be a checking crew to verify the quality of work, and to correct deviations from standard procedures. Approximately ten per cent of the plots should be randomly selected for checking.

Undiscovered errors can disrupt procedures and increase the costs of computing and compiling the entire inventory; the data-processing program demands error-free cards. Therefore, in addition to field checks, machine-error checks (Smith, 1965) should be used. In fact, machine-error checks, which compare inventories tree by tree and plot by plot, have been an important factor in encouraging better measurement, the use and development of better tools for tree measurement, standardization of field instructions, and improvement of coding systems for tree and plot descriptions. It should be emphasized that machine-error checking should be done before the field crews leave an area so corrections can be made with a minimum of effort.

The usual practice is to remeasure plots at three- to ten-year intervals, and for large inventories, it must be decided whether to remeasure the complete system in one year, or to measure part of the system each year during the cycle of measurement.

Table 16–1 gives an example of growth calculations procedures for a one-fifth-acre permanent sample plot.

17

Stand Structure, Density, Site Quality, and Yield

17—1. STAND STRUCTURE

Stand structure is the distribution of species and tree sizes on a forest area. The structure of a stand is the result of the species' growth habits and of the environmental conditions and management practices under which the stand originated and developed. There are two typical stand structures, even-aged and uneven-aged, although under natural forest conditions there are all gradations between the two. A brief treatment of certain mensurational aspects of these two structural types follows; for additional silvicultural and management detail reference should be made to Meyer, Recknagel, Stevenson, and Bartoo (1961), Smith (1962), and Davis (1966).

17—1.1. Even-aged Stands. An even-aged stand is a group of trees that has originated within a short period of time. The trees in an even-aged stand thus belong to single age class. The limits of the age class may vary, depending on the length of time during which the stand formed. A natural stand may seed-in over a period of several years. Rarely will an age class be only one year, except in the case of a plantation. More commonly, the age class for an even-aged stand will extend to ten or even twenty years. In some cases, a stand may appear even-aged because the trees show size uniformity. For example, stands growing slowly on poor sites may consist of trees of widely diverse ages, yet have little variation in size. Even-aged stands may be composed of shade-tolerant or -intolerant species, although even-aged stands of intolerant species are more common. Even-aged stands arise out of, or are perpetuated by, environmental conditions that allow trees to become established within a comparatively short, definable period. An even-aged forest may consist of several even-aged stands belonging to different age classes.

The trees in an even-aged stand are fairly consistent in height, with variations depending on their crown position as dominant, codominant, intermediate, or suppressed. The diameters in an even-aged stand show wider variation, although following a typical pattern. Most trees cluster near the average diameter, with decreasing frequencies at larger and smaller diameters. As even-aged stands grow older, the diameter class distribution changes. The total number of trees in the stand decreases, with numbers of trees appearing in larger diameter classes not previously represented. Figure 17–1 shows the diameter distribution of an even-aged stand at several ages. Several investigators have found that the diameter distributions of even-aged stands follow definite laws, and that the relationship of number of trees and diameter can be described by computed values (Baker, 1923; Anderson, 1937; Meyer, 1930; Schumacher, 1930; Schnur, 1934; and Schnur, 1937). Although the general distribution of number of trees plotted over diameter classes has usually been noted as a skewed (but nearly normal) distribution, studies by Gingrich (1967) have demonstrated that for upland forests of the central hardwood region (United States): "When the average stand diameter is large enough [8 inches, in his study] to accommodate the frequency curve in [its] positive range . . . , a normal diameter distribution exists." The stands studied did not demonstrate significant kurtosis (peakedness). From an analysis standpoint it is worth noting that numerous studies have shown that estimated parameters of the typical even-aged structure (measures of variation, skewness, and kurtosis) are more closely related to average diameter than to stand age or a measure of site quality, though undoubtedly both of these have a considerable effect on the distribution. Thus, average tree diameter is a basic and very useful means of characterizing an even-aged stand.

17–1.2. Uneven-aged Stands. A stand consisting of trees of many ages and corresponding sizes is said to be uneven-aged. The trees in an uneven-aged forest originate more or less continuously, in contrast to the single reproductive period characterizing an even-aged forest. This continuing source of new trees produces, in an undisturbed stand, trees of ages varying from germinating seedlings to over-mature veterans.

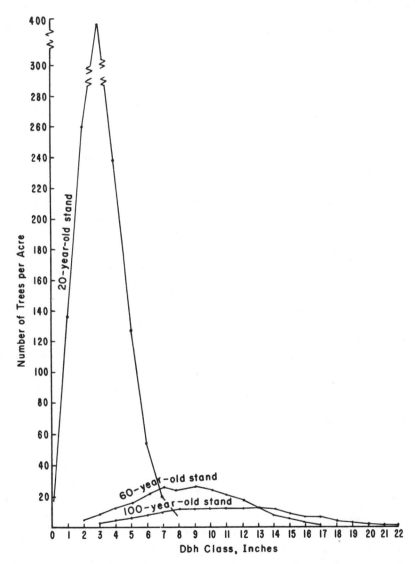

Fig. 17–1. Examples of diameter distributions at three ages in mixed oak stands; site index 80 (Schnur, 1937).

In an uneven-aged forest, the trees in the crown canopy are of many heights, resulting in an irregular stand profile as viewed from a vertical cross-section. The more shade-tolerant species tend to form uneven-aged stands. Cutting methods which remove only scattered trees at short intervals maintain forest conditions favorable to shade-tolerant species and an uneven-aged stand.

The typical diameter distribution for an uneven-aged stand is a large number of small trees with decreasing frequency as the diameter increases, as shown in Fig. 17-2. The diameter distribution for small areas

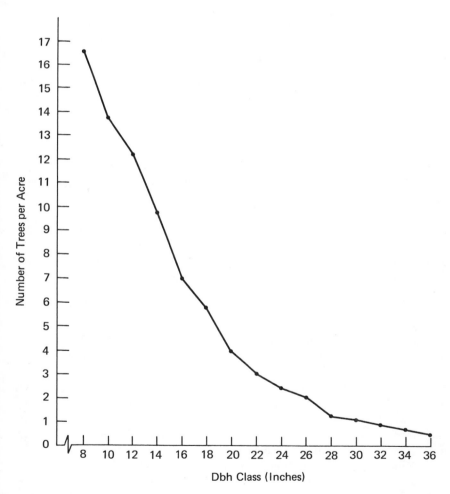

Fig. 17–2. Diameter distribution per acre for an uneven-aged virgin stand of beech–birch–maple–hemlock (adapted from Meyer and Stevenson, 1943).

of uneven-aged forests may show considerably greater irregularity. As the area of the uneven-aged stand or forest increases, the irregularities tend to even out and the inversed-J-shaped diameter distribution of an uneven-aged forest becomes apparent. Combining equal areas of all age classes for a theoretical fully regulated [1] even-aged forest will also produce the distribution typical of an uneven-aged forest. The actual forest structure on any unit area of land, however, is radically different.

Meyer (1953), basing his work on the investigations of De Liocourt (1898), studied the structure of what he termed a balanced uneven-aged forest. His definition of a balanced uneven-aged forest is "one in which current growth can be removed periodically while maintaining the diameter distribution and initial volume of the forest." Meyer states that a balanced uneven-aged forest will tend to have a diameter distribution whose form can be expressed by the exponential equation:

$$Y = ke^{-aX} \tag{17-1}$$

where:

Y = number of trees per diameter class

X = dbh class

e = base of natural logarithms

a, k = constants for a characteristic diameter distribution

Research has shown that the typical uneven-aged distribution can be characterized by determining values for the constants a and k in equation 17–1; a determines the rate by which numbers of trees diminish in successive diameter classes, and k indicates the relative density of the stand. Meyer's work demonstrated that these constants are rather well correlated, positively. Therefore, high values of a, indicating a rapid reduction in trees for increasing diameter, are generally associated with high values of k, indicating a relatively high density of small timber, and vice versa.

A diameter distribution can be tested for conformity to the definition of a balanced structure by checking the linearity of a trend line when number of trees is plotted over diameter class on semilogarithmic paper, as shown in Fig. 17–3.

A balanced distribution implies that the number of trees in successive diameter classes follows a geometric series of the form $m, mq, mq^2, mq^3,$ . . . , where q is the ratio of the series and m is the number of trees in the largest diameter class considered. The constant q, then, is the ratio of trees in successive diameter classes.

Although the determination of a and k could proceed using the techniques of non-linear regression made feasible by recent advances in the

---

[1] An even-aged forest in which all age classes in the rotation are represented by equal areas.

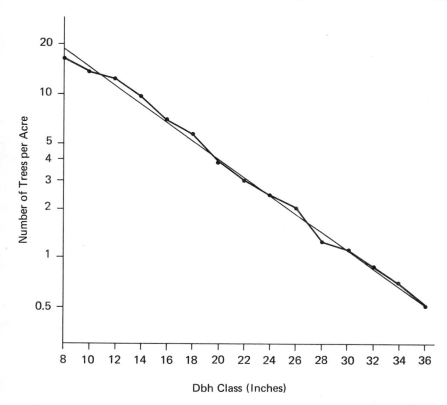

Fig. 17–3. Number of trees per acre by diameter classes represented on semi-log paper using the data shown in Fig. 17–2. The logarithmic least-squares equation (unweighted) was log $Y = 1.72242 - 0.05563X$.

application of electronic computers, it is worthwhile to discuss the approach taken in most of the literature on the subject, i.e., the application of graphical and/or linear least-squares techniques involving the logarithmic transformation of equation 17–1.[2] If this is done, one obtains:[3]

$$\log Y = \log k - aX \log e \qquad (17\text{–}2)$$

[2] The graphical approach is described by Meyer (1953); only the linear least-squares approach is described in the following paragraphs. Either approach is useful as a preliminary step to the non-linear solution, to obtain initial estimates of the constants a and k.

[3] If natural logarithms are used:

$$ln\ Y = ln\ k - aX, \text{ leading to } k = e^{b_0}.$$

Since $a = b_1$ directly, no detransformation is needed. It should be noted that either logarithmic approach involves a bias—"logarithmic transposal discrepancy"—(Meyer, 1953) of the same type discussed in Section 9–5.1.

which can clearly be handled by simple linear regression, since by re-definition:

$$Y' = b_o + b_1 X \tag{17-3}$$

where:

$Y' = \log Y$
$b_o = \log k$
$b_1 = -a \log e$

The constants a and k can then be determined by:

$$k = \text{antilog } (b_o) \tag{17-4}$$

and:

$$a = \frac{-b_1}{\log e} = \frac{-b_1}{0.43429} \tag{17-5}$$

It is basic to the concept of a frequency distribution that the number of trees in any diameter class of width h, is given (approximately) by the equation:

$$n_i = h Y_i \tag{17-6}$$

$$= hke^{-aX_i} \tag{17-7}$$

where:

n_i = number of trees in the ith class
X_i = midpoint of the ith class
Y_i = ordinate value on the curve corresponding to X_i
h = class width

Therefore, by definition:

$$q = \frac{n_{i-1}}{n_i}$$

$$= \frac{hke^{-a(X_i-h)}}{hke^{-aX_i}}$$

$$q = e^{ha} \tag{17-8}$$

In stand structure analyses of this type, it is imperative to note that the constant k varies with both stand area and the width of the diameter class, that q is a function of class width, and that a is not dependent on either stand area or class width. The exponential equation 17-1 is usually written with the tacit assumption that the class width is one and that the data (number of trees in this case) are on a unit area basis. For data grouped into classes h units wide, representing totals from a stand of area A acres (or hectares), one can calculate a k' using the logarithmic least-squares approach and then find the basic k from the equation:

$$k = \frac{k'}{hA} \qquad (17\text{--}9)$$

When using the ratio, q, especially in comparing stands, a common class width must be assumed. It, therefore, seems reasonable to define q as the ratio of numbers of trees in successive diameter classes of width *one*, and adjust q, calculated on any other basis, back to the unity basis. For this purpose, it is easily shown that:

$$q_h = (q_{h'})^{h/h'} \qquad (17\text{--}10)$$

where q_h and $q_{h'}$ are calculated using diameter class of h and h' units, respectively.

For a numerical example we will use the data represented in Figs. 17–2 and 17–3. Using two-inch diameter classes, the logarithmic least-squares equation was:

$$\log Y = 1.72242 - 0.05563\, X$$

Therefore, using equations 17–4 and 17–9:

$$k' = \text{antilog } (1.72242) = 52.77$$

$$k = \frac{52.77}{(2)(1)} = 26.38$$

using equation 17–5:

$$a = \frac{-(-0.05563)}{0.43429} = .1281$$

and using equation 17–8:

$$q = e^{2(.1281)} = 1.29$$

A q of 1.29 is, therefore, appropriate for the distribution as represented (two-inch diameter classes); however, we can calculate a "standard" q using equation 17–10:

$$q_1 = (1.29)^{1/2} = 1.14$$

For details regarding the management potential of uneven-aged structure analysis, the reader is referred to the writings of H. A. Meyer and his students. Ecological applications have also been described by Leak (1964), and Schmelz and Lindsey (1965).

17–2. STAND DENSITY AND STOCKING

Measures of stand density and forest stocking are both used to depict the degree to which a given site is being utilized by the growing trees or simply to indicate the quantity of wood on an area. However, a distinction is usually made between the two terms. As described by Gingrich (1967):

Stand density is a quantitative measurement of a stand in terms of square feet of basal area, number of trees, or volume per acre. It reflects the degree of crowding of stems within the area. *Stocking,* on the other hand, is a relative term used to describe the *adequacy* of a given stand density in meeting the management objective. Thus, a stand with a density of 70 square feet of basal area per acre may be classified as overstocked or understocked, depending upon what density is considered desirable.

Stand density can be expressed, as above, in absolute units per unit land area of such stand parameters as volume, basal area, crown coverage, number of trees, etc., but often it is expressed on a relative scale as a per cent of some "normal" (full or desirable) density, or as a per cent of the average density. When expressed in this form, it should be clear that "relative density" exists as a term transitional between "stand density" and "stocking" as defined above. Stand density is also expressed as an index derived using more involved concepts (Sections 17–2.2, 17–2.3, 17–2.4, 17–2.5).

17–2.1. Relative Density. For many forestry purposes, volume is the ultimate expression of stand density. Ideally, then, relative density is determined by comparing the volume of an observed stand with the volume of some standard, such as the volumes of fully stocked stands for specified ages and site qualities as given in a yield table. For example, a 50-year-old stand of white pine on site index 58 land in Massachusetts was measured and its volume was found to be 4500 board feet per acre. A normal yield table showed theoretically full stocking for this age and site to be 6290 board feet. The relative density is then (4500/6290)(100) = 71.5 per cent. Note that relative density percentages using volume depend on the volume unit chosen. For example, board-foot density percentages will differ from cubic-foot density percentages for the same stand. Density as measured by relative volumes has several disadvantages. Volumes as expressed for the standard or fully stocked stand may be based on different merchantability limits, different log rules, or different volume units from the stand under investigation, making valid comparison difficult. In addition, stand volume estimates are too expensive if only a measure of relative density is needed.

Instead of volume, stand basal area can be used in a similar way as a density measure. The advantage of basal area is that it is easily determined and is quite consistent for fully-stocked stands for specified ages and sites. Since relative density depends on the unit of volume used, even for the same stand, relative density using basal area need not be the same as that using volume.

The number of trees per unit land area can be used as another measure of stand density. At any age, there can be a wide range in the number of trees per unit land area, so that frequency by itself is of little value. For a useful descriptive measure of stand density, number of trees must be qualified by tree sizes. The stand structure as shown in a stand table describes this but is too cumbersome for practical use as a stand density description. A useful measure of density for even-aged stands based on number of trees is Reineke's stand density index (Reineke, 1933).

17–2.2. Stand Density Index. Stand density index is the number of trees per acre that a stand would have at a standard average dbh. The stand density index for a stand is obtained by referring to a stand density index chart for the species. As shown in Fig. 17–4, the chart consists of a series of lines representing the relationship between number of trees per acre and average stand diameter. The chart can be constructed by

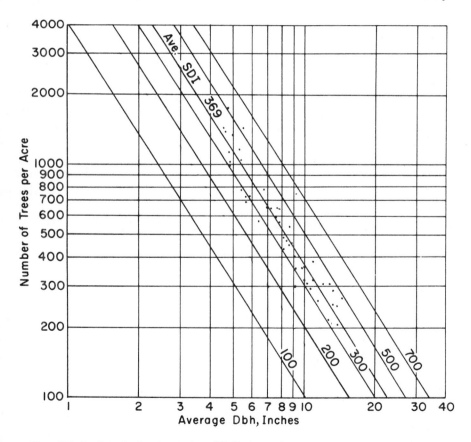

Fig. 17–4. Stand density index (SDI) chart for white pine in southeastern New Hampshire. Equation is $\log N = -1.598 \log D + 4.165$. Based on 53 sample plots.

plotting the logarithm of number of trees per acre over the logarithm of the average stand dbh on rectangular coordinate paper. The natural values are plotted on logarithmic paper in Fig. 17–4, yielding the same results. The number of trees and the average stand diameters are obtained from a series of sample plots. Average stand diameter is taken from the average basal area of the trees tallied. An average relationship for all the observations will be defined by a straight line. This line represents the average stocking of all plots. The number of trees indicated by the intersection of this line and the ordinate at the standard dbh is the average stand density index. A series of parallel lines is then constructed to intersect the standard diameter ordinate at specified numbers of trees per acre. The numbers at these intersections are the stand density index values for the set of parallel lines. If the average stand density index line is taken as 100 per cent, other index lines can be expressed in percentages instead of numbers of trees.

The stand density index for a stand is determined by plotting the position of the observed number of trees and the average stand dbh per acre on the stand density index chart for the species. The stand density index is indicated by the closest line to the plotted point or can be found by interpolation between the index lines. For example, the stand density index for a white pine stand of 14.6 inches average dbh, with 265 trees per acre, on Fig. 17–4 is about 480.[4] The equation form of the average stand density index line is $log\ N = a\ \log\ D + b$, where N = number of trees per acre and D = average stand dbh. Reineke found that the a constant was -1.605 for several species. Other investigators noted that the linear relationship expressed by the equation holds for many species and that the slope differs little although the b constant varies considerably. The average stand density index line for Fig. 17–4 has the equation $\log\ N = -1.598\ \log\ D + 4.165$, based on a least-squares solution for 53 plots. Stand density index is not strongly correlated with age or site. Stands of the same age and on the same site may have different numbers of trees and average stand diameters. This quality of independence of age or site makes stand density index an additional valuable parameter in describing a stand, especially in yield table construction (see Section 17–4).

17–2.3. Tree-area Ratio. The tree-area ratio is a measure of density first proposed by Chisman and Schumacher (1940) as a measure which is independent of stand age and site quality and is appropriate for even- or uneven-aged stands. It is based on the concept that if the space on the

---

[4] Using the technique of translation of axes (see Section 17–3.3), the stand density index can be *calculated* from the formula $\log\ \mathrm{SDI} = \log\ N - a(\log\ D - \log\ 10)$. For this example then, $\log\ \mathrm{SDI} = \log\ 265 + 1.598(\log\ 14.6 - 1)$, leading to $\mathrm{SDI} = 485$.

ground, Y, occupied by a tree of diameter at breast height, d, can be expressed by the relation:

$$Y = b_o + b_1 d + b_2 d^2 \qquad (17\text{--}11)$$

then the total area of growing space represented on a plot or unit of ground area can be found by summing over all the trees on the plot or unit area. Thus, a measure of growing space utilization can be obtained by adding over all trees (n) on a unit area, leading to:

$$\text{tree area} = b_o n + b_1 \Sigma\, d + b_2 \Sigma\, d^2 \qquad (17\text{--}12)$$

After the constants b_o, b_1, and b_2 are obtained by least squares, the contribution to tree area of a single tree of diameter, d, can be found by letting $n = 1$, $\Sigma d = d$, and $\Sigma d^2 = d^2$.

Using data obtained from sample plots (preferably adjusted to the appropriate unit area basis) the constants in equation 17–12 are obtained by the method of least squares, minimizing the sum of squared residuals:

$$\sum_{i=1}^{N} (1 - b_o X_o - b_1 X_1 - b_2 X_2)^2 \qquad (17\text{--}13)$$

where:

X_o = number of trees per plot (or unit area)
X_1 = sum of diameters per plot (or unit area)
X_2 = sum of squared diameters per plot (or unit area)
N = number of plots in the sample

It is important to note that "normal equations" derived from this minimization differ from the usual ones in that the column vector to the right of the equal sign becomes ΣX_o, ΣX_1, ΣX_2 rather than ΣY, $\Sigma X_1 Y$, $\Sigma X_2 Y$.

If the data used to derive the coefficients b_o, b_1, and b_2 in equation 17–12 came from stands which were deliberately chosen to be "full" or "normally" stocked, then the application of the regression equation to other stands and substitution of n, Σd, and Σd^2 will provide a tree-area figure which will reflect the proportion of *full stocking* demonstrated by that stand. On the other hand, if the data used to derive the coefficients came from stands having a range of densities, substitution into the equation for a given stand will reflect the proportion of stocking as compared to the *average stocking* of the basic data.

Although some studies (Lynch, 1958; Beers, 1960) have found that certain of the independent variables in the basic tree-area ratio model (equation 17–12) contribute nonsignificantly and might be dropped from consideration, Gingrich (1967) shows on logical grounds that all three independent variables should be retained. For further treatment the reader should refer to the basic references cited. It should be understood that the tree-area ratio is firmly established as a useful measure of stand density, and that the final form of the regression equation is somewhat dependent on the use to which the measure is put.

17–2.4. Crown Competition Factor. A measure of density, which in final form is similar to the tree-area ratio, although considerably different in derivation, is the crown competition factor (CCF) proposed by Krajicek, Brinkman, and Gingrich (1961). The authors claim that CCF is independent of site quality and stand age, and should be suitable for use in both even- and uneven-aged stands.

The development of a CCF formula for a species or species group would proceed as follows, using the example given by Krajicek et al. (1961):

1. Measurements of crown width and dbh are taken on a satisfactory number of truly open-grown trees, carefully selected to insure that they have developed in an undisturbed, competition-free environment.
2. For this measured sample the relation of crown width (CW) to dbh (d) is found by least squares. Example: $CW = 3.12 + 1.829d$.
3. A formula for the crown area of individual trees expressed as a per cent of one acre is derived and called "maximum crown area" (MCA) since it indicates the maximum proportion of an acre that the crowns of trees of a given dbh can occupy. Example:

$$MCA = \frac{\pi(CW)^2}{4} \cdot \frac{100}{43560} \qquad (17–14)$$

$$= 0.0018 \, (CW)^2$$

Substituting the regression relating CW to dbh:

$$MCA = 0.0018 \, (3.12 + 1.829d)^2$$
$$= 0.0175 + 0.0205d + 0.0060d^2$$

4. By adding the MCA's for all trees on the average acre of forest land an expression of stand density, called crown competition factor (CCF) is obtained. Thus, using the example, the CCF for a specific stand could be determined by substituting in the following equation:

$$CCF = \frac{1}{A} \, (0.0175 \, \Sigma \, n_i + 0.0205 \, \Sigma \, d_i n_i + 0.0060 \, \Sigma \, d_i^2 n_i) \quad (17–15)$$

where:

$\quad n_i$ = number of trees in the ith dbh class
$\quad d_i$ = midpoint of the ith dbh class
$\quad A$ = stand area in acres, taken to be unity if a per-acre stand table is the basis for the data to be substituted

It should be clear that any combination of MCA's that sum to 100 (CCF = 100) represents a closed canopy and reflects a situation where the tree crowns just touch and are sufficiently distorted to completely cover each acre of ground. However, the authors of this index (Krajicek, et al., 1961) state:

> It should be emphasized that CCF is not essentially a measure of crown closure. Theoretically, complete crown closure can occur from CCF 100 to the maximum for the species (in oaks, approximately CCF 200). Instead of estimating crown closure, CCF estimates the area available to the average tree in the stand in relation to the maximum area it could use, if it were open grown.

17–2.5. Point Density. The previously described measures of density are usually employed to determine density of a stand in general or "on the average." Somewhat more specific measures of density have been developed to describe the degree of competition on a given point or tree in the stand. An example of point density is a technique developed by Spurr (1962) called the "angle-summation method." "This method," Spurr explains, "should have its utility in such studies as the correlation between tree growth and density around that tree, the correlation between establishment of natural regeneration and point density, and the selection of plus trees in forest tree improvement research."

In the angle-summation method a point or tree is chosen, upon which we wish to determine the degree of competition from surrounding trees. Using the basic theory of Bitterlich's angle count method (horizontal point sampling as described in Chapter 14) *each competing tree* is imagined to be "borderline" from the chosen point or tree and, thus, to have a specific basal area factor. Spurr's point density measure then is obtained by appropriately summing a series of basal area per acre estimates made using these trees. Other measures of point density are described and evaluated by Opie (1968) and Gerrard (1969); further treatment is beyond the scope of the present work.

17–2.6. Forest Stocking. In an excellent discussion of stocking and density, Bickford et al. (1957)[5] accept the *Forestry Terminology* (1958) definition of stocking: ". . . an indication of the number of trees in a stand as compared to the desirable number for best growth and management: such as well-stocked, over-stocked, partly stocked." And, although they point out that there are varying shades of meaning from the viewpoint of the silviculturist, economist, or forest manager, the most common connotation of "forest stocking" is in the sense of "best growth." That is, the terms "overstocked" and "understocked" represent upper

---

[5] This article is the report of a special committee of the Society of American Foresters, appointed to study the subject of forest stocking.

and lower limits of site occupancy within which there exists a degree of stocking where forest growth will be optimum. Ideally, the forest manager should be able to recognize this optimum stocking under the complete range of stand composition and conditions he will encounter. Many attempts have been made to quantify forest stocking so that its relation to growth can be more readily determined. Based on the repeatedly shown concept that gross increment varies very little over a wide range of stand density, the work of Gingrich (1964, 1967) culminated in a stocking chart, Fig. 17–5, which has found considerable usage in applied forest management in the central United States.

The chart was developed using (1) a tree-area ratio equation (see Section 17–2.3) derived from data for stands which were deliberately chosen to be "fully stocked," and (2) an equation based on the crown-competition factor (see Section 17–2.4) using data from open-grown trees. Thus, in Fig. 17–5 the A line (100 per cent stocking) ". . . represents a normal condition of maximum stocking for undisturbed stands of upland hardwoods of average structure," and the B line represents the lower limit of stocking for full site occupancy (Gingrich, 1967). The entire range of stocking between A and B is called "fully stocked" because the growing space can be fully utilized. It follows that stands having a combination of basal area and number of trees per acre falling outside this range will demonstrate gross increment less than the potential of the site, due either to over- or understocking.

Application of the stocking chart to determine a prescription of silvicultural treatment is in itself simple. For example, if stand measurements indicate a basal area per acre of 80 square feet, and 175 trees per acre, an average diameter of 9.2 inches is indicated (in Fig. 17–5). Following the "9.2 line" down to the point where it crosses the B level, one finds that a basal area of 65 square feet is the minimum basal area to maintain full stocking at that average diameter. Therefore, silvicultural treatment which removes 15 square feet of basal area without materially changing the average stand diameter leaves a stand which will still fully utilize the site and produce wood efficiently. For greater detail on application the reader is referred to the handbooks written by Roach and Gingrich (1962, 1968).

17–3. SITE QUALITY

A knowledge of the growth responses of forest trees to the factors of the environment is important to forest management. The forester can use this knowledge to encourage the growth of desirable species, either by modifying the environment or by concentrating on sites having desirable environmental characteristics. In the past, the forester has

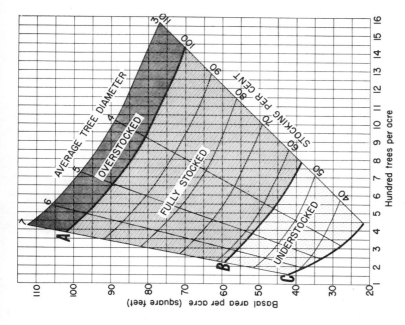

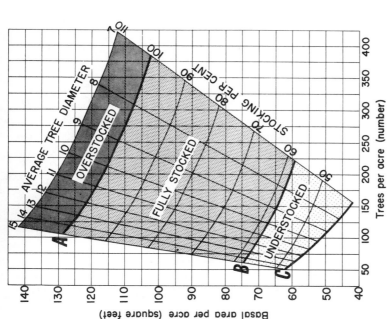

Fig. 17–5. Relation of basal area, number of trees, and average tree diameter to stocking per cent for upland hardwood stands. Tree-diameter range 7–15 (left), 3–7 (right). The area between curves A and B indicates the range of stocking where the trees can fully utilize the growing space. Curve C shows the lower limit of stocking necessary to reach the B level in 10 years on average sites. (Source: Gingrich, 1964.)

been restricted in his ability to modify the environment on a given site to changing stand density and structure. In the future, he may be able to extend this to fertilization and irrigation practices when the economic climate is propitious. At present, the application of the knowledge of site-growth relationships consists of the encouragement of a species on sites where its establishment is readily achieved or where its growth potential can be fully realized.

The relationship of the growth of forest trees to their environment, or, as it is commonly referred to, their site, is a difficult one to measure. The factors of the site and the plants themselves are interacting and inter-dependent, making it difficult to assign cause and effect relationships. A considerable amount of effort has been directed toward investigating the characteristics of the soil in an attempt to find some one environmental factor to serve as a reliable indicator of site quality. This approach has been found practical but frequently leaves unassigned a sizable amount of variation in the growth parameter employed. To understand fully the growth of trees in relation to environment, individual site factors cannot be studied in isolation. The interdependencies and influences of the other factors may be masked and, consequently, not recognized. Even if the primary interest lies in studying one factor of the site, it must be done with recognition of the effects of the other factors.

The productivity of a site for tree growth is usually evaluated on a stand basis. Considered in this way, site quality expresses the average productivity of a designated land area for growing forest trees. A common way of expressing relative site quality is to set up from three to five classes, or ordinal ranks, such as Site I, Site II, and Site III, designat-ing comparative productive capacities in descending rank. The charac-teristics of each class must be defined to enable any area to be classified. To a large extent, the definitions are in qualitative terms so that the ranking of a site is quite subjective. Wherever possible, attempts are made to introduce numerical definitions to improve the precision of site quality ranking.

Site quality can be evaluated in two general ways:

1. By the measurement of one or more of the individual site factors considered closely associated with tree growth. This approach evaluates site quality in terms of the environmental causal factors themselves.
2. By the measurement of some characteristics of the trees or lesser vegetation considered sensitive to site quality. This approach as-sesses site quality from the effects of the environment on the vege-tation.

17–3.1. Measurement of Site Factors. Of the numerous environmental factors influencing tree growth, the important relationship between soils and tree growth has been so apparent that attention has been directed to it for a long time. An excellent summary of work in this field has been given by Coile (1952). Continuing work by other investigators has progressed along similar lines for an increasing number of species in different localities. They have shown that the soil characteristics significantly related to tree growth are not the same everywhere. Relative wetness, sandiness, depth, amount of clay in the A and B horizons, nutrient levels, soil temperature, and other characteristics have different proportionate effects, depending on the kind of soil and species involved. Evaluating site quality from soil characteristics has several advantages. The soil is comparatively stable and changes slowly. An evaluation of site quality from soil characteristics can also be made regardless of the presence or absence of the forest. An area may support a dense forest or be cut over, but the site quality based on the soil will be little affected.

The usual form of soil-site quality investigation has consisted of a multiple regression analysis with height or site index as the dependent variable and a number of soil and other environmental characteristics as the independent variables. A commonly used approach is to use the model:

$$\log H = b_o + b_1(1/A) + b_2(B) + b_3(C) + \ldots + b_n(N)$$

where:

$$H = \text{height}$$
$$A = \text{age}$$
$$B, C \ldots N = \text{soil or other environmental factors}$$
$$b_o \ldots b_n = \text{constants to be determined by least squares}$$

Environmental factors other than soil characteristics have also been studied in their relation to growth. These include aspect, slope, elevation, photoperiod, air temperature, etc. Hills (1952) has prepared a site evaluation system which considers the integrated result of all environmental factors in expressing site quality.

A major difficulty in this type of analysis pertains to the numerical coding of qualitative variables to enable the regression approach. Such procedure can lead to difficulty because the arbitrary assignment of numbers to discrete classes and subsequent computations, by assuming a continuous scale, implies a scale of equal units which may not represent the actual relation between the original discrete classes. Thoughtful assignment of numerical codes to qualitative variables will make the subsequent regression analysis more meaningful. For an example of such coding refer to Beers, Dress, and Wensel (1966).

17–3.2. Measurement of Vegetative Characteristics. The characteristics of the vegetation which can be used to express the quality of a site are the quantity of wood produced, size characteristics of the trees, and the species of plants naturally occurring on the area.

Since the concept of site quality refers to productivity, its most direct measure is the quantity of wood grown on an area of land within a given period. It is widely assumed that the measurement of site quality in this way (using volume growth, for example) is of limited value because of the difficulty in development and application. The value of using volume growth to define site quality, however, has been reiterated by Mader (1963). The work of Stage (1966) has indicated one feasible approach based on volume growth potential estimated from relations involving stand height, age, and a relative measure of site quality. It is evident that the use of volume growth to assess site quality will develop with the increased application of data-processing equipment and analysis techniques to carefully garnered forest growth data, but apparently no specific approach has been widely adopted.

The sizes which trees will attain according to their age is also affected by site quality. The most useful tree-size characteristic for site evaluation is tree height. Diameter is less reliable since it is more sensitive to stand density.

The relationship of tree height to age, called *site index*, has been used for many years in evaluating site quality for even-aged stands of single species or nearly pure composition. The height of the dominant and codominant trees has usually been taken as representative of stand height for site index work. This choice is not without its limitations. It relies on the subjective decision as to which are dominants and which are codominants. In addition, the crown position of a tree and its height growth may be affected by stand alterations, such as cuttings. Other stand height measures, such as the average height of a specified number of the largest trees or the height of the tallest tree, have been suggested as alternative parameters. Unless otherwise specified, site index is generally defined as the average height that the dominant and codominant trees on an area will attain at key ages such as 50 or 100 years. For example, site index 70 on a 50-year basis means that the dominants and codominants reach an average height of 70 feet in 50 years. Site index 120 on a 100-year basis means an average height of 120 feet in 100 years. Site index curves are prepared for even-aged stands, as shown in Fig. 17–6, to allow site classification for a stand at any age. To assess the site quality of an area, it is necessary only to determine the average height of the dominant and codominant trees and their average age and to locate the position of these coordinates on the site index chart for the species. The site index for the stand can be read from the closest curve. For an average height of the dominants and codominants of 65 feet and stand age of 40 years, the site index for white pine in the southern Appalachians from Fig. 17–6 is 75. Total age or age at dbh level can be used in the preparation of site index curves. Husch (1956) has pointed out

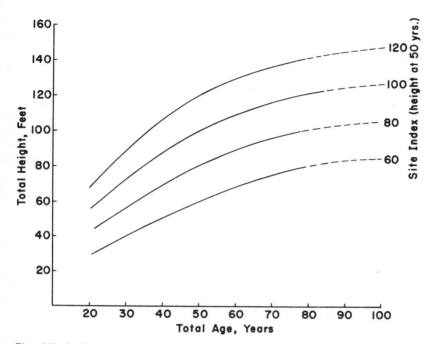

Fig. 17–6. Site index curves for natural stands of white pine in the southern Appalachians (Doolittle and Vimmerstedt, 1960).

several advantages of using age at dbh instead of total age. Measuring age at dbh eliminates the necessity of adding arbitrary corrections to convert age at increment-boring level to total age; it measures tree age after the initial period of establishment and adjustment has passed; it utilizes a standard and conventional point for age determination.

It is important to understand that site index varies according to species. Site index charts are prepared for individual species or for typical forest types, such as the charts prepared by Schnur (1937) for mixed oak forests in the Central States. A single forest area may have different site index values, depending on the species and site index chart. To help solve this problem, regression formulas can be derived relating the site index or height of one species with that of another. Examples of this type of study are those of Foster (1959), Deitschman and Green (1965), and Norman and Curlin (1968).

The relationship of age and total height expressed by site index has enjoyed widespread popularity for several reasons. Height has been found closely correlated to the ultimate measure, volume. In addition, the two requisite measurements, height and age, are quickly and easily determined. Height growth has been considered only slightly affected by stand density, although some studies have shown that stand height and site index in some cases are related to stand density (Husch and Lyford, 1956; Gaiser and Merz, 1951). Finally, site index has been popular because it provides a numerical expression for site quality rather than a generalized qualitative description.

In uneven-aged stands of several species, height in relation to age cannot be used to express site quality. The height growth of a species in this type of stand is not closely related to age but more to the varying stand conditions by which it has been affected during its life. The classic concept of site index has consequently been restricted to species normally occurring in even-aged stands. McLintock and Bickford (1957) considered several alternatives for evaluating site quality in uneven-aged stands in their study of site quality for red spruce in the northeastern United States. They concluded that the relationship between height and dbh of the dominant trees in a stand was the most sensitive and reliable measure of site quality. Site index according to this concept is then defined as the height attained by dominant trees at a standard dbh. The site index for a tree of any age can be read from the height-dbh curves for the range of site indexes, as shown in Fig. 17–7. This chart utilizes a standard dbh of 14 inches.

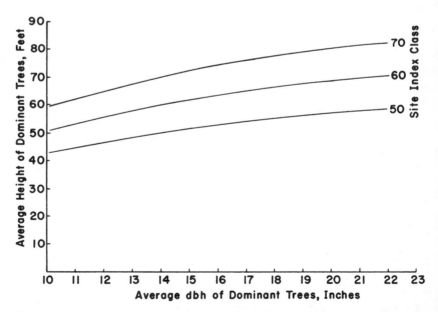

Fig. 17–7. Site index curves for uneven-aged stands of red spruce (McLintock and Bickford, 1957).

Another approach to site quality evaluation makes use of the composition of plant communities on an area of land. This system is based on the theory that certain key species in the forest reflect the overall quality of a site for a tree species or forest type. As Westveld (1954) points out: "The concept . . . recognizes that plant communities are distinct entities developed and arranged in accordance with definite biological laws; they are not mere aggregations of plants brought together by chance. Such communities are well differentiated and are very constant for the same site." Site classification systems based on this concept have been most successful in relatively undisturbed northern forests in Finland and eastern Canada where the forests are extensive and the species few (Ilvessalo, 1937; Sisam, 1938). These systems utilize measures of presence and relative abundance of characteristic species in the minor forest vegetation, called plant indicators, as indicative of the quality of the site for specified tree species. An additional premise is that these shorter-lived plants are more useful site quality indicators than the trees themselves, since they are more sensitive and will, after a disturbance of the forest, return to an equilibrium with site conditions more rapidly than trees.

In summary, it has been proven that there does exist a valid correlation between plant indicators and site quality, but it must be kept on broad terms. The general applicability of indicator plant systems has several limitations. It is restricted to forests of simple composition such as occur in northern latitudes; it requires considerable ecological knowledge on the part of the forester; and it must be recognized that the lesser vegetation is affected by forest composition, stand density, and past management as well as site quality. In addition, the lesser vegetation is shallow-rooted and does not indicate conditions in deeper soil horizons, although these soil conditions affect tree growth. In spite of these limitations, indicator plants can be of general assistance in site quality evaluation.

17–3.3. Preparation of Site Index Curves. The preparation of site index curves for even-aged stands is based on the average height and age measurements of the dominant and codominant trees on a series of sample plots. If temporary sample plots are used, there should be a sufficient number and distribution to cover equally the range of age and site classes found under natural conditions. For reliable relationships, a total of at least 100 plots is necessary, although more are desirable.

Using such sample data, graphical techniques have traditionally been used to construct the desired series of site index curves. In recent years regression techniques have been employed to remove the subjectivity involved in the handfitting of curves. One commonly used approach is described in the following paragraphs.

Using field data involving total tree height and total tree age (plot averages or individual tree data) obtained from selected dominant or codominant trees, site index curves similar to those shown in Fig. 17–6 can be derived. The procedure is as follows:

1. Transform the height and age data to logarithm of height and reciprocal of age and fit a simple linear regression, obtaining numerical values for the constants a and b in the model

$$\text{logarithm of height} = a + b \left(\frac{1}{\text{age}}\right) \tag{17–16}$$

The resulting equation represents the "average" site index curve for the data.

2. Locate points needed to draw a specified site index curve by moving the Y axis to the key age (by mathematical translation) and then, by definition, the Y intercept is the log of site index. For example, if the key age is 50 years, equation 17–16 is translated to become:

$$\log \text{height} = \log \text{site index} + b \left(\frac{1}{\text{age}} - \frac{1}{50}\right) \tag{17–17}$$

Thus, for a curve where the regression coefficients are:

$$a = 1.950 \quad \text{and} \quad b = -4.611$$

$$\log \text{height} = \log \text{site index} - \frac{4.611}{\text{age}} + .09222 \tag{17–18}$$

and the curve for site index 80, for example, can be found by substituting various ages into the following equation, solving for log of height, and then finding height:

$$\log \text{height} = \log 80 \quad - \frac{4.611}{\text{age}} + .09222$$

$$= 1.90309 - \frac{4.611}{\text{age}} + .09222$$

$$= 1.99531 - \frac{4.611}{\text{age}}$$

3. Locate other site index curves by substituting the pertinent site index number in equation 17–18 and proceeding as described in step 2.

It is often useful to calculate site index from the fitted equation rather than to read a graph. For this purpose, equation 17–17 is rearranged, by solving for log site index, to become:

$$\log \text{site index} = \log \text{height} - \frac{b}{\text{age}} + \frac{b}{\text{key age}} \tag{17–19}$$

For the example used in step 2, the resulting equation is:

$$\log \text{ site index} = \log \text{ height} + \frac{4.611}{\text{age}} - \frac{4.611}{50}$$

For a given plot one can substitute values of average tree height (as a logarithm) and average tree age and obtain logarithm of site index, and then, using anti-logs, the site index can be estimated.

More recently, the fitting of more sophisticated models to the height-age relationship has become common. Brickell (1968), for example, used the model:

$$H = a(1 - be^{-kA})\frac{1}{1 - m} \qquad (17\text{--}20)$$

where:

H = total tree height

A = total tree age

e = base of natural logarithms and a, b, k, and m are coefficients estimated by non-linear regression procedures. A set of polymorphic site index curves were then developed from the fitted least-squares equation.

17–4. YIELD TABLES AND FUNCTIONS

A *yield table* is a tabular presentation of volume per unit area and other stand characteristics of even-aged stands by age classes, site classes, species, and density.

Obviously, this definition is not applicable to uneven-aged stands. Volumes cannot be shown at specified ages for an uneven-aged stand, since there is no one representative average age. A type of table has been prepared for uneven-aged stands, showing the volumes produced in growth for given periods with a certain level of growing stock on land of different site qualities (Meyer, 1934). Yield records for uneven-aged stands over long periods are required for preparing this kind of table. Accumulated information of this type is limited in the United States. Consequently, little effort has been devoted to the preparation of yield tables for uneven-aged stands. The increased availability of permanent plot records portends to accelerate this area of research.

Even-aged yield tables are prepared from yield studies of the relationship between a dependent variable, such as volume, basal area, or number of trees, and independent variables describing stand conditions, such as age, site quality, and stand density. Site quality is most often measured in terms of site index, although discrete site quality classes have been used. Density has been most commonly measured in terms of basal area, although stand density index is often more convenient to use.

Yield tables are valuable in such forest management activities as regulating the cut, determination of length of rotation, and forest valuation.

Growth estimates can also be derived from yield tables, as discussed in Section 16–3.1.

Although the tabular form of yield relationships has endured years of use in forest management activities, the past decade has seen a proliferation of studies which emphasize the formula form. The conclusion is inescapable that the construction techniques employed for most of the older yield tables are made obsolete by the modern, mathematically sophisticated approaches. However, regardless of the method of analysis used, the basic nature of yield tables is worthy of discussion. Only even-aged yield tables are described; uneven-aged yield relationships are briefly treated in Section 17–4.2.

17–4.1. Even-aged Yield Tables. Yield tables for even-aged stands are of several types, depending on the independent variables used: *normal, empirical,* and *variable density.*

Normal yield tables show the relationship on a per unit area basis, between the two independent variables, stand age and site index, and one or more dependent variables. An example is show in Table 17–1. This table has been prepared for one site index and shows values for a number of dependent variables according to age. Similar tables have been prepared for other site index levels.

This type of table originated before analytical methods for handling three independent variables were available. Since normal yield tables use only two independent variables, they are conveniently constructed by graphical methods. The density variable is held constant by attempting to select sample plots of the same density. The density required has been called *full or normal stocking.* Full or normal stocking is supposed to describe the density of a stand which completely occupies a given site and makes full use of its growth potentialities. Since it is difficult to describe quantitatively full stocking, qualitative and somewhat subjective guides must be used. For example, the guides might be: completely closed crown canopy, no openings in the stand, and regular spacing of the trees. Such specifications leave much to the judgment of the individual in choosing so-called fully stocked stands for samples.

The stand parameter values for successive ages, shown in normal yield tables prepared from a number of sample plots, are averages derived from many stands considered fully stocked at the time they were sampled. Each stand in which these sample plots were taken may have shown varying patterns of development over its life. In past years, some stands may have been over- or understocked in terms of the definition of normality. When data from these samples are compiled, average relationships are developed which represent the development of a theoretically fully stocked stand over its entire life. It is quite unlikely that any existing stand will show the same pattern as is represented in a normal yield table. In reality,

Table 17-1
Example of Normal Yield Table

Yield per Acre for Fully Stocked Spruce–Aspen Stands; Good Site–Index 80[5]

| | | | | | Tolerant Softwoods, Mainly Spruce | | | Intolerant Hardwoods, Mainly Aspen | | | Entire Stand |
| | | | | | Volume Inside Bark | | | | | | |
Spruce, Total Age (Years)	Height, Average Dominant (Feet)	Number of Trees	Average Dbh (Inches)	Basal Area (Sq. ft.)	Entire Stem (Cu. ft.)	Merch. Stem[1] 12"+ (Cu. ft.)	Scribner Rule[2] 12"+ (Bd. ft.)	Basal Area (Sq. ft.)	Composition[3] (%)	Volume to Basal Area Factor[4] (Units)	Basal Area (Sq. ft.)
30	23	1091	1.6	16	155	0	0	88	83	16.7	104
40	34	1379	2.5	49	620	5	0	88	64	19.9	137
50	45	1344	3.3	79	1280	20	0	85	52	22.6	164
60	58	1091	4.1	100	2010	55	150	82	45	25.0	182
70	70	845	5.0	114	2740	105	600	79	41	27.1	193
80	80	643	6.0	125	3445	310	1,540	76	38	28.7	201
90	87	484	7.1	133	4060	835	3,490	71	35	30.1	204
100	93	376	8.3	140	4565	1645	7,020	66	32	31.3	206
110	98	307	9.3	145	4995	2520	11,180	60	29	32.3	205
120	102	264	10.2	150	5370	3325	15,590	53	26	33.2	203
130	106	238	10.9	153	5680	3995	18,980	45	23	34.0	198
140	109	220	11.4	156	5945	4460	21,320	36	19	34.7	192
150	112	208	11.8	158	6165	4810	23,060	26	14	35.3	184

[1] 1-foot stump, 4-inch top inside bark.
[2] 1-foot stump, 6-inch top inside bark.
[3] Hardwood composition by basal area.
[4] × basal area = total cubic volume.
[5] Note: In this study, site index is defined as the height attained by the average dominant spruce at 80 years of age.
SOURCE: Macleod and Blyth, 1955.

very few stands are encountered which can be called fully stocked. Both under- and overstocked stands can be encountered, with understocking the usual case.

The volume of an existing stand may be estimated from a normal yield table, by measuring its age, site index, and relative stocking percentage or normality. Relative stocking can be measured by comparing the volume, basal area, or number of trees per acre for a stand with the yield table values shown for a stand of the same age and site index as discussed in Section 17–2.1. There is little point in using volume to measure normality when volume is the parameter to be estimated. Basal area has been found to be the most satisfactory basis for expressing relative stocking. It is easily and quickly determined and is closely related to volume. The stocking or normality percentage times the yield table volume estimates the volume of the existing stand. This naturally assumes that relative stocking in basal area equals relative stocking in volume. This may be a tenable assumption for volume in cubic feet but can lead to serious error for board-foot estimation. Normality percentages for the same stand calculated from basal area, cubic feet, and board feet can give widely differing results.

McArdle, Meyer, and Bruce (1949) utilized the same data for a conventional yield table and prepared a form of normal yield table based on average dbh rather than age. They utilized the idea that stands of the same average dbh are similar, even though differing in age and site class. The resulting yield table then relates all of the normal yield-table variables to average stand diameter. Table 17–2 reproduces this table. To use the table, the average diameter and number of trees per acre are determined for the stand under investigation. Volume per acre is obtained by multiplying the volume per tree from the table by the number of trees per acre as found from field sampling.

Because of the several subjective decisions necessary in their preparation and use, normal yield tables have been challenged; indeed, the entire normality concept has been seriously questioned in recent years (Nelson and Bennett, 1965). To overcome the fully stocked assumption of normal yield tables, the two types of tables described below have been used.

An *empirical yield table* is similar to a normal yield table but is based on sample plots of average rather than full stocking. The judgment necessary for selecting fully stocked stands is eliminated, simplifying the collection of field data. Resulting yield tables show stand characteristics for the average stand density encountered in the collection of the field data.

When stand density is used as an independent variable, *variable density yield tables* result. Tables then show the yields for various levels of stocking. This approach also has the advantage of not requiring samples to be fully stocked. Sample plots of any density can be used since the density is measured as a variable for the solution.

Table 17-2
Revised Douglas Fir Yield Tables

Based on average diameter instead of site and age.

Average Dbh of Stand[1] (Inches)	Normal No. of Trees per Acre	Normal Height of Trees of Average Dbh (Feet)	Total Stand[2] and Entire Stand (Cu. ft.)	Volume Per Tree — 5 Inches Dbh and Over to a 4-Inch Top (Cu. ft.)	Volume Per Tree — 7 Inches Dbh and Over to a 4-Inch Top (Cu. ft.)	Volume Per Tree — 12 Inches Dbh and Over to a 4-Inch Top (Cu. ft.)	Volume per Tree, 12 Inches Dbh and Over — Int. 1/8-Inch Rule[3] (Bd. ft.)	Volume per Tree, 12 Inches Dbh and Over — Scribner Rule[4] (Bd. ft.)
2	4466	22						
3	2387	31						
4	1530	39	1.8	0.9	0.2			
5	1084	47	3.2	2.1	1.1			
6	818	55	5.1	3.8	2.6	0.3		
7	644	62	7.6	6.2	4.9	1.1	5	3
8	524	69	10.9	9.4	8.0	2.5	18	11
9	437	76	14.9	13.4	12.1	5.3	35	23
10	371	83	19.6	18.0	16.7	9.5	66	43
11	320	90	25.2	23.6	22.7	15.1	102	67
12	280	97	31.5	29.8	29.3	21.7	148	99
13	248	104	38.5	36.6	36.5	29.5	224	149
14	221	110	46.6	44.3	44.3	38.3	274	184
15	198	117	55.5	52.8	52.8	48.0	347	236
16	180	123	65	62	62	58	432	296
17	164	130	76	72	72	69	521	359
18	150	135	87	83	83	81	618	429
19	138	141	99	95	95	93	724	510
20	127	147	112	108	108	106	836	593
21	118	152	126	121	121	119	956	683
22	110	157	142	136	136	134	1075	779
23	102	162	158	152	152	150	1205	886
24	96	167	175	169	169	168	1339	999
25	91	171	193	186	186	185	1485	1125
26	85	176	213	205	205	204	1653	1262
27	80	180	234	227	227	227	1826	1405
28	76	185	256	249	249	249	2031	1562
29	72	189	279	271	271	271	2249	1730
30	68	194	302	293	293	293	2476	1905

[1] Weighted by basal area.   [2] Total stand, i.e., trees over 1.5 inches dbh.   [3] To 5-inch top.   [4] To 8-inch top.

SOURCE: McArdle, Meyer, and Bruce, 1949.

Mulloy (1947) has prepared variable density yield tables using stand age and stand density index as the two independent variables. Site quality has been accounted for by preparing yield relationships for discrete site classes. Table 17–3 shows the yields of even-aged stands of jack pine for a

Table 17–3
Variable Density Yield Table
Jack Pine—Medium Site—100 SDI[1]
Timigami, Ontario

Age (Years)	Total Volume (Cubic feet)	Current Annual Increment (Cubic feet)	Mean Annual Increment (Cubic feet)
10	185	23.5	18.5
20	420	24.0	21.0
30	660	15.5	22.0
40	815	11.9	20.4
50	934	11.3	18.7
60	1,047	10.3	17.4
70	1,150	10.3	16.4
80	1,253	10.3	15.7

[1] Volumes for other stand density indices can be obtained by pointing off two places in the stand density index and multiplying times the tabular values.
SOURCE: Mulloy, 1944.

stand density index of 100. Site as a variable has been held constant for the relationship. This yield table is applicable only to the jack pine cover type in Ontario for average site conditions.

With the increased use of statistical techniques, yield studies involving more than two independent variables can be carried out. MacKinney, Schumacher, and Chaiken (1937) used age, stand density, site index, and a stand composition index as independent variables. This resulted in a more general type of variable density yield table. In a later study MacKinney and Chaiken (1939) used age, site index, and stand density as independent variables; Smith and Ker (1959) used site index, age, maximum height, average stand diameter, basal area per acre, and number of trees per acre in preparing yield equations by multiple regression.

17–4.2. Yield Functions. Most of the early normal yield tables used in America were prepared by graphical procedures described by Bruce (1926) and Reineke (1927), and improved upon by Osborne and Schumacher (1935). Departure from the graphical approach was evident in the classic study by MacKinney et al. (1937), who used the least-squares regression technique applied to a logarithmic transformation of the Pearl-Reed logistic curve. The multiple regression applications by Schumacher (1939),

Smith and Ker (1959), among others, further demonstrated the superiority of sound statistical techniques over the purely graphical approach for the preparation of yield tables. The fact that regression techniques provide a "yield formula" as well as yield tables was recognized as a distinct advantage especially in early computer applications. Through all this development, however, a major problem was ignored or overlooked—because yield functions (which predict stand volume at a specified age) and growth functions (which predict volume growth over shorter periods) were often derived independently, summation of a succession of periodic *growth estimates* added to an initial volume would not necessarily lead to the final stand volume indicated by the *yield function estimate*. The application of calculus to growth and yield studies led to the resolution of this inconsistency between growth summation and terminal yield. The independent, essentially simultaneous works of Buckman (1962) and Clutter (1963) began a new era in yield studies. A brief description of their work is appropriate.

Working with even-aged red pine, Buckman (1962) emphasized that growth and yield are not independent phenomena and should not be treated as such. Furthermore, he employed methods of calculus which had been neglected in virtually all previous yield studies of this type. Beginning with the basal area *growth equation* of the form:

$$Y = b_o + b_1X_1 + b_2X_1{}^2 + b_3X_2 + b_4X_2{}^2 + b_5X_3 \qquad (17\text{--}21)$$

where:

Y = periodic net annual basal area increment (i.e., $\dfrac{dX_1}{dX_2}$, change in basal area with respect to age)

X_1 = basal area in square feet per acre
X_2 = age in years
X_3 = site index

yield tables were prepared by iterative solution and cumulation; that is, the least-squares fit of equation 17–21 is solved for a particular site, age, and stand density; basal area growth is then added to the stand density, one year is added to age, and the equation is again solved. Addition of the n successive annual growth estimates to the initial basal area provides a yield estimate n years hence.

Clutter (1963) working with loblolly pine (even-aged) clearly indicated the relation between growth and yield models by the definition:

> Such models are here defined as compatible when the yield model can be obtained by summation of the predicted growth through the appropriate growth periods or, more precisely, when the algebraic form of the yield model can be derived by mathematical integration of the growth model.

In the research reported by Clutter a yield model was first prepared of the form:

$$\ln V = a + b_1 S + b_2 (\ln B) + b_3 A^{-1} \qquad (17\text{--}22)$$

where:

$\ln V$ = logarithm to the base "e" of volume
A = stand age in years
S = site index in feet
B = basal area per acre in square feet

and differentiated with respect to age, obtaining:

$$\frac{dV}{dA} = b_2 V B^{-1}(dB/dA) - b_3 V A^{-2} \qquad (17\text{--}23)$$

where:

dV/dA = rate of change of volume with respect to age or instantaneous rate of volume growth
dB/dA = rate of change of basal area with respect to age or instantaneous rate of basal area growth

Since the rate of basal area growth is not ordinarily available, regression analysis was used to obtain dB/dA as a function of age, site, and basal area. The model finally adopted was:

$$dB/dA = -B(\ln B)A^{-1} + c_o A^{-1} B + c_1 BSA^{-1} \qquad (17\text{--}24)$$

Substituting this relation for dB/dA in equation 17–23 led to the equation:

$$dV/dA = -b_2 V(\ln B)A^{-1} + b_2 c_o V A^{-1} + b_2 c_1 VSA^{-1} - b_3 V A^{-2} \quad (17\text{--}25)$$

Using the form of this equation as a model, and based on data gathered on permanent sample plots, a least-squares regression equation was obtained, thus relating volume growth with present basal area, age, site index, and volume (estimated using equation 17–22). Subsequent integration of this regression equation led to the final yield function, from which volume yield at some future time could be predicted from given initial age, basal area and volume, projected age, and site index.

Virtually all published studies of growth and yield have been undertaken for even-aged stands. The application of recent growth and yield model theory to uneven-aged stands is quite feasible, however, as shown by Moser (1967). Moser proposed a growth model (a generalization of Von Bertalanffy's growth-rate function) which, when mathematically integrated, provides a yield function in which time is represented by the variable "elapsed time from an initial condition." Using annual remeasurements of permanent plot data, methods were evaluated for the development of compatible growth and yield functions for uneven-aged stands.

No serious study of growth and yield should be undertaken without prior examination of the dissertations of Turnbull (1963) and Pienaar (1965). A major contribution of these works is that forest-growth phenomena are studied from a basic standpoint in order to develop the general quantitative growth theory of even-aged forest stands, and to develop "biomathematical growth models," as opposed to empirical and semi-empirical regression models that abound in forestry literature.

18

Developments of Interest to Forest Mensuration

18–1. INTRODUCTION

Recent developments and techniques within the traditional field of forest mensuration have been covered in the preceding chapters. It is worthwhile at this time to mention several new procedures not treated elsewhere in this text. We refer to systems analysis and operations research which are approaches to problem solving that characteristically depend on model building and an array of techniques that include simulation and mathematical programming (linear, parametric, dynamic, etc.). Forest mensurationists should be aware of these and other new developments in decision making. It is most probable that knowledge of, and skill in, the use of these techniques will before long be considered an absolute requirement and a basic tool of forest mensuration.

These new procedures cannot be called developments in forest mensuration; rather, they are applications of externally devised procedures, usually of a mathematical or statistical nature, to which mensurationists have been drawn by their interest in, and understanding of, these latter disciplines. The new techniques have developed outside the area in which forest mensurationists have traditionally worked and it is only recently that specific applications to classical mensurational problems have been attempted. In a reverse direction, mensurationists have taken an interest in and, in fact, have been called upon to use these techniques for the solution of a variety of problems outside the usually accepted bounds of forest mensuration. Again, this has occurred principally because of the numerical skills of mensurationists which enable them to understand and apply these techniques.

This chapter will touch on only the basic ideas of some of these new developments with the hope that the interested reader will refer to the cited and rapidly growing literature on these topics. These topics will be considered individually for ease of presentation and not because they are intrinsically separate and distinct. Actually, they are interrelated, as will become apparent. Indeed, it may become difficult to decide where one ends and another begins. An excellent example is afforded by operations research which draws upon all the techniques in varying combinations to solve problems. These techniques are new and evolving and, consequently, it is difficult to give clear-cut definitions. Even among those actively working with these techniques there are still differences of opinion on precise definitions.

18–2. SYSTEMS ANALYSIS AND DESIGN

Systems analysis and design is the name given to a general approach aimed at understanding more clearly the combination of things or parts which, taken together, form a complex whole which can be designated as a system. Perhaps the main feature of the systems approach is that it tries to isolate the essence of a complex physical or conceptual entity or system, describe its structure, and explain its internal cause-and-effect relationships. Jones and Gray (1963) succinctly define a system as "an organized arrangement of interacting components whose unique circuitry (interrelationships) confers capabilities lacking in any of its isolated components." In other words, the capabilities of the entire system can be greater than the sum of the capabilities of the individual components. Systems occur in nature or they may be consciously designed by man. They are so ubiquitous that it is difficult to conceive of something which cannot be described as a system or part of a system. All living organisms are systems with subsystems of organs, tissues, cells, etc. Associations of living organisms such as human society,· a forest or forest type can be thought of as systems. The natural laws which control our physical environment similarly can be thought of as forming a system. Man-made systems are all around us. A machine, such as an automobile, is an excellent example of an engineered system. The organization of a company or industry for the manufacture and distribution of goods forms a system, as does a forest managed to produce wood products and other goods and services.

Under the systems approach, *analysis* tries to separate the components of the system and study their individual characteristics and behavior. *Synthesis,* on the other hand, tries to understand the behavior of the entire system from knowledge of the components and how they are inter-related and function in the system. The combination of analysis followed by synthesis forms a methodology which has been given the name of systems analysis.

In the application of systems analysis it has been found useful to represent the relationships between components and their assemblage in a system using both qualitative and quantitative mathematical models. A system can be represented qualitatively by a verbal description or, better, by a block diagram. The representation of a system by a verbal model or description is by no means new and has been done intuitively as long as man has been a rational creature. Formal, qualitative representation of systems by diagrams is of more recent origin. Each component is represented by a box. Inputs to the components are indicated by entering arrows, outputs are represented by exiting arrows. The box itself represents the function which is executed by this component. The entire system is synthesized by the connection of these components.

A system is represented quantitatively by some form of mathematical model, usually an equation. The equations commonly utilized in forest mensuration to represent relationships between variables are mathematical models of designated systems. A more detailed discussion of mathematical models is given in the following section. For a comprehensive treatment of systems analysis the reader is referred to Hare (1967).

As will become apparent, systems analysis forms a basic part of the other techniques mentioned in this chapter.

18–3. MATHEMATICAL MODELS

Mathematical modeling is a new name for an old practice. Models to represent functional relationships in quantitative form have been used since the dawn of numerical concepts. Both the ancient Pythagorean theorem, relating the lengths of sides of a right triangle, and the modern theory, relating mass and energy in the classic $e = mc^2$, are examples of mathematical models.

Mathematical models have long been used in forest mensuration. In trying to show the quantitative relationship between variables, model equations have been devised, such as the yield function of Schumacher (1939), $\log X = a + b \, (1/T)$. This model states the system-relating volume of a stand, X, to age of that stand, T. Assuming the model represents the situation, the specific function is then defined by the constants, a and b, found from empirical observations. This function has implicit in it a fundamental characteristic of models. That is, the model is less complex than real life but at the same time is sufficiently complete to yield useful information approximating reality. In the example shown, obviously the yield of a stand is dependent not only on its age but on many additional factors, such as site quality, density, competition, past treatment, etc. However, these other factors are not included in the model from a desire of simplicity or because they are assumed to be related to age, are not easily or conveniently measured, or are unrecognized. The model thus shows a simplified conception of a system which may leave out many actual relationships or even show an artificial relationship.

Mathematical models may be either deterministic or statistical or probabilistic. A deterministic model shows a relationship between variables without any random elements. The yield equation shown above exemplifies this. In a statistical model the relationships between variables are in terms of probability distributions.

A good summarization of model building from a forestry economics point of view is given by Chappelle (1966), but his observations can also be considered applicable to all quantitative functional relationships.

18–4. SIMULATION

Simulation is one of the techniques used for decision making. The term "simulation" means to reproduce the behavior of a system in the form of a model which emulates, but not necessarily reproduces, real life, and to operate this model to obtain alternative solutions. Simulation, then, is the technique of performing experiments on a model of a system. Simulation techniques do not generate optimal solutions but, rather, show alternative results that allow the investigator to make a decision on the levels of his input variables that are best for his purposes. The resulting decisions may or may not be the same as the optimal solution. For comprehensive treatment of simulation the student is referred to Tocher (1963), Charafas (1965), Naylor, Balintfy, Burdick, and Chu (1966), and Mize and Cox (1968).

The application of simulation studies to forestry problems is in its infancy. A concise summary of their applications to date is given by Newnham (1968). Using his categories, simulation has been applied to forestry in studies of:

1. Forest sampling (Palley and O'Regan, 1961; O'Regan and Palley, 1965; Arvanitis and O'Regan, 1967).
2. Forest management operations (Gould and O'Regan, 1965;

O'Regan, Arvanitis, and Gould, 1965; Clutter and Bamping, 1965; Grevatt and Wardle, 1967; and Hool, 1968).
3. Fire protection (Kourtz, 1966).
4. Insect populations (Watt, 1963).
5. Stand growth (Newnham and Smith, 1964; Smith, Newnham, and Hejjas, 1965).
6. Harvesting machines (Newnham, 1966).

Simulation studies require the construction of a model to describe the system under investigation. It is obvious that this requires a clear understanding of the system and the objectives of the study. To accomplish this the system is best described preliminarily on a qualitative basis using a block or flow diagram. From this a mathematical model is constructed, describing the operation of the system in terms of the individual elements of the system. This simulation model need not completely represent all the elements in the real-life system. Rather, for practical purposes, it should consist only of the important ones with the trivial or non-influential elements eliminated.

After the model has been constructed, it is then operated to simulate the actual behavior of the system. The operation consists of feeding input data into the model, and observing the solutions. If the behavior of the input variables is not precisely known, then random observations are taken from the probability distributions associated with these variables. By repeating the operation for various levels and combinations of the input variables a series of solutions can be obtained. The solutions in conjunction with the input data are then compared to decide on the most satisfactory configuration of the input variables.

Simulation studies are usually carried out on digital computers since they normally require much calculation. However, the concept of simulation is independent of electronic computers and simpler studies can be executed without them.

18–5. MATHEMATICAL PROGRAMMING

Mathematical programming is a general term including several techniques aimed at preparing a program or schedule of actions to be taken, their timing and quantities or levels, to achieve the stated objectives within a system. In mathematical programming the system is described by a mathematical model which allows the objective to be stated in quantifiable terms. Dantzig (1963) has shown that under this general category of mathematical programming can be included linear, linear parametric, non-linear, and dynamic programming, network analysis, game theory, queuing theory, inventory control, and Markov chains. It is probable that applications of all of these programming developments will be made to forestry. Network analysis is a valuable tool for formulating, executing, and controlling projects, which is being increasingly used (Husch, 1969). Up to the present, however, linear programming has received the greatest attention and, consequently, will be briefly described here.

The purpose of linear programming is to determine the optimal allocation of limited resources to satisfy a given objective when there are competing uses or activities needing these resources. The given objective may be to maximize the yield or output, or to minimize the effort, cost, or required input of a system. For detailed treatment of the subject the reader is referred to such texts as Hadley (1962), Dantzig (1963), Spivey (1963), Llewellyn (1964), and Frazer (1968).

Linear programming has been found applicable in solving a wide variety of problems in which the common factor is the necessity for allocating resources to different uses or activities. Applications in forestry have so far concentrated on problems of forest and land management or regulation (Jones, 1960; Curtis, 1962; Leak, 1963; Loucks, 1964; Wardle, 1965; Kidd, Thompson, and Hoepner, 1966; Littschwager and Tcheng, 1967; and Navon, 1967) and forest industry (Arimizu, 1956; Row, Fasick, and Guttenberg, 1965; and Fasick and Sampson, 1966).

The investigations of linear programming in forest management have been directed toward the basic problem of deciding how much to cut, from where and at what time, to meet some specified objective and at the same time satisfy certain restrictions or requirements. The usual objective has been to maximize the total yield of a forest. To satisfy the chosen objective, linear programming is used to arrive at a cutting schedule taking into consideration the size of the forest, its volume and growth, chosen rotation or cutting cycle, the number of cutting periods, and such restrictions as the necessity of equal volume or value yields or improvement in the age class distribution by the end of the rotation.

In other forest industry applications linear programming has been used to decide on the best way to utilize or process the varying sizes and grades of logs to maximize the quantity or value of the several possible products or their combinations.

Linear programming requires that a mathematical model called the objective function be constructed to describe the problem. As the name of the technique implies, all the mathematical functions in this model must be linear.

The simplex algorithm is the basic method which can be used in solving any linear programming model. The method, described in any of the suggested references, is an algebraic procedure which approaches the optimal solution by iteration. It is well adapted for computer solution and computer programs have been prepared and are available. For some special linear programming problems, commonly referred to as the "transportation," "transshipment," and "assignment" problems, short-cut solutions can be used.

A limitation of the linear programming procedure just described is that all the coefficients in the mathematical model must be assumed to be constant when actually they may not be known or constant. Parametric linear programming is a procedure in which these coefficients are allowed to vary with consequently varying behavior of the objective function. Navon and McConnen (1967) utilized this procedure in formulating policy for the management of forest lands. Non-linear programming is another extension which has been developed to permit the mathematical model of the objective and restraint functions to express non-linear relationships.

Another assumption in linear programming is that there is precise knowledge of all future states at all stages in a schedule or program even though some of these future stages may depend on decisions made at preceding stages. Thus, in a forest regulation problem one would have to make the assumption that growth and allowable cuts per acre at future times are precisely known, although we can be sure that previously taken decisions at earlier stages in the schedule will not permit predicting this with certainty. To allow the determination of a sequence of interrelated decisions, which will maximize or minimize an objective function, when future systems states are variable, the technique of dynamic programming has been developed. An interesting application of dynamic programming to the forest regulation problem is given by Hool (1966).

18–6. OPERATIONS RESEARCH

Operations research can be described as a scientific approach to decision making regarding the operation of organizational systems. The breadth of the field is demonstrated by the inclusiveness and imprecision of the definition. Since the development of operations research as a recognized field, a methodology and body of techniques have evolved which give coherence to this decision-making approach. Suggested general references on operations research are Hillier and Lieberman (1967), and Ackoff and Sasieni (1968).

Operations research is of recent origin, beginning with work by the British and United States military during World War II, when it was developed for solving logistic, strategic, and tactical military problems. Since that time it has been applied to civilian as well as military problems that involve the conduct and coordination of operations or activities within any kind of organization.

The operations research approach to problem-solving is well described by Hillier and Lieberman (1967), from which the following summary has been drawn. They describe the methodology as:

1. Observation and formulation of the problem in the context of the entire system.
2. Construction of a mathematical model which includes the essential elements that will allow a solution relevant to the real-life situation and the decision maker's objectives. Testing and modification of the model until considered valid for the problem.
3. Development of procedures for obtaining solutions to the model.
4. Developing a solution that either gives an optimal value to a chosen measure of the system or yields alternative values which can be evaluated for their desirability.

Operations research utilizes all the techniques previously mentioned such as systems analysis, model building, simulation, and mathematical programming. It also commonly requires a team approach, since any single individual is unlikely to have all the knowledge and skills necessary for the solution of an operations research problem.

The application of operations research to forestry problems has been growing in recent years. Indeed, most of the previously cited studies on the forestry applications of systems analysis, simulation, and mathematical programming can also be considered as examples within the realm of operations research. Broido, McConnen, and O'Regan (1965) have summarized a number of recent studies on the minimization of forest fire costs, strategy of insect pest control by chemical methods, use of linear programming in forest management, and simulation studies as examples of the application of operations research.

Dress and Hall (1964) discussed the use of operations research in forest management and pointed out the natural ties between forest mensuration and operations research. It is certain that the use of operations research and its specialized techniques will expand in forestry. The forest mensurationist will need to know how to utilize these tools in the solution of measurement problems.

Appendix

Table A–1
Some Converting Factors for Common Units of Measurement

A. Length

	mm.	cm.	m.	km.	in.	ft.	yd.	rod	chain	mile
1 millimeter	1	0.1	0.001	—	0.0394	0.0033	—	—	—	—
1 centimeter	10	1	0.01	10^{-5}	0.3937	0.032808	0.010936	—	—	—
1 meter	1,000	100	1	10^{-3}	39.3701	3.28083	1.09361	0.19884	0.04971	0.00062
1 kilometer	10^6	10^5	1,000	1	39,370.1	3,280.83	1,093.61	198.838	49.7096	0.62137
1 inch	25.40005	2.540005	0.02540	—	1	0.08333	0.02778	0.00505	—	—
1 foot	304.8006	30.48006	0.30480	$.3048 \times 10^{-3}$	12	1	0.33333	0.060606	0.01515	0.000189
1 yard	—	91.44018	0.91440	$.9144 \times 10^{-3}$	36	3	1	0.18182	0.04545	0.000568
1 rod	—	502.92	5.02921	0.00503	198	16.5	5.5	1	0.25	0.003125
1 chain[a]	—	2,011.68	20.1168	0.02012	792	66	22	4	1	0.0125
1 mile[b]	—	—	1,609.347	1.6093	63,360	5,280	1,760	320	80	1

[a]There are 100 links per chain; each link = .66 feet or 7.92 inches; 1 furlong = 10 chains.
[b]1 international nautical mile = 1852 meters.

Table A–1 (Continued)

B. Area

	cm.^{2}	m.^{2}	hectare	km.^{2}	in.^{2}	ft.^{2}	yd.^{2}	chain^2	acre	mile^2
1 centimeter^2	1	0.0001	10^{-8}	—	0.15500	0.001076	1.196×10^{-4}	—	—	—
1 meter^2	10,000	1	0.0001	10^{-6}	1,549.997	10.76387	1.19599	0.00247	0.000247	3.861×10^{-7}
1 hectare[a]	10^8	10,000	1	0.01	15.50×10^6	107,638.7	11,959.9	24.7104	2.471044	0.0038610
1 kilometer^2	10^{10}	10^6	100	1	—	10,763,867	1,195,985	2,471.04	247.104	0.38610
1 inch^2	6.4516	6.4516×10^{-4}	—	—	1	0.006944	0.7716×10^{-5}	—	—	—
1 foot^2	929.034	0.092903	—	—	144	1	0.11111	0.000230	0.000023	—
1 yard^2	8,361.31	0.836131	—	—	1,296	9	1	0.002066	0.000207	—
1 chain^2 [b]	—	404.687	0.040469	0.0000405	627,264	4,356	484	1	0.1	0.000156
1 acre[c]	—	4,046.87	0.404687	0.0040469	6,272,640	43,560	4,840	10	1	0.001562
1 mile^2	—	258,999.7	258.9997	2.590	—	27,878,400	3,097,600	6,400	640	1

[a] 1 hectare = 100 are.
[b] 1 square chain = 10,000 square links.
[c] 640 acres = 1 section; 36 sections = 1 township (6 × 6 miles).
Basal area per unit land area converting factors:
1 square foot per acre = .2296 square meters per hectare.
1 square meter per hectare = 4.3560 square feet per acre.

Table A–1 (Continued)

C. Volume

	c.c.	liter[b]	m.^{3}	in.^{3}	ft.^{3}	yd.^{3}	oz.[a]	pint[a]	qt.[a]	gal.[a]	qt.[c]
1 cubic centimeter	1	0.001	0.000001	0.061023	—	—	0.033814	0.002113	0.001057	—	0.00091
1 liter	1,000.027	1	0.001	61.0237	0.035315	0.0013	33.8147	2.11342	1.05671	0.264178	0.90810
1 cubic meter	10^6	999.973	1	61,023.7	35.3145	1.308	—	—	1,056.68	264.170	908.08
1 cubic inch	16.3872	0.016387	16.38×10^{-6}	1	0.000579	21.43×10^{-6}	0.554113	0.034632	0.017316	0.004329	0.01488
1 cubic foot	28,317	28.316	0.028317	1,728	1	0.03704	957.5	59.8442	29.9221	7.48052	25.714
1 cubic yard	764,555	764.56	0.76456	46,656	27	1	—	—	—	—	—
1 ounce[a]	29.5737	0.29573	29.57×10^{-6}	1.80469	0.00104	—	1	0.0625	0.03125	0.00781	0.02686
1 pint[a]	473.179	0.473167		28.875	—	—	16	1	0.5	0.125	0.42968
1 quart[a]	946.359	0.94633	0.000946	57.75	0.03342	—	32	2	1	0.25	0.85937
1 gallon[a]	3,785.43	3.78533	0.003785	231	0.13368	—	128	8	4	1	3.43747
1 quart[c]	1,101.23	1.1020	0.001	67.2006	0.03889	—	—	—	1.16365	0.29091	1

[a]United States fluid measure. British Imperial gallon = 277.42 in.^{3} = 1.2009 U.S. Gal.
[b]Volume of 1 kg. of water at 4°C and 760 mm. pressure.
[c]U. S. dry measure. 32 quarts = 1 bushel.
Volume per unit land area converting factors:
1 cubic foot per acre = 0.06997 cubic meters per hectare.
1 cubic meter per hectare = 14.29 cubic feet per acre.

Table A-1 (Continued)

D. Mass

	grain[a]	ounce[a]	pound[a]	ton[a,b]	gram	kilogram	metric ton
1 grain[a]	1	0.002286	0.000143	—	0.64799	—	—
1 ounce[a]	437.5	1	0.0625	—	28.34953	0.028350	—
1 pound[a]	7,000	16	1	0.0005	453.592	0.453592	0.0004536
1 ton[a,b]	—	32,000	2,000	1	—	907.1849	0.90718
1 gram	15.43236	0.035274	0.002205	—	1	0.001	—
1 kilogram	15,432.4	35.27396	2.204622	0.001102	1,000	1	0.001
1 metric ton	—	—	2,204.62	1.102311	—	1,000	1

[a]Avoirdupois system.
[b]U. S. ton; 1 imperial ton = 2240 pounds.
Mass per unit land area converting factors:
1 U. S. ton per acre = 2.241 metric tons per hectare.
1 metric ton per hectare = .44609 U. S. tons per acre.

Table A–2
Areas of Some Plane Figures

Figure	Diagram	Formula
Rectangle		$A = l\,w$
Parallelogram		$A = b\,h$
Triangle		$A = \dfrac{b\,h}{2}$ or $A = \sqrt{S(S - a)(S - b)(S - c)}$ where $S = \frac{1}{2}(a + b + c)$
Trapezoid		$A = \frac{1}{2}(a + c)\,h$
Circle		$A = \pi r^2$ or $A = \dfrac{\pi D^2}{4}$ where $r = \dfrac{D}{2}$ Circumference $= 2\pi r = \pi D$
Circular sector		$A = \dfrac{\theta r^2}{2}$ where θ is in radians $A = \dfrac{\theta \pi r^2}{360}$ where θ is in degrees
Circular segment		$A = (\frac{1}{2}) r^2 (\theta - \sin\theta)$ where θ is in radians
Ellipse		$A = \pi a b$ Perimeter $= \pi(a+b)\left[1 + \frac{1}{4}\left(\dfrac{a-b}{a+b}\right)^2 + \frac{1}{64}\left(\dfrac{a-b}{a+b}\right)^2 + \ldots\right]$
Parabola		$A = (\frac{2}{3}) l\,d$ Length of arc $= l\left[1 + \frac{2}{3}\left(\dfrac{2d}{l}\right)^2 - \frac{2}{5}\left(\dfrac{2d}{l}\right)^4 + \ldots\right]$

Table A–3
Volume and Surface Areas of Some Solids

The following symbols are used in the formulas:

V	= volume	L	= slant height
A_b	= area of the base	P_b	= perimeter of lower base
A_m	= area of a midsection parallel to A_b and A_u	P_u	= perimeter of upper section
		P_r	= perimeter of right section
A_u	= area of an upper section	S_l	= lateral surface area
A_r	= area of a right section	S_t	= total surface area
h	= altitude	d	= distance from base to intermediate section

Solid	Diagram	Formula
Prismoid		$V = \frac{h}{6}(A_b + 4\,A_m + A_u)$ $S_l = \frac{1}{2}(P_b + P_u)\,L$ $S_t = S_l + A_b + A_u$
Prism or cylinder		$V = A_b\,h$ $S_l = P_r L$ $S_t = S_l + 2\,A_b$
Pyramid or cone		$V = \frac{1}{3}\,A_b\,h$ $S_l = \frac{1}{2}\,P_b\,L$ $S_t = S_l + A_b$
Frustum of cone or pyramid		(treat as prismoid or) $V = \frac{h}{3}(A_b + \sqrt{(A_b)(A_u)} + A_u)$ $S_l = \frac{1}{2}(P_b + P_u)\,L$ $S_t = S_l + A_b + A_u$
Sphere		$V = \frac{4}{3}\,\pi r^3$ $S_t = 4\,\pi r^2$

Table A–3 (Continued)
Volume and Surface Areas of Some Solids

Solid	Diagram	Formula
Paraboloid		$V = \frac{1}{2} A_b h$ $S_l = \left(\frac{2\pi r}{12 h^2}\right)\left[(r^2 + 4h^2)^{\frac{3}{2}} - r^3\right]$ $S_t = S_l + A_b$
Frustum of paraboloid		$V = \frac{A_b + A_u}{2} d$ $S_l = $ surface $acb - gck$ $S_t = S_l + A_b + A_u$
Neiloid		$V = \frac{1}{4} A_b h$
Frustum of neiloid		$V = \frac{d}{6}(A_b + 4A_m + A_u)$

Table A-4(a)
Areas of circles in square feet for diameters in inches

Diameter	0.0	0.1	0.2	0.3	0.4	0.5	0.6	0.7	0.8	0.9
0	0.000	0.000	0.000	0.000	0.001	0.001	0.002	0.003	0.003	0.004
1	0.005	0.007	0.008	0.009	0.011	0.012	0.014	0.016	0.018	0.020
2	0.022	0.024	0.026	0.029	0.031	0.034	0.037	0.040	0.043	0.046
3	0.049	0.052	0.056	0.059	0.063	0.067	0.071	0.075	0.079	0.083
4	0.087	0.092	0.096	0.101	0.106	0.110	0.115	0.120	0.126	0.131
5	0.136	0.142	0.147	0.153	0.159	0.165	0.171	0.177	0.183	0.190
6	0.196	0.203	0.210	0.216	0.223	0.230	0.238	0.245	0.252	0.260
7	0.267	0.275	0.283	0.291	0.299	0.307	0.315	0.323	0.332	0.340
8	0.349	0.358	0.367	0.376	0.385	0.394	0.403	0.413	0.422	0.432
9	0.442	0.452	0.462	0.472	0.482	0.492	0.503	0.513	0.524	0.535
10	0.545	0.556	0.567	0.579	0.590	0.601	0.613	0.624	0.636	0.648
11	0.660	0.672	0.684	0.696	0.709	0.721	0.734	0.747	0.759	0.772
12	0.785	0.799	0.812	0.825	0.839	0.852	0.866	0.880	0.894	0.908
13	0.922	0.936	0.950	0.965	0.979	0.994	1.009	1.024	1.039	1.054
14	1.069	1.084	1.100	1.115	1.131	1.147	1.163	1.179	1.195	1.211
15	1.227	1.244	1.260	1.277	1.294	1.310	1.327	1.344	1.362	1.379
16	1.396	1.414	1.431	1.449	1.467	1.485	1.503	1.521	1.539	1.558
17	1.576	1.595	1.614	1.632	1.651	1.670	1.689	1.709	1.728	1.748
18	1.767	1.787	1.807	1.827	1.847	1.867	1.887	1.907	1.928	1.948
19	1.969	1.990	2.011	2.032	2.053	2.074	2.095	2.117	2.138	2.160
20	2.182	2.204	2.226	2.248	2.270	2.292	2.315	2.337	2.360	2.382
21	2.405	2.428	2.451	2.474	2.498	2.521	2.545	2.568	2.592	2.616
22	2.640	2.664	2.688	2.712	2.737	2.761	2.786	2.810	2.835	2.860
23	2.885	2.910	2.936	2.961	2.986	3.012	3.038	3.064	3.089	3.115
24	3.142	3.168	3.194	3.221	3.247	3.274	3.301	3.328	3.355	3.382
25	3.409	3.436	3.464	3.491	3.519	3.547	3.574	3.602	3.631	3.659
26	3.687	3.715	3.744	3.773	3.801	3.830	3.859	3.888	3.917	3.947
27	3.976	4.006	4.035	4.065	4.095	4.125	4.155	4.185	4.215	4.246
28	4.276	4.307	4.337	4.368	4.399	4.430	4.461	4.493	4.524	4.555
29	4.587	4.619	4.650	4.682	4.714	4.746	4.779	4.811	4.844	4.876
30	4.909	4.942	4.974	5.007	5.041	5.074	5.107	5.140	5.174	5.208
31	5.241	5.275	5.309	5.343	5.378	5.412	5.446	5.481	5.515	5.550
32	5.585	5.620	5.655	5.690	5.726	5.761	5.796	5.832	5.868	5.904
33	5.940	5.976	6.012	6.048	6.084	6.121	6.158	6.194	6.231	6.268
34	6.305	6.342	6.379	6.417	6.454	6.492	6.529	6.567	6.605	6.643
35	6.681	6.720	6.758	6.796	6.835	6.874	6.912	6.951	6.990	7.029
36	7.069	7.108	7.147	7.187	7.227	7.266	7.306	7.346	7.386	7.426
37	7.467	7.507	7.548	7.588	7.629	7.670	7.711	7.752	7.793	7.834
38	7.876	7.917	7.959	8.001	8.042	8.084	8.126	8.169	8.211	8.253
39	8.296	8.338	8.381	8.424	8.467	8.510	8.553	8.596	8.640	8.683
40	8.727	8.770	8.814	8.858	8.902	8.946	8.990	9.035	9.079	9.124
41	9.168	9.213	9.258	9.303	9.348	9.393	9.439	9.484	9.530	9.575
42	9.621	9.667	9.713	9.759	9.805	9.852	9.898	9.945	9.991	10.038
43	10.085	10.132	10.179	10.226	10.273	10.321	10.368	10.416	10.463	10.511
44	10.559	10.607	10.655	10.704	10.752	10.801	10.849	10.898	10.947	10.996
45	11.045	11.094	11.143	11.192	11.242	11.291	11.341	11.391	11.441	11.491
46	11.541	11.591	11.642	11.692	11.743	11.793	11.844	11.895	11.946	11.997
47	12.048	12.100	12.151	12.203	12.254	12.306	12.358	12.410	12.462	12.514
48	12.566	12.619	12.671	12.724	12.777	12.830	12.882	12.936	12.989	13.042
49	13.095	13.149	13.203	13.256	13.310	13.364	13.418	13.472	13.527	13.581
50	13.635	13.690	13.745	13.800	13.854	13.909	13.965	14.020	14.075	14.131

Table A–4(b)
Areas of Circles, (a) in square feet for circumferences and diameters in inches, and (b) in square meters for circumferences and diameters in centimeters

Diameter ins./cm.	Circumference ins./cm.	Area sq.ft.	Area sq.m.	Diameter ins./cm.	Circumference ins./cm.	Area sq.ft.	Area sq.m.
1	3.14	0.005	–	51	160.22	14.186	0.240
2	6.28	0.022	–	52	163.36	14.748	0.212
3	9.42	0.049	0.001	53	166.50	15.321	0.221
4	12.57	0.087	0.001	54	169.65	15.904	0.229
5	15.71	0.136	0.002	55	172.79	16.499	0.238
6	18.85	0.196	0.003	56	175.93	17.104	0.246
7	21.99	0.267	0.004	57	179.07	17.721	0.255
8	25.13	0.349	0.005	58	182.21	18.348	0.264
9	28.27	0.442	0.006	59	185.35	18.986	0.273
10	31.42	0.545	0.008	60	188.50	19.635	0.283
11	34.56	0.660	0.010	61	191.64	20.295	0.292
12	37.70	0.785	0.011	62	194.78	20.966	0.302
13	40.84	0.922	0.013	63	197.92	21.648	0.312
14	43.98	1.069	0.015	64	201.06	22.340	0.322
15	47.12	1.227	0.018	65	204.20	23.044	0.332
16	50.26	1.396	0.020	66	207.34	23.758	0.342
17	53.41	1.576	0.023	67	210.49	24.484	0.352
18	56.55	1.767	0.025	68	213.63	25.220	0.363
19	59.69	1.969	0.028	69	216.77	25.967	0.374
20	62.83	2.182	0.031	70	219.91	26.725	0.385
21	65.97	2.405	0.035	71	223.05	27.494	0.396
22	69.12	2.640	0.038	72	226.19	28.274	0.407
23	72.26	2.885	0.042	73	229.34	29.065	0.418
24	75.40	3.142	0.045	74	232.48	29.867	0.430
25	78.54	3.409	0.049	75	235.62	30.680	0.442
26	81.68	3.687	0.053	76	238.76	31.503	0.454
27	84.82	3.976	0.057	77	241.90	32.338	0.466
28	87.96	4.276	0.062	78	245.04	33.183	0.478
29	91.11	4.587	0.066	79	248.18	34.039	0.490
30	94.25	4.909	0.071	80	251.33	34.907	0.503
31	97.39	5.241	0.075	81	254.47	35.785	0.515
32	100.53	5.585	0.080	82	257.61	36.674	0.528
33	103.67	5.940	0.086	83	260.75	37.574	0.541
34	106.81	6.305	0.091	84	263.89	38.484	0.554
35	109.96	6.681	0.096	85	267.04	39.406	0.567
36	113.10	7.069	0.102	86	270.18	40.339	0.581
37	116.24	7.467	0.108	87	273.32	41.282	0.594
38	119.38	7.876	0.113	88	276.46	42.237	0.608
39	122.52	8.296	0.119	89	279.60	43.202	0.622
40	125.66	8.727	0.126	90	282.74	44.179	0.636
41	128.81	9.168	0.132	91	285.88	45.166	0.650
42	131.95	9.621	0.138	92	289.03	46.164	0.665
43	135.09	10.085	0.145	93	292.17	47.173	0.679
44	138.23	10.559	0.152	94	295.31	48.193	0.694
45	141.37	11.045	0.159	95	298.45	49.224	0.709
46	144.51	11.541	0.166	96	301.59	50.266	0.724
47	147.65	12.048	0.173	97	304.73	51.318	0.739
48	150.80	12.566	0.181	98	307.88	52.382	0.754
49	153.94	13.095	0.189	99	311.02	53.456	0.770
50	157.08	13.635	0.196	100	314.16	54.542	0.785

Table A–5
Circular- and Square-Plot Dimensions

Area		Radius of Circular Plot		Side of Square Plot		Diagonal of Square Plot	
Acres	*Sq, Ft.*	*Feet*	*Chains*	*Feet*	*Chains*	*Feet*	*Chains*
(English System)							
1.00	43,560	117.75	1.784	208.71	3.162	295.16	4.472
.50	21,780	83.26	1.262	147.58	2.236	208.71	3.162
.25	10,890	58.88	.892	104.36	1.581	147.58	2.236
.20	8,712	52.66	.798	93.34	1.414	132.00	2.000
.10	4,356	37.24	.564	66.00	1.000	93.34	1.414
.05	2,178	26.33	.399	46.67	.707	66.00	1.000
.01	435.6	11.78	.178	20.87	.316	29.52	.447
.001	43.56	3.72	.056	6.60	.100	9.33	.141
(Metric System)							
Hectares	*Sq.M.*	*Meters*		*Meters*		*Meters*	
1.00	10,000	56.41		100.00		141.42	
.50	5,000	39.89		70.71		100.00	
.25	2,500	28.21		50.00		70.71	
.20	2,000	25.23		44.72		63.24	
.10	1,000	17.84		31.62		44.72	
.05	500	12.62		22.36		31.62	
.01	100	5.64		10.00		14.14	
.001	10	1.78		3.16		4.47	

References Cited

ABETZ, P., and MERKEL, O. 1962. The accuracy of tree height measurements with the Blume-Leiss hypsometer. *Allg. Forst-u Jagd-Ztg.* **113**:277–85.

ACKOFF, R. L., and SASIENI, M. W. 1968. *Fundamentals of operations research.* New York: John Wiley & Sons.

ALDRICH, R. C. 1966. Forestry applications of 70 mm. color. *Photogramm. Eng.* **32**:802–10.

ANDERSON, R. T. 1937. The application of Fourier's series in forest mensuration. *Jour. Forestry* **35**:293–99.

ANUTSCHIN, N. P. 1960a. *Forest mensuration.* Moscow, U.S.S.R.

———. 1960b. Determination of the current accretion of plantations by lateral, surface of trees. Fifth World Forestry Congress, Seattle. Sp/71/1, U.S.S.R.

ARIMIZU, T. 1956. Application of linear programming to forestry. (1) Optimum mixture of logs in the sawmill. *Tokyo Univ. Forestry Bull.* no. 11.

ARVANITIS, L. G., and O'REGAN, W. G. 1967. Computer simulation of economic efficiency in forest sampling. *Hilgardia* **38**:133–64.

ASHLEY, M. D., and ROGER, R. E. 1969. Tree heights and upper stem diameters. *Photogramm. Eng.* **35**:136–46.

ASSMAN, E. 1943. Untersuchen über die Höhenkurven von Fichtenbestanden (Investigations of the height curves of spruce stands). *Allg. Forst-u. Jagd-Ztg.* **121**:29–32.

ATTIWILL, P. M. 1966. A method for estimating crown weight in Eucalyptus, and some implications of relationships between crown weight and stem diameter. *Ecology* **47**:795–804.

ATTIWILL, P. M.. and OVINGTON, J. D. 1968. Determination of forest biomass. *Forest Science* **14**:13–15.

AVERY, T. E. 1968. *Interpretation of aerial photographs.* 2nd ed. Minneapolis: Burgess Publishing Co.

AVERY, T. E., and MEYER, M. P. 1962. Contracting for forest aerial photography in the U.S. *U.S.F.S. Lake States For. Exp. Sta. Sta. Paper no. 96.*

BADAN, H., HENSON, W. H., and STEWARD, A. 1961. Un. compas forestier enregistreur; nouvelle application de la mecanographe daus les inventaires forestiers. (A recording caliper; new application of mechanization in forest inventory) IUFRO, Tagungshericte Wien. 25/7–S/1.

BADGLEY, P. C., and VEST, W. L. 1966. Orbital remote sensing and natural resources. *Photogramm. Eng.* **32**:780–90.

BAKER, F. S. 1923. Notes on the composition of even-aged stands. *Jour. Forestry* **21**:712–17.

BAKER, F. S. 1960. A simple formula for gross current annual increment. *Jour. Forestry* **58**:488–99.

BARNES, G. H. 1945. Cubic foot scaling and utilization of logging waste. *Timberman* **46**:66–72.

———. 1962. Yield of even-aged stands of western hemlock. U. S. Dept. Agric. Tech. Bull. no. 1273.

BARNES, R. M. 1963. *Motion and time study.* New York: John Wiley & Sons.

BARTOO, R. A., and HUTNIK, R. J. 1962 Board foot volume tables for timber tree species in Pennsylvania. *Pennsylvania State Forest School Research Paper no. 30.*

BASKERVILLE, G. L. 1965. Estimation of dry weight of tree components and total standing crop in conifer stands. *Ecology* 46:867–69.

BEERS, T. W. 1960. An evaluation of site index for mixed oak in the Central Hardwood Region. Ph.D. thesis. Lafayette, Ind.: Purdue University.

———. 1962. Components of forest growth. *Jour. Forestry* 60:245–48.

———. 1963. Empirical substantiation of the (double rising)/(double effective) method of diameter growth estimation. *Jour. Forestry* 61:278–80.

———. 1964. Cruising for pulpwood by the ton without concern for tree diameter: point sampling with diameter obviation. Lafayette, Ind.: Purdue University Extension Mimeo F–49.

BEERS, T. W., DRESS, P. E. and WENSEL, L. C. 1966. Aspect transformation in site productivity research. *Jour. Forestry* 64:691–92.

BEERS, T. W., and MILLER, C. I. 1964. Point sampling: research results, theory, and applications. *Purdue Univ. Agric. Exp. Sta. Res. Bull. 786.*

———. 1966. Horizontal point sampling tables. *Purdue Univ. Agric. Exp. Sta. Res. Bull. 808.*

BEERS, T. W., and MYERS, C. C. 1965. The use of permanent points—good or bad? Proc. Conference on C.F.I. Michigan Tech. Univ., pp. 182–97.

BEHRE, C. E. 1935. Factors involved in the application of form-class volume tables. *Jour. Agric. Res.* 51:669–713.

BELYEA, H. C. 1931. *Forest measurement.* New York: John Wiley & Sons.

BENSON, A. O., and WOLLIN. 1941. Grading northern hardwood logs. U.S.F.S. For. Prod. Lab.

BERGSTRAND, E. 1959. *The Geodimeter system.* New York: Geodimeter Co.

BESLEY, L. 1967. Importance, variation, and measurement of density and moisture. Wood Measurement Conf. Proc. Tech. Rep. no. 7. University of Toronto: Faculty of Forestry.

BICKERSTAFF, A. 1948. Increment hammer. Forest Service Canada. *Silv. Leaf. no. 26.*

BICKFORD, C. A. 1957. Converting factors for stacked wood. U.S.F.S. Northeast. For. Exp. Sta. Res. Note no. 72.

BICKFORD, C. A., et al. 1957. Stocking, normality, and measurement of stand density. *Jour. Forestry* 55:99–104.

BITTERLICH, W. 1947. Die winkelzählmessung. (Measurement of basal area per hectare by means of angle measurement.) *Allg. Forst-u. Holzwirts. Zfg. 58:*94–96.

———. 1955. Schallmesstechnik in der Forsteinrichtung (The use of distance measurements by sound in forest management). *Allg. Forstztg.* 64:14–25.

———. Sektorklpuuen aus Leichtmetall (Calipering forks made of light alloys). Wien: *Holz–Kurier* 14:15–17.

BLASCHKO, R. 1964. The use of modern instruments for measuring distances in forestry. *Allg. Forstztg.* 75:148–50.

BOWER, D. R., and BLOCKER, W. W. 1966. Accuracy of bands and tape for measuring diameter increments. *Jour. Forestry* 64:21–22.

BRAATHE, P., and OKSTAD, T. 1964. Trade of pulpwood based on weighing and dry matter samples. *Meddel. Norske Skogforsok.* 72:5–64.

———. 1967. Trade of pulpwood based on weighing and dry matter samples. XIV IUFRO Congress. Sect. 41. Vol. IX:236–42.

BRICKELL, J. E. 1968. A method for constructing site index curves from measurements of tree age and height—its application to inland Douglas-fir. U.S.F.S. Intermt. For. and Range Exp. Sta. Paper INT–47.

BRIEGLEB, P. A. 1942. Progress in estimating trend of normality percentage in second-growth Douglas fir. *Jour. Forestry* 40:785–93.

BROIDO, A., McCONNEN, R. J., and O'REGAN, W. G. 1965. Some operations research applications in the conservation of wildland resources. *Management Sci.* 11:802–14.

BRUCE, D. 1916. The Biltmore stick and the point of diameter measurement. *Proc. Soc. Amer. Foresters* 11:226–27.

————. 1925. A formula for the Scribner rule. *Jour. Forestry* **23**:432–33.

————. 1926. A method of preparing timber yield tables. *Jour. Agric. Res.* **32**:543–57.

Bruce, D., and Schumacher, F. X. 1950. *Forest mensuration.* 3rd ed. New York: McGraw-Hill Book Co.

Buckman, R. E. 1962. Growth and yield of red pine in Minnesota. U.S. Dept. Agric. Tech. Bull. no. 1272.

Cable, D. R. 1958. Estimating surface area of ponderosa pine foliage in central Arizona. *Forest Sci.* **4**:45–49.

Calkins, H. A., and Yule, J. B. 1935. The Abney level handbook. *U.S.F.S.*

Campbell, R. A. 1962. A guide to grading features in southern pine logs and trees. *U.S.F.S. Southeast. For. Exp. Sta. Paper no. 156.*

————. 1964. Forest Service log grades for southern pine. *U.S.F.S. Southeast. For. Exp. Sta. Res. Paper SE–11.*

Carron, L. T. 1968. *An outline of forest mensuration with special reference to Australia.* Canberra: Australian National University Press.

Casey, R. S., and Perry, J. W. 1951. *Punched cards.* New York: Reinhold Publishing Co.

Chacko, V. J. 1961. A study of the shape of cross-sections of stems and the accuracy of caliper measurements. *Indian For.* **87**:758–62.

————. 1962. Sampling in forest inventories. *Indian For.* **88**:420–27.

Chamberlain, E. B., and Meyer, H. A. 1950. Bark volume in cordwood. *Tappi* **33**:554–55.

Chapman, H. H., and Demeritt, D. B. 1936. *Elements of forest mensuration.* Albany: J. B. Lyons Co.

Chapman, H. H., and Meyer, W. H. 1949. *Forest mensuration.* New York: McGraw-Hill Book Co.

Chappelle, D. E. 1966. Economic model building and computers in forestry research. *Jour. Forestry* **64**:329–33.

Charafas, D. M. 1965. *Systems and simulation.* New York: Academic Press.

Chisman, H. H., and Schumacher, F. X. 1940. On the tree-area ratio and certain of its applications. *Jour. Forestry* **38**:311–7.

Clark, J. F. 1906. Measurement of sawlogs. *Forestry Quart.* **4**:79–93.

Clemence, G. M. 1952. Time and its measurement. *Amer. Sci.* **40**:260–69.

Clutter, J. L. 1963. Compatible growth and yield models for loblolly pine. *Forest Sci.* **9**:354–71.

Clutter, J. L., and Bamping, J. H. 1965. Computer simulation of an industrial forestry enterprise. *Proc. Soc. Amer. Foresters:* 180–85.

Cochran, W. G. 1963. *Sampling techniques.* 2d ed. New York: John Wiley & Sons.

Coile, T. S. 1952. Soil and growth of forests. *Advances in Agronomy* **4**:330–98.

Considine, P. M. 1948. *Industrial weighing.* New York: Reinhold Publishing Co.

Cooper, C. F., and Smith, F. M. 1966. Color aerial photography: toy or tool? *Jour. Forestry* **64**:373–78.

Cummings, W. H. A. 1941. A method of sampling the foliage of a silver maple tree. *Jour. Forestry* **39**:382–84.

Cunia, T. 1964. Weighted least squares method and construction of volume tables. *Forest Sci.* **10**:180–91.

————. 1965. Continuous forest inventory, partial replacement of samples and multiple regression. *Forest Sci.* **11**:480–502.

Curtis, F. H. 1962. Linear programming the management of a forest property. *Jour. Forestry* **60**:611–16.

————. 1965. Tree weight equations—their development and use in forest management planning. *Proc. Soc. Amer. Foresters:* 189–91.

Curtis, R. O. 1967. A method of estimation of gross yield of Douglas fir. *Forest Sci. Monograph* 13.

Curtis, R. O., and Bruce, D. 1968. Tree heights without a tape. *Jour. Forestry* **66**:60–61.

DANIEL, T. W. 1955. Bitterlich's Spiegelrelaskop—a revolutionary general use forestry instrument. *Jour. Forestry* **53**:844–46.

DANTZIG, G. B., 1963. *Linear programming and extensions.* Princeton, N. J.: University Press.

DAUBENMIRE, R. F. 1945. An improved type of precision dendrometer. *Ecology* **26**:97–98.

DAVIS, K. P. 1957. *American forest management.* New York: McGraw-Hill Book Co.

———. 1966. *Forest management: regulation and valuation.* 2d ed. New York: McGraw-Hill Book Co.

DAVIS, R. E., FOOTE, F. S., and KELLY, J. W. 1966. *Surveying theory and practice.* New York: McGraw-Hill Book Co.

DAWKINS, H. C. 1957. Some results of stratified random sampling of tropical high forest. Seventh British Commonwealth Forestry Conf. Item 7(iii).

———. 1963. Crown diameters: their relation to bole diameter in tropical forest trees. *Commonwealth Forestry Rev.* **42**:318:33.

DEITSCHMAN, G. H. and GREEN, A. W. 1965. Relations between western white pine site index and tree height of several associated species. *U.S.F.S. Intermt. For. and Range Exp. Sta. Res. Paper INT–22.*

DELIOCOURT, F. 1898. De l'aménagement des sapiniéres. *Bull de la Société Forestiére de Franche-Compté el Belfort.* Besancon, France.

DEMING, W. E. 1950. Some theory of sampling. New York: John Wiley & Sons.

DICKERSON, L. M. 1942. An inexpensive planimeter. *Jour. Forestry* **40**:19–22.

DIETZ, P. 1966. Die Vermessung von Industrieholz nach Gewicht. (The measurement of industrial wood by weight). *Inst. fur Forstbenutzung und Forstliche Arbeitsw. der Univ. Freiburg.*

DILLER, O. D., and KELLOG, L. F. 1940. Local volume table for yellow poplar. *U.S.F.S. Central States For. Exp. Sta. Tech. Note no. 1.*

DILWORTH, J. R., and BELL, J. F. 1968. Variable plot cruising. Corvallis, Ore.: O.S.U. Book Stores.

DOEBELIN, E. O. 1966. *Measurement systems: applications and design.* New York: McGraw-Hill Book Co.

DOOLITTLE, W. T., and VIMMERSTEDT, J. P. 1960. Site index curves for natural stands of white pine in the southern Appalachians. *U.S.F.S. Southeast. For. Exp. Sta. Res. Note no. 141.*

DRESS, P. E., and HALL, O. F. 1964. The mensurational implications of the use of operations research in forest management. *Proc. Soc. Amer. Foresters:* 218–20.

DUERR, W. A. 1938. Comments on the general application of Gehrhardt's formula for approach to normality. *Jour. Forestry* **36**:600–604.

ECKEL, L. H. 1953. The hatchet planimeter. *Forestry Chron.* **29**:273–77.

ELLIS, B. 1966. *Basic concepts of measurement.* Cambridge: At the University Press.

ENGHARDT, H., and H. J. Derr, 1963. Height accumulation for rapid estimates of cubic volume. *Jour. Forestry* **61**:134–37.

FOOD AND AGRICULTURE ORGANIZATION. 1958. Lignometer, forest survey instrument. *For. Equip. Notes A.11.58.*

FASICK, C. A., and SAMPSON, G. R. 1966. Applying linear programming in forest industry. *U.S.F.S. Southern For. Exp. Sta. Res. Paper SO–21.*

FENDER, D. E., and BROCK, G. A. 1963. Point center extension: a technique for measuring current economic growth and yield of merchantable forest stands. *Jour. Forestry* **61**:109–14.

FENTON, R. H. 1948. Wood content of stacked 4-foot round pulpwood in Connecticut. *U.S.F.S. Northeast. For. Exp. Sta. Paper no. 17.*

FERREE, M. J. 1946. The pole caliper. *Jour. Forestry* **44**:594–95.

FFOLLIOTT, P. F., and WORLEY, D. P. 1965. An inventory system for multiple use evaluations. *U.S.F.S. Rocky Mt. For. and Range Exp. Sta. Res. Paper RM–17.*

FINNEY, D. J. 1947. Volume estimation of standing timber by sampling. *Forestry* **21**:179–203.

———. 1948. Random and systematic sampling in timber surveys. *Forestry* **22**:64–99.

———. 1950. An example of periodic variation in forest sampling. *Forestry* **23**:96–111.

———. 1953. The estimation of error in the systematic sampling of forests. *Jour. Indian Soc. Agric. Stat.* **5**:6–16.

FOGELBERG, S. E. 1953. Volume charts based on absolute form class. Ruston: Louisiana Tech Forestry Club of Louisiana Polytech. Inst.

FORBES, R. D., and MEYER, H. B. (Eds.). 1955. *Forestry handbook.* Soc. Amer. Foresters. New York: The Ronald Press Co.

FOREST PRODUCTS LABORATORY. 1958. Overall work plan for development of log and bolt grades for hardwoods. *U.S.F.S. For. Prod. Lab. Rep. TGUR–16.*

———. 1966. Hardwood log grades for standard lumber. *U.S.F.S. For. Prod. Lab. Res. Paper FLP-63.*

FOSTER, R. W. 1959. Relation between site indexes of eastern white pine and red maple. *Forest Sci.* **5**:279–91.

FRAYER, W. E. 1966. Weighted regression in successive forest inventories. *Forest Sci.* **12**:464–72.

FRAZER, J. R. 1968. *Applied linear programming.* Englewood Cliffs, N. J.: Prentice-Hall.

FRIES, J. 1965. Eigenvector analyses show that birch and pine have similar form in Sweden and in British Columbia. *Forestry Chron.* **41**:135–39.

FRIES, J., and MATERN, B. 1965. On the use of multivariate methods for the construction of tree taper curves. Stockholm: Paper no. 9, I.U.F.R.O. Advisory Group of Forest Stat. Conf.

FRITTS, H. C., and FRITTS, E. C. 1955. A new dendrograph for recording radial changes of a tree. *Forest Sci.* **1**:271–76.

FURNIVAL, G. M. 1961. An index for comparing equations used in constructing volume tables. *Forest Sci.* **7**:337–41.

GAINES, E. M. 1962. Improved system of grading ponderosa pine and sugar pine saw logs in trees. *U.S.F.S. Pac. S.W. For. and Range Exp. Sta. Tech. Paper no. 75.*

GAISER, R. N., and MERZ, R. W. 1951. Stand density as a factor in measuring white oak site index. *Jour. Forestry* **49**:572–74.

GARAY, L. 1961. An introduction to tarif volume tables. Univ. of Washington: *For. Biom. Res. Group Rev. Paper no. 1.*

GARLAND, H. 1968. Using a polaroid camera to measure trucked hardwood pulpwood. *Pulp and Paper Mag. Canada* **69**(8):86–87.

GARRISON, G. A. 1949. Uses and modifications of the "moosehorn" crown closure estimator. *Jour. Forestry* **47**:733–35.

GEHRHARDT, E. 1930. Ertragstafeln für reine und gleichartiger Hochwaldbestände von Eiche, Buche, Tanne, Fichte, Kiefer, gruner Douglasie und Larche (Yield tables for pure and homogeneous stands of oak, beech, fir, spruce, scotch pine, Douglas fir, and larch). Berlin: Springer–Verlag.

GERRARD, D. J. 1966. The construction of standard tree volume tables by weighted regression. University of Toronto: *Tech. Report no. 6.*

———. 1969. Competition quotient: A new measure of the competition affecting individual forest trees. *Mich. State Agric. Exp. Sta. Res. Bull. 20.*

GEVORKIANTZ, S. R. 1950. Converting International ¼-inch gross sawlog scale to peeled total volume in cubic feet. *U.S.F.S. Lake States For. Exp. Sta. Tech. Note no. 329.*

———. 1956. Short cuts in scaling—converting stacked cordwood to board feet. *U.S.F.S. Lake States For. Exp. Sta. Tech. Note no. 468.*

GEVORKIANTZ, S. R., and OCHSNER, H. E. 1943. A method of sample scaling. *Jour. Forestry* **41**:436–39.

GEVORKIANTZ, S. R., and OLSEN, L. P. 1955. Composite volume tables for timber and their application in the Lake States. *U. S. Dept. Agric. Tech. Bull. no. 1104.*

GIERUSZYNSKI, T. 1959. *Pomior drzew drzewostanow.* Warsaw: Panstwowe Wydaunictno Rolnicze i Lesne.

GINGRICH, S. F. 1964. Criteria for measuring stocking in forest stands. *Proc. Soc. Amer. Foresters:* 198–201.

————. 1967. Measuring and evaluating stocking and stand density in upland hardwood forests in the Central States. *Forest Sci.* 13:38–53.

GIRARD, J. W. 1933. Volume tables for Mississippi bottomland hardwoods and southern pines. *Jour. Forestry* 31:34–41.

GODMAN, R. M. 1949. The pole diameter tape. *Jour. Forestry* 47:585–89.

GOULD, E. M., JR., and O'REGAN, W. G. 1965. Simulation, a step toward better forest planning. *Harvard Forest Paper 13.*

GRAVES, H. S. 1906. *Forest mensuration.* New York: John Wiley & Sons.

GREVATT, J. G., and WARDLE, P. A. 1967. Two mathematical models to aid in nursery planning. Vienna: I.U.F.R.O. Congress.

GROSENBAUGH, L. R. 1948. Improved cubic volume computation. *Jour. Forestry* 46:299–301.

————. 1952a. Shortcuts for cruisers and scalers. *U.S.F.S. Southern For. Exp. Sta. Occ. Paper no. 126.*

————. 1952b. Plotless timber estimates—new, fast, easy. *Jour. Forestry* 50:32–37.

————. 1954. New tree-measurement concepts: height accumulation, giant tree, taper and shape. *U.S.F.S. Southern For. Exp. Sta. Occ. Paper no. 134.*

————. 1955. Better diagnosis and prescription in southern forest management. *U.S.F.S. Southern For. Exp. Sta. Occ. Paper no. 145.*

————. 1958. Point-sampling and line-sampling: probability theory, geometric implications, synthesis. *U.S.F.S. Southern For. Exp. Sta. Occ. Paper no. 160.*

————. 1963a. Some suggestions for better sample-tree measurement. *Proc. Soc. Amer. Foresters:* 36–42.

————. 1963b. Optical dendrometers for out-of-reach diameters: a conspectus and some new theory. *Forest Sci. Monograph* 4.

————. 1964. STX-FORTRAN 4 PROGRAM—for estimates of tree populations from 3P sample-tree-measurements. *U.S.F.S. Pac. S.W. For. and Range Exp. Sta. Paper PSW–13.*

————. 1965. Three-pee sampling theory and program "THRP" for computer generation of selection criteria. *U.S.F.S. Pac. S.W. For. and Range Exp. Sta. Paper PSW–21.*

————. 1966. Tree form: definition, interpolation, extrapolation. *Forestry Chron.* 42:444–57.

————. 1967. The gains from sample-tree selection with unequal probabilities. *Jour. Forestry* 65:203–6.

GUTTENBERG, S., FASSNACHT, D., and SIEGEL, W. C. 1960. Weight-scaling southern pine sawlogs. *U.S.F.S. Southern For. Exp. Sta. Occ. Paper no. 177.*

GUTTENBERG, S., and REYNOLDS, R. R. 1953. Cutting financially mature loblolly and shortleaf pine. *U.S.F.S. Southern For. Exp. Sta. Occ. Paper no. 129.*

HADLEY, G. 1962. *Linear programming.* Reading, Mass.: Addison-Wesley Publishing Co.

HALL, O. F., and RUDOLPH, T. D. 1957. Weight loss of stored jack pine pulpwood. Univ. of Minnesota Forestry Note no. 57.

HANKS, L. F., and THOMPSON, G. W. 1964. Aerial stand volume tables for Iowa hardwoods. *Iowa State Jour. Sci.* 38:415–26.

HANSEN, M. H., and HURWITZ, W. N. 1943. On the theory of sampling from finite populations. *Annals Math. Stat.* 14:333–62.

HANSEN, M. H., HURWITZ, W. W., and MADOW, W. G. 1953. *Sample survey methods and theory.* 2 vols. New York: John Wiley & Sons.

HARDY, S. S., and WEILAND, G. W. 1964. Weight as a basis for the purchase of pulpwood in Maine. *Univ. Maine Agric. Exp. Sta. Tech. Bull. 14.*

HARE, V. C. 1967. *Systems analysis: a diagnostic approach.* New York: Harcourt Brace Jovanovich.

HEINSDIJK, D. 1965. Zero sampling units in forest inventories. *Bol. Setor Invent. Flor. Secão Pesgu. Flor. Brasil no. 8.*

HELLER, R. C. 1965. Aerial remote sensing research in forestry. *Proc. Soc. Amer. Foresters:* 162–68.

HENRICKSEN, H. A. 1950. Hojde-diameter diagram med logaritmisk diameter (Height-diameter diagram with logarithmic diagram). *Dansk Skovforen. Tidsskr.* **35**:193–202.

HERRICK, A. M. 1940. A defense of the Doyle rule. *Jour. Forestry* **38**:563–67.

———. 1946*a*. Composite volume tables for Indiana hardwoods. Purdue Univ. Extension Leaflet 273.

———. 1946*b*. Grade yields and overrun from Indiana hardwood sawlogs. *Purdue Univ. Agric. Exp. Sta. Bull. 516.*

———. 1955. How to grade hardwood sawlogs. *Purdue Univ. Agric. Ext. Ser. Bull. 346.*

———. 1956. The quality index in hardwood sawtimber management. *Purdue Univ. Agric. Exp. Sta. Bull. 632.*

HILGER and WATTS. 1965. Symposium on electronic distance measurement, Oxford University. London: Hilger and Watts.

HILLIER, F. S., and LIEBERMAN, G. J. 1967. *Introduction to operations research.* San Francisco: Holden-Day Co.

HILLS, G. A. 1952. The classification and evaluation of site for forestry. Ontario Dept. Lands and Forests. Res. Rep. no. 24.

HIRAI, S. 1950. Studies on the weight-growth of forest trees (II). *Picea excelsa* of the Chichibu University Forest. *Tokyo Univ. Forestry Bull. no. 38.*

HIRAI, S., and AIZAWA, E. 1966. Studies on the weight growth of forest trees (VIII). Two artificially planted *Populus* species. *Tokyo Univ. Forestry Bull. no. 62.*

HIRATA, T. 1955. Height estimation through Bitterlich's method, vertical angle count sampling. *Jap. Jour. Forestry* **37**:479–80.

HIRSCH, S. N. 1965. Infrared line scanners—a tool for remote sensing of forested areas. *Proc. Soc. Amer. Foresters:* 169–72.

HOLSOE, T., and LONGACRE, G. V. 1949. Board foot-cubic foot ratios. *West Virginia Agric. Exp. Sta. Res. Briefs no. 3.*

HONER, T. G. 1965. Volume distribution in individual trees. *Pulp and Paper Magazine of Canada,* Woodlands Section Index 2349 (F–2).

HOOL, J. N. 1966. A dynamic programming Markov chain approach to forest production control. *Forest Sci. Monograph 12.*

———. 1968. An univariate allocation algorithm for use in forestry problems. *Jour. Forestry* **66**:492–93.

HOOL, J. N., and BEERS, T. W. 1964. Time-dependent correlation coefficients from remeasured forest plots. *Purdue Univ. Agric. Exp. Sta. Res. Prog. Report 156.*

HUMMEL, F. C. 1951. Instruments for the measurement of height, diameter, and taper on standing trees. *Forestry Abs.* **12**:261–69.

———. 1953. Uses of the "volume/basal area line" for determining standing crop volumes. London: Rep. For. Res. Comm. 1951/52.

———. 1955. The volume/basal area line; a study in forest mensuration. London: For. Comm. Bull. no. 24.

HUSCH, B. 1947. A comparison between a ground and aerial photogrammetric method of timber surveying. Master's thesis. Syracuse: New York State College of Forestry.

———. 1956. Use of age at dbh as a variable in the site index concept. *Jour. Forestry* **54**:340.

———. 1962. Tree weight relationships for white pine in southeastern New Hampshire. *Univ. New Hampshire Agric. Exp. Sta. Tech. Bull. no. 106.*

———. 1963. *Forest mensuration and statistics.* New York: The Ronald Press Co.

———. 1966. Standardization in forest resource surveys. Proc. of Sixth World Forestry Congress. Madrid.

———. 1969. A manual for the application of network analysis techniques to the planning, execution and control of UNDP projects. FAO, Rome.

———. 1970. Planning a forest inventory. FAO, Rome.

HUSCH, B., and LYFORD, W. H. 1956. White pine growth and soil relationship in southeastern New Hampshire. *Univ. New Hampshire Agric. Exp. Sta. Tech. Bull. no. 95.*

IIZUKA, H. 1964. Study on weight growth of stem by growth curves. *Kyushu Univ. Forestry Rep. no. 20.*

ILVESSALO, Y. 1937. Perä-pohjolan luonnon normaalien metsiköiden kasvu ja kekitys (Growth of natural normal stands in central north Finland). *Comm. Inst. Forestalis Fenniae* **24**:1–168.

INSTITUTE OF FOREST PRODUCTS. 1957. Conversion factors for Pacific Northwest forest products. Seattle: Inst. For. Prod.

INTERNATIONAL BUSINESS MACHINES CORP. 1959. IBM port-a-punch. Unit Record Bull. I.B.M. Co.

IUFRO. 1959. The standardization of symbols in forest mensuration. International Union of Forest Research Organizations.

IVANJUTA, V. M. 1964. A universal mensuration instrument and methods of using it. (Russ.) *Lesn. Z., Arhangelsk* **7**:47–52.

JACKSON, A. G. 1911. The Biltmore stick and its use on national forests. *Forestry Quart.* **9**:406–11.

JACKSON, W. L. 1962. Guide to grading defects in ponderosa and sugar pine logs. U.S.F.S. Pac. S.W. For. and Range Exp. Sta.

JANSSON, T. 1964. Purchase of pulpwood on the basis of the wood's absolute dry weight. *Skogen* **51**:102–3.

JEFFERS, J. N. R. 1956. Barr and Stroud dendrometer, Tupe F.P. 7. London: Rep. For. Res. For. Comm., 1954/55:127–136.

JENSEN, C. E. 1964. Algebraic description of forms in space. U.S.F.S. Central States For. Exp. Sta.

JENSEN, V. S. 1940. Cost of producing pulpwood on farm woodlands of the Upper Connecticut River Valley. *U.S.F.S. Northeast. For. Exp. Sta. Occ. Paper no. 9.*

JOHNSON, F. A. 1966. Bark factors for douglas fir. *U.S.F.S. Pac. N.W. For. and Range Exp. Sta. Res. Note no. 34.*

JOHNSON, F. A., and HIXON, H. J. 1952. The most efficient size and shape of plot to use for cruising in old-growth douglas-fir timber. *Jour. Forestry* **50**:17–20.

JOLLY, N. W. 1951. The volume line theory in relation to the measurement of the standing volume of a forest (with particular reference to *Pinus radiata*). S. Australia Woods and Forests Dept.

JONES, R. W., and GRAY, J. S. 1963. System theory and physiological processes. *Science* **10**:461–66.

JONES, T. A. 1960. Linear programming applied to a wood supply problem. Purdue University: Proc. For. Manag. Control Conf.

JONSON, T. 1910. Taxatoriska undersökningar om skogsträdens form. I. Granens stamform (Forest mensurational investigations on forest tree form. Spruce stem form.) *Skogsvårdsf. Tidskr.* **8**:285–328.

———. 1911. Taxatoriska undersökningar om skogsträdens form. II. Tallens stamform (Forest mensurational investigations on forest tree form. Pine Stem form.) *Skogsvårdsf. Tidskr.* **9**:285–329.

———. 1912. Taxatoriska undersökningar öfver skogsträdens form. III. Formbestämning a stående träd (Forest mensurational investigations concerning forest tree form. Form determination of standing trees). *Svenska Skogsvårdsf. Tidskr.* **10**:235-75.

KAIBARA, I. 1957. Jukohscope. Tokyo: Taican Corp.

KEEN, E. A. 1950. The relascope. *Empire For. Rev. 29, no. 3.*

KENDALL, R. H., and SAYN-WITTGENSTEIN, L. 1959. An evaluation of the relascope. Dept. North. Affairs and Nat. Res. Canada. For. Res. Div. Tech. Note no. 77.

KER, J. W. 1951. A test of the accuracy of tree height measurements taken by Abney level and chain. *B.C. Lumberman* **35**:59–60.

KIDD, W. E., JR., THOMPSON, E. F., and HOEPNER, P. H. 1966. Forest regulation by linear programming—a case study. *Jour. Forestry* **64**:611–13.

KIPPEN, F. W., and SAYN-WITTGENSTEIN, L. 1964. Tree measurements on large-scale, 70 mm. air photographs. Dept. For., Canada, For. Res. Branch Pub. no. 1053.

KISH, L. 1965. *Survey sampling*. New York: John Wiley & Sons.

KITTREDGE, J. 1944. Estimation of the amount of foliage of trees and stands. *Jour. Forestry* 42:905–12.

KONDOR, G. 1964. New tree caliper, an accurate and fast tree-diameter measuring device. *Forestry Chron.* 40:401.

KORF, V. 1953. *Dendrometrie*. Prague, Czechoslovakia.

KOURTZ, P. H. 1966. A cost effectiveness study of a lookout-aircraft forest fire detection system. Master's thesis. University of California.

KOZAK, A., and SMITH, J. H. G. 1966. Critical analysis of multivariate techniques for estimating tree taper suggests that simpler methods are best. *Forestry Chron.* 42:458–63.

KRAJICEK, J. E., BRINKMAN, K. A., and GINGRICH, S. F. 1961. Crown competition—a measure of density. *Forest Sci.* 7:36–42.

KUCHLER, A. W. 1967. Vegetation mapping. New York: The Ronald Press Co.

KULOW, D. 1966. Comparison of forest sampling designs. *Jour. Forestry* 64:469–74.

LAAR, A. VON. 1962. A comparative test of the accuracy and efficiency of two hypsometers. *South Afr. Forestry Jour.* 43:22–25.

LABAU, V. J. 1967. Literature on the Bitterlich method of forest cruising. *U.S.F.S. Pac. N.W. For. and Range Exp. Sta. Res. Paper PNW–47.*

LAHIRI, D. B. 1951. A method of sample selection providing unbiased ratio estimates. *Bull. Inst. International de Statistique* 33:133–40.

LANE, P. H. 1964. Grades for inland douglas fir saw logs in standing trees. *U.S.F.S. Pac. N.W. For. and Range Exp. Sta. Res. PNW–19.*

LANGE, K. D. 1962. Selling stumpage by weight in the South: a case study. *Jour. Forestry* 60:816–20.

LANGLEY, P. G. 1965. Automating aerial photo interpretation in forestry—how it works and what it can do for you. *Proc. Soc. Amer. Foresters:* 172–77.

LARSON, P. R. 1963. Stem form development of forest trees. *Forest Sci. Monograph* 5.

LEAK, W. B. 1963. Estimating maximum allowable timber yields by linear programming. *U.S.F.S. Northeast. For. Exp. Sta. Res. Paper NE–17.*

———. 1964. An expression of diameter distribution for unbalanced, uneven-aged stands and forests. *Forest Sci.* 10:39–50.

LEARY, R. A., and BEERS, T. W. 1963. Measurement of upper-stem diameter with a transit. *Jour. Forestry* 61:448–50.

LEMMON, P. E. 1957. A new instrument for measuring forest over-story density. *Jour. Forestry* 55:667–69.

LESCAFFETTE, J. 1951. Une propriété des arbres et des peuplements—la surface génératrice (A property of trees and stands—the generating surface). *Soc. For. Franche-Comté. Bull.* no. 25:712–25.

LEXEN, B. 1941. The application of sampling in log scaling. *Jour. Forestry* 39:624–31.

———. 1943. Bole area as an expression of growing stock. *Jour. Forestry* 39:624–31.

LIMING, F. G. 1957. Homemade dendrometers. *Jour. Forestry* 55:575–77.

LITTSCHWAGER, J. M., and TCHENG, T. H. 1967. Solution of a large-scale forest scheduling problem by linear programming decomposition. *Jour. Forestry* 65:644–66.

LLEWELLYN, R. W. 1964. Linear programming. New York: Holt, Rinehart, and Winston Co.

LOCKARD, C. R., PUTNAM, J. A., and CARPENTER, R. D. 1963. Grade defects in hardwood timber and logs. U.S. Dept. Agric. Handbook no. 244.

LOETSCH, F. and HALLER, K. A. 1964. Forest inventory. Vol. 1. Munich: BLV Verlagsgesellschaft.

LOVENGREEN, J. A. 1952. Hojdemalere. Afprovning af forskellige Hojdemaalere udfort af Statens forstlige Forosogsvaesen (Hypsometers. Tests of various instruments carried out by the Danish State Forest Experiment Station). *Dansk Skovforen. Tidsskr.* 37:590–601.

LOUCKS, D. P. 1964. The development of an optimal program for sustained-yield management. *Jour. Forestry* **62**:485–90.

LUSSIER, L. J. 1961. Work sampling applied to logging. A powerful tool for performance analyses and operations control. *Pulp and Paper Mag. Canada* **62**:130–40.

LYNCH, D. W. 1954. What is an acceptable allowable error and sample size in sample log scaling or tree measuring. *U.S.F.S. Intermt. For. and Range Exp. Sta. Res. Note no. 14.*

———. 1958. Effects of stocking on site measurement and yield of second-growth ponderosa pine in the Inland Empire. *U.S.F.S. Intermt. For. and Range Exp. Sta. Res. Paper no. 56.*

LYONS, E. H. 1964. Recent developments in 70 mm. stereo-photography from helicopters. *Photogramm. Eng.* **30**:750–56.

———. 1966. Fixed airbase 70 mm. photography, a new tool for forest sampling. *Forestry Chron.* **42**:420–28.

MAASS, A. 1939. Tallens form bedömd av diametern 2.3 meter från marken (Stem form of pine as determined by diameter 2.3 meters above ground). *Svenska skogsvfören. Tidskr.* **37**:120–40.

MACKINNEY, A. L., and CHAIKEN, L. E. 1939. Volume, yield and growth of loblolly pine in the Midatlantic Region. *U.S.F.S. Appalachian For. Exp. Sta. Tech. Note no. 33.*

MACKINNEY, A. L., SCHUMACHER, F. X., and CHAIKEN, L. E. 1937. Construction of yield tables for nonnormal loblolly pine stands. *Jour. Agric. Res.* **54**:531–45.

MACLEOD, W. K., and BLYTH, A. W. 1955. Yield of even-aged, fully-stock spruce-poplar stands in northern Alberta. Dept. North. Affairs and Nat. Res. Canada. Tech. Note no. 18.

MACON, J. W., and GEVORKIANTZ, S. R. 1942. Estimating volume on the spot. *Jour. Forestry* **40**:652–55.

MADER, D. L. 1963. Volume growth measurement—an analysis of function and characteristics in site evaluation. *Jour. Forestry* **61**:193–98.

MADGWICK, H. A. I. 1964. Estimation of surface area of pine needles with special reference to *Pinus resinosa. Jour. Forestry* **62**:636.

MAEGLIN, R. R. 1967. Effect of tree spacing on weight yields for red and jack pine. *Jour. Forestry* **65**:647–50.

MANUAL OF COLOR AERIAL PHOTOGRAPHY. 1967. Washington, D. C.: Amer. Soc. Photogramm.

MANUAL OF PHOTOGRAMMETRY. 1966. Washington, D. C.: Amer. Soc. Photogramm. Vols. I and II. 3d ed.

MANUAL OF PHOTOGRAPHIC INTERPRETATION. 1960. Washington, D. C.: Amer. Soc. Photogramm.

MARQUARDT, D. W. 1963. An algorithm for least-squares estimation of nonlinear parameters. *Jour. Soc. Indust. Appl. Math.* **11**:431–41.

MARQUIS, D. A., and BEERS, T. W. 1969. A further definition of some forest growth components. *Jour. Forestry* **67**:493.

MARTIN, W. H., and SIMARD, H. 1959. Weight as a basis for wood measurement. *Pulp and Paper Mag. Canada* **60**:149–59.

MATÉRN, B. 1958. On the geometry of the cross-section of a stem. *Meddel. Statens Skogsforskningsinst.* **46**:1–28.

MCARDLE, R. E., MEYER, W. H., and BRUCE, D. 1949. The yield of Douglas fir in the Pacific Northwest. U. S. Dept. Agric. Tech. Bull. no. 201. Rev.

MCGEE, C. E. 1959. Weight of merchantable wood with bark for planted slash pine in the Carolina sandhills. *U.S.F.S. Southeast. For. Exp. Sta. Res. Note no. 128.*

MCLINTOCK, T. F., and BICKFORD, C. A. 1957. A proposed site index for red spruce in the northeast. *U.S.F.S. Northeast. For. Exp. Sta. Paper no. 93.*

MCNISH, A. G. 1964. Lasers for length measurement. *Science* **146**:177–82.

MESAVAGE, C. 1947. Tables for estimating cubic foot volume of timber. *U.S.F.S. Southern For. Exp. Sta. Occ. Paper no. 111.*

——. 1965a. Aids for using Barr and Stroud dendrometers. *Proc. Soc. Amer. Foresters:* 238–44.

——. 1965b. Three-P sampling and dendrometry for better timber estimating. *South. Lumberman* **211** (Dec. 15):107–9.

——. 1967. Random integer dispenser. *U.S.F.S. Southern For. Exp. Sta. Res. Note SO–49.*

MESAVAGE, C., and GIRARD, J. W. 1946. Tables for estimating board foot volume of timber. Washington, D. C.: U. S. Forest Service.

MESAVAGE, C., and GROSENBAUGH, L. R. 1956. Efficiency of several cruising designs on small tracts in North Arkansas. *Jour. Forestry* **54**:569–76.

METEER, J. W. 1953. Continuous inventory management and growth studies. *Jour. Forestry* **51**:410–14.

——. 1966. Butt log tree grades analyzed. Michigan Tech. Univ. Ford Forestry Center Res. Note no. 2.

MEYER, H. A. 1940. A mathematical expression for height curves. *Jour. Forestry* **38**:415–20.

——. 1942. Methods of forest growth determination. Pennsylvania State College School Agriculture. *Agric. Exp. Sta. Bull. no. 435.*

——. 1953. *Forest mensuration.* State College, Pa.: Penns Valley Publishers.

——. 1956. The calculation of the sampling error of a cruise from the mean square successive difference. *Jour. Forestry* **54**:341.

MEYER, H. A., RECKNAGEL, A. B., STEVENSON, D. D., and BARTOO, R. A. 1961. *Forest management.* 2d. ed. New York: The Ronald Press Co.

MEYER, H. A., and STEVENSON, D. D. 1943. The structure and growth of virgin beech-birch-hemlock forests in northern Pennsylvania. *Jour. Agric. Res.* **67**:465–84.

MEYER, W. H. 1930. Diameter distribution series in even-aged forest stands, Yale Forest. *Yale Univ. School of Forestry Bull. no. 28.*

——. 1933. Approach of abnormally stocked stands of Douglas fir to normal conditions. *Jour. Forestry* **31**:400–406.

——. 1934. Growth in selectively cut ponderosa pine forests of the Pacific Northwest. U. S. Dept. Agric. Tech. Bull. no. 407.

——. 1942. Yield of even-aged stands of loblolly pine in northern Louisiana. *Yale Univ. School of Forestry Bull. no. 51.*

MIHAILOV, I. 1953. *Dendrometrie.* Skopje, Yugoslavia.

MILLER, C. I. 1949. A methods study of the cumulative volume tally sheet. *Jour. Forestry* **58**:889–92.

——. 1952. The determination of simple methods for obtaining form-class of individual trees. Purdue University Agricultural Experiment Project no. 644. (Mimeographed.)

——. 1959. Comparison of Newton's Smalian's, and Huber's formulas. Dept. of Forestry and Conservation, Purdue University (mimeograph for limited distribution).

——. 1963. Faster point sampling. *Jour. Forestry* **61**:299–300.

MINOR, C. O. 1960. Estimating tree diameters of Arizona ponderosa pine from aerial photographs. *U.S.F.S. Rocky Mt. For. and Range Exp. Sta. Res. Note no. 46.*

MIZE, J. H., and COX, J. G. 1968. *Essentials of simulation.* Englewood Cliffs, N.J.: Prentice-Hall.

MOESSNER, K. E. 1962. Preliminary aerial volume tables for Pinyon-Juniper stands. *U.S.F.S. Intermt. For. and Range Exp. Sta. Res. Paper no. 69.*

MOSER, J. W., JR. 1967. Growth and yield models for uneven-aged forest stands. Ph.D. thesis. Purdue University.

MOSER, J. W., JR., and BEERS, T. W. 1969. Parameter estimation in nonlinear volume equations. *Jour. Forestry* **67**:878–79.

MOSER, J. W., JR., and HALL, O. F. 1969. Derived growth and yield functions for uneven-aged forest stands. *Forest Sci.* **15**:183–88.

MOTT, P. G. 1966. Some aspects of colour aerial photography in practice and its applications. *Photogramm. Record* **5**:221–39.

MOUNTAIN, H. S. 1949. Determining the solid volume of four foot pulpwood sticks. *Jour. Forestry* **47**:627–31.

MULLOY, G. A. 1944. Empirical stand density yield tables. Dept. Mines and Res. Ottawa, Canada, Silv. Res. Note no. 73.

———. Empirical stand density yield. Dept. Mines and Res. Ottawa, Canada, Silv. Res. Note no. 82.

NASH, A. J. 1948. The Nash scale for measuring tree crown widths. *Forestry Chron.* **24**:117–20.

NAVON, D. I. 1967. Computer-oriented systems for wildland management. *Jour. Forestry* **65**:473–79.

NAVON, D. I., and McCONNEN, R. J. 1967. Evaluating forest management policies by parametric linear programming. *U.S.F.S. Pacific S.W. For. and Range Exp. Sta. Res. Paper PSW–42.*

NAYLOR, T. H., BALINTFY, J. L., BURDICK, D. S., and CHU, K. 1966. *Computer simulation techniques.* New York: John Wiley & Sons.

NELSON, T. C., and BENNETT, F. A. 1965. A critical look at the normality concept. *Jour. Forestry* **63**:107–9.

NEWNHAM, R. M. 1966. A simulation model for studying the effect of stand structure on harvesting pattern. *Forestry Chron.* **42**:39–44.

———. 1968. Simulation models in forest management and harvesting, *Forestry Chron.* **44**(1):7–12.

NEWNHAM, R. M., and SMITH, J. H. G. 1964. Development and testing of stand models for douglas fir and lodgepole pine. *Forestry Chron.* **40**:494–502.

NORMAN, E. L., and CURLIN, J. W. 1968. A linear programming model for forest production control at the AEC Oak Ridge Reservation. Oak Ridge National Lab. Rep. no. ORNL–4349.

NORTHEASTERN FOREST EXPERIMENT STATION. 1965. A guide to hardwood log grading (revised). U.S.F.S. Northeast. For. Exp. Sta.

NYLINDER, P. 1958. Variations in weight of barked spruce pulpwood. Stockholm: Uppsats. Instn. Virkeslära K. Skogshögsh no. 15.

———. 1967. Weight measurement of pulpwood. Stockholm: Rapp. Instn. Virkeslära K. Skogshögsk no. R57.

OPIE, J. E. 1968. Predictability of individual tree growth using various definitions of competing basal area. *Forest Sci.* **14**:314–23.

ORE, O. 1948. *Number theory and its history.* New York: McGraw-Hill Book Co.

O'REGAN, W. G., and ARVANITIS, L. G. 1966. Cost effectiveness in forest sampling. *Forest Sci.* **12**:406–14.

O'REGAN, W. G., ARVANITIS, L. G., and GOULD, E. M., JR. 1965. Systems, simulation, and forest management. *Proc. Soc. Amer. Foresters:* 194–98.

O'REGAN, W. G., and PALLEY, M. N. 1965. A computer technique for the study of forest sampling methods. *Forest Sci.* **11**:99–114.

OSBORNE, J. G. 1942. Sampling errors of systematic and random surveys of cover type areas. *Jour. Amer. Stat. Assn.* **37**:256–64.

———. 1946. Volume sampling procedure. U.S.F.S. Forest Survey Techniques Confer.

OSBORNE, J. G., and Schumacher, F. X. 1935. The construction of normal-yield and stand tables for even-aged timber stands. *Jour. Agric. Res.* **51**:547–64.

PALLEY, M. N., and O'REGAN, W. G. 1961. A computer technique for the study of forest sampling. I. Point sampling compared with line sampling. *Forest Sci.* **7**:282–94.

PANSHIN, A. J., DEZEEUW, C., and BROWN, H. P. 1964. *Textbook of wood technology.* Vol. 1. 2d ed. New York: McGraw-Hill Book Co.

PARDÉ, J. 1955. Un dendromètre Blume-Leiss (The Blume-Leiss hypsometer). *Rev. For. Fran.* **7**:207–10.

———. 1961. *Dendrometrie.* Imprimerie Louis-Jean Gap.

PARKER, D. C., and WOLFF, M. F. 1965. Remote sensing. *Science and Technology,* July: 20–31.

PATRONE, G. 1963. *Lezioni di dendrometri.* Florence: B. Cappini and Co.

PHIPPS, R. L., and GILBERT, G. E. 1960. An electric dendrograph. *Ecology* **41**:389–90.

PIENAAR, L. V. 1965. Quantitative theory of forest growth. Ph.D. thesis. University of Washington.

POPE, R. B. 1962. Constructing aerial photo volume tables. *U.S.F.S. Pac. N.W. For. and Range Exp. Sta. Res. Paper no. 49.*

PRODAN, M. 1965. *Holzmesslehre.* Frankfurt on the Main, Germany: J. D. Sauerlander's Verlag.

RAPRAEGER, E. F. 1950. The cubic foot as a national log-scaling standard. *U.S.F.S. Northern Rocky Mt. For. and Range Exp. Sta. Sta. Paper no. 24.*

RASPOPOV, I. M. 1955. K metodike izucenija proekcii kron derevjev (A method of studying the crown projection of trees). *Bot. Z.* **40**:825–27.

REINEKE, L. H. 1927. A modification of Bruce's method of preparing timber yield tables. *Jour. Agric. Res.* **35**:843–56.

———. 1932. A precision dendrometer. *Jour. Forestry* **30**:692–97.

———. 1933. Perfecting a stand density index for even-aged forests. *Jour. Agric. Res.* **46**:627–38.

ROACH, B. A., and GINGRICH, S. F. 1962. Timber management guide for upland Central hardwoods. U.S.F.S. Central States For. Exp. Sta. 33 pages.

———. 1968. Even-aged silviculture for upland central hardwoods. U. S. Dept. Agric. Handbook No. 355.

ROBINSON, D. W. 1969. The Oklahoma State angle gauge. *Jour. Forestry* **67**:234–36.

ROBINSON, J. M. 1967. The history of wood measurement in Canada. Ottawa: For. Mgt. Research and Services Inst. Internal Rep. FMR–7.

ROGERS, E. 1952. Large-scale airphotos tested in forest survey prove unsatisfactory. *U.S.F.S. Northeast. For. Exp. Sta. Res. Note no. 12.*

ROW, C., and FASICK, C. 1966. Weight scaling tables by electronic computer. *For. Products Jour.* **16**(8):41–45.

ROW, C., FASICK, C., and GUTTENBERG, S. 1965. Improving sawmill profits through operations research. *U.S.F.S. Southern For. Exp. Sta. Res. Paper SO–20.*

ROW, C., and GUTTENBERG, S. 1966. Determining weight-volume relationships for saw logs. *For. Products Jour.* **16**(5):39–47.

SAMSET, I. 1962. The weight of a complete Norway spruce tree: a preliminary study at Silderika. *Tidsskr. Skogbr.* **70**:342–48.

SATOO, T. 1962. Notes on Kittredge method of estimation of amount of leaves of forest stand. *Jour. Jap. Forestry* **44**:267–72.

SATTERLY, J. W. 1921. The hatchet planimeter. Univ. Toronto Math. Series No. 2.

SAYN-WITTGENSTEIN, L. 1965. Statistics—salvation or slavery. *Forestry Chron.* **41**:103–5.

SAYN-WITTGENSTEIN, L., and ALFRED, A. H. 1967. Tree volumes from large-scale photos. *Photogramm. Eng.* **33**:69–73.

SCHIFFEL, A. 1899. Form und Inhalt der Fichte (Form and volume of spruce). Mitt. aus d. forstl. Versuchsan. Österreiche 24.

SCHMELZ, D. V., and LINDSEY, A. A. 1965. Size-class structure of old-growth forests in Indiana. *Forest Sci.* **11**:259–64.

SCHNUR, G. L. 1934. Diameter distribution for old-field loblolly pine stands in Maryland. *Jour. Agric. Res.* **49**:731–43.

SCHNUR, G. L. 1937. Yield, stand, and volume tables for even-aged upland oak forests. U. S. Dept. Agric. Tech. Bull. no. 560.

SCHUMACHER, F. X. 1930. Yield, stand, and volume tables for Douglas fir in California. *Calif. Agric. Exp. Sta. Bull. no. 491.*

———. 1939. A new growth curve and its application to timber yield studies. *Jour. Forestry* **37**:819–20.

SCHUMACHER, F. X., and HALL, F. S. 1933. Logarithmic expression of timber-tree volume. *Jour. Agric. Res.* **47**:719–34.

SEIP, H. K. 1964. *Tremaling.* Skogbruk og Skogindustri, vol. 3. Norway.

SHIGO, A. L., and LARSON, E. vH. 1969. A photo guide to the patterns of discoloration and decay in living northern hardwood trees. *U.S.F.S. Northeast. For. Exp. Sta. Res. Paper NE-127.*

SHIUE, C. J. 1960. Systematic sampling with mutiple random starts. *Forest Sci.* **6**:42–50.

SINGER, J. 1964. *Elements of numerical analysis.* New York: Academic Press.

SISAM, J. W. B. 1938. Site as a factor in silviculture. Its determination with special reference to the use of indicator plants. Dominion Forest Service. Canada. Silv. Res. Note no. 54.

SMIRNOV, V. V. 1963. The quantities of needles in spruce stands. *Lesn. Hoz.* **16**:17–19.

SMITH, D. M. 1962. The practice of silviculture. 7th ed. New York: John Wiley & Sons.

SMITH, J. H. G., and BAILEY, G. R. 1964. Influence of stocking and stand density on crown widths of douglas fir and lodgepole pine. *Commonwealth Forestry Rev.* **43**:243–46.

SMITH, J. H. G., and KER, J. W. 1959. Empirical yield equations for young forest growth. *British Columbia Lumberman.* Sept.

SMITH, J. H. G., KER, J. W., and CSIZMAZIA, J. 1961. Economics of reforestation of douglas fir, western hemlock, and western red cedar in the Vancouver Forest District. *Univ. of British Columbia Forestry Bull. no. 3.*

SMITH, J. H. G., NEWNHAM, R. M., and HEJJAS, J. 1965. Importance of distribution and amount of mortality can be defined by simulation studies. *Commonwealth Forestry Rev.* **44**:188–92.

SMITH, R. N. 1965. Programming for error detection. Proc. Conference on C.F.I. Michigan Tech. Univ., pp. 151–65.

SOCIETY OF AMERICAN FORESTERS. 1958. Forestry terminology. Washington, D. C.: Soc. Amer. Foresters.

SOEST, J. VAN, and TIEMENS, F. 1953. De hoogtemeter van Blume-Leiss (The Blume-Leiss hypsometer). *Ned. Boschb. Tijdschr.* **25**:279–82.

SPIVEY, W. A. 1963. Linear programming, an introduction. New York: Macmillan Co.

SPURR, S. H. 1952. *Forest inventory.* New York: The Ronald Press Co.

———. 1960. Photogrammetry and photointerpretation. 2d ed. New York: The Ronald Press Co.

———. 1962. A measure of point density. *Forest Sci.* **8**:85–96.

STAGE, A. R. 1957. Speedy scaling of low value log-loads: *U.S.F.S. Intermt. For. and Rance Exp. Sta. Res. Note no. 50.*

———. 1966. Simultaneous derivation of site-curve and procedures. *Proc. Soc. Amer. Foresters:* 134–36.

STEVENS, S. S. 1946. On the theory of scales of measurement. *Science* **103**:677–80.

STOFFELS, A. 1955. L'exactitude des mesurages à l'aide due dendrometre modifié de Christen (The accuracy of measurements made with the modified Christen hypsometer). *Schweiz. Z. Forstw.* **106**:385–93.

STOFFELS, A., and VAN SOEST, J. 1953. Principiele vraagstukken bije proefperken. 3, Hoogteregressie (The main problem in sample plots. 3, Height regression). *Ned. Boschg.-Tijdschr.* **25**:190–99.

STOTT, C. B. 1968. A short history of continuous forest inventory east of the Mississippi. *Jour. Forestry* **66**:834–37.

STRAND, L. 1957. "Relaskopisk" hoyde-og kubikkmassebestemmelse. (Relascopic height and cubic volume determination). *Norsk Skogbruk* **3**:535–38.

SUKHATME, P. V. 1954. *Sampling theory of surveys with applications.* Ames: Iowa State College Press.

SWAN, D. A. 1959. Weight scaling in the Northeast. *Amer. Pulpw. Assn. Tech. Release no. 59–R5.*

TARAS, M. A. 1956. Buying pulpwood by weight. *U.S.F.S. Southeast. For. Exp. Sta. Sta. Paper no. 74.*

———. 1967. Weight scaling: its past, present and future. Faculty of Forestry, Univ. of Toronto, Wood Measurement Conf. Proc. Tech. Report no. 7.

TARDIF, G. 1965. Some considerations concerning the establishment of optimum plot size in forest survey. *Forestry Chron.* **41**:93–102.

THOMSON, G. W., and DEITSCHMAN, G. H. 1959. Bibliography of world literature on the Bitterlich method of plotless cruising. Iowa State Univ. Agric. and Home Eco. Exp. Sta.

TOCHER, K. D. 1963. *The art of simulation.* New York: D. Van Nostrand Co.

TRIMBLE, G. R., JR. 1965. Timber by the pound not a desirable trend for hardwood sawlogs. *Jour. Forestry* **63**:881

TROREY, L. G. 1932. A mathematical expression for the construction of diameter height curves based on site. *Forestry Chron.* **18**:3–14.

TUOVINEN, A. 1965. A study at Kemyärvi Oy on measuring birch pulpwood by weight. Helsinki: *Tied. Metsäteho,* no. 245.

TURNBULL, K. J. 1963. Population dynamics in mixed forest stands. A system of mathematical models of mixed stand growth and structure. Ph.D. thesis. Univ. of Washington.

TURNBULL, K. J., and HOYER, G. E. 1965. Construction and analysis of comprehensive tree-volume tarif tables. Resource Management Report no. 8. State of Wash., Dept. of Nat. Resources, Olympia, Wash.

TURNBULL, K. J., LITTLE, G. R., and HOYER, G. E. 1963. Comprehensive tree-volume tarif tables. State of Wash., Dept. of Nat. Resources, Olympia, Wash.

TURNBULL, K. J., and PIENAAR, L. V. 1966. A non-linear mathematical model for analysis and prediction of growth in non-normal and thinned forest stands. Stockholm: Int. Advisory Group Forest Statisticians no. 9.

U. S. DEPARTMENT OF THE INTERIOR. 1947. Manual of instructions for the survey of public lands of the United States. Washington, D.C.: Government Printing Office.

U. S. FOREST SERVICE. 1964. National forest log scaling handbook. U.S.F.S. Washington, D. C.

VAUGHN, C. L., WOLLIN, A. C., McDONALD, K. A., and BULGRIN, E. H. 1966. Hardwood log grades for standard lumber. U.S.F.S. For. Prod. Lab. Res. Paper FPL–63.

VEZINA, P. E. 1962. Crown width-d.b.h. relationships for open-grown balsam fir and white spruce in Quebec. *Forestry Chron.* **38**:463–73.

VUOKILA, Y. 1955. The Finnish curve calipers. *Jour. Forestry* **53**:366–67.

WAHLENBERG, W. G. 1941. Methods of forecasting timber growth in irregular stands. U. S. Dept. Agric. Tech. Bull. No. 796.

WALTERS, C. S., and HERRICK, A. M. 1956. A comparison of two log-grading systems. *Univ. of Ill. Agric. Exp. Sta. Bull. 603.*

WARDLE, P. A. 1965. Forest management and operational research: a linear programming study. *Management Sci.* **11**:B260–B270.

WARE, K. D. 1964. Some problems in the quantification of tree quality. *Proc. Soc. Amer. Foresters:* 211–17.

———. 1967. Sampling properties of three-pee estimates. Paper presented at 1967 Soc. Amer. Foresters-Canadian Inst. Forestry Meeting, Ottawa, Canada.

WARE, K. D., and CUNIA, T. 1962. Continuous forest inventory with partial replacement of samples. *Forest Sci. Monograph 3.*

WATT, K. E. F. 1963. Dynamic programming, look ahead programming and the strategy of insect pest control. *Canadian Entomologist* **95**:525–36.

WATT, R. F. 1950. Growth in understocked and overstocked western white pine stands. *U.S.F.S. Northern Rocky Mt. For. and Range Exp. Sta. Note no. 78.*

WENDEL, G. W. 1960. Fuel weights of pond pine crowns. *U.S.F.S. Southeast. For. Exp. Sta. Res. Note no. 149.*

WESLEY, R. 1956. Measuring the height of trees. London: *Park Administration* **21**:80–84.

WESTVELD, M. 1954. Use of plant indicators as an index to site quality. *U.S.F.S. Northeast. For. Exp. Sta. Paper no. 69.*

WHEELER, P. R. 1962. Penta prism caliper for upper-stem diameter measurements. *Jour. Forestry* **60**:877–78.

WILJAMAA, L. E. 1942. A simple but practical Finnish instrument for measuring tree diameters. *Jour. Forestry* **40**:506–7.

WILSON, R. C. 1967. Space photography for forestry. *Photogramm. Eng.* **33**:483–90.

WINER, H. I. 1961. Notes on the analysis of pulpwood logging in the Southeast. Southeast. Tech. Comm. Amer. Pulpwood Assn. Logging School. Georgetown, S. C.

WRIGHT, W. J. 1962. Motion and time study techniques and their application to forest operations in northern Ireland. Master's thesis. University of California.

YATES, F. 1946. A review of recent statistical developments in sampling and sampling surveys. *Jour. Royal Stat. Soc.* **109**:12–30

———. 1948. Systematic sampling. *Royal Soc. of London Philos. Trans.* **241**:345–77.

———. 1949. Sampling methods for censuses and surveys. London: Charles Griffin and Co.

———. 1960. Sampling methods for censuses and surveys. 3d ed. London: Charles Griffin and Co.

YERKES, V. P. 1966. Weight and cubic-foot relationships for Black Hills ponderosa pine sawlogs. *U.S.F.S. Rocky Mt. For. and Range Exp. Sta. Res. Note RM-78*.

———. 1967. Effect of seasonal stem moisture variation and log storage on weight of Black Hills ponderosa pine. *U.S.F.S. Rocky Mt. For. and Range Exp. Sta. Res. Note RM-96*.

YOUNG, H. E. 1954. Photogrammetric volume determination of huge pulpwood piles. *Photogramm. Eng.* **20**:808.

———. 1964. The complete tree concept—A challenge and an opportunity. *Proc. Soc. Amer. Foresters:* 231–33.

YOUNG, H. E., and CARPENTER, P. M. 1967. Weight, nutrient element and productivity studies of seedlings and saplings of eight tree species in natural ecosystems. *Univ. Maine Agric. Exp. Sta. Tech. Bull. no. 28*.

YOUNG, H. E., ROBBINS, W. C., and WILSON, S. 1967. Errors in volume determination of primary forest products. School of Forestry, Univ. of Maine (Mimeographed).

YOUNG, H. E., STRAND, L., and ALTENBERGER, R. 1964. Preliminary fresh and dry weight tables for seven tree species in Maine. *Univ. Maine Agric. Exp. Sta. Tech. Bull. no. 12*.

ZENGER, A. 1964. Systematic sampling in forestry. *Biometrics* **22**:553–65.

ZILLGITT, W. M. 1946. A quick method of estimating cull in northern hardwood stands. *U.S.F.S. Lake States For. Exp. Sta. Tech. Note no. 255*.

ZILLGITT, W. M., and GEVORKIANTZ, S. R. 1946. Estimating cull in northern hardwoods, *U.S.F.S. Lake States For. Exp. Sta., Sta. Paper no. 3*.

ZOBEL, B., RALSTON, J., and ROBARDS, J. H. 1965. Wood yields from loblolly pine stands of different age, site and stand density. School of Forestry, North Carolina State Univ. Tech. Rep. no. 26.

Index